BODYCAGE

By Rehana Incognito

Rehana Incognito

All rights reserved, no part of this publication may be reproduced by any means, electronic, mechanical photocopying, documentary, film or in any other format without prior written permission of the publisher.

Published by
Chipmunkapublishing
PO Box 6872
Brentwood
Essex CM13 1ZT
United Kingdom

http://www.chipmunkapublishing.com

Copyright © Rehana Incognito 2008

Edited by Rochelle Taylor

Chipmunkapublishing gratefully acknowledges the support of Arts Council England.

BODYCAGE

Dedicated in honour, awe and respect of Miss Debbie-Lee... who shined as the perfect example of triumph, humbly... with warmth and humour, transcending the greatest challenge in her life. With loving guidance and encouragement to celebrate and share who I am as a human being, I learnt we don't need to search for treasures at the end of rainbows, but that we are standing in them all the time, dancing in them... Only needing a good storm of rain... and the right angle of perspective, to see them!

Rehana Incognito

BODYCAGE

PART ONE

Rehana Incognito

BODYCAGE

CHAPTER ONE

1963

Start from the beginning? How far in the beginning? Like - "In the beginning was the Word and the Word was with God"? Well, perhaps not... of course that's already been used ... in a *really big* way, so I'll be serious.

Thinking again... it *is* serious and I'll hope my words don't read as egotistical, let alone alluding to blasphemy for touching near the use of some hugely important opening clues, contained with all that wisdom, in one such Great Book itself. Important enough all the same to think back now how our every word starts us off on a journey to create something, somehow and somewhere in a world where we so often feel like the only animal unknowing of who or what it really is... or even where it fits in. Not just the words which start in our own minds and hearts, but those said *to* us... those we have gone over and over in a crazy old place we've found ourselves in, building and building, creating and creating whatever kind of world we can make for ourselves.

So... the first things I can remember, however vaguely from the mind of a child? hmmm? I keep thinking of that chintzy song from the 1980s. Oh yeah, "Life in a Northern Town". Now I remember... by the "Dream Academy", of all names. I should have known, and perhaps just noticed, something noteworthy about an academy of dreams!

"In winter nineteen sixty three
It felt like the world would freeze
With John F Kennedy...y...y...

Rehana Incognito

And The Beatles."

Standing in a short, neat row like the rest in our Northumbrian pit village, our little terraced house stood bedecked in snow. Perhaps it did resemble an idyllic, Dickensian Christmas card just somewhat. However, the scene from behind the warmly lit windows was far from anything like Yuletide merriment. The only clinking glass to be heard was sadly, every breakable object in the house being hurled at each other by my brawling parents.

Madly scrambling up the stairs, Karen and I heard the Christmas tree ornaments shatter around us... exploding like fireworks against the wall as we fled. Our bedroom door slammed shut just in time to hear the hallway mirror come crashing down in a million pieces. Huddled with my big sister against the window ledge, we pressed our faces against the frosty glass. Karen said she could see the shape of the Virgin Mary in the patterns of muted light being cast across our bedroom wall.

"Aah divn't knaa who she is," I whispered, trying to discern anything to even resemble a human being. The flickering forms actually terrified me. They could be the shadows of the gnarled, bony fingers of nasty little hobgoblins whom Karen told me lived under my bed. Every night I would check for them before cocooning myself deep beneath the covers, taking extra care to ensure that my hands were safely tucked away... lest they should be grabbed!

"Ye knaa nowt anyway!" Karen said in her strong Northumbrian accent, thumping a fist on my head as an explanation mark, reminding me that I really did know NOWT. We whiled away another night of our parent's battle time, living out fantasies in a world of toys and Fairy Princesses while the threats, screams and crashes went on and on from below.

Heeding Karen's warning not to go downstairs lest I 'get a hit 'n aall', I listened as every scream from my mother and bellowing yells of my father resounded through my body. Those cries of threats and abuse seemed to scratch themselves deeply into a part of me I could not have known existed. Playing over and over again like the break in a record, they truly were serving the very same purpose - to ruin what should or could have been a beautiful song.

Relief came with a shuddering slam of the front door. Dad had fled. At last I would be able to creep downstairs to find my Mam, perhaps to offer a comforting cuddle and survey the damage. But picking our way down a stairway strewn with shards of glass, we found our mother nowhere in sight. She was off, out that door... after him in the hottest pursuit.

With her fire fuelling a blindly raging inferno, Mam had clearly had enough. An astrologer might well quip - "What more could one expect when the warm, gentle flame of the Aries 'Fire' is fuelled by the wild, wicked wind of the Gemini 'Air'?" My Arian mother had indeed been possessed by Mars, the God of War, as she chased the 'sustenance' of her burning vitality - her Gemini husband. All of which I knew nothing about, though certainly it all came cascading back when the time was ready. (Takes a moment to say a silent prayer to Linda Goodman whose books on her startling, life-long studies of astrology and humanity's beautiful personal connections to all of those "signs" took me through great journeys of understanding. Like holding the hand of a wonderful friend sent straight from Heaven, she gently and humorously showed a way for us with such wisdom, strength and care.)

Rehana Incognito

My mum knew too where to find him, licking his wounds, whilst trying to obliterate any memory of the responsibilities of a wife and children. There at the Red Lion, whatever was left of the housekeeping money was about to be squandered again on drink. Now, as an Aries woman myself, I would not like to have been in his shoes when a wife with fire shooting from her eye sockets walked through the door of that pub...

Time, it seemed, would afford opportunity enough for many re-enactments of that scene... in my own life, and in the lives of too many of us. And Time, it seems, affords me now the opportunity to take my turn to hold some hands, to wander through an understanding of many of the conundrums we face and work through in life. In this particular one, it appears, I took on more than many would have signed up for.

As the snow deepened, the faces of weather-weary people must have begun to look longingly at posters springing up here and there.
'COME TO SUNNY AUSTRALIA' they beckoned... with glossy pictures of happy families strolling along palm-lined beaches. A new life, promising jobs in a land of milk and honey began to tempt so many of those lost in the gloom of this miserable winter and economic recession.
Australia enjoyed an economic boom though, with vast mineral deposits being discovered all over the country. New industries spawned everywhere, requiring a vast influx of migrant labour to fuel a growing economy. In this bitter winter the lure was to prove irresistible to millions of families across Europe, including, it seemed... ours.

BODYCAGE

Our Aunt Alison had rushed from across the street to join us, picking our way across the carnage that was once a cosy living room. Along with half the village it seemed, she had heard that Howard and Jean were fighting again. With our little hands clutching tightly to hers, we traipsed across the house to find my little sister, Colleen, still fast asleep. She must have become quite adept at sleeping through the battles. Aunt Alison shook her head in disbelief.

"By... your Mam's got an aaful temper. There's nowt left here that's not smashed! Aah wish your Da wasn't taking ye aall away from us, Pet. Australia's an aaful lang way from us. Aah knaa we'll never see ye aall again."

"Where's *Osst*... what's it called again?" I chirped at her. "Won't we be able to catch a bus and come back to see you, Aunty... if it's such a laang way away?"

"No, Hinny," she giggled down, "it's too far to go on a bus. You'll all be going on a big, bonny boat."

"Aah can tek mah goldfish alaang though, can't Aah? Aah'll hang him on a *laaaaang* string in the water behind the big, bonny boat."

"No, Pet. He'll have to bide here with us."

The truth had now dawned about my parent's recent fights. With my father's decision that we immigrate 'Down Under'... to Australia, our world really was about to turn completely upside down. Should my mother decide we were not to accompany him, he was willing to journey alone... of course on the understanding that he would pave the way for a better life when we eventually joined him. Mum fought him with a passion, he all the more persisted. To survive without him would have been a miserable struggle. Finally, not trusting his decision to travel alone, she relented. We prepared to leave all that we knew and understood of our beloved

Rehana Incognito

Northumberland behind. Painfully, she took the risk to give up our familiar world to follow my father's dreams.
 Time would have it too, that I might understand the all-consuming force which would compel *me to* forsake all. To be willing to sacrifice anything... clinging to my last gasp of a man's 'life-giving air'. An air which I felt sure was the source of my own warm, inner flame, believing I would perish without it. I would surely learn the pain of watching that flame die to a flickering ember, as the 'sustaining' beloved withdrew from my life and question what to do with the whole experience.

 The Australian Government in due course authorised our immigration documents. The grand sum of ten pounds for our 'assisted passage' had been paid. Dad's decision had been final. We would soon be taken to our 'new and better life in the sun'. By March of 1964 it still felt like the world froze, just like in the song. Or at least it looked like a freeze-frame as Mum, with aching heart, lumbered her three little bairns into a waiting taxi. Looking up at our now empty house in the crisp morning air, she recalled in twisted anguish each piece of her precious furniture being sold for next-to-nothing.
 Just like the furniture, we too were about to disappear out of sight and around the bend of our cobbled street. The taxi grumbled as it lurched forward into the snow... like a huge, ugly beast that had just devoured its sullen cargo. Crunching its way along the frosty roads we were soon delivered to the train at Newcastle-Upon-Tyne. From there we clattered through the night to London to join (as it turned out) our 'plane to the 'Underworld'. I could forget the big, bonny boat!
 We were off to a world where nobody knew us. Only my dad's step father came to see us off at the station. He kindly handed a little souvenir pen through the

BODYCAGE

carriage window with the Queen's coronation portrait on it... I should imagine for me to remember where I was from and to write home. My father's painful decision was too much for any of our other relatives to witness. Years later I learned that Aunt Alison sat sobbing, hidden behind a hedge that morning, watching her closest sister and family vanish from her world.

How my own heart ached with every clickety-clack, clickety-clack as the train sped us through England... further and further from all we knew and found familiar. Upon reaching King's Cross Station it appeared that the whole world was caught up in the same madness. Everywhere mothers and fathers with small, bewildered children milled about in the chaos of luggage and overladen baggage carts.

In reality many were indeed like us. Their ten pounds had been paid to transport entire families off to feed the industries in 'boom towns' all over Australia. Towns like Wittenoom Gorge, which later became infamously known for the outbreak of Mesothelioma - a deadly disease caused when asbestos fibres awaken from a long slumber hidden in people's lungs, slowly choking the life from their helpless hosts.

Dad tried to keep us all laughing and calm as Mum's nervousness about the flight had already overwhelmed her. She had mistaken the wing of the aircraft for another plane being perilously close to ours. There was sure to be a crash! If that were not enough, she was soon paralysed with fear as Dad convinced her we would all be safe... as "parachutes were to be found beneath the seats - should we need to leap from the plane!"

Mercifully, her hysteria calmed during take off, as Dad explained how we would arrive in Australia... upside down. Indeed, I too was enthralled as he explained how people would be at hand when we landed in Perth to "tip us back up the right way". I could hardly wait for that!

Still dazed and half asleep, we landed in Bombay to refuel. A thick, heavy wall of heat almost sent us reeling back into the plane. The flies and stench of that city assaulted us like the opening of the gates to hell. All memories of a frozen England were put out of my mind for many years.

That heat served only as a foretaste of the inferno awaiting us in Perth, Western Australia. And, as the T-shirts say-

*"W.A. IS A GREAT PLACE.
10 BILLION FLIES CAN'T BE WRONG!"*

It seemed that was true. As we arrived, a welcoming reception of all 10 billion of the filthy dirty things plastered us at once as we stepped, albeit right way up, onto the tarmac.

With flies becoming too familiar, too quickly... encrusting our eyes with their disgusting bodies, we made our way through the terminal on a hot summer's day. We all vomited.

Along with other migrant families we were taken by bus to a refurbished army camp. Graylands Migrant Hostel was to serve as home until suitable work and accommodation could be found for us. With its rows and rows of semi-cylindrical tin huts it looked like a bizarre Stalag!

Immediately Mum saw that we could easily become lost. Being still unable to read at that time, she taught me to recognize the number of our hut as "an O on top of an O, next to another O on top of an O". That

BODYCAGE

seemed the easiest way for a five year old to understand the number 88! It was put to use many times in my hapless wanderings... usually trying to find the way out and a bus to Northumberland.

There in the camp, it was some time before we even felt that we were foreigners in this country... that ordeal was yet to come. Everyone was either English, Scottish, German or Italian. Actually we seldom even spoke to other English children as they had difficulty understanding our broad Northumbrian brogue. It seemed our parents, too had a similar problem. Several of the European parents mistook our accent for German.

Seemingly, World War Two's anti-German sentiments still ran high amongst many of these people. Often, they would be 'off hand' with us, leaving Karen and I just SHOUTING whatever it was we were trying to convey. They would just SHOUT back. Mostly we got our message through, or Karen would just clobber them... to my dismay. We became a formidable team at Graylands Hostel!

Still, the realisation of being seen as 'different' played on my mind. It had been the first recollection of racism as such. A racism which seemed all the worse (if that were possible) as it was being meted out by white people to instil a sense of difference between other *white* people- Something already questionable... even to a five year old.

Soon enough, as we ventured from the hostel, we all learned the pain of insults and taunts. Sometimes hurled at us, sometimes muttered beneath the breath, we heard the words "Pommy Bastards, Filthy Poms" or the simple generic term for the lot of us – "Bloody immigrants".

The Italians, the Germans, the Dutch and all else, were surely enduring their own pains at these indignities. Thankfully perhaps, most would not have even understood that they were being insulted. However, we surely did... and it began to hurt deeply. Having thought we were decent, honourable people like anyone else, we were now aware of grown adults letting us feel that we were in some way inferior.

Looking back it is easy to see what a young and isolated country Australia was. Easy too to understand how an irrational fear of foreigners 'overrunning the country to take all the jobs' may have developed. But still, as a child, it became easy to resent these people as merely the 'descendants of convicts from the vilest slums of Britain' I quickly learned. We had begun to lament with other foreigners about the uncouth, uncultured behaviour of the Aussies.

For years it was hard to conceive of how they could have been so cruel... and even more difficult to forgive. To me, the influx of immigrants had brought a wealth of cultural (and culinary) delight to this country... only now to be so richly enjoyed and appreciated - even by the bigots! Dad did not help either by explaining that Aussies were 'the most well balanced people on Earth'; "They've got a chip on each shoulder!" he loved to remark.

So there we remained... in Tin Hut Land, for almost one year. Standing in tiring queues in the cafeteria and shower blocks, we watched along with other disgruntled foreigners all the displaced and dissatisfied of Europe coping with their frustrations. Often we banded together with other families to discuss our hopes, dreams and fears about our new life in this land. Soon Mum and Dad had befriended some good-natured Aussies they had met on a train. Anyway, as Dad often said to Mam "it's a migrant camp not bloody Changi prison."

BODYCAGE

At last we were getting out of the camp more often. With newly found friends we soon discovered another side to the Australian character. A character forged around the enjoyment of an easy-going, care-free lifestyle, based on heaps of enjoyment of life in the Great Outdoors.

Many balmy evenings were spent absorbing the pleasures of our new life whilst languishing on the banks of the Swan River. There we would stand waist deep in tepid waters... trawling our nets along to scoop out a bounty of fresh shrimps and big, blue crabs. There our feast was devoured well into the night with our few Aussie friends, as the torch lights of the nocturnal fishers danced across the black expanse of water.

Still, however, few of the other children had befriended us. I had become accustomed to that, so spent most of my time stalking Karen... forever afraid to leave her side. *She* always seemed to know what she was doing... I had not a clue. Apart from that I was small for my age, becoming too timid and 'soft'. Should anyone have wanted to steal a toy from me... it was theirs. They could kick all the sand in the pit in my face if they wanted to. And often they did. But when Karen was around she would clip them for me, or knock them down. Yippee, she could always save me! So that was the state of affairs as the first day of school approached.

Karen and I were separated early in the day, after we had dutifully sung "God Save The Queen" in the playground. I hadn't learnt the last line as "long to reign over us" sounded like "long to rhinoceros" as the Australian children pronounced it. So I sang that and no one noticed at all. With dried out leaves whipping around our feet in the maddening hot wind, we too scattered in a swirl of confusion into little groups to be herded towards our classrooms.

Realising that I was now on my own, I gazed cautiously at all and everyone in these new surroundings. Remaining 'low-key' for the day, I dreaded the thought of being hit by some other child through some hideous misunderstanding. Karen would not be there to sort it out. Perhaps I had remained too inconspicuous that morning, as the teacher had omitted my 'rotation' from one play activity to the next. I could hardly have cared less as I honed my fishing skills in a tank of metallic prey. These could gleefully be hoisted from the tank by my little magnet-on-a-string fishing line with great gusto... until the following day as I played (pretending to be invisible) my little fishing game. Only then to be apprehended by 'Miss' and moved on to the next activity - building blocks... with which I was hopeless! Whilst feeling sure that little boys all around me were building scale replicas of the Sydney Harbour Bridge, I could build NOTHING!

Soon came the day we can all relate to - the "What do you want to be when you grow up" day. Listening to all the usual responses like... "I want to be a ballerina, Miss" or "I want to be a fireman, or a nurse..." My mind raced frantically as my turn approached. It harkened back to the silly 'mouth-stretching' exercises we had started to do. "Open your mouths very wide, girls and boys." Miss would say. "Wide like crocodiles now, come on. We want to be able hear you *PRO-NOUNCE* your words very clearly when you speak." Australians seem to be the only people in the world who can string whole sentences together without actually opening their mouths properly at all. It took years to realise why and several mouthfuls of those 10 billion flies just whipping into my gob at every opportunity!

BODYCAGE

Believing that developing this crocodile mouth was of enormous importance, I began stretching my mouth so wide it would often bleed, leaving my mother to wonder if I had been hit again. I had almost decided to announce that "I would like to be a crocodile when I grow up," as my turned came about. Fortunately, at the last moment I abandoned my reptilian aspirations, standing up to announce to Miss and the class-
"When I grow up I want to be a Princess!"
 My heart sank. I gazed confusedly at all the snickering faces around the classroom as my heart leapt up to lodge itself like a stone in my throat. Even the beloved Miss laughed.
"Don't be silly," she said, "You can't be a Princess when you grow up. For goodness sake, you're a little boy, Ian!"
 That was the first I could recall of any remark about a difference in gender roles... or how certain behaviours were expected if one was a boy or a girl. The difference in our bodies had always been noticeable, but until then had not been associated with the things we could actually do with them.

Although I was aware of body parts like those other little boys, no association had been made with any need to join them in their types of behaviour. When girls were asked to move to one side of the classroom and boys to the other... often I would trot off with the girls. No-one understood my confusion and indignity at being hauled over to sit with 'the rest of the boys.' Who could have, really? But what did I care?
"If I want to be a Princess when I grow up, I will!" I thought to myself. And that, despite having met the wickedest Queens along the most crooked paths, I am still working on!

CHAPTER TWO

1966
Following the first year at school, news finally came that we would be leaving the migrant camp. Dad had been allocated a job in a town in the state's far North West. Soon our belongings were packed for another plane ride, with the promise of a real, new house and a normal life.

How ironic it was that we should leave one little mining town in the North of England only to find ourselves in a mining town in the North of Australia. "Not a great improvement really", we thought. However, we were abuzz with the prospect of setting up a new home and starting the 'better' life in where else but Wittenoom Gorge!

Another plane door was soon to open on yet another fiercely hot wind-lashed tarmac. The blast of hellish heat assaulted us as the plane disgorged its cargo. Each gust of hot air seemed to torment all the more, whipping at our flesh with its swirling clouds of red dust... interspersed with wisps of blue asbestos dust blowing all about the town from the asbestos slag heaps, dotted around the mines.

The township itself looked like a cross between the surface of Mars, Beirut and hell itself, greeting us with homes that resembled row upon row of shabby chicken coops

"We're going home. THAT'S IT!" Mum tried to bundle us back into the mining company bus, throwing luggage haphazardly on top of us. Just as quickly, Dad hauled it back out again.

"We're here now and we CAN'T go home yet. We're stopping here, and THAT'S IT!"

BODYCAGE

Unfortunately, that was it and there we did stop, realising fully that my parents had made a huge mistake. There would soon be much cause to lament having left England, that "Land of the Angels" the Romans had named it, after the fair people inhabiting this island of misty forests, so I'd been told and just accepted. Well, that at least explained Anglia!

Here we were now, with only fast-fading memories of that home which offered all the peace, security and familiarity we longed for...quickly becoming a mythical, longing memory to a young child baking in heat, blasted by red dust. Further into the uncertainty we went, slowly sinking in dread of the unknown.

Through the eyes of the first seafarers to skirt the shores of Australia, this land seemed, for the most part, a desolate sandpit. Through their eyes it was a hell on Earth, suitable only as a dumping ground for criminals. For me it was place which came to offer and teach most of what my life would become and so much of what I could make of it. For that I can only be truly grateful.

Little could those early settlers, cast upon such hostile shores, have known of the teaming life-support system beyond their perception. A system which had supported the Aboriginals for about seventy thousand years before... in a land they only knew of as 'The World'... a world of which they were as much a part as the air they breathed.

How incredible now, to look back and ponder which words and concepts we ourselves choose to use to describe a condition which just *is*. Then allowing those very concepts to give 'reality' to a world we ourselves have created! Rich, colourful symbols are always there, only waiting for us to open our minds and hearts to their interpretation - when the time is right, to make of our own world a heaven or hell.

Dad was not about to stay around long enough to give his new job a chance. On the pretext of seeking a better job in the city, he abandoned us... promising to send for us when he could arrange (again) a better life. Mum was terrified and home-sick, with no-one but three small children to comfort her and one more now on the way.
At least the fighting had stopped, so we did not miss Dad that much. There was, however, a new school for Karen, Colleen and I to start. All three would soon be off hand-in-hand to school. With our little heads shrouded in green, net hoods to protect us from flies, we looked like tiny aliens. Far preferable at least were the little hoods than contracting the disease (carried by flies) causing blindness in local children. The paradise scene, the promise of the immigration posters, this was not.

The new school itself was little more than yet another jumble of pre-fabricated asbestos buildings, set in the middle of a dusty field. The entire town looked like it had been assembled overnight, indeed it probably was. Just a big, ugly monster drawing asbestos fibres from the rocks beneath that Mars-like surface of the desert. Who knows how many slumbering Aboriginal 'spirit totems' were disturbed? The Aboriginals were despatched long ago... they could not tell us, but something was amiss.
The foreigners and their families fed the industries, whilst being introduced to life Down Under the hard way. Years later Wittenoom would be bulldozed to the ground. In the manner of Chernobyl, the government ordered that metres of dirt be heaped upon it to batten

BODYCAGE

down the deadly fibres... released from their subterranean entombment.

However, the outskirts of town presented a whole new world to discover. The rustic beauty of the Kimberly region forever changed her face with her many moods showing as light grew and faded across the ancient rock formations. There we learned to swim in the panoramic, crystal-clear gorges hewn from rocks and cliff faces eons ago, floating on our backs to gaze up at the rocky cavernous walls surrounding us with strange lizards flicking out their tongues and quickly darting back into their hide-outs.

Karen and I, with a troupe of little friends, once found an old raft. It was fashioned from oil drums slashed together by ropes. We climbed on, negotiating our way along a ravine filled with emerald green water... disappearing to shadowy depths. Huge, ragged cliffs loomed above us as we made our way towards a cave which came into view from around a tight bend. Clambering from the raft we stumbled into the shallow cave to stand face-to-face before several enormous, mouthless beings.

The faces of the 'Wandjina', Creator Gods, stared from soulless eyes... eyes which may have rested cloistered on their gallery walls for centuries. Did they peer back at us too in amazement, wondering what had happened to long-absent artists paying respects with offers of a quick touch-up of their paint work? Who, they must have wondered, were these pasty, white little strangers? Certainly not the children who'd lived there thousands of years, with skin so blue-black it could reflect the sunshine and the clouds! With our skin so pale, only sunburnt faces betrayed the truth... that we ourselves were not mysterious spirits of the dead.

Rehana Incognito

I had made a note to try to learn more about the paintings of these creatures. Perhaps, across the centuries, a message was to be heard. From their Dreamtime they had created the world, with no need of mouths with which to speak they had somehow sung and danced the world and its beings into creation. Only with their very thoughts, from a world of dreams, would they create... instantly understood and interpreted... from those very minds... *lives* which would spring into form. The spirits dreamed and sang forth the landforms, the water, the people, the plants, the kangaroo, the emu, the raucous hordes of gigantic black parrots swirling over us and mankind - the custodians of it all! And in return the Aboriginal people replayed the songs and dances for millenia more. Each of the dreaming songs and dances of all the life and land around them kept their lives vital and in harmonised to attract the energies of those same songs and dances- Never forgetting to return to the sacred caves... even to touch up the paintwork!

Of all of that I knew little yet, but how I stand now in awe of a world abuzz with the knowledge of these principles - known to cultures thousands of years before our own, expressed in appropriate form and language for each successive society. From the words of the Holy Books, the teachings of Buddha, the gentle Jesus or the Sufi poets to the majestic cave paintings of Neolithic man... the same message is always there. Only now are we starting to grasp their full splendour with support and validation of scientific study into these formerly 'mystic' processes to make sense of this world and this life.

BODYCAGE

In Wittenoom we could feel tropical thunderstorms, booming so hard from the heavens that they pounded their force right through our bodies. Or we could watch a bushfire, rage across the countryside, clearing away the brittle, the dry and the obsolete. Then we could watch in awe as lush new growth shot forth... greener and stronger from its blanket of nutritious ash. Again it began its cycle of total renewal from seeming death, dark decay and devastation under that scorched up earth... all over again to push through the surface and become as beautiful as the native orchids, ancient and majestically offering themselves to the glory of the work of the Sun to finish their own growth through such works I could not begin to understand either!

1966 saw me turn seven years old, making good progress at school with Karen remaining my only real friend. With other children around, I remained distant, making my own versions of their games to enjoy alone rather than join in. Despite how I may have felt about my true gender 'on the inside', certain nuances and incidents told me too that I was unlike other boys. Already, for a couple of Christmases, Karen and I had swapped the likes of her magical, musical jewellery box for my very unwanted train sets and cars!
 Other children's awareness of this difference became obvious. I tried to remain as inconspicuous as possible. Sometimes Australian children would still taunt us about being Poms, always said with a despising tone. Karen would continue to clobber them in her tomboyish way!
 Often, being singled out as different was unavoidable. With the occasional battering now and then, a little more abuse was added to my lot. Mostly I told my mother I had fallen from my bike, although, often enough, it looked like I had fallen *under* a bus! This

abuse, I soon realised was reserved for any child who may have seemed different in some way. *Any* way, actually! It was the teasing of a child who may have been fat, a different colour, handicapped... or simply poor.

That pain seemed all the worse whilst we were so far away from home, without the support of relatives... or a father figure. This abusive behaviour I can now understand in the ignorance of children, but when adults inflicted it... it would take years to learn how to forgive.

Karen, undoubtedly endured her own personal hells, with the abuses of the local Pommy Haters. In turn she vented her anger on me... reduced to a human punching bag for the slightest perceived misdemeanour. I felt totally betrayed, at a loss, to arrive home from school only to find no sanctuary there either.

Like any other child devoid of resources to process every pain, fear and indignity... without even words to give our agonies a name, all I could do was hold it inside. There, like the asbestos fibres, they wait until their time is ripe to unleash turmoil in our lives. Any expression of tears or fear would be met only with more taunting. Ever quicker, I learnt to keep it hidden inside.

With Mum lost in her own nightmare of cultural dysphoria, loneliness and now her new-born baby, Gemma, to cope with... isolation overwhelmed me. Feeling so small and insignificant that year, I began to save pocket money and any other small coins to be found. I used to put my odd coins into the big, yellow ceramic Labrador dogs with the harnesses on them in front of shopping centres and such, which someone had explained were the 'Blind Dogs'. I'd pitied the poor dogs, believing the unfortunate things were led about

BODYCAGE

by those harnesses... being blind of course! When Karen finally asked me why I kept giving all my pocket money to blind people it came as quite a revelation to realise it was not the dogs who were blind at all. So I withheld further donations, in the belief that the blind *people* would have been well cared for by all the dogs I'd inadvertently bought for them. Now that enough spare cash had been collected, I sat at the kitchen table, proudly counting it out for Mum.
"I've got eight pennies, two sixpences and one shilling here. Let me see, that makes two shillings, err... sixpence and...mmm another twopence. Well, I have *a lot* of money here, Mum! Do you think I've got enough for you to buy me a ticket home to England?"
 Gazing down at my pitiful collection of coins, she could only laugh. Australia had recently converted to using dollars and cents! No one had bothered to inform me. So, the coins which had earlier held the promise of buying a ticket to freedom, was now a handful of useless metal! Mum had appreciated the effort though, and was pleased that I had mastered the skill of addition in the old currency... albeit too late.

Following almost a year of this existence in Wittenoom, news came from Dad that he had found a job and new home for us in the South West. We were to join him there in a large country town called Bunbury.

My sisters and I could hardly contain our excitement as Mum herded us up the stairway, onto the plane and out of there. Baby Gemma too could at last have a break from the cruel heat which left her constantly irritable and covered in a nasty heat rash. Landing in Perth a few hours later, a three hour train ride awaited us. The antiquated 'Australind' rattled its way through the *green* countryside of the lush South West. With such relief we gazed from the windows to see sheep and cows!

The delightful old 1930s rattler chugged into Bunbury by lunchtime where dad met us at the station. He had purchased a small car in which he drove us around for a brief tour. Bunbury was to be our home for the next decade. With its glorious beaches, pretty, neat houses and tidy gardens, Bunbury looked like Paradise to us. We all wondered if this was the time we had waited for... to live like a real family at last, a white picket fence perhaps? ... and the 'Brady Bunch' next door?

Again there was a new school to start. Again we were the new kids. Not only that but we were the dreaded Poms! The taunting began all over again. Just like in Wittenoom, Karen continued to take out her frustrations on me. And still no sanctuary would be found at home. The neighbours were a family of small-minded and xenophobic Aussies of the decidedly red-necked variety... they hated the sight of us and let us quickly know.

Our lovely new back garden was mainly a sandy scrap of land, with the only grass which really stood a chance was struggling to survive growing over the septic tank and a lonely Hills Hoist clothesline was the only garden feature. Karen soon had me tied to that, calling it a tree, where, with shorts hoisted up so tightly, exposing my bare buttocks, one by one my father's darts were hurled at me. The tiny, writhing (decidedly pathetic) blond St Bartholomew was being sentenced to death by piercing of the arrows! Hardly could I have felt more alone and despondent - strapped to that clothes line . I cried out to the crowd of 'Romans' who had gathered in the arena to watch my 'public execution'... but no one from the jeering crowd would help.

BODYCAGE

If Karen were not to be found inflicting some hideous torture on me, our parents were now inflicting their own tortures upon each other. Marital and parental responsibilities had again become too much for my father. Soon enough, the carefree life of an unmarried playboy dangled alluringly before his eyes. One by one his drunken mates coaxed him from home. Soon, he would return from his trips to the pub less and less. Sometimes not returning for days.

For most women in the 1960's, spousal abandonment was devastating to their families. It was no different for my mother. What little welfare was available for 'deserted wives' left her with little recourse other than to pull her husband back into our lives. With no one to help us return to family support in England, again she fought him like a wild animal. The more she pleaded the more he turned to his other women and the drink... escaping responsibilities, squandering his paycheque. A wife and children were clearly in the way of his preferred lifestyle.

With Mum feeding baby Gemma her bottle he was grabbing at her throat as she pushed the baby into my arms asking me to run as fast as I could away from him off into the night. It was then she felt too that he would kill us all in a drunken, blind rage.

Somewhere far from my house I was still struggling through the dark streets with my heavy little sister as another neighbour was driving home from work and found us. He helped us into his car, taking us back home to calm down my parents. Whatever was said, I really don't know but he left for good shortly after that. He had finally disappeared completely from our lives, mercifully, for good. We were on our own.

I was glad he left anyway. Most of the dreaded fighting at home had stopped. So, unfortunately, had our main source of income. His child support payments stopped soon after his disappearance...of course without a trace.

My father's actions heralded the introduction to the pain and anguish inflicted on so many by these types of men - Men who put their own desires for sexual variety and irresponsibility before the welfare of wives and children. It pained me to know that he raised a family in this world only to abandon us in a foreign country and that pain stayed, notching its groove into my record for a long, long time.

Most of my mother's friends were also in similar situations. A bunch of distraught, abandoned women, struggling to understand their predicament... and how to survive whilst raising their children. That was our peer group- abandoned women and children, left by 'those bastards' to fend for ourselves, or become prey for the other 'bastards' to come along. We had learnt early to expect little more of the ones who would call themselves *'men'*.

With little understanding and even less resources with which to cope, Mum set about trying to find a new partner. Someone, perhaps, who could provide for us... and be a father. Those attempts brought only a succession of losers into our home. Losers who saw a beautiful, vulnerable, young woman... still innocent enough to believe their stories. Stories like how they would stand by her and her children. Which of course they did... until they had sufficiently enjoyed the cosiness of her home and all the sex to be had for the price of a few lies!

Then, just as Mum felt she was getting somewhere, they too would disappear. Afraid of commitment and responsibility, they would vanish in rapid succession from our lives. Half of them returning to wives they had somehow forgotten to tell Mum about.

BODYCAGE

Returning from school one day, it was hardly surprising to find my mother crumpled and sobbing on the kitchen floor.
"What's wrong, Mum. What's the matter with you?" Never before had I seen someone look so lost and broken.
"There's no food in the house, Love. I've nothing to give you all for dinner tonight." Realising there would be no money in the house for groceries, I rummaged through the pantry to find a small bag of rice. A glimpse inside the fridge revealed half a jar of turkey spread.
"Come on Mum. Get yourself up. There's some rice here and turkey spread. I can make us something out of that and get us all fed."
Busying myself to prepare the 'turkey feast' I chirped happily about my day at school. Anything to distract her attention from the agonies which had left her now whimpering softly at the table... trying to pull herself together before my sisters arrived home too. Perhaps that incident had made her all the more aware of her desperation. She was a young woman, alone in a foreign country... raising four small children. No one in her family had the funds to help us return to England and she had neither the time nor skills to find employment. She was a 'Deserted Wife'.
The term had a stigma to it, like a dirty word. People then, with just a glance, could make a woman feel that she had done something wrong. "What had she done to cause her man to run off?" she knew they wondered, with their hushed voices and snide comments.
I would notice them look across their shoulders on the bus at us, happy and smug as they returned to their 'Brady Bunch' homes... which seemed like an alien world to us. She lived like that for so long, knowing only that she had become a 'Deserted Wife'. And how I pitied her.

Rehana Incognito

 Weeks later, upon returning from school, I found Mum asleep on her bed. Baby Gemma wailed in her crib. Rushing to check her, I found her soaked. Her plaintiff cry told me she was famished... Mum must have been asleep for hours! Something surely must be wrong.

 Running back to Mum, I shook her head from side to side. She was dazed, only half able to lift the lids of her tear-filled eyes... choking out some garbled, slurred words. Panicking, I fled the house, literally flying through our neighbour's front door. With legs feeling like dragging lead, Mrs Freeman hurried me back along our garden path.

 "Does your Mum have any tablets in the house, Ian?" Mrs Freeman asked. She appeared totally calm, seeming to know that something like this would happen.

 "Yes" I replied "they're in the bathroom cupboard. I'll get them." To my horror, on picking up the bottle with the unpronounceable name, I found it empty. My mother had tried to escape her pain in a huge overdose of tranquilizers. That's all the doctors would prescribe. There was no help, no therapy. Women were advised to simply take tablets to numb their tormented minds.

 Our kind neighbour induced Mum to vomit with several glasses of salted water ferried back and forth from the bathroom. She sat by her side long enough to wait for Karen's return, explaining to her that we must all try to help more while Mum was in this difficult condition.

 Gazing into my mother's baleful eyes, looking so much like my own that I could clearly see myself... I absorbed her pain as the dutiful sponge a child can be. Absorbing the pain and storing it, who knows where for a future reference in the "things we are destined to try to fix" catalogue perhaps!

BODYCAGE

For my part, with a keen eye for bargains, shopping became an excellent chore. I took that on gladly and even managed to spare a little money from the housekeeping. Delightedly too, I fussed over my toddling little sister, gleefully taking care of her every need.

Karen and Colleen were surely pleased at my taking so well to household duties, as day by day Mum's strength returned. All the time her own personal flame of life burned ever brighter with a new sense of strength and determination, yet tempered now with a hardness etched on her face and soul.

This strengthened determination - never to be a victim again, I would need to learn too. Still being little more than this willowy, elfin, creature... moving timidly through a world which still seemed alien to me... a hunger to surpass all the misery gnawed.

With the perpetual look of an anxious deer, I would hurry home from school. Knowing that soon behind me the insults would be hurled... along with rocks and other little projectiles stinging my legs and cracking against my head.

Sunday school presented some respite. We bundled off early to give Mum some quiet time, to rest peacefully... believing that we might learn some hope for a better life from those well-meaning tutors at a local church. There I learned that I should always be good, do what I was told, and all good things would happen for me. I was glad it was just that simple, ready to take on all of life's new twists and turns, so sure it would all be just fine.

"Dear God," I promised every night in my prayers, "I'll be good and try my hardest not to do wrong. Just please make them stop hitting and teasing me. And please can you help Mum find a nice man to look after us all?" I asked, asked and asked, but the answer never seemed to come.

Father Raymond really taught us to pray well. He was very helpful with his tuition. Sitting close, supporting me on the little pew, it never occurred to me to question why his hands kept kneading my little bottom. It must have occurred to someone though... Father Raymond was arrested and imprisoned for molesting children at the Church of England Boys Society, and Sunday School in 1969.

BODYCAGE

CHAPTER THREE

1969
Being the odd one out at school sometimes had advantages. Although the teasing and bullying was beyond my control, I was at least thankful not to be chosen to play on any sports teams. I hated it! Being smaller than average and lacking any skills, I did not want to join in their roughness anyway. I hope none of those boys ever thought they had hurt my feelings. They did choose me once to join a football game, though... substituting with another miniscule boy - as a *goalpost*!

I often wondered, when they were being so hurtful, just how less-than-human they presumed me to be. Did they ever wonder who, inside this soft little body, perceived as so different from theirs, I might be? Perhaps, if they looked further, they would have found that I could draw well... and swim. An even closer look might have shown how well I could care for sick birds and animals brought to me, before their release again to freedom. Maybe I'd even be a good friend to know. For the most part, they didn't want to know.

So when they had banded into a gang, to outsmart each other with the most painful insults they could hurl, I froze... holding the tears and hurt inside. To myself, I could only wonder why on earth they could come up with nothing original. I had heard it all before! My armour was forming.

By now I had discovered an ally. One to become a comrade in arms throughout life. A friend to rely on in the worst of situations - a sense of humour. Attempts to find laughter in anything had to be better than dwelling on, or even acknowledging, painful experiences. They were nightmares, brushed aside - impossible for a child to process alone anyway. Just like any other clown, tears remained hidden behind the lonely mask I still wore with shame.

People somehow began to laugh around me more often than at me... Even a lot of teachers, surprised that an observant sharp wit would engage them in entertaining banter for the 'unruly mobs'. Sadly, most of the humour went over kid's heads, but the teachers had taken notice. New friends were soon made, if for little other reason than to be popular with teachers too.

Sometimes I was even invited to join some team games with boys. Being really fast with ball games, some teams were genuinely glad to have me. And I could certainly run! As all went well for such a short time, I developed kidney failure. Two bouts of acute nephritis saw me hospitalised for almost four months. Perhaps that was some indication that all was not as it should have been below my waist . I later learned in studies of the metaphysical relationship of events in our lives on parts of our own bodies that it is fear which causes problems in the kidneys. (Says another little prayer of thanks for the wonderful works of Louise Hay on all of that subject and more.)

On release from hospital, weeks were spent confined at home... living like a recluse, joyously pampering the birds and animals I had missed so much in hospital. Their company was my greatest joy and pleasure. Knowing they could never hurt me, and needing my care so totally, I took their little lives so seriously.

The whole neighbourhood was abuzz when our pet duck hatched out her nine little ducklings. Karen and I dug out a little pond for them in the back garden where we showed them off to neighbourhood kids. Early one morning I bounded to the hutch to feed them. The mother was panting and quacking wildly as she paced urgently along the wire. Every duckling lay dead... their little necks broken and twisted.

A scrawled message taped to the hutch door read "Bye-bye Babies. Ha-ha Ian". Again... frozen, numbed inside, I lay out each little body in a shoe-box lined with cotton wool. Grief-stricken, I dug a grave near their little pond, setting them to rest, sadly weeping to myself how sorry I was.

"I can try to be happy that God has taken them from this world, safely into His," I prayed. "They, at least, had been released from the insanity." Funny how one of the boys at the school bus stop next day kept smirking, gauging to see how much the pain of this act I would register. Sorry to disappoint him... I would register NONE!

The situation again soon changed... with the onset of puberty - unfortunately not mine, but that of my peers. They began developing the usual signs of bodily changes, blossoming into young men and women. I was not. Still I remained an androgynous waif (to say the least)... leaving me ever-conspicuous as the odd one out, different from the other boys.

Again the difference of soft, gentle behaviour marked me as target for new, more spiteful abuse. It becomes more imaginative as the brutes get older! Little respite still could be found in my own home. With teenage sisters bearing witness to the development of other boys, where I was not, they too were relentless with their teasing. Pleading with God, I begged to know why this was happening to me.

The pain and confusion was clear to see on my mother's face too. Her friends would often point out that I should be starting to look 'masculine' by now.

"Perhaps you should get him to join a football club, Jean." Mum would look at them as if they were quite insane! Still, I considered these people to be so tactless to cause Mum pain too. However, one of her friend's husbands eventually took me to a Boy Scouts meeting, whereupon I messed up every activity. They must have taken one look at me and decided to deny membership. Thankfully, I never heard from them!

1972
At thirteen years old I felt completely alone, wondering if only my few little pets understood me, or even cared. In this sorry, misfit state, I knew inside there just was no man growing in me at all. My only recourse, I felt, would be to end my life. In view of my 'good behaviour' throughout my span of thirteen years, I felt sure there would be a welcome for me at heaven's door.

So much time had been spent avoiding school, wandering about town and hiding in sand dunes. There I would contemplate the surest way to end my life, involving as little inconvenience to others as possible.

Perched on the edge of a pier, I gazed into the waters of the almost deserted marina... pondering the consequences of jumping from tall buildings or flinging myself beneath a train.

A loud pop was suddenly heard as the water's surface broke just metres before me. Then another and another. A family of dolphins had stopped to gaily cavort. Like clowns, with their permanently-fixed grins, discarded beer bottles and rubber tyres were tossed into the air, catching my attention. Delightedly, in our alien communion, with a smile to match theirs, the spirits of the loneliest child in town were lifted. Feeling less alone, I watched them disappear from view along the river. Not telling many people of my secret little spots to find the dolphins coming close, I often swam out to them, never too far from the shore to dive deep below and around them, sometimes just giving them

BODYCAGE

long strokes... which they didn't mind at all... or getting my arms right around the smaller ones for a hug and short ride through the surf. Learning earlier that a family of dolphins had appeared at a spot where locals often fed them fresh fish, proudly presenting their very new-born calf to the group of teenage boys there that day, their inter-species trust had been cruelly betrayed when the boys killed it with a brick. I made sure these ones knew they could trust and enjoy my friendship without bringing anyone else along.

As dusk drew near, I headed for the bus stop, resolving to plot my demise another day. Hurrying along the beach-front, a man's voice called from a car parked close to a cliff.

"Excuse me, could you tell me how to get to Koombana Bay from here?"

Looking toward him all thought of my solemn sojourn vanished from mind. Of course I knew where Koombana Bay was. It was another nearby spot where I could sneak away for secret liaisons with my dolphin friends. They always seemed to find me, ready to wade into the sea, splashing around, stroking their shiny soft skin.

Like the dolphins, this man too, had mysteriously appeared... with a smile just as wide and appealing. The tall, rugged blond angel leaned toward me across his jeep. With his long, wavy hair and good looks, it was impossible not to be drawn to him.

"Koombana Bay is over that way," I gestured toward the distance. "It's a bit hard to explain, but I can draw you a map if you have a pen." I quickly blurted, amazed that I had thought of a means to hold his attention. Moving toward his car, I noticed he'd hardly taken his attention from me. Clambering into the jeep, I hurriedly scrawled a simple map as he explained the circumstances of his arrival in Bunbury.

Rehana Incognito

Introducing himself as Jim, he explained his plans to house-sit a boat over the summer. Happily we chatted, for what seemed like ages, even sharing a few laughs. As a warm fire now sparked within, I would have done anything to hold his companionship even longer. Jim must have sensed some intensity... mentioning how much he too enjoyed the company. With hand resting on my long, golden (and hairless) leg, Jim decided at last to ask my name.
"It's Ian," I replied.
"Gee, you've really got quite a sense of humour. Ian's a boy's name!" Sitting back with a smirk, he awaited a reply.
"Of course it's a boy's name. That's what I am. I know I don't look much like one... I don't feel like one either. But that's what I am alright... a boy!"
Jim's hand remained fixed on my thigh. With his gentle, relaxed manner I didn't really expect him to move it. Nearly blacking out with anxiety, my heart pounded as Jim's other hand ran through my long, sun-bleached hair. His puzzled, lost look almost caused me to laugh... 'til he said the words which would always remind me that some people could see who I really was.
"Well, uhhh...you look like a beautiful girl to me. And besides, look what you've done." Wondering what I had done, I followed his gaze in the direction indicated. There, I noticed the bulge... straining to escape his shorts. As if that day was not hot enough, I felt myself truly on fire now. The fire burned from my mind, burned up across my thighs... meeting somewhere in my groin. Having not yet had an erotic thought, I still somehow knew that the overflowing bulge was something with which I wanted better acquaintance!
Clearly, Jim too, wanted me to become well acquainted with it. With one hand unleashing it, the

other placed mine gently upon it as he drew me closer. A little of the sea breeze brushed across my searing cheeks. What I now found resting in my hands felt so warm, intriguing, and delicious-looking... I could think of nothing but eating it.

And so I did - soon realising the power I had to make this man squirm with pleasure. The burning sensations throughout my body increased with the feelings of bliss. Soon I felt an unfamiliar warmth in my loins. My body had awakened to sex.

Not pausing for a moment to consider our actions, we arranged another meeting the following evening, to spend some time on the boat. With a quick goodbye peck on the cheek, I leapt from the car, I ran (almost skipping) to the bus stop... back to the loathsome home life.

After hardly sleeping at all that night, I awoke surprisingly fresh... feeling inspired enough to make an appearance at school. I wanted to tell the world about my new friend, and what we'd done. They could be as rotten to me as they wanted, because now I had someone who cared... and wanted me. I felt empowered, like somehow I had absorbed strength from my time with Jim. Catching up with lessons that day served well to pass the time before our rendezvous.

At last the clock above the teacher's head struck 3.30. The siren wailed our freedom for the weekend. Running home, I contemplated swiping a pair of Karen's panties to wear for the date then dashed through the house almost forgetting in such haste to scratch out a note for Mum. "I'm staying over at a friend's to study. Back tomorrow." She wouldn't, mind or even question me.

Rehana Incognito

Bolting out the door, I headed briskly for the bus to town. To the beat of my footsteps, a poem memorised years before pounded in my head.

"Two steps down and into the garden,
through the gate and into the lane.
Nobody's seen me. Nobody's seen me.
All by myself... I'm out in the rain."

Springing from the doors of my own "Streetcar Named Desire", the bus emptied me into the presence of the widest smile I'd ever seen. Climbing into the jeep with Jim, it all seemed like a dream... safely diving into his world of masculine strength and security. It was truly hard to believe this was really happening, let alone that he had actually turned up.

Sharing the steering of the boat, we commenced a journey along the bay, navigating the brown, muddy waters of the Collie River... laughing and joking as the scenery drifted by. In an isolated grove we anchored the boat, hidden near sand dunes by the mouth of the river. We lay upon the deck, watching a huge golden sun sink into the reddening swirls of a wondrous West Aussie sunset.

After an eternity of small talk, Jim leaned across, brushing his fingers lightly across my lips. "They look so nice and soft. Would you mind if I kissed them?" Would I mind? Having spent half of the previous afternoon with his penis in my mouth, I figured I'd at least give that a try!

The gentle nibbling and sucking on my lips felt so good. Drawing his tongue into my mouth again evoked that feeling of power, fulfilment, engulfing him. As he licked and chewed his way along my neck, I writhed... burning again. Glad that he'd given my lips a break, I felt them, wanting to absorb every feeling connected with this newness...They were swollen and tender. For days they looked like they'd been stung by wasps! Breathing ever heavier now, Jim slid a hand slyly under my T-shirt to pinch and stroke a hardening nipple.

Still confused with the barrage of new sensations, I felt that heat again sear from my neck to groin. Throwing back my head, all conscious awareness of the world quickly faded. Arching my back, I gasped, slowly starting to grind my pelvis against his. Rolling onto my stomach, to hide my own embarrassing arousal, I dangled my leg into the water over the side of the boat.

Whipped by the sea-breeze, the cool, choppy water partially soothed my fire. Gazing into its dreamy depths... my body feeling like a bridge between two worlds... part of me wanting to slip overboard to be caressed, enfolded by the supporting waters. With one leg slightly adrift, the other sprawled on deck, Jim's hand slid gently into my cut-off jeans... firmly kneading my buttocks. He drew me back from taking the plunge into the safe waters I'd always known onto a new path taking me to endless new destinations and perils along the way.

Placed in a vulnerable position seemed preferable to lying face up. I couldn't stand the thought of exposing the 'less than subtle' reminder of the truth... that this was just a fantasy. A fantasy that I was this man's 'girlfriend'.

Assured that he was now in complete control, I could hardly care anymore what he might do. Being so sweet and gentle, even with his now full erection probing against my exposed buttocks, this still felt oddly, just right. *Nothing*, however, could have could have prepared me for the pain involved in his next manoeuvre. A rod of burning steel seemed to shoot through my entire body. Stifling a scream, clutching at the side of the boat, I almost lost consciousness for the full three minute ordeal.

Being now sick from the lurching roll of the boat, the feeling of having been impaled by a roll of linoleum dispelled any notion of this being a pleasurable 'first time'. However, as the waves of pain ebbed, I did ponder the dynamics of what had just happened. Accepting the part I had played in needing him 'inside', at any cost, it did feel to me that we were making love. At least from that first, painful experience, there was no doubt in my mind about my preferred sexual role. Its expression, to me, felt as it should be... instinctively or otherwise - it was female. Innocence had been given away on a windy, summer night. Given to a twenty four year old man, who cared not in the least what had just transpired between himself and a thirteen year old boy.

Seeing Jim frequently, some form of emotional stability took form in my world. More concentrated effort was put in with studies, with Jim encouraging me... even not to skip classes to be with him. He also began to clothe me with surprise little gifts of androgynous clothes... mainly, I'm sure, so that we'd attract little attention together. The clothing was hardly unusual in the seventies... with cheese-cloth Indian tops, love beads and baggy pants, I hardly looked any different to most teenage girls.

I began to feel like part of the world around me, where other teenagers had started to date. Jim had also bought me a ring... engraving our names on the inside, adding some validity to our relationship. Like my sisters, I too had a boyfriend. I had ached for this caring, affection and security... now it was mine. What Jim was thinking, I never asked, nor was I told. Years of further experience with men and their desires, taught me he was like so many who could not care through whom or what sexual gratification was obtained.

BODYCAGE

Returning to the city at the end of summer, Jim left an address to write and arrange to be together again. Being naive, I let him go happily, sure that he would stay in touch and find a way for us to be together. Good God, I was deluded! Taking myself to the movies, all alone, feeling like a tragedy, I had heard that "Jonathan Livingston Seagull" was the most incredibly beautiful and meaningful film to see. Possibly I'd thought that going off to watch a meaningful film would be good experience for me to try to understand what could be so amazing about the life of a seagull called Jonathan, set to Neil Diamond's songs and soundtracks. So off I went, sitting alone in the theatre, mesmerised by the beauty of the seashores, with surreal sunsets set to music. By the end of the film, with the song "Be" ringing over and over in my mind as the image of a brilliant white, lonesome seagull soared across the fiery reds and golden sunset of heaven, it became the first film I'd ever seen which actually left me sitting there crying for whatever reason I was far from being able to know.

"Lost...
On a painted sky
Where the clouds are hung
For the poet's eye
You may find him
If... you may find him
There...
On a distant shore
By the wings of dreams
Through an open door
You may know him
If ...you may. Be."

Those words and feelings stayed.... they are here still.

Rehana Incognito

One letter did arrive, which I answered immediately. It came back within a week, marked: "Not here. Please return." The panic and dread which came over me felt like losing my link to reality. The weekend could not come quick enough as I lied to my mother to escape for a couple of days. Hitch-hiking to Perth, I traced the address he had left... only to find he was unheard of there. He had lied.

Dejectedly I wandered to Scarborough Beach Road to find the coast and hitch a ride South. Dark clouds, from out of nowhere, blocked the sun, emptying their miserable drizzle... spitting at my face. All by myself I was indeed out in the rain.

Feeling totally abandoned as the rain just as abruptly stopped, I trudged to the water's edge, crunching through the thin, crusty layer of dampened sand. Pondering what to do, I sat to watch the quickly fading sun... wishing I could just look up to see Jim in his jeep... coming to rescue me. There in the sand my heart sank in unison with the sun. Its golden light caressed the choppy water as I caught a glimpse of my pals - the dolphins... a whole troupe caroused past, leaping from the waves. Calling out a silent greeting from my heart, I ached to swim out and join them, knowing they had heard me... they always could. The huge orange sun melted into the horizon, blazing in and out of billowing, emptied puffs of clouds whose colours defied description. Again the rest of "Be" rang over and over....

"Be...
As a page that aches for a word
which speaks on a theme that is timeless...
While the Sun God will make for your day
Sing...

BODYCAGE

As a song in search of a voice that is silent...
And the one God will make for your way."

Again the tears welled up as I felt a shadow flickering over me. My heart shuddered in the hope that it might be Jim. Yet some 'thirty something' man approached and sat by my side. After some trivial conversation, I explained my predicament of living some 200 kilometres away, with no way to get back in the evening.
"Well, Ian. You should come back to my house, have something to eat and have a shower. After that I might enjoy a ride down to Bunbury. Might even have you home in time to get your homework done for school in the morning." His eyes sparkled from behind his thick glasses at the thought of my being a schoolkid.
 Relieved, however, at his offer I let him lead me to his car. With his trembling hands and stuttering along the way I should have guessed that something was amiss. However, being brought up to respect and obey adults, I went haplessly along... not even knowing what a paedophile was.
 Whilst the man busied himself in the kitchen, he suggested I take a shower. Compliantly, I did. With eyes closed, head lathered in shampoo, I suddenly realised I was not alone. This vile creature's hands groped and grabbed at every part of my body. Freezing, not knowing what to do, I just wanted him to stop rubbing his penis all over me. Apart from that, he began tugging and clawing at parts of me I didn't even want to acknowledge possession of!
 With frantic effort I grabbed the shower nozzle to rinse soap from my eyes, trying all the while to get some bearing on this mess. With no point fighting him, I realised that I was pinned, stomach pressed against the stark, cold tiles. With resolve, I went to 'that

place'... away from my body. Away where I went during the screams and thumps of my parent's fighting, during the maddening taunts and bullying of other children. With the body left behind, I drifted to another world as the ugly mix of soap, sperm and blood dribbled down my legs. Flinging me around, clasping my face close to his he spluttered through the mist. "You won't tell anyone about this will you, Ian?" We could both be in a lot of trouble. Besides, you do want me to give you a lift home, don't you?"

Wanting only to get away from him as quickly as possible, I let him drive me the silent 180km home. Asking to drop me off where no one could see his car, he switched off his lights, turning into the darkness of the nearby racecourse. With hardly a word being exchanged during the long drive, he stunned me by asking, as I scrambled from the car, if I'd like to visit him again?!

How I wished then to have some one dear to me... close enough to tell of what I had just gone through. Leaping from the car, I wondered, fleeing into the night... should I call the police and give them his details? They would be certain to pay him a visit. Of course I could not. It, too, would be kept inside... right there with the anguish and pain of the cruel deaths of the ducklings. No one would see that pain.

Being so distraught at losing Jim, and the violation at the hands of this dirty man, school work became a gratifying distraction. Somewhere I noticed a man in a T-shirt... emblazoned on the front were the words "Wissen ist Macht". Daring to ask the meaning, I learned that it was German, meaning "Knowledge Is Power".

How fortuitous to find this reminder from the Universe! Already doing well at high school French, I took on German as well. I would do my best to learn all I could.

BODYCAGE

From there the feeling of strength crept slowly through. After German came Japanese and, after years to come spent living in Europe, came Italian and Dutch. At that point I should have trained as an ambassador for the United Nations! However, it would be years yet before I'd be confident enough to say 'NO' in any tongue or appreciate the creative power hidden in our every word no matter what the language.

Doing well now in school earned some merit with teachers and students. Many teachers, I'm sure, were aware of my difference and could clearly see the implications of being 'singled out'. Their care, consideration and a little extra support was much appreciated.

"Ian Davies, you're like a gazelle in motion jumping those hurdles!" The physical education teacher remarked as I puffed and panted at the end of the 100 metre race. His smile fed the growing inner strength as I noticed his gaze scan the length of my long legs... dripping with sweat.

"That's no surprise," I mused with him, "I always feel like I'm on the run. At least I'm starting to look the part!" Perhaps I should also have fled from him... there he was every time I stepped from the showers after sports class. His gaze was not restricted to my performance on the racetrack. He would observe my every move like an exhibit in the zoo, tracing each step from the shower to drying off and quickly dressing - always waiting 'til last, lest I be teased about my underdeveloped body!

His sexual attraction was not the only one I noticed in high school. As boys developed their macho behaviour in an adolescent hierarchy, they too showed signs of their own confusion about me... and their sexual attractions.

Rehana Incognito

Andy Bailey was a boy in my school year with Klinefelter's Syndrome. His ungainly body was topped with a below-normal sized head, which mercifully contained a smart enough mind to stay within the 'normal' school system. 'Pin Head', they loved to call him. However, the boys would afford him little opportunity to study in peace... teasing him mercilessly. Who could be the cleverest of heroes to reduce Andy to a mass of tears? Extra points were awarded to he who could make Andy pee his pants in terror.

On his behalf I often pleaded with the more sensible students to let him be left alone... to give him a chance. My pleas served only all the more, to draw attention to myself as to why I would not partake in his torments.

Andy's pleas, and my own, were to no avail as he was removed from school before the end of his first year - in an ambulance. We gazed from the window as they drove him off... the ambulance lights twinkling and sirens wailing like the sparks and screams in his head... where the circuits had finally shorted out.

Andy never returned to our school of course. Later we heard that, at the age of fourteen, he had taken his own life. How hopeless my world felt to know that kids in their early teens were capable of driving another to their death. Still, he had finally escaped his tormentors... now they would need someone else upon whom to hone their skills. Surely, I felt, I would be next.

Fortunately though, my difference did not always attract simply ridicule or abuse. Some of the older boys had indeed been observing me in that manner which confused their adolescent minds. Often they would hold eye contact for just a little longer than expected, only to avert their gaze rapidly if I noticed - sometimes too, I caught their nervous or embarrassed smiles!

BODYCAGE

Danny was one of these toughest of boys, whom once I found to be standing before me as I dashed from the shower after sports class. Inching toward him, clutching a towel across my groin, Danny held his gaze fixed to my every move as I approached my belongings.

This young man I had seen pulverise adversaries for the slightest infraction of mysterious rules and regulations set up to control their alien empire. He would just as easily intimidate teachers. Still, he had done no harm to me in the past... but the look on his face, as I slipped on my shorts, told me something was a little out of the ordinary. With not a word yet said, I leaned forward to tie my shoe laces, wishing only to look up and find him gone.

Danny, with the physique of a bear, leaned forward to slip an arm under my shoulder... pulling me up, almost level with his face.

"You didn't like what happened to your little friend, did you Ian?" My mind didn't want to accept that this was really happening. The world went blank as I became only aware of his cold, glazed eyes... and the smell of marijuana on his breath. "Some of the guys might start the same treatment with you. I can stop that, real easy. But there's something you're gonna have to do for me."

"I don't know what you want from me, Danny. I don't even know what you guys are on about half the time anyway." Pushing my shoulders down he had me seated with his belt buckle and zipper facing straight into my eyes. There was really no mistaking what he wanted as he pushed my face roughly into his swelling groin. Clearly he could offer me protection from situations I had seen reduce a child to insanity in weeks.

With the other students already gone and plenty of time before the janitor would come to lock up, I opted to try to please him... in whatever way. That I must have practiced well enough - Danny seemed pretty smug as he straightened up his clothes, putting his hand to my cheek in a gentle mock slap. There I was left alone to ponder what had happened... and left alone (for the most part) too, continuing my studies with minimal hindrance from the testosterone-crazed bullies.

It seemed good enough to know now that knowledge is indeed strength, but I'd sadly learned too, that prostitution can offer a lot of protection.

At the end of summer 1974, I progressed to Technical College to study the catering industry whilst still finding time to explore sexual experience with men who found themselves drawn to me. Still yearning to have someone with whom to share love, to protect me and care, it was easy to confuse their desires as being fulfilment of my needs. It took so long to find out that is all it really amounts to. The best thing about the whole Hotel Management and Catering course tho was a field trip to a meat processing plant. It was on that day, after completely revolting and horrifying myself at the entire process of butchery and dismemberment of fellow defenceless mammals that I went cold turkey (sorry!) on eating meat, not touching it again even once for thirty years now!

BODYCAGE

CHAPTER FOUR

1975
With all going well in the first year of college, we hardly expected the explosive turn in the life of my big sister - now pregnant at the age of sixteen to an older neighbourhood boy from a better home than ours. My mother's despair was clear to see - unsure as to whether we could support this child or give it up to the adoption service. In an already crowded home, we decided to do our best to keep it.

Geoff was born in due course to a mother who was little more than a child herself. Still, his arrival in our world offered a whole breath of hope with his innocent presence... all new, swathed in total bliss. His gurgles of delight at anything which caught his eye infected me, giggling along with him. How I longed to remember a time when I too knew nothing of the dysfunction all around. For now, it seemed that's all there was.

With plenty of live-in babysitters, Karen took to the night as often as time would allow. Allowing herself again to become further prey to an endless stream of hounds, who feigned an interest to care for her and her tiny son. His own father had vanished at the first hint of responsibility... random support payments appeared for the times he had work. Like my own father's commitment to child rearing, support payments soon stopped.

Mum had found some extra work to help Karen set up an apartment of her own. It hardly came to pass in time as my studies began to fail. On most of the nights of Karen's absence, baby Geoff's needs for feeding and changing would wake me up several times. I also took turns, only to struggle out of bed, arriving late to classes in which I would be semi-comatose by 10 A.M.

Rehana Incognito

Along with the constant lateness, I fell further and further behind with study... eventually dropping out all together. We decided to move back to the city once Karen had found her new home. We planned to find a larger house and better chances for us all to find work, pitching in together to keep trying to make this 'better world' for ourselves still. It always seemed to materialise before us in some magical way... only to vanish before our eyes as we reached out to claim it. Then back to the misery of feeling that the whole world had a conspiracy against us.

Somehow we did get moved into a bigger house in Perth. Setting about straight away to find work, an amiable personnel manager at David Jones department store hesitatingly offered me a position in the cosmetics department.

"Would you mind at all?' she asked as I almost leapt from my chair with excitement. Mind? It was like a dream come true! I hadn't even dared to ask if there might have been a position for me there, expecting to end up somewhere dreary like *hard*ware or *soft* furnishings. Endless images flashed through my mind of all the creative fun I could have with the gorgeous beauties at the make-up counters. Gratefully, I was swept into it.

Being the first male to work in that department was wild. I was forever astounded that women would constantly prefer to ask my opinion of a shade of lipstick or blush. As if I'd known then what would match their blouses or hair colour! Like the girls at the counters, I quickly learned to earn my $60 a week, bluffing it as they did... and how useful was all that knowledge to be one day! Big thanks to all those girls at every cosmetics stand at David Jones department store. If only they knew I have them to thank for learning to cleanse, tone and moisturise, keeping my skin as soft and glowing as it needed to be for what was still to come.

At home I felt totally used and unappreciated, contributing week after week to Mum's unending projects to beautify her home. Never, it seemed would it be 'just right'. Curtains went up only to be yanked down a week later, followed by the carpet and furniture in her never-ending quest to create her vision of perfection in her exterior world. She would be up til late at night at times, with my sisters and me, dragging furniture all over the house until she felt it had found just the right place. I had to wonder whether she just had an innate gift for Feng Shui or if it was merely a reflection of her own house in her mind being not quite how she wanted it. Finding myself doing the same thing throughout my life, I learnt it was the latter. Adding the touch of Feng Shui seemed to make it all the more legitimate for me. Anyway, Mum's still at it today, as I fill my spare room with her countless impulsively purchased, unsuitable goodies!

Life at home stifled me. It felt like a dead-end, facing daily the fact that my mother took out each frustration and demand on me as she would have with my father. "You're just like him!" she'd scream with bitterness when I couldn't agree to her increasing demands. There I was left in adolescence, feeling as I often had as child... wondering how on earth I could be 'just like' a man I could barely recall a thing about!

Frantically I began to save for an airline ticket as a desperate urge to 'go home' compelled me. Home, to me, was the only memory of a place where all seemed real, unchanging and comforting in a world of familiarity. The memory of life in Northumberland, before we went 'upside down', was drawing me back... to see if it could again be found.

Rehana Incognito

Mum, of course was infuriated - I too, was 'abandoning her, leaving her to suffer without my income'... "Just like him!" Thank God, before Mum's guilt trip had almost dissuaded me from moving on, Colleen too found a job as a salesgirl. With further income in the household, Mum at least began to understand the draw to the homeland. Were she not herself feeling trapped in Australia, she too would have made the return. At least one of her children would make it there... it seemed some comfort to her in the end. I said goodbye to my family at Perth Airport on a drizzly, grey August day in 1977.

1977

Arriving on, what was for England, a hot summer's night, the Tube spat out me and my luggage at King's Cross Station. The smell there was instantly familiar as I recalled the bustling scene of our arrival there from Newcastle thirteen years before. There we were hurried through with so many others to our life in Australia.

Brimming now with the excitement of reaching the company of friendly Northumbrians, cobbled streets and green forests, I didn't notice that someone had just walked off with my luggage! There, I arrived back on the platform at dawn at Newcastle Central Station with only a flight bag of survival goods, which I'd kept mercifully close on a strap across my shoulder.

The stolen clothing was dreadful enough to consider replacing, the loss of important documents was going to be a problem, but the loss of treasured photos of a life I'd had for eighteen years, ate away at me. Perhaps that entire loss was a portent of things to come, things to change and things best forgotten, or at least put behind.

BODYCAGE

Standing in line to buy the ticket home, sadness overwhelmed me at the loss of so many memories. Counting reassuringly again through my change in pennies and pounds, I wondered how a thief could take almost all a traveller had without even a thought. A traveller who, at eighteen, looked only fifteen and was feeling very disheartened at the 'welcome' home.

Everyone seemed pleased with the return home of one of the 'Lost Tribe' as I settled in at Aunt Alison's. Soon enough I was inundated with a supply of clothes from well meaning uncles and cousins, all happy to see me again and help me return to their idea of a normal life. There was even talk of finding me a job 'down the pit'! The thought of disappearing into a coal mine miles out beneath the North Sea sent me scuttling out for the job section of the newspaper!

Under 'Hospital Appointments' I found an advertisement for nurses, training provided, at St Nicholas Hospital in Gosforth, Newcastle. On calling them, I learned it was a psychiatric hospital with a general nursing ward too. That sounded like quite an opportunity to grow and learn, I figured, but without all the hassle of hideous open wounds, broken limbs and mangled accident victims. Sailing through a hastily arranged interview, I joined the class of student nurses at the end of summer.

Following two week's introductory training we commenced work on the wards - my first allocation being to Ward 21... Acute Disturbed Males. Just the place for someone who's been dealing with the acutely disturbed for years, I figured. On the first day of duty, with still no uniform, I wandered about... finding activities to occupy the patients.

A somewhat scrawny, middle aged porter appeared late one evening to remove the body of a patient who had passed away earlier in the day. Pushing the trolley past me as I leaned against the wall, whilst vaguely participating in a board game, I couldn't help but notice how he looked like Josef Goebbels. From behind his tiny, round glasses he noticed my bewildered gaze, offering back a knowing wink and nod, enquiring if I was 'alright today?'

As he chauffeured the corpse along the hallway I overheard him nudging the Charge Nurse with a glance at me - "Doesn't seem ought much wrong with that lad. What's he in here for?" he hissed through his thin lizard lips, as I feigned further interest in the game. "He seems quite bright 'n all".

"That's a relief to know", replied the Charge. "He's actually a new nurse... started today!"

That was the first I'd realised how often the staff who are drawn to this work can be as bizarre as the patients. Time and time again I'd hear it said - "You end up thinking it's normal after being surrounded by the insane after a while". Soon enough it did seem that way... only the degree of madness and how dangerous one might be to another had any bearing on my perception of what insanity might be.

Over the next three years I witnessed every degree of mental disorder and their treatments. From the depressed housewife to homicidal, and suicidal, teenagers... I dealt with them all, each leaving their scars of tortured hopelessness deeply etched in my psyche.

So many souls driven to insanity by the pressures of life, the cruelty of others or the confusions of religion... all became a breeding ground, perpetuating a horrid picture of a world in which I felt it a hopeless nightmare to try and conduct a life. In a way they presented a microcosm of the entire world's tragedy, condensed into the rambling Victorian structures of St Nick's. The nurses, whisking through the gloomy corridors, must

BODYCAGE

have seemed like angels, or envoys from another world amongst them... in the world of the sane. I was left with few illusions about human nature and behaviour.

Whilst supervising bathroom activities on a frosty, winter's morning, a grey-faced patient approached... blankly staring out from his world... through the eyes of a dead fish!
"Nurse, this razor's blunt," he muttered in a monotone, robotic voice. Dangling the safety razor perilously before my face his expressionless face mouthed further. "You'd better put a new one in... or I'll cut myself Nurse."
"I've just changed all the blades myself Alec... and, err... I haven't got the key on me now to open the razors anyway." A vein pounded heavily, making a criss-cross where his full frontal lobotomy traversed a bald forehead. Menacing! Yes, that's how Alec McGowan looked, looming at me through the steam of the green tiled bathroom. Beads of condensation now poured down the brow of this man who had burnt to death his mother and aunt, only to spend the rest of his life in institutions - they nagged too much he'd said.
  Thoughts of him grabbing a blade as I tried to change it raced through my mind. My heart thumped as I envisioned struggling with him as my hands became shredded by the slashing blade.
Sensing the fear as my own attack and defend mode took hold, Alec began to bellow into my face.
"O.K! O.K!" he bellowed, brandishing the razor in a fist made ready to plummet through my skull. A strong arm reached from behind him, pulling his own behind his back as the razor clinked across the floor. Still stoned with fear, I stared in amazement as Eric, a student

nurse one year ahead of me, marched him to the sanctity of his favourite white, padded cell for a while to calm down.

Trotting proudly back into the bathroom, Eric grabbed me on both the shoulders. Giving a little shake 'back to life'. Eric apologised for being late for his shift, leaving me to face that ordeal on my own.

"Thanks a lot for your help. Do you think that might have gotten out of hand if you hadn't stopped him?" I asked, feeling like a complete geek.

"It already was out of hand," Eric laughed. "You've got to watch Alec like a hawk... and *NEVER* stop in the bathroom on your own with him. Promise me that now! And I'll go off and write up a report."

The White Knight who had just saved me turned to leave. I murmured something, hoping he'd turn around. There, riveted to the gaze of his huge blue eyes, lost in a tussle of black, curly hair... I stumbled over my words. After a teeny forever it came.

"Thanks for helping me there, Eric. I... err... wonder if I could take you for a drink sometime?" He was actually the most handsome and sexy man I'd ever seen, so was beside myself with excitement as he called back - "Well, I've nought on tonight. Fancy a drive out to a pub in Whitley Bay then?"

"Aye," I muttered in disbelief as he disappeared in the bathroom mist.

The rest of that shift dragged by, as I contemplated bundling up on the back of Eric's motorbike... and a chance to put my arms around him, at least. I was almost pissed off when we reached the coast, slowly lowering my arms from around his waist. The time in the pub was like a slow torture, stumbling over banal conversation, Eric's eyes perusing the attributes of each passing female and a bunch of local Whitley Bay lads who turned to watch when ever I either went to the

BODYCAGE

bar or just squirmed around in my seat, feeling both nervous and excited to be sitting there with Eric. On Eric's trip to the bar he came snickering like he'd just discovered the secret to life. "You'll never believe what those lads are arguing about over there." I just shook my head as if he were talking about aliens. "They are having a bet whether you are a lad or a lass!" I turned my attention to their little side of the bar and could indeed hear their voices getting louder. Thick as bricks, one was saying "It's a lad", the other saying louder than him "it's a bloody lass." Eric must have heard my sigh of relief when he suggested we leave.
"Let's get away early, then. You're on the 7 o'clock 'n all aren't you?"
"Uh, huh, I am," I stammered.
"Well, you'll want to be wide awake when Alec comes at you with that razor again, won't you?!" Was he teasing me, aware of my hopelessness in those situations? Teasing me he was... and the tone of his voice and the smirk on his face left no doubt that he was flirting as well.

On reaching the nurses home, where I was now in residence... perhaps with Dutch courage or desperation... I brazenly asked if he'd stay in my room rather than take the long ride home.
"It'll be a lot easier for you to get to the ward from there in the morning too," I offered, already knowing that he'd accept the invitation. It felt like a major lottery win when he chirped back -
"SURE!"
"But all I've got is a s-single bed ... there ain't no room for your sweet head," I drunkenly slurred the words to that stupid song as we fumbled our way up the stairs. Eric just snickered, surely thinking me to be quite mad. After quickly washing and allowing him to share my

toothbrush, we squeezed into the s-s-single bed... which was really quite roomy, but I pondered every excuse to touch him... anywhere. Expecting him to just roll over, curl up and doze off, I gazed across at this dream... just lying there.

He seemed so grown up to me, so confident and aloof... secure with his place in the world already, at nineteen! Such a stark contrast to the lonely, confused, inadequate and insecure person I felt I was. And every pretty nurse in the hospital wanted to dated him, in fact most had! But here he was, alone in my bed, with me wondering what on earth could ever make me think that he would want me... So in total unawareness, I could use him.... absorbing from him all that I didn't even accept I was missing in myself.

Still face to face, my wonderings were answered, as he softly... in a half-sleep... murmured.

"You know, Ian. You're a very unique person. I enjoy your company...but please don't take this wrong... I'm not gay, like. Nowt like that. But I feel attracted to you. Like I would be to a lass."

I could see that he was struggling with himself - looking now like a lost child too, struggling for the words to describe something neither of us understood. Feeling just as hopeless, I made the brave move to comfort him. Sliding my arm across his and around his shoulder, I gently pulled him closer in a tender hug. Unbelievingly, his beautiful lips landed on mine like a butterfly with an electric cattle prod attached. I was just stunned.

Now drawn so close we sunk together into one entity in the soft, cosy mattress. For the first time this kiss of a man felt so different. Different from the uncomfortable experiences I could associate with homosexual contact in the past - when more and more I would turn my head away, avoiding contact with the lips. Kissing Eric felt like oxygen being pumped into my fire, and the burning transformed me into a new, living flame... flickering in the half-light. The flame licked at his body consuming him in the warmth, burning us both in the passion. His 'kiss of life' sent me a-soaring as I thought back to our chat in the pub about Star Signs.

"So you're an Aquarius, Eric? They're weirdos aren't they?... Always attracted to the bizarre and off-beat," I laughed. "My nephew, Geoff's an Aquarius. So I like them of course! An Air sign from what I remember, always refreshing... like fresh air," I rambled.

"Or a howling gale if you're not careful," came his reply, which left me momentarily stumped. The air continued to fuel my fire. "Burn Baby, burn!" I whispered to myself.

With all the cares of our work far behind us, and the chaos and despair of our patients asleep on the ward, we escaped to a world where only we existed... finding total bliss and solace in each other's arms. Arms which reached across to squeeze me tight as he rolled himself onto me. The bedding fell to the floor as the central heating radiator rumbled its presence. The windows in the room had completely fogged as we'd generated enough heat to render it useless!

Snow built up on the window ledge from the pregnant clouds as we rolled about on that bed. Tuned in to an all night disco station, I mouthed every pathetic word as we danced the dance the Universe had provided for us that night. Donna Summer moaning "Love to Love You" must have been more than either of us could bear. Giving no thought to tomorrow, Donna enticed the two writhing forms deeper into the intertwining oneness. The oneness of the greatest passion of all... where only the feeling of two hearts beating in unison to the rhythm of their sexual mechanics, would lead to total sexual ecstasy. At least it seemed that way to me, lying there like the star of my own Hollywood movie, in a role which was screening in my head alone!

Upon awakening, after a deep one hour of sleep, Eric had little to say. He scrambled into his clothes... hurriedly hiding his nakedness, as if to hide the nakedness of his own soul from the ravages of a nocturnal succubus. Trembling, as I grabbed for my own clothes... watching him as he sullenly dressed... I anxiously waited for him to comment on our night together, to show some more tenderness... to ask when we could be together again. He showed nothing.

Hardly knowing what to do or say, I watched him leave after a quick splash in the sink. Thinking he would walk out the door without a word, I blurted.

"Aren't you talking to me this morning then?"

"Oh... aye. I'll see ye." Stony reply, not even a glance! There on the ward, he avoided contact with me the entire shift. Deciding not to pursue the matter any further, I returned miserably to my room. Pushing the sleep button on the radio, I crawled into bed feeling nothing but loneliness and a desolate sense of confusion. What more torment could I have expected than to realise what was playing on the radio...

'I can't stand the rain...on my window... bringin' back sweet memories.'

How apt and how silly that crazy song by "Eruption" (of all names!) now seemed. I'd rocked out every heart-wrenching emotion to it on the dance floor only nights before with other disco queens at Newcastle's first real gay, mixed nightclub, dancing ourselves dizzy as another song told us to do. Now lying in the darkness, with orange sparkles of the street light reflecting the raindrops on my window, I gazed at "the pillow... where his head use to lay" like he'd been there all my life, getting swept away in the full flow of drama and meaning this song held for me. Reaching my arms

BODYCAGE

around it, I hugged it to my face, hoping to smell a trace of Eric. Through the muffled sounds I heard the words again and again...
'I just can't stand the rain.'
One tragic song after another played through the night, but even those sounds were preferable to hearing other nurses coming and going, giggling 'good nights' to their lads. Preferable too, to the now pounding rain, turning my beloved pure white snow to the grey slush I'd trudge through to work in the morning.

Wondering how to get through the craziness of work, feeling like a zombie myself, Eric added to the misery by completely avoiding any contact again. Shattered through lack of sleep, over-anxious and hopelessly confused, I knew I'd have to confront him. Somewhere I'd catch him alone, plead for some understanding or reason behind a situation I felt to be horribly wrong... and tragically, needed to 'fix'.

My chance came as I found Eric alone in the treatment room. Busily he sorted through bottles of Valium, Inderal and all manner of mind numbing and mood altering drugs in the room we called the 'Candy Store'. None of those drugs could have helped me cope with the treatment Eric was about to administer to me.

"Eric, do you want to talk to me about the other night?" I stammered, half closing the door behind me.

"About what, Ian? Nothing happened the other night... except I made a mistake." He fumbled with the pill bottles, squirming and clearly wishing that I'd just vanish.

"Well what do you expect me to do now, Eric? It felt so special, what happened...err... the other night. It meant something to me!"

My words surely looked like the desperate plea they were, spilling from the mouth of someone clearly advertising that they too were desperate and pleading. Such a pitiful and broken person could hardly inspire the attraction of anyone... let alone comfort and compassion. Especially from Eric.

"I just want to forget about it, *aalreet*!" He had snapped back in a more guttural Northumbrian tone. I knew he meant it.

"Just forget about it." And, as a casual after thought, he softly added, barely audibly... "I'm sorry I used you."

The Candy Store simply turned to darkness for me, as tears streamed down my reddened cheeks. Slamming the door of the medicine chest, Eric pushed by me. Tightly he pulled closed the door to the room as if to entomb me and what I represented to him.

Standing there, mouth agape in disbelief, I noticed a shadow through the marbled glass panels of the door. My heart thumped in the hope that Eric was back, he'd changed his mind and realised he did care for me. The doorknob slowly twisted as I joyously stood back to stare into the deadened eyes of Alec McGowan, closely set in his ghoulish face.

"Got any sweets for me, Nurse?" I couldn't have imagined worse. I could happily have clawed open the medicine chest and filled Alec with the whole lot. Angrily, I felt my nails biting into the flesh of my palms. A fleeting, fruitless interlude with a man of my dreams had been replaced with a vision of my worst nightmares!

Fumbling through my pristine, white nurse's jacket, I found some mints.

"He's a Polo for you, Alec." I handed him the packet. Gleefully he took them, delightedly unwrapping them with the relish of a child. Slipping my arm under his, I led my mindless automaton back to his room. Like a macabre bride escorting her twisted groom to the

BODYCAGE

honeymoon suite, I wondered if this was really all I deserved?

Mid morning the ward phone rang as we sat for our tea break. Over the raucous blare from the radio of BBC1's "Everything Stops For Tea" and the chatter of nurses and cleaners, I heard the Charge call out to Eric.

"It's for you bonny lad! There's a young lass on the phone askin' for ye."

How painful to endure that added indignation. Seeing Eric at work every day began to gnaw at me with hopelessness beyond comprehension. Every thought brought me back to the longing for him... to retrieve and relive that feeling of wholeness, of total bliss and security in the arms of another... the feeling that I had found 'home'.

Almost nightly, I'd saunter out with a couple of very 'out' gay nurses and lesbian friends. Tiring of gay bars and clubs around Newcastle we'd venture further by train to the next city... like Durham or Middlesbrough. The quest seemed never to end, whether in clubs on Tyneside or bars in Edinburgh. Always looking for that elusive 'high' of the 'right guy' or the 'right' encounter to make the misery of being 'gay', lonely and misunderstood disappear for that all too brief moment of oblivion.

We formed a merry band of Fairies and Dykes, rampaging across the countryside - a campy version of the hideous medieval 'Harrying of The North'... only more rape and pillage than shedding the blood of 'those cursed Northerners'! Even as I danced myself dizzy with 'Liz'... who was really Chris - with his bejewelled fingers looking for all the world like 'Miss Taylor', or Tony... the over-the-top and effeminate 'Mother' of us all, I still felt uncomfortable.

Rehana Incognito

In 1979 the fabulous Casablanca opened just above the Haymarket Metro Station. With hundreds of others, I queued for hours to pay the one pound entrance fee to Newcastle's first all-Gay nightclub. Watching all the bonny lads and lasses falling for other bonny lads and lasses, we danced out lyrics to every song... knowing every word by heart. Just before the last slow dance, when we'd all hoped to find someone to take us in their arms, Gloria Gaynor would belt out "I Will Survive" for every tragic queen to swamp the dance floor in a stampede I often felt I might not survive!

From time to time, the crowds would find themselves enthralled by a visiting drag show, usually up from London for a weekend break. So many of them seemed little more than parodies of women, with so much of their performance reliant upon the denegration of femininity. Whoever 'Simone' was or where she came from I'll never recall, but her appearance at the 'Cass' surely etched a lasting impression. Never before had I seen someone so perfectly pretty and feminine in every respect, moving with the grace of a prima ballerina... only to learn that she was once a 'man'.

"Some man she must have been!" Liz snickered as Simone swished regally by during her interval. In one sweeping glance like a searchlight across her body, I registered every detail. With her bodily structure, facial features - even the elegant, slender hands... Simone was a clone of myself, with longer hair and make-up!

During the course of that winter I watched the performances of several other such 'artistes', wondering all the more if there might indeed be a third gender category into which people with bodies like us must fall? And, as they seemed to project a successful transformation, so then... I felt, might I.

The cabaret performers, week after week, fostered my hopes of one day finding an escape from a body which served now only as a cage. In their beautiful costumes, glittering with colours, sparkling with jewels... they were elegant birds set free to be and express what they wanted to be. I felt like a child standing outside a party to which there was no invitation, heart despondent... wondering how to get in.

But who in the world could I talk to about this? My gay friends would surely laugh and my relatives lived such uncomplicated lives it would throw them into one hell of a conundrum! As wonderful as they were, they could certainly have offered little support or understanding. My family in Australia had enough difficulties already, I felt. One more complication would not have been gladly received.

Still, at this time, I had developed no facial hair and to give any resonance of depth to my voice required considerable strain! To top it all, I noticed that a 'lump' had developed directly beneath each of my nipples. With a pluck of courage I explained the presence of the lumps to a sympathetic gay doctor over lunch in the hospital cafeteria. Kindly, he referred me to an endocrinologist at the Royal Victoria Infirmary. Again I felt the flurry of excitement that another step might be drawing closer to the hoped for release.

Rehana Incognito

BODYCAGE

PART TWO

Rehana Incognito

BODYCAGE

CHAPTER ONE

1979
"Young man, what you seem to be developing there is breast tissue." the grey-haired, bespectacled specialist abruptly pointed out, prodding about my chest with his clammy, wizened hand. "If you'd like to take this prescription for testosterone, they should disappear in a matter of weeks. Hormonal imbalances occur from time to time, but usually in adolescents. Perhaps yours has been a little prolonged."
Without much further questioning, I folded the prescription... half taking note of his mention of it being derived from a male animal. Probably a rat, I thought. Should have me feeling like a normal, red-blooded male in no time. But is this what I want? The doctor had told me what was wrong. How could I question a doctor's advice? I would take the testosterone and see if some bizarre metamorphosis would transform me into a 'normal' male.
Traipsing to the pharmacist at the RVI, I felt ashamed that I had lost the courage to blurt out the whole story... to tell him the truth about how I felt. He seemed so assertive and sure as he scratched out the script that I felt almost secure with his belief. So, willingly conceding (for now) that this was my only support, I filled myself up with 'Extract de Rat'!
I don't know if those hormones were driving me nuts or whether it was the hopeless situation with Eric, but life turned crazier by the moment. The most horrendous winter since 1963 depressed us all. Each song on the radio seemed directed at me as a cruel reminder of my crummy life!
"I can't stand the rain... on my window...bringin'
back sweet memories."

That song still tormented me all day and more so... all night! Pushing psycho geriatrics around on my next ward assignment, the very effeminate nurse Wally and I would chorus together...
"My head is sayin' fool forget him...
my heart is sayin' don't let go.
Hold on to the end...
that's what I intend to doooo.
Hopelessly devoted to yoooou."
As Olivia Newton-John wailed her hit from Grease, Wally and I lived each moment of the 'he done me wrong' dramas of our hopeless courtships. Oh, how it seemed misery loved company indeed... and how easy it was for 'like to find like'!

With Christmas and New Year came the chance for plenty of overtime. Not being swept up by seasonal spirit either, the chance of making extra money cheering patients was irresistible. With the other nurses, each ward was gaily decked, patients spruced up for their families and Christmas revelry enjoyed, for a time at least, with minimal upsets. And around the corner was the occasion for us to forget all the madness of our working life... the staff New Year's Eve party.

Dawn, another nurse from the Acute Disturbed Females ward, had retired her four women charges to bed, one of whom had just told her that her nerves were bad and the doctor says she has to have them out! As strained and fatigued we were, we staggered from punchbowls to scotch bottles. For hours we danced, like Wally and I, living out the tragic bleakness of each song like a scratched record of life's cruel realities.

As midnight approached Wally swished by with a gentle stroke of both our heads... making his way no doubt for a suitable man with whom to see in the New Year. For me it was Dawn. She didn't seem to be looking elsewhere either. We hugged tightly.

FIVE... FOUR... THREE... TWO... ONE! I planted the biggest kiss, smack on her lips... thinking I'd faint or be struck by lightning.

"Wow Ian, that was a surprise!" Dawn laughed, arms clasped still tightly around my waist. Oh God, I hoped she wasn't expecting much more, but blurted out all the same -

"I hope all your dreams come true... and you get all you want."

"I hope I want everything I get." she cheekily replied as we swung each other around in a clumsy but genuine embrace. With the laughter, the alcohol and closeness to another body, I began to enjoy this moment. Only to confuse it all with yet another try to analyse an unfamiliar process.

Was the 'rat's piss' testosterone kicking in, I wondered? Being a gorgeous young woman, admired even by me... from afar... I resolved it to be a nasty little case of 'Venus Envy'. Perhaps I just wanted to be part of her, feel her and absorb a little of the essence of who she was... and all I wanted to be.

From far across the room I noticed Eric. Standing jaw agape, slightly leering at us, he was clearly aghast at what he'd just witnessed. Out of sheer vindictiveness I kissed Dawn once again, forgiving myself quickly for the one and only time I would take advantage of a woman!

By 2am nurses had wilted into the darkness of the wards or made their way home. Some of us still danced on, soliciting hugs and kisses where ever they might be found. On a refill trip to the punchbowl, I noticed the half-sleeping form of Eric, slumped in an easy chair. Dangling from his limp hand was his only companion at this wee hour - a big frosted, electric blue balloon... dejectedly tugged up and down. Truly, it seemed like his only friend, bound haphazardly by its long white ribbon to his whimsical control.

In the dim light I peered ever closer into his half-closed eyes. There peered back with the eyes of a hurt, lost child... a child who drew pity with a helpless gaze which clearly expressed regret at doing something terribly wrong. Responding to that look I took the chance to challenge.

"What's wrong, Eric? Is there something you want to say to me now? Now that we're both drunk enough to say what we want... and blame it on the drink."

"I really do want you, Ian. In fact I'm nuts about you... I just look at you and want you." Hanging his head he choked, "That's why I turn away. I can't face it." Dangling that balloon up and down as he spoke, controlling it, giving it life as I stood like a motionless, void of feeling statue before him... he rambled on.

"Nowt could ever come of it with us. We're both only nineteen... and who would understand or accept it? I don't even bloody understand!" My hero started to look even less impressive as he made his excuses about why we could not enjoy the greatness of love together. A love I felt was all that mattered, making everything feel alright and find its own way through. This and other myths I well and truly thought myself ready to live by.

Eric rose from the chair, leeringly swaying toward me. Leaning him gently back against the cold blackened window, I rested him on the sill for support as his head slumped onto my shoulder. Muffled through my heavy sweater I made out his words.

"Can I come back and spend the night in your room with you... just this once?"

BODYCAGE

"Do you know, Eric... The harder you try to pull that balloon back down, the harder it's going to want to bounce right back up again and hit you in the face."

How I'd have loved to just pounce on his gorgeous body right there and then. However, I responded in a way I could never have imagined.

"I couldn't stand to be with a guy as gutless as you! You're not going to get a chance to be another bastard that used me!" Walking away, head held high... for that moment at least... I felt pride was worth more than a night in the sack with a drunk.

After nearly three years in a mental hospital I felt grateful not to have become a patient. Learning the skills of psychiatric and general nursing presented plenty opportunity to grow, whilst the only major effect of the testosterone was to reduce the size the 'lumps' beneath each nipple. Lots of swimming took care of a noticeably increased libido and slight broadening of my shoulders. Some little blond facial 'fuzz' started to appear on my upper lip and chin.

That was hardly the great metamorphosis I'd expected, especially having seen women more masculinized than I had any chance of being! However, with frequent outbursts of temper and impatience, I discontinued the use of testosterone after a few short months. A bad bout of acne disappeared at the time of its cessation, leaving me now with a voice like a cross between Marlene Dietrich and Lauren Bacall... or at least like the heaviest of smokers, which I was not. Thoughts of pursuing my plan to change gender again played on my mind.

This I could never do in provincial Northumberland... my relatives would surely die of shock! After moving into my Bewick Court apartment, it seemed the whole world was gay. This centrally located building came to be known as 'Homosexual Heights', where I could never have looked out of place... but surely felt I was. From Homo Heights I'd need to escape too, lest the gay neighbours also turn their backs on me.

Hesitatingly, with memories of my mother's departure from England, I sold off cheaply all my furniture and tossed a coin. Heads, I'd try to establish myself in London and assume a new life. Tails would mean a return to Australia. There at least was family, whereas in London I knew no one. It was Tails... my ticket was soon booked for a return to Perth. Looking from the window across a grey, drizzly London I did feel glad not to be starting a life in that grimness.

Still, I had my reference as a good and capable nurse and one really inspiring lesson from it all I can never forget. I call it the "Gift of Grace", because that was her name. A lovely elderly lady with a hideous terminal cancer I cared for during my general nursing experience. Grace always had a dignity about her frail presence, forever apologising for the dreadful smell which, once experienced stays with you forever, as a result of her cancer. Sharing many fleeting chats during the busy times of my ward duties, I always gave her that extra care and attention as her time to leave this world clearly drew nearer. Sadly, as she had slipped into unconsciousness near the end of my late shift, I was asked to stay with her until she took her last breath.

Quietly I sat by her bedside, just being there, comforting any need which might arise and gently holding her hand which had clearly worked so hard serving the lovely family who all came one by one to say their goodbyes. She neither recognised nor was able to even acknowledge anyone due to her laboured, deep and rattly slumber. One by one they kissed her goodbye, thanked her for being a loving mother, sister and friend and offered their thanks to me for keeping her so comfortable.

Many times, Grace would take one big breath, then stop as I just prayed that she would let go and release herself, only to agonisingly start her laboured breathing again. Suddenly however, she popped up her head and opened her eyes.

"Oh, it's you Ian, Pet. Am so glad it's you." She squeezed my hand tightly.

"Don't you worry about all this... It is so lovely...all so lovely." She looked off into some imaginary distance, smiling with such serenity and peace as the last breath softly sighed from her, sinking back into the pillow. I sat for what seemed like forever as the room and myself felt nothing but peace and such a lightness, that I almost felt I had sailed somewhere with her. On reporting this to the night sister, she had told me I must have imagined my conversation with Grace due to my being tired and overworked as such an exchange would have been impossible due to Grace's condition. I do know it did happen and can never be more grateful to Grace for her gift, which will stay with me, comforting forever. That's what 'Grace' is to me - an unconditional gift from Love, so when we are lost in fogs of doubt... there is something more hopeful to hold tight in our minds, to believe in no matter what appearances tell us to the contrary. Thank you to her, where-ever she may now be... you were truly my 'Amazing Grace'.

1980

Swallowing a sleeping pill for the twenty four hour flight to Perth, I wondered how or if I could broach my desire to change with my family. Would they cope or even be supportive? Arriving back in Perth it took little time to realise they were so lost in their own needs not to even bother mentioning it. To make it worse they taunted me constantly as to why I wasn't dating a girl. It hardly seemed timely to let them know I wanted to be one!

A few months of hard labour at a geriatric hospital quickly earned me enough money to join a nurse returning to live in Melbourne. Tracey filled me with excitement every day about how Melbourne was so elegant, more European and still close enough to my family. I was easily convinced to try the relocation with plenty of help and encouragement from Tracey.

1981
Shortly after arriving in the "Garden State" - where I'd sensed a blossoming of sorts - I composed a letter to my sister Karen. It felt quite bizarre to explain such feelings as 'changing' sex and mostly I wanted her to understand. I could not bear the thought of losing contact with her little son, Geoff. She wrote back to say that she had told Mum. After several furtive calls to Karen and Mum, I saddened at their icy dismissals. Dejected and distraught, I felt answerable to no one. With mind made up I went ahead.
Tracey made me so comfortable in her home, a terraced Victorian cottage kept always pristine by her former lesbian partner. She moved out as we moved back in, leaving me totally at ease to clarify my intentions about what I was hoping to achieve with all this gender business with Trace.
She was a lesbian. I might of known she'd have seen more in me than anticipated... as she snickered, "Honestly, Ian...do you think I didn't know? I thought you were such a sexy thing all along. You're sort of like an honorary woman already aren'tya?!" In whatever

perverse way, that was a great help. But there was more to come, for which I'm extremely grateful. With the sharing of clothes, building of confidence and even her flirting, I felt I'd make it for certain. If a lesbian found me attractive something must surely be right... or horribly wrong!

The only record album I'd brought from England was the collection of Fleetwood Mac's greatest hits. Over and over I'd play it whilst dancing alone with the words of "Don't Stop... ...Thinkin' about Tomorrow" ringing in my head. It remained a happy little theme song for a while until Trace walked in on me dancing out a frenzied lip-sync of "Rhiannon"... which I'd somewhere read was about a white witch... of all things.

'Would you stay if she promised you heaven?..
Will you ever win?...
Rhiaaaaaanon..'

"That's who you are, Girl. *RHIANNON*! Will you ever win...?" she chimed along with a giggle as my christening dance whirled and wound on across the living room floor. Tracey's eyes glimmered with delight as the words of the song spun themselves around me.

'Dreams unwind...
Love's a state of mind...'

Riannon I became (dropping the "h"), dancing and singing myself into existence like a White Witch Wandjina, the Creator Gods and Goddesses. I wondered over and over...
"Would I stay for the promise of heaven?" Would I ever win... and what was really the battle to be won anyway?" Riannon, the 'Magic Maiden' was weaving

her*self* into my being, soaking herself and expanding into tiny spaces of my soul I could not see or barely be aware of yet dancing the spell to find out and experience all it means to be a woman.

With my nursing records all in my male name, I wondered how to obtain a nursing job and continue with my change. Changing my records would be extremely complicated as, to be truthful, would be nursing patients in my circumstances. Another way to earn a living would need to be found. Just as this appeared to be my downfall, a chance introduction to a friend of Tracey's led to my rescue.

Mischief was in the air, I felt. Tracey was very evasive as I pressed for more details about where we were heading as the tram clattered along the sedate avenue of St Kilda Road. We jumped off near the corner of Fitzroy Street, Tracey trundling me along behind her to the foyer of an elegant old apartment building.

Buzzer pressed, a sultry cooing voice bade us walk up to the first floor. There, on the landing to greet us, two fat little corgis frolicking at her feet, stood Lady Felicity Bancroft. "Dahhhling, sooo lovely to meet you!" she purred with a regal extension of her hand. Shaking it gently, I was agog to notice every finger glittering with diamonds and gold.

Mesmerized, Felicity led me to a sumptuous antique sofa where Trace had already perched. It almost swallowed us as I watched the Rubenesque blonde throw back her hair, puff out her abundant chest to begin what seemed like an audience with the Queen.

"Tracey tells me that you're planning to have a sex-change. How wonderful, Darling," she chortled as if she heard that every day. "Well my Love, you look so nervous and timid. Do you have any idea what you are going to face? And do you know what it'll look like when the surgeons are finished down there?"

BODYCAGE

"No Felicity, I'm not really sure about any of it... really. But anything's got to be better than what's there now... I've no use for that!"
"Well" she said, hoisting a large skirt past her thighs "If that's what you want, you'd better have a look at what you're going to get." I almost jumped to run as Tracey firmly grasped my arm in assurance to stay. Here was a woman who looked as if she'd easily have given birth to four children, telling me she too was a sex-change! I *was* speechless.
"Yes, Darling my doctor was one of the most skilled plastic surgeons in Australia. Of course it was done years ago. But look at the thing... it's like a little Barbie doll's pussy isn't it?" Beckoning me forward to take a peek I was still horrified at the thought of Barbie having genitalia. But still I braced myself for a peek at the surgeon's skill. I thought it looked like a horrible axe wound and figured that it signified the authenticity of the workmanship. I wanted that surgeon's number!
"Yes, it does look like the real thing." I eventually muttered. "Well, what I mean is...err, it IS real. Or as real as it's going to be..." I hoped not to have been offensive.
"Yep, it's as good as a bloody good'un."
I had to laugh - Tracey was right... and she should know.
Graciously, I declined Felicity's further offer to 'feel what it's like inside'. Her 'show and tell' was enough for me. Nightmarish visions of it might ensue for weeks. So, what more could I say?
"Well, thanks a lot for showing me the workmanship, Felicity. That was very kind of you... I look forward to having one of my own some day."
"Sweetie, don't you realise? That's just the thing... Don't you know how long this is all going to take? It's not like going to the dentist to get a tooth out, Love!

Rehana Incognito

There's two years of psychiatric assessment ahead of you... *and* you have to live and work as a woman... *And* hold down a steady relationship! Then, if you get through that, there's a long wait for a surgeon... if you're getting it done on Medicare. Other than that you'll have to come up with thousands to get it done privately." On she rattled as my head spun, no longer hearing a word she said.

Kindly she noticed my bewilderment as I envisioned every nightmare scenario that just might happen. Felicity promised to help with guidance and explain everything later... 'When it's not all too overwhelming.'

"Riannon," Tracey chirped in, undoubtedly sensing despondency, "Lady B used to work for the board of assessors... dealing with people in your situation. She knows who's bullshit and who's not". She then apologised for the little surprise, explaining that she just wanted me to feel natural and relaxed, without the worry and wonder about what Felicity might think. Tracey also explained she'd met 'Lady B' at a lesbian club and had a brief affair during her 'Lesbian phase'.

"Just a crazy little moment of girly madness really, Darling," chortled her Ladyship. "I just experimented with my sexuality for a while. It wasn't for me, Love. I could never give up dick for anybody. Besides, they have their purpose in my life just now..." She abruptly halted her words, leaving me to wonder what on earth she was leading to.

However, she delightedly continued to enthral me with the details of the 'T.S scene', referrals to doctors I might see... even what to wear when I meet them!

"Don't ever let them catch you in jeans... no matter how good you think you look in them. They'll take that as a sign that you're more comfortable in male attire. Crazy as it seems, I'll warn you about things like that."

BODYCAGE

God, did I appreciate it. I loved my jeans and could have jeopardised everything by flaunting my legs and bum! I wondered what to do with all the clingy jeans Tracey had passed on to me. They were some of the few articles of clothing she had which were remotely feminine! I'd play their game though, and enjoy every moment of my friendship with my new mentor, whose warm hearted interest was clearly maternal.

"How on earth did you get to be 'Lady' Bancroft though?" I ventured to ask on the way out the door, having also noticed her addressed as such on a red-letter bill from the gas company. "Wouldn't you have to have been married to a Lord?" Her reply was astounding.

"Love, it's all bluff in this world. You can call yourself anything you want... people are so gullible, they'd believe anything... 'You gotta have a gimmick... if you don't have a gimmick... ladedadedadadadedo..." She bumped and ground her way across the landing. "Works wonders for hotel reservations and gets the best seats in any restaurant!"

From Gypsy Rose Lee to deposed aristocracy in a split second! Felicity was a fine actress in ways I continued to discover for months. In fact she could have been a movie unto herself. She'd clamoured to the top of Melbourne's social set and travelled the world as a cabaret performer, now supplementing her income doing the voice overs for tacky foreign porno movies... being both the male *and* female performers!

Before ballooning to her current proportions, Felicity's exotic strip shows had earned her many wealthy suitors, photos of whom she delighted in showing in her scrap book of memorabilia. Perusing each page of promotional shots, newspaper clippings and all manner of evidence of glamour... I was captivated.

Every image presented, along with the splendid trappings of her home, fed a burning to succeed as she had... in every way and more. I sat there in her 'Jeanie's bottle' filled with the promise of magic to come, hopelessly attempting to absorb it all. Quizzically, my gaze fell upon a row of photos framed upon the mahogany mantle piece. Each frame held the picture of a little blonde girl, from black and white baby and toddler shots, to a gangly, yet sensuous teen. Noticing my curious gaze, Felicity unashamedly explained they were her! She had created her own past from images of total strangers and I have no doubt that she thoroughly believed in her own legend.

Felicity's care and very presence reassured me that I was not unique in this conundrum. Undoubtedly she too was the genuine case of the 'one in thousands', destined for a metamorphosis from an expression of male to the totally female. I wondered then of the others who remained caged in bodies serving only as prisons to a spirit needing desperately to live its 'Truth'. Wondering too, why it should be so painful and cruel, any meaning at all would be long in coming. And I wish I hadn't wondered about most of the others I met.

CHAPTER TWO

1982

Armed with Felicity's information about doctors, and the promise of a job in a restaurant she was soon to open, I left feeling hopeful of a means in sight to change my life. With so many images of exciting possibilities playing over in my head I could barely sleep. Questions of whether I could succeed began to gnaw at me. Could I even get through my period of 'trial'? A job, perhaps, I could well hold down but the thought of anyone having me as his girlfriend (in this condition!) was hard to imagine.

Two or three years living like this would be nothing short of hellish. Drifting in and out of sleep I envisioned a magic pill... which I could take in the evening, blissfully fall asleep to awaken in a totally transformed and beautiful body. Yes... a body like that of any other woman. This one had to be a mistake... as I'd dreamt as a child...it's a mistake and I'll wake up one day to find the nasty dream is over.

I awoke to find that any dream was my only escape for now. The nightmares began when I awoke. After the first restless night, my goal was to make an appointment with a Doctor Harvey. He, I was told, was very understanding in providing medical care for many of the transsexual cabaret performers. His secretary found an appointment for that very afternoon. Unbelievingly grateful that this was under way, I thanked God that this exciting, though uncertain journey had begun. Unsure of what lay ahead, I felt sure it had to be better than the past.

The tall, gangly Doctor Harvey was quite an entertainer too. His plush, wood-panelled office looked out across the bay at South Melbourne. Gazing at yachts and boats skimming across the waves, I sat back assuredly as he wrote out his referral. He recommended that I consult with a Professor Walters with the department of Obstetrics and Gynaecology at the Royal Women's Hospital.

"You'll have no problems with all of this at all, I can assure you," he said with all the charm of a games show host. "You'd better get on with changing your name on your documents though. Your Medicare card is going to be seen a lot over the next few months. It'll raise a few eyebrows the way it is."

"Oops, I'd forgotten about that. And thanks very much for the encouragement. I felt like you'd tell me to go home and forget it!"

"Oh come on! You'll just sail through it. You look most of the way there already." He seemed so at ease about it all, I wondered if it was like having a tooth pulled after all. "You'll make your transition with no trouble at all."

"But Doctor, I didn't tell you... I want to be a black woman!"

"Get out of here! We can't do that one yet, but at least you have a sense of humour to get you through. Stay in touch and let me know how it all goes."

Clutching the coveted referral for assessment, I leapt into Tracey's little Morris Mini, crunching a bumper in front of me and a fender to my rear in hasty effort to get home. Not that I was careless about other cars, just an easily distracted driver and still am really. Thankfully, I've never had an accident, though probably caused thousands! Fleeing another trail of destruction, I wasted no time in calling the Professor to arrange an appointment.

"The first available appointment is in six weeks, Riannon," the receptionist explained. "Would you prefer a morning or afternoon appointment?" Oh God, I wondered how could there be so many transsexuals in Melbourne that he could not see me for *six* weeks?! Impatient little vixen that I was! Sensing the air of despondency, the receptionist politely pointed out that the clinic was tied to the infertility program, treating all manner of gynaecological problems as well as transsexuals. I'd just have to be patient and use this time to plan a sensible transition period.

Without family support there was no need to go on living a life unsuited to my feelings any more. Now nothing could hold me back from pursuing this goal while each piece of the puzzle began to fit in just right way. No longer feeling I'd be an embarrassing upset to anyone, I was ready to press on.

No longer would I wear my gender-ambiguous clothes which left the question of my gender to the state of mind of the observer.

No more to be a woman in their eyes... if they thought so. Or a man if they chose. It had become too hard an act... and only an act... to present as male. I felt no more real than a cartoon character parody of anything that could even try to be masculine.

Felicity made a gift of a huge bundle of lovely clothes. Her taste was impeccable. Swathed in quality, beautiful clothes, from someone who knew how to bring out my best in everything, added to the comfort I began to enjoy. With Tracey's 'ambiguous' stuff and all my own old clothes bundled into plastic bags, I lumbered them off to the Goodwill bin. No longer would I wear anything to make me feel ungainly, even ridiculous, again. In tight black ski pants, white sneakers and a bulky, pink knitted sweater, I slammed shut the bin lid on that part of my life. Another was about to swing open.

Rather than visit the gay club, Pokey's, to celebrate this momentous step, Tracey decided to escort me to Tangles. This was right next to the St Kilda waterfront. A nightclub where the glamorous Melbourne version of 'Les Girls' performed almost nightly. A place where I'd be inconspicuous enough to mix with the predominantly (I'd assumed) straight crowd. There, I'd need not worry if people were to wonder about me. The drag show made it somehow 'safe' and, as it transpired, every freak in Melbourne was there anyway!

Tracey made quite an effort to 'femme herself up', which I appreciated a lot. We set out thinking we looked like Madonna with the hair suitably gelled into tangles, lots of beads and here and there a crucifix or two. Setting off for the tram to St Kilda, Tracey had more trouble with the high heels than I did! Worse still, seated on the tram, a spotty-faced adolescent asked if she was a 'drag queen'?! "A what?" she asked incredulously. We fell about laughing as 'Spots' took another seat far away from us.

Rolling into Tangles, we found the cabaret already under way. The lights were down, a carnival of music played. We unobtrusively darted for the bar bobbing down here and there as spotlights darted around us like fugitives from a prison camp. With so many eyes upon us, we felt we were stealing the show. Fumbling through the crowd, I felt the occasional nip on the bum.

"Are you doing that, Trace?"

"Doing what?"

"Pinching and grabbing at my arse."

"No, idiot! They're grabbing mine too. Can you blame them? We look like a couple of streetwalkers."

"That doesn't mean they have a right to help themselves like that."

"You're gonna have a lot to learn about men, Girlfriend!"

By time we'd reached the bar barely an eye was on the cabaret performers. Cat calls and wolf whistles came from everywhere. People turned to look all the more at the cause of such commotion. It was us... and the glamour pusses knew it, scowling down from their mighty podium. It appeared we were stealing their show after all. However, as we got right to the bar, another commotion was in progress.

"Get outa that seat, ya ugly bastard. Don'tya know how to treat a fuckin' lady?" A huge, manly, jewel-encrusted fist hoisted a wimpish looking man from a bar stool... by his neck! With a hefty stab of a five inch stiletto, the hapless character was despatched, tumbling from his perch.

BODYCAGE

"Well! I can't believe the nerve of these guys," she said, dusting her hands of the affair with a quick adjustment of the coif of her wig. "And what's your name, Love? Haven't seen you here before."

Oh God, those parrot-like, painted eyes were fiercely focused on me. "Err, my name's... (what the hell is it?)...Riannon! Was that man making a nuisance of himself with you? He certainly seemed to have caused you some upset."

"He didn't upset me, Love. He just didn't realise who the hell I am. I'm Lexi... Lexi Roper, and this is where I always bloody sit. Nice to meet ya, Rina."

I dared not correct her.

"Well you look great, by the way," I grovelled "And it's nice to meet you too. We haven't been here before, so I'll be sure to remember that's your spot!" We then fled to the other side of the club, making sure all night to keep well clear of Lexi Roper.

The rest of the cabaret show was well performed and mesmerising. The performers, exquisite and professional, held their audience captivated and spellbound. Other 'trannies' we met found it hilarious that Tracey was not actually one of us, with many offering make up and hair tips throughout the night!

As for the glamorous Show Queens, they paraded by, noses in the air with little more than an all encompassing cursory glance. All the while nodding approving smiles to the many admirers, whilst occasionally extending a courteous hand. With their heavily painted faces, bulging silicone implants straining from their outfits, they slunk through the crowds. The carnival played on.

During the Showtime intervals a disco played. Very odd couples appeared on the dance floor. Just standing there, sipping a double gin, I wondered which women might have been real and which were not.

Most, obviously were not. Still, none had trouble finding partners to get them onto the floor. I noticed Lexi's dance card seemed heavily booked!

One, I noticed danced alone. With a show of her own going on, this older 'lady' paraded on the dance floor in skin tight G-string leotards. Changing from one silvery, spangly outfit to the next throughout the night, I cringed as people snickered at her. She remained oblivious, flinging her arms like a windmill in a show choreographed for the rhythm of her own drum.

Leaning across the bar I called to the barman for another double gin.

"Did you hear what that bitch just said about you, Shari?" I swung around to see Lexi standing next to me and an approaching show goddess. "She just told that barman you've got a double chin !"

"Who the hell do you think you are, you fucking bitch?" the lovely Shari drunkenly hissed and slurred. "You come into our club after we've stood up there all night making these bastards horny... then you walk out with them. I've got a good mind to just..." She started to lunge at me as Lexi piped in.

"Just a minute, Love." Lexi pulled her back as she got just too close. "I was just kidding. Rina's a good kid. She didn't say anything about ya double chin. She was just ordering a drink."

"You're a fuckin' shit stirrer, Roper! I could have done the bitch in through you. *AND WADDAYA MEAN, I'VE GOT A FUCKIN DOUBLE CHIN*? I haven't got a double chin have I, Love?" she turned to ask, sweeping her garish claws along the sagging flesh of her neck. With a furtive shake of the head from side to side, I affirmed her delusion. In their world where looks were the stakes of survival, why could I not help but think of Barry Manilow singing about the faded 'Lola'... painted feather in hair 'n all ?!

BODYCAGE

The rest of that night was a bit of a blur, not in the least because I drank way too much, but someone had also spiked my drink. Feeling the music start to slur in my head and everyone moving in slow motion around me, my tunnel of vision seemed to be getting narrower. Feeling confused I felt the need to get to the bathroom and get some water either all over me or in me. Grabbing my purse I aimed for the Ladies, noticing one after the other knowing smirk from the faces of those glamorous show goddesses. Sliding slowly to the floor, losing my grip on the sink, I felt two long, slender arms slide under my shoulders and lift me back up. "Stay awake, stay awake," said this tall, doe-eyed girl who'd rushed into the loo behind me.

"So, you got your special welcome to their crazy little empire too, did you? You're lucky. If they'd felt really threatened by you they'd have made sure you got really hurt... Sad old bitches." Telling me her name was Roula, I could hardly have been more grateful as she stayed with me until the water had flushed some of the drug through and I'd tidied myself up enough to get out of there.

Roula steadied me as I found Tracey at a table in a darkened corner being chatted up by two token 'lesbians'. There they were, two big burley guys in matching Tina Turner wigs, mini skirts and fishnet stockings, stroking each other's legs, gazing longingly into each other's eyes. Perhaps not believing their luck that Tracey was showing them some interest, I heard them saying more than a few times how much they love being lesbians. Well, I guess if a guy can't find his ultimate lesbian fantasy he can just clad himself up as one and *be* his lesbian fantasy!

Mercifully this Gender Cornucopia was getting ready to spew out its assorted contents. I'd chatted to Roula for a little while and realised she was my age and in just the same circumstances. I popped her number into my purse and promised to call during the week to swap notes as Tracey shook off her "lesbian" admirers and headed for the front door in the hope of finding a taxi. Roula had her *dad* waiting in his car outside for her! The sweet Philippina receptionist and cloakroom girl passed a consoling smile, handing back my jacket. Next to her a stocky girl with a shock of long red hair was piling herself into a huge leopard print coat which was way too over the top for this time of year. "Love your coat," I still sort of half drunkenly slurred as she swung round almost knocking me out with her over-revealed bust. "Well, I need my heavy one cos am walking home from here and gotta pick up my rent money," she replied in a voice like the girl who reads the weather on Channel Seven. If it wasn't for the fact that she looked like Bette Midler with a five o'clock shadow and balls, I'd never have known that voice wasn't a biological woman's.

"Rent money, at this time on Sunday morning?" I stupidly enquired.

"Love, where the fuck are you from? This is St Kilda. I am walking home, dressed like this... whadda ya think? I am going to *make* the rent on the way home. Wanna come?"

Tracey by then had pulled me back, but knew the redhead's name as Loren, telling her she'd get me home to her place. Promising that she would give me Loren's number if she wanted to get to know me better, Loren said that was fine and strutted out into the night. Tracey looked out after her, coming back in to say there were no taxis at the stand as a tall blond guy walked into the reception area right behind us.

"You girls want a lift? Got the whole night free if you're not too far away." What a dream come true he was. Tracey and I didn't think twice about getting in his car.

BODYCAGE

He was a well-known footballer from a top league Melbourne team and had been "for a laugh at the trannies" with his mates who for some reason just weren't yet ready to leave. Hans got us home in twenty minutes and of course we invited him in. With Tracey knowing very well that my luck had really changed after she'd threatened to find and smash whoever had slipped me the pill, she went off to bed to leave Hans and myself sitting on the sofa, cups of tea in hand and not really knowing what to say. We both just giggled like two teenagers on our first date. And in a way, I was!

I can't recall much about that time, sitting there with Hans, as I was so tired and had way too much to drink (aside from having some weird chemical still swirling in my system). However, I did quickly realise from what he'd said about his mates and the "trannies" that he had not realised I might be one of them. Yes, we kissed and cuddled and both our hands wandered....a lot! But, as he didn't know about my situation and I had no idea how to gage his reaction nor had the experience to tell him... I didn't let it go any further. Thinking I must be a girl of impeccable virtue, he did get up to go at about sunrise, shocking me by asking if he could leave me his number if I'd like to catch up with him again. I stuffed it under the cushion of the sofa where I slid off to sleep after telling him just to let himself out.

CHAPTER THREE

A kind of nauseating aroma of over-buttered crumpets, tainted with an excessive slathering of vegemite and strong tea wafted me out of a semi coma on the sofa. Tracey merrily manifested through my bleary-eyed blinks, thrusting the TV dinner tray under my nose as I groaned and turned my head into the cushions sinking into the back of the sofa.
"Where's Prince Charming, then?" she asked as I turned over to see the apparition of what must have been Melbourne's only diesel housewife, stood with her cropped, jet black spiked hair, fishnet Army Surplus top, khaki jeans and a frilly Australiana apron of Cockatoos, Gum Nuts and Kangaroo Paws.
"You mean I *hadn't* dreamt that?" I half muttered, sliding my hand around under the cushions to see if I'd actually dreamt Hans had left his number. I found a piece of ratty, damp cardboard and my heart went a'racing! Yes, there it was.... his name and his number.
"Give him a call... He's bloody gorgeous. It's the weekend and he might be free. Gotta run... enjoy ya brekky." Tracey popped the tray on a side table next to the sofa and hauled over the phone for me too before grabbing her jacket and helmet to tear off for her weekend leaving me with a very mischievous grin.
As her Kawasaki 'whatever' rattled to life then screamed off down the side driveway, I had a chuckle that she at least had something hot and throbbing between her legs... and I'd kind of missed it last night which was all a bit sad. As my senses took hold with a couple of crumpet bites and a few sips of tea, I still just kept staring at the piece of paper (half an Emu Bitter beer coaster actually) with the name and number. Gazing from the coaster to the phone, the phone to the

BODYCAGE

coaster several times, a full fantasy about him coming to pick me up and driving somewhere nice for the day, holding each other's hands and falling in love, flashed through my head. I just ached to call and see if those heady feelings from last night might still be alive with him too. I had already planned our children's names, the floral arrangements at our white wedding and a life together as I dialled the number. It started to ring as my heart again pounded. Phew, the answer machine came on to my relief, with his name and voice saying,

"Hi. It's Hans.... I am not home. So, make my day and leave me a message." Thankfully he hadn't given me the number for a weight loss clinic or some other dirty trick.

Just as quickly as I'd envisioned our perfect life together in a split second of phone dialling, I swung totally the other way. The newspapers snap a picture of us sipping cappuccinos at an Italian cafe on the coffee strip on Lygon Street.

"Premier League Footy Player Scores Girl With Extra Tackle" screams The Melbourne Herald Sun, as Truth newspaper reporter chases us both down the street with a microphone in Hans' face snarling - "Is it true your girlfriend was really a man?" Slamming the phone down before the beep and flinging the coaster into my remaining tea, I watched it slowly sink to the bottom of the mug along with all my hopes and dreams of being the most intriguing Footballer's Wife, years before that show's time! Realising I just couldn't do it to him or cope with the aftermath of embarrassment myself, I felt certain too that even if I'd had the nerve to tell him, he'd not be likely to take it well or know how to cope. His career would indeed be ruined.

Stumbling to the shower, I peeled off my clothes and grabbed the facial scrub to wash away the last night's makeup... Watching the mix of brown foundation, some shades of eye colours and lipstick streaking down my body like a living water colour, it snaked its way over my tiny bumps of breasts, down a long shapely pair of legs and swirling down the plug hole. Stealing shy glances at my own body in the smoky, steamed up mirror along the shower wall, it almost looked so perfect. Stroking the softness of my skin, I wondered too why it had never developed a coarser texture of any man my age... and why the little blond hairs all down my forearms were barely even visible 'til they caught some soap suds.

Running a hand, too small and elegant to be anything but a girl's, over an ever-curvy butt and sliding the hair which had now past my shoulders over to one side, I looked up again to realise that I had *become* 'The Battle of the Sexes' all in one body as I stood starring in my own semi soft porn "Watercolour Challenge"! Angling my body away so as only to see myself from behind and my side, how I now wished even more that I did not have to see what I was still stuck with between my legs. Yet not hating myself or my body for how it was, nor having weird desires to mutilate myself, which so many have claimed to feel. No, I just saw it as a place I was stuck living in... Which just wasn't right for me to get through this life and do and feel all I wanted to feel.

My body and gender issue just seemed like a really great stage spectacular where I knew there should have been wonderful music and beautiful colours yet I was watching it in black and white with no sound. Still, I managed a smirk, realising that perhaps I was more a bizarrely built house with my mother's wiring and father's plumbing... one by one, the tiles were probably starting to slip from the roof too!

BODYCAGE

Feeling admittedly just a little bitter and sorry for myself that my lovely picket fence dream had gone down the plug hole along with last night's slap, I resolved to spend a couple of weeks in the house, taking stock of where I was going and what I was doing. Really though, I only found myself watching endless episodes of the Japanese soap opera "Oshin", both laughing and crying, railing and rejoicing at the trials, joys, tragedies and triumphs in her life as a wretched-little-girl-turning-supermarket-tycoon in pre and post war Japan . Apart from that, Tracey had come home from the hospital one day with heaps of old Cosmopolitan and Vogue magazines after taking pity when she'd found me surrounded by a snow storm of tissues, gibbering on the floor one evening after Oshin's sister had died of consumption after being worked to death in a factory or something equally as hideous and soul-destroying.

After two weeks of boredom and self pity, I remembered somewhere in the carnival and carnage of the night at Tangles that Lexi Roper had shoved her phone number in my purse, asking if I'd like to come to her house to answer the phone for her...for some reason other than that she liked my voice. Rummaging through the Black Hole that my handbag had too quickly become, I found Lexi's number scratched on the inside of a matchbox folder. Like Pandora, opening her box to untold mischief, I'd resigned myself to 'stick with my own kind... with what might be safe and familiar.' As foolhardy as Pandora herself, I felt excited to call Lexi and see what that whole box of tricks might hold for me. 'Tricks'... now that jogged my memory a bit. Lexi had said she ran an escort service from her home and had wanted me to play receptionist for her. Knowing for sure I'd need the money as I couldn't manage on the dole, it was too much to resist. I let the

Rehana Incognito

fingers do the walking...and dialled away into another adventure.

"Playtime Transsexuals, can I help you?" she'd nasally rasped. Wow, this is a *real genuine business woman,* I'd thought as she generously invited me over for what was promising to be a busy night for some reason. "Get off the tram at the second stop on Fitzroy Street and give me a call from the phone box over the road when ya get there to make sure I'm free."

I was *in* and soon to be on my way to her magical wonderland, yet wondering why Lexi had said she might not be free when I got there. Knowing it was in the thick of the red light area and dodgy with drug dealers and streetwalkers to boot, I still busied myself trying to get dressed and ready in time to trundle to St Kilda before it got too dark. Just throwing on tight jeans and a baggy top, no makeup and little beach sandshoes, I decided to leave myself looking as unglamorously androgynous as possible... as that's how I felt. Not wanting anyone chatting me up on the way or mistook for a street walker and questioned by St Kilda police (who forever patrolled the streets and would ask uncomfortable questions) while I either waited or walked up Grey St to Lexi's, I kept my head low and ignored the passing toots of the occasional lone male driver while I waited for the tram.

Well, I'd waited ages and then got stuck in a jam of trams outside Flinders Street Station as a football crowd milled over the streets, onto trams and into the station, making it well after sunset as I spilt out with a mob of footy revellers on Fitzroy Street. Mercifully Lexi answered the phone right away, giving me instructions for the 5 minute walk up the hill to turn a corner somewhere up the top on the right. I could not bolt up that hill quick enough. In my haste and nervousness I'd somehow entwined the phone cord in my handbag

BODYCAGE

strap while fumbling with the phone card, dropping the whole lot. Suddenly in a panic and a flustered, nervous wreck, I turned myself in the now almost complete darkness along Grey Street.

Finding Lexi's quaint little weatherboard 'miner's cottage' tucked in amongst a dozen or so others with neat, well grown-in gardens and a kaleidoscopic array of hanging flower baskets rocking back and forth in the breeze, I bobbed between them to press her front doorbell. The door quickly drew back, only half opening, as a long scarlet talon-like hand and that rasping parrot voice invited me to step in. Peeping into the dimmed light I could vaguely make out heaps of overstuffed deco style furniture, heaps of ornaments and tiffany lamps. It was starting to feel like being beckoned into the Addams Family's parlour as I half gave a thought to just turning around and heading straight home. But, like all those tiny little moths circling in crazy, fuzzy, out-of-control, ever-spiralling orbits around the bare light bulb on the front veranda, before being fried to death and plastered over the shade, I was drawn, stepping past her threshold with the door quickly shutting behind me.

There, resplendent in the half-light, stood Lexi in her long red, shaggy fur coat, high heels and fishnet stockings... though without her wig. Her dishevelled tufts of thin red hair were somewhat damp with sweat and one of her earrings had come completely unfastened, hanging loosely from her ear lobe. She seriously looked like Chewbacca with alopecia crossed with The Joker from Batman as she enquired if I'd thought the soft pink "champagne" light bulbs, strategically positioned to spotlight her at the front door, had the desired effect of softening "the look"? Well, it didn't. She just looked as ghoulish and as comical as I describe, so I turned to one of the

glamorous movie star photos she'd had in a frame where I sat and asked if it was a glamour shot of her.
Clearly the flattery helped and she really thought I meant it, as she said it was actually a publicity shot of Jean Harlow and I explained that I couldn't see very well anyway. Still feeling something of a sense of dread, I half expected, as she curled the sides of her mouth to smile, that blood would come from the corners as a dirty, blood-stained set of fangs might appear, like the hideous kiss of the Funnel Web Spiderwoman. Then she showed me all the photos of her which she did have, framed on every available surface throughout the living room. There was Lexi in her furs, Lexi in big fluffy jumpers, Lexi in swimwear.... with full face of showgirl makeup, killer "mall hair" wigs and highest of high heels... even at the beach!
"Didn't you sink into the sand in those heels?" I asked, staring closer at the pic before putting it back in its spot. She replied that she didn't ever actually go on the beach but only walked up and down the St Kilda waterfront and the pier, picking up blokes and having a laugh. Truly frightening, I thought and wondered how she had never been assaulted before remembering her hoisting of a man twice her size from a bar stool at Tangles and jettisoning him into the oblivion of the night.

In a few of the pictures was another kind of dowdy looking character in plain print frocks, baggy track suit tops and not a sign of makeup, with a hard face and very lost look about her. Kind of like shots of Edna Everage with her tragic shadow of a friend and "bridesmaid", Madge Alsop, forever kept in sight but forever humbled and frumpy to make Edna appear even more magnificent. Trying to keep the flattery alive, I asked if it were her sister?

BODYCAGE

"That sad fucking old thing is Myrna...Myrna the Murderer. Lives in the spare room since she got out on parole." Lexi gestured to a firmly shut side door off the back veranda as I squeaked – "Is she in?"
Lexi replied that Myrna was out visiting some criminals at a cheap hotel near the beach and would be back later for a "double". I didn't dare ask what that was, though actually thought at the time it might actually have been a drink.

Furnished with a very expensive crystal glass of a heady red wine myself, Lexi led me through the house for a tour whilst rushing back and forth to an ever-ringing phone, reeling off the same patter every time.

"Yes, I'm very passably feminine, long red nails, fishnet stockings, 38-27-36... 8 and a 1/2."

I nearly choked, realising it wasn't her shoe size she meant there and glanced down at the bulge stacked haphazardly into a diamante-encrusted g-string. Like the deranged Pollyanna I may well have been, I foolishly asked why they'd want to know about that "8 and a 1/2" if she'd gone to so much trouble to be a "girl".

"Love, what the fuck do you think they're coming here for? If they wanted a woman they'd be home with their fucking wives. They're here for *this*!" She roared, cupping her crotch in a move which would make Michael Jackson's grab look like a demure Japanese schoolgirl's giggle. My head now reeled with another million questions about the whole scene as she ushered me into what she'd called "The Mug Room"... where she "did the mugs". With not a sink full of dirty cups and saucers in sight, I figured the "mugs" must be the clientele and stumbled into the room.

Struggling to heave open a door over laden with yet more fur coats and a rack of gaudy shoes over a shag pile carpet, Lexi led me into the inner sanctum of her twisted weatherboard temple of love. A wrought-iron Victorian style bed bedecked with piles of lace, silken cushions and pillows, stood in the middle of a cramped room of dressers and mirrors, dimly lit lamps and walls plastered in paintings and prints of various women in sensuous poses. As my eyes squinted around the room I took another step forward as the hideous sight of a rack of terrifying eyes, ghoulish gashes of lips and long straggles of hair on mottled bright white heads faced me eye-level along the wall. As my whole little life just about flashed by, jumping nearly out of my skin at this macabre collection of shrunken heads which would not have looked out of place hanging in the doorway of a head-hunter's hut, I covered my eyes before peeping through my fingers to see that they were actually shop dummy display heads with all Lexi's wigs on them and vile faces she'd painted on herself with coloured marker pens!

Venturing to run my fingers through some of the array of fibres on the wigs, I felt the build-ups of hairspray and sweat from many a hot day or night out in those, although Lexi explained that most of her "mugs" loved to wear those wigs more often than she actually did. Wiping my hands quickly on my jeans and feeling a little queasy at the hygiene questions such behaviour might just pose, I shuddered to think whatever else was going on in that room when she went in with someone willing to spend his money on such pursuits. As the phone rang yet again, with Lexi giving the street name and house number this time... I knew I was about to wonder no more. It was not just escort she did, but a little cottage industry of a brothel in her home... how thick could I have been?

Like a clockwork Barbie doll, Lexi had thrown on a wig, set all the lighting right in the bedroom and thrust the phone into my hand, bundling me off into the kitchen to hide myself as she ran to her position in the soft pink glow in front of the door awaiting the bell. Peeping around the door, nervously holding the phone and praying it would not ring, the door bell did with its campy Big Ben chime. Lexi thrust a stocking clad leg forward to give him a good eyeful, luring him to fall through the door after it before she'd stepped back to stand in her spotlight for her gentleman caller to behold in all her glory. Busily, she swished him to the room, he with head down and exaggerated manly swagger, showing a clear discomfort and perhaps some clue and embarrassment that what he was doing was something he really felt ashamed of, knowing that he had to take at least those last few steps with his facade of masculinity intact before doing what he felt compelled to do. Clearly hearing Lexi brusquely mutter something about "money up front" and "business before pleasure, darling", she raced from the room, stuffing wads of twenty dollar notes into an already cash-crammed teapot on her shelves cluttered with old fashioned brand names of Australian biscuit tins.

"See ya in a half hour...You heard what to say on the phone... Just give them the spiel...Don't give the address, but tell them where to call from when they get to St Kilda"... And off she flew into her boudoir.

She was gone before I could even ask what more I should say... like what they'd get for their money et cetera. So I stood there in the kitchen, totally stunned 'til the phone rang, clutched tightly in my hands. Nervously I went through much of the spiel as Lexi had done but was asked so many confusing questions about what goes on that I just kept saying he'd have to call her back in half an hour and speak to her himself. I mean, how could I have had a clue what "is she fully functional" meant? I thought she looked pretty alive to me and able to hold down a relatively normal conversation, get down to the supermarket and cook a basic meal and everything, so naturally said that I thought she was indeed very fully functional, wondering if they thought she was some sort of robot that had been switched off for a while or just newly serviced.

As the phone didn't ring for a few minutes, and the picture was so bad on the little portable TV in the corner of the kitchen which was to keep me entertained whist Lexi entertained, I tried to listen out to what I could hear from the room. Half out of curiosity and half out of wondering if I could see how this guy looked out of his clothes, I have to admit, I tiptoed across the living room, stopping with every creak of a floorboard to be sure I'd not been heard. Creeping closer to the door I could see enough light coming from the old-fashioned big keyhole beneath the huge ornate doorknob, just screaming for me to risk a Pandora-esque peep at what might be going on.

Squatting down in front of the door, I got to eye-level and peeped through the keyhole. Lexi could not have arranged it better- the view was pure porno panorama. The guy stood naked by the side of the bed, heaving Lexi's semi-solid breasts up and down, exposing a ghastly slash of a red welted scar beneath each as testimony to a botched up boob job. Lexi's long, sausage-like fingers with the huge stuck-on red nails were stroking his penis and cupping his scrotum as with her other hand she lifted her tight, shiny black mini skirt. This cute, slightly rugged boy-next-door guy sat down on the bed with Lexi standing before him as a statue in a temple, grinning down at his mortal wonderment like a man-woman two-faced god, holding all the power of night and day, good and evil, creator and destroyer, male and female enshrined in one body with all the adorning accessories. The awestruck gaze

BODYCAGE

on his face as he stared up at her, slowly approaching with an intrepid hand the bulge in her black, lacy knickers, turned to absolute rapture as he gasped in amazement when Lexi flipped down those panties to allow a very eager, swollen willy of her own to bounce forth with its unleashed freedom, practically knocking him over!

"Oh wow, that's what I call *fully functional,*" he gasped, going straight for the grab, drawing it close, kissing it and gazing in enamoured wonderment. Totally hypnotised by her ghastly little snake, it charmed him like a mesmerized, humble devotee seeing for the first time 'The Holy of the Holies.' That rotten phone rang again and I quickly tiptoed across the creaky boards in time to answer it before it rang too many times. After giving a quick spiel as before, I left it off the hook and crept back to my naughtiness at the keyhole.

With her happy worshipper now flat on his back as Lexi fondled him, she was kind of smothering him with her breasts as she deftly materialised a condom from nowhere, ripped off the cover and leaned forward as I expected her to pop it over him. She didn't. She stood up and quickly rolled it tightly over and down her own excited member, as the guy grabbed it like a dying man and sucked it as though her balls may have been full of the elixir of life. After a brief satiation of sucking a 'girl's penis' he was on his hands and knees in no time flat with Lexi leaping just a bit too eagerly, for any lady I knew, to position herself behind him.

Well, that was all my illusions shattered about why a totally straight-looking man, like I'd seen most days of life, would be coming to see someone *acting* and *dressing* like a woman yet playing the role of a big, old girlie tart himself behind closed doors! I quickly headed straight back to the tortured scene on the telly with the dreadful reception, trying to make out as much of the sounds and images on the screen as I could of the scene just spied through Lexi's bedroom keyhole... All just as meaningless and as out-of-tune to the station as the television was!

Long since, I'd read it was said that Julius Caesar was known as being 'every woman's man and every man's woman', but then I had no idea of the games these men played to balance out their lives, putting themselves together again through power exchange games of surrender and conquer! I recalled that the virtuous, stoic matriarch's of Ancient Roman society had also said that "men would prefer a piece of rotted, mouldy cheese, crawling with maggots when given the fresh new curds of a virginal, pure young bride." Mouldy cheese, matrons and maidens aside, all I'd thought then was that they were a twisted, sick bunch not far removed from a big old dog who, after a bath and a scrub, could not wait to go out and roll themselves in a pile of dung!

The bedroom door flung open exactly after the half hour he'd paid for. Again, like He-Man, Master of the Universe, he swaggered behind Lexi to the front door, with head kind of low. With a quick "see ya" each, he couldn't get out quick enough as I heard the old metal garden gate slam before Lexi even closed the front door. I darted to the front room window to watch him wandering down the road and thought of all those Greek and Roman myths and legends I'd read through High School. Thinking of the poor warriors, off to be slaughtered in some hatefully barbaric battle, paying their homage visits to shrines of the Goddesses...the Goddess of Love, leaving a small donation of a coin for protection and to be perhaps even loved and comforted before heading his way with a final act of compassion and comfort from the Sacred prostitutes installed at such places so long ago.

So, like a warrior striding back into his battles with the world after a sacred visit and odd little sacrifice at this 'Shrine of Hermaphrodite', perhaps he was off too to face his battles in his little world. There, like the many others I'd meet and see coming and going along that little footpath to the sacred inner sanctum, perhaps he'd somehow felt he had used this mythically gorgeous vision of a creature to fulfil a balance of some deeply confused and destabilised symbols of masculinity and femininity. Somewhere in his own mind and interpretation of this world of many other symbols of what is male or female, strong or weak, dominating or yielding...he had made his journey somewhat more meaningful to himself for the experience.

Lexi for her part had made a few shekels and gotten her rocks off for her trouble. It was all totally alien and bewildering to me, just as I thought those men traipsing down the garden path to Lexi's front door were no different to the tiny moths, being drawn ever closer to their own destruction... frying themselves alive in a frenzy they could not control but had become tragically drawn too.

Thoughts stayed in my mind for long after, of how these interactions of men coming into these 'secret', strange worlds of symbols, tied in with sex and what people thought sex may have been all about. The confusion, the guilt... the countless cries out of "oh God..." which seemed as close as we might ever be to a spiritual thought, and not to mention of course, the ritual cleaning... like trying to scrub away what had just happened. It's startling to think it only takes the reversal of two letters to turn the word 'sacred' to the word 'scared' and see how the two are so closely entwined as we try to put our lives together like a big Humpty Dumpty cracked egg, unable to find the pieces or recall how we got broken. Then all we end up with *is* this big, cracked egg anyway! As Chairman Mao is known to have said – 'To make an omelette, you got to break a few eggs'. So I guess I'd called for my next non-stick, Teflon frying pan and was turning on the gas myself. Thankfully a key came in the front door, as Myrna the Murderer came home on time for the "double".

"Myrna" came as equally a shock to me as I no doubt was to "her". Turning to see me standing there with a phone dangling in my hand like a big plastic wedding bouquet and a try-not-to-look-shocked smile, Lexi introduced me again as Rina-who's-come-to-do-the-phones. Myrna gave a sort of mumbled shrug, not daring to catch my eye with head hung down, bolting in a hideous bomber parka, dirty jeans and sneakers in a rush to the "sleep out" room built on the back veranda. I caught a glimpse of filthy nails, chewed right down to the chipped, garish bits of nasty, red nail polish still on the fingers. Right now, having since seen "Silence of the Lambs", it felt quite likely that I had just met the cast! Lots of crashing and banging of cupboard doors came from the sleep out as the phone scared the life out of me again with its shrill ring. I passed it to Lexi as I figured it was the "double" turning up at the phone box, ready to be summoned for service. It was, and Lexi told him to stop in at the pub on the corner to grab a quick drink as Myrna was running a few minutes late.
Lexi's face had turned as hard as granite, it could have split and fire shot from her forehead with fury. A stream of filthy language spewed from her lips telling Myrna what an ungrateful, useless, worthless person she was and what a privilege it was to live in her little cottage

there in St Kilda with all this work available and that would be the only sex or attention ever to come Myrna's way! Lexi then taunted Myrna about all the beatings inflicted by the police when taken into custody for soliciting back in the old days (well, the nineteen seventies and sixties!) and how the police had forced Myrna to perform sex acts with them and photographed Myrna all dressed up from the top as a woman but with the skirt up and panties down...just for a laugh.

She said I too should be grateful for people like her who "had paved the way and gone through all this with how police treated us in the past, so we could have a better life". Feeling sure Myrna was about to be dragged from the hideaway in a 'Mommy Dearest' frenzy, wire coat hangers flashing and powder bleach flung all over the bathroom floor 'n all, I lunged for my huge grass-woven carry-all bag and bolted to the front door.

"Look, I'll leave you girls to it, Lexi....am sure he'll be here soon and then I'll have missed the last tram home.....so I'll scoot off now, ok?"

"She's no fucking 'girl'... she's a tragic old bloke and will be out on his arse...and *rah-RAH-RAH*....." The language and manner had changed to the tone of a 'rough-nut' Australian truck driver with the voice of a deranged Dalek on high voltage venom. (I didn't know what else was said as I was down the path and at the end of the street before her front door had shut). Brushing past some cute guy as I turned the corner I caught a whiff of whiskey on him. He turned in to Lexi's street and I knew who he must be and where he was heading. I could hardly wait for the long, slow tram ride home to ponder what kind of world I was letting myself into or even knowing what other choice to get by I might even have.

Rehana Incognito

All along I'd probably just hoped that it would have been like a never-ending Dolly Parton "Smokey Mountain Christmas Special", with beautiful, glamorous clothes, makeup and music, everyone friendly and full of love... simply all things nice. This world of vile, dysfunctional men, dressing as women acting out their painful, ugly pasts and making a lot of money whilst entertaining a twisted view of anything *I'd* thought sex was about, seemed far away from my lonely little dream. It stunned me as betraying and shocking as the hapless victims of Nazi brutality arriving at a concentration camp to hear a full, welcoming orchestra playing wonderful music. To be lulled at the sight of the neat, fake facades of shops and amenities around the camps to mask what was really going on. I felt just as sickened at the perverseness of it all.

Still, with my personal documents not yet changed to show 'female', there was no choice about work and the Gender Board had stipulated that to be considered and receive assessment and treatment, a 'patient' must live and work as a member of the 'opposite sex'. My personal documents all being in a male name were of no use to get a job as a female of course so I called Loren for advice. Thankfully, she even offered to come with me to the city and go from step One - the deed poll office to change my name, to steps Two, Three, Four and forever it seemed where my deed poll would be embarrassingly shown to everyone in order to get a new driver's licence, bank details and all.
So, accepting Lexi's apology by phone on that Sunday night and learning that Myrna the Murderer had fled back "up bush" the night before, I agreed to keep working for Lexi until I either got a "normal" job or Felicity's restaurant opened. More interestingly though was the drama of why Myrna had fled "up bush". She

BODYCAGE

had nowhere else to go in any big city as she was too well known...even when dressed as a guy...which for all intents and purposes she was. She had been given new identity documents some 10 years before, after having given information to the police in another state in exchange for a lenient sentence in a case involving several "high profile" (with low lives) paedophiles who had been convicted and charged with the disappearance, rape and kidnapping of many young boys. This ring of indescribable trash of humanity had involved Myrna and "one of the girls" to lure the young boys with a feeling of security or the promise of sexual adventures to get into their cars.

Personally, I cannot even bring myself to now to write about what was done to these children, but I do know that Myrna, despite the short period of incarceration, was as much responsible for those boys who did indeed die during their ordeal at the hands of their captors. The torment she wore and the life of a rat, forever on the run would be punishment albeit unfitting, forever. It made the every episode of "Prisoner Cell Block H" I rushed home even from a dinner party at times to watch (pre video days!) seem like a schoolgirl's holiday camp really. Still... it was getting close to 9 o'clock, I put down the phone on Lexi as the theme tune to "Prisoner" was starting...

"He used to bring me roses...
I wish he could again...
but that was on the outside...
and things were different then...
On the inside the roses grow,
they don't mind the stony ground...
but the roses here are prisoners too...
'til morning comes around..."

Rehana Incognito

Somehow, I must have fallen asleep during "Prisoner" and realised I'd have a whole week again to wonder about all those hard-done-by-bitches and tragic wenches of Wentworth Detention Centre. Thankfully, I thought, trudging back to bed cocooned in a thick quilt to get up early to dispose of my old identity in the city in the morning, I still had my daily episodes of the Japanese soap opera "Oshin" to keep me going with melodrama every night at 5 on the Special Broadcasting Service! I went to sleep, humming the "Prisoner" theme tune with a dreamy picture forming and unfurling in my head also with some sound track... blurring in and out of the picture of Bette Midler's "The Rose" as I pulled the quilt tighter around me against the chill of the night....

"just remember in the winter...
far beneath the bitter snows...
lies the seed that with the sun's love ...
in the spring becomes the rose."

Loren met me on the steps 'under the clocks', that traditional city meeting place for Melbournians in front of Flinders Street Station which showed the next departure times for the trains. She'd dressed up, as Melbourne girls were more prone to do than most other Aussies for going "into town". In a long white frock and low-cut top, bouncing her chest a little bit more than was really necessary, we headed down the steps. Making sure that any male passenger on his way up the stairs had noticed, Loren flung her hair back like a wild filly, smiling with content at her 'conquests' each time one had gotten an eyeful... (Which was easy to notice, as their heads usually bounced up and down in the direction they were looking). She showed me to the office of Births, Deaths and Marriages, otherwise known as the offices of Hatch, Match and Dispatch)

where I took my documents for the Deed Poll. On stuffing my birth certificate discretely under to the young girl behind the glass window, I walked off as she took it for some stamping or another... but suddenly I heard –
"Excuse me... hello? Just a minute... you seem to have given me the wrong person's documents, Love."
By then, the other people waiting on the ghastly, green vinyl chairs along the wall for their turn in the queue were all ears to hear what I'd done wrong. Loren was doubled over, stifling her laughs, but her big back and shoulders shook up and down betraying her, as I moved back to the window. In her little black-rimmed glasses, tapping her pen against the counter she announced loudly to all-
"I think you've given me your brother's or husband's papers. These all have a man's name on them."
In the loudest of whispers to make myself audible through the little grill, I tried to explain... "Erm... the name is mine.... on the documents. I need to change it to the name on the deed poll form...ok?"
"Well...OK... I suppose... no worries, but that's a funny thing that your parents had given you a boy's name isn't it?"
Not believing this young girl had still not worked it out, I beckoned her closer, cupping my hands over the speaking grill, attempting a loud whisper...
"I AM a boy...still... I need these forms to show a new identity." Wishing that the ground would open and swallow me, I turned to see everyone just staring; the clerk just gave me the weirdest of looks. She quickly disappeared behind closed doors returning with the same weird, unchanged look two minutes later, handing me the completed form with my new name on it. Loren was beside herself with glee at my humiliation but was quickly put in her place when I reminded her

that it was not that bad as the clerk did think I was some poor girl changing her name because her parents must have cruelly given her a boy's name! She'd be sure to get me back, I guessed, as we jumped the tram for the next port of call... the bank.

Clattering down Collins St, a burly young guy had sat himself in front of us, mesmerised as ever at Loren's overabundant exposure of cleavage, his attention not unnoticed by Loren. She gave her chest the biggest bouncy heave at every clunk of the tram as our stop approached. The boy was hypnotised and had embarrassedly put his jacket over his lap. Collecting ourselves to get off as the tram slowed down, Loren gave a quick gaze around, noticing we were the only ones in the back of the tram. Leaning very close to him she said just loudly enough for me to hear...
"Quickly darling... give us a flash of your lovely cock." He too quickly gazed around with a cheeky little smirk and went to undo his zip. Just as he was about to give her his big treat, she leaned back to him as the doors slid open, deepening her voice to a husky drawl, to roar...
"...and I'll show you mine!"
I almost fell to the street, running off as quickly as I could, alone, to the bank not even daring to look back to see if Loren was behind me. Already flustered and a total nervous wreck with that performance and the embarrassment at the registrar's office, I now had to explain the same thing to another bank clerk.
Loren had reached my side just as the young, mousy-looking, female clerk at the information desk had called my turn. Giving Loren the most chilling glare I could muster, hoping she'd behave in the bank and embarrass me no further, I explained to this girl what needed to be changed on my bank records. This young

clerk obviously had her own opinions of "diversity", acceptance perhaps, as well as basic understanding and good manners. She took my deed poll and bank book, going from desk to desk throughout the bank, pointing over to where I stood, trying to pretend I was not noticing, as she giggled and smirked to everyone she was clearly enjoying telling what must have been the story of the month at the bank. Necks craned and eyes squinted over the tops of computer screens as they were clearly trying to make out which of the people standing around me she was talking about before she eventually made her way back to me with a loud voice saying -
"*MISS* Davies... your new passbook is here for you." She watched me walk towards her, trying to hold my head high, as all the staff had stopped to watch or hear what I might say. As I approached the desk with my head down, reaching out for the new passbook she was about to hand me, another hand reached over mine and grabbed it harshly from her. Loren herself passed the book to me hissing over the counter -
"Listen you ugly little bitch... She *might* well be what you know... but look at her! Every guy in town today's going to be staring at her everywhere she goes... All day today and all day tomorrow... And you'll still be an ugly little nobody of a bank clerk stuck in here!" I was already heading for the door, wondering if all those clerks were just staring at me because they knew about my past or really were enjoying the view of my bum in very tight jeans. I didn't care really, having already relished the taste of enough men hitting *on* me instead of just hitting me! Loren caught me shaking on the corner by an ATM.
"Well, I won't show my face in there ever again. But thanks." And I didn't...but took Loren to lunch after she'd slipped her card into the ATM, punched in her

numbers then loudly announced her wonderment at the machine 'spitting out bloody twenty dollar notes from the wall without even needing to suck a cock'.
"Miss *Davies,* now is it? I'm gonna call you Bette."
"Don't bother, she was Bette *Davis.*" I hurried her along the street hoping for no more incidents.
"Oh well... thought she made a movie about you anyway....'All About Ian'!!" More maniacal laughter as we battled through the shoppers.
 I got on with the rest of the name changes without further incident. Then it was back home in time to see Oshin's gorgeous and beloved eldest son, Yuu, writing beautiful letters from the Japanese war front in the Philippines, slowly dying of some heinous illnesses and starvation before ever getting home to his dear mother. Going through nearly another box of tissues with that one, I called Roula again for a bit of cheering up, arranged to go shopping and borrow her copy of "April Ashley's Odyssey" to absorb all I could about other people who "might" be like me and just be that little bit surer that I was, hopefully, on the right course. I decided to keep up the work on Lexi's phone for the time being, meeting lots of the other "girls" in the neighbourhood and from the drag shows at Tangles. Also got to know the fabulous 'show Goddesses' of the amazing Pokeys Revue on Sunday nights. I really hope someone, somewhere has immortalised those girls (perhaps there's a shrine in a Melbourne gay bar...or at least a humble website!) as their shows were sheer genius for the time, bringing the glamour and drama into our real Melbournian world of shows like Dallas and Dynasty. Amazingly a lot of the shows had their genesis in the mind of the wonderfully, delightful Miss Terri 'Tinsel', who had come up with the likes of her "Alien" meets "Chicago" type drag shows whilst high and away in other worlds herself on

morphine and methadone in and out of consciousness in hospital after her sex-change surgery. Nothing like lying there and thinking the nurse coming at you with a syringe is a giant lizard about to spew green acid saliva over you and eat you alive... but that was Terri.

Although finding enough to identify with in April Ashley's story... her world of high society contacts, glamour and travel hadn't even registered as a hope or chance for anyone like me. I loved the fact that she too was a Northerner and had made it through to who she believed she was, though I felt her lifestyle was so far removed from the likes of me, that I couldn't help but wonder if the fact that she had some celebrity status had granted her a lot more acceptance from people who knew of her past than someone less known. From where I was seeing it at that time, I knew to keep very low-key and not let it be known... or go right over the top like those hard drag queens and hookers, compromise my personality, and fight for every scrap of dignity I would need. My personality and what good qualities I had were not going to change, I'd decided. Keeping my mind focused on the nicer ladies in my life, absorbing all their successful and endearing qualities, I knew I had the looks and body to go with them.... so kept at it.

1984
Apart from Roula and Felicity, I was hard pressed to find any others from the trans-community who lived anything like my dreamt-of 'normal' world, living a 'real' life. Even to people like Loren, who I guess had a good heart really and meant very well (although she was vulgar and crude at times with a mind like a man in a sewer) I was a *freak* to them. They would constantly mock me for wanting to go all the way... have the complete surgical change to have my body fully as I

wanted it to be. Always it was the same negativity, reminding me that I'd never be a "woman"... that I'd only ever be used by men... they'd always go crawling back to their wives and girlfriends, who would "throw on the tears" and get their man back every time. I tried to convince these friends that it was for me...I didn't care about those men...but secretly I'd hoped that it might be different for me, wanting to believe that people fall in love with a soul...and look past all kinds of things when they find who they really love. And I just couldn't then recall where I'd read that love does not recognise what is of race and creed or man or woman... we just fall in love. So, somewhere, deep down, I wanted to believe it would be so with me and I had started young enough to be a success with it all... with plenty of time!

Making my way to Lexi's one evening, I crossed to Grey St as cars cruised by me in a world of my own, trying to catch glimpses of a heaven-sent sunset. Sometimes the cars slowed, a window would wind down and ask if I was "doing business". I always hung my head shyly, shaking a quick and big "NO". Even though a lot of the men who had stopped were really very attractive and I'd have loved a romp in the hay with many of them! I just wondered all the time why they would be out looking to *pay* for some sex. Clueless Pollyanna continued to the top of the hill on Grey St, confidently proud that she looked great enough for men to even want to pay for and felt even more reassured that she was making the right decision with her life!

Almost to Lexi's corner, a huge tranny came lumbering along the road, hammering furiously at the window of a rapidly departing car. It was "Lurch" or Lorraine, a very unattractive man, convinced of his transgender status,

soliciting motorists on the streets as he himself had become a 'working girl'.
"Come back....Come back, Love." She'd bellowed at him. "It's alright... I've had the operation... I'll give you head for twenty bucks. *COME BAAAaaaack!*"
The mortified, desperate gutter crawler caught a break in the traffic and screeched into it, escaping his pursuer. Lurch glanced up as a sneer hissed from a mouthful of very bad teeth. In clingy snakeskin pants, with gnarled dirty hands and long, sharp red false nails, *Trannysaurus Rex* stumbled ungainly on its way through her *Gender Dysphoric Park* to look for more prey. She'd trail these creeps in the hope of making some money and even paying her for sex... which often enough they actually did, shattering my delusions that any of the attention from these blokes actually counted for much. I felt somewhat disheartened to suddenly realise that! I was not really sure what mattered more to Lurch. Getting a bit of extra cash or having someone actually give her some sexual attention? Throwing her an understanding smile, I appreciated her "G'day, Love" as she headed for another car as I crossed to Lexi's street.
Another few strides and I was almost to Lexi's corner when another apparition loomed from the church doorway through her hunting ground. Yet another rasping voice hissed my name as I looked up to see the *lovely* Shantelle in the highest of white plastic heels, gigantic white plastic hoop earrings, green lurex tights, skin tight blue sweater (off both shoulders) and what looked like the remains of a skinned road kill Afghan hound spiked on her head. Standing like a cross-dressed sentry on her lonely vigil, surveying her turf whilst waiting for the endless stream of punters to drive by, she must have thought me an entertaining piece of prey to fall into her path to hone her skills on.

Rehana Incognito

Most of the clientele would have known she was really a man... most of the time by day, dressing as the sex goddess by night, with the most incredible reputation for fooling those who did not know. Shantelle could actually perform complete 'vaginal' intercourse without even actually having to *have* a vagina by manipulating the penis of some naïve punter with a well greased-up hand soaked in Vaseline. Amazing, I'd thought, that any guy would be foolish enough to pay money for something he could probably have done better with his own hand anyway... but it just went to show the power of suggestion made for a satisfactory illusion in his mind that what he thought he was actually doing...was real!

'Trick sex' was a trick *for* the Tricks and something I was *never* going to risk a try. Enough 'girls', I'd learnt, had tried that one, been caught out and risked being beaten half to death by a guy who may not have been pleased to find out the 'woman' he'd paid for a *good* time might well have had a bigger willy than him! (Is that why they get so mad?!). To me she was just another nasty piece of work from the scene at Tangles and am sure somewhere she had a heart, even though I am totally sure I saw her slip her hand into one of her 'friend's' handbags one night and take her purse!

"*HIIIiiiiiiii, Girrrrl*. Haven't seen you at the club much lately. Thought you musta left us and gone off to be a real woman already," she sneered down at me from on high as I tried to hurry past.

"No Shanny, I got sick of Tangles and go to straight places only now. Tangles isn't really for me... you know..."

"Yeah? What makes you think you're so special?" She stepped down, grabbing at my arm. "Don't think you'll fit in any better at your straight places, Love. Some guy will find out the score and tell everyone where you

BODYCAGE

go... or some jealous slag or a gay guy will recognise you. Then your little charade will be all over. It's happened to heaps of queens I know, so you must be living in a fucking dream!" She ranted on as I walked away as fast as I could while she smeared on another gash of crimson lipstick like a child filling between the outlines of drawn on lips, extending almost up into her nostrils.

Back over my shoulder I found the courage to belt back...

"Well, I don't care... it's better than trying to fit in with a bunch of cross dressers and cock-suckers trying to pretend *they* are straight!" Wondering what I'd risked by my defiance of the Wicked Queen of Darkness herself, she screeched on.

"How straight do you think your world is anyway...? I know you're off to Roper's place. Won't be long before you realise you'll make more money in her fucking bedroom than on her phone! You're fucked, Rina... *FUCKED!*"

"It's *Riannon...* See ya later Shanny."

"You're fucked whatever you want to call yourself. Don't think having your operation will change a thing. Women are second class citizens and you'll be nothing but a second class woman... to everyone. You'll see." She was still railing as I disappeared from her vision and the last thing I heard was "When ya lose yer balls, you'll lose yer brains too...just like the rest." With a furtive glance back as I heard the heels a' clatter thinking she was after me, it was a relief to see her services to the community were required as a car had slowed to her post... a window slipping down, ready to talk business.

Off the hook from that ugly scene, I hurried along Lexi's little street knowing for sure I would not last much longer with that scene. Quickly enough I'd become an outcaste within a minority of a Transsexual Empire with it's inverted, reversed and convoluted standards of how I'd expected things to be. Most of those types had wanted to stay as they were... perpetually in the pre-operative condition. Not even sure why they'd wanted to be called "pre op" transsexuals anyway... They always intended to be *never-to-be-operated* transsexuals! They had no desire to change, and why should they? Happy with their male equipment, and happy to use it as any other man might, enough of them had partners who were abundantly happy with that state of affairs. As abundant too it seemed these type of men were, it was not for me. Plenty were after me and persuasively attractive propositions at times they were too, but I knew soon enough what they were after and I found it abhorrent. No, they could worship at another Shrine of Hermaphrodite to look for the balance of male and female energy (or symbols subconsciously associated thereof!) outside of themselves elsewhere.

Just three more doors to Lexi's and a light splash of water hit my bare arms. Before I could even look up to see if it had started to rain on this clear night, I was drenched in a torrent accompanied by another tirade from an elderly lady with a garden hose in hand. Swinging the hose wildly at me, up and down from head to toe, she shrilled,

"Go ply your filthy trade elsewhere you dirty hussy." She hurried along from behind her well watered hedges and roses. Trying to explain that I was just visiting a friend in the street, she ignored my pleas. "Oh God, stop squirting me!! I'm soaked through." Parting my hair through the drizzle down my face I could see such contempt and felt overcome with grief that this old lady had already judged me as less than a piece of dirt to be hosed from her front path before even getting to

BODYCAGE

know me. Lexi had a great laugh as I squelched through the door. "Ran into Lizzie did you?" she grinned sarcastically, throwing me a towel.
"Who's Lizzie?" I asked, dabbing at the wet patches.
"Well, girl...you're the biggest 'Prisoner' fan I know... Thought you'd have recognised one of your idols right away. She's the actress who plays Lizzie Birdsworth in your favourite show. Didn't you recognise her in her civvies?"
Oh, now that I saw her face again and heard the voice over in my head, I realised I had indeed been abused and assaulted by one of my favourite TV characters and it all felt worthwhile – 'Went*worth* Detention Centre worthwhile', I figured and with all the sordidness and drama around me feeling like somehow I'd materialised into some kind of excessively perverse and pornographic episode of the show itself!
However, with Lexi there was always plenty of action. When she'd made a few dollars, the phone would be unplugged and off we'd go to spend it. She was a compulsive shop-a-holic for sure, but unfortunately also a compulsive shop*lifter!* Her performances in the more ritzy Toorak boutiques were outrageous. To the dismay of sales girls and shoppers alike, she got away with murder. Taking back often stolen clothes and accessories and getting refunds or swaps, she'd prowl through racks of clothing, just for laughs, making horrible manly grunts and growls, leaving people gazing around the shop wondering where the "man" was making the noises. All the while she'd be bundling designer gowns and all else she could stuff into her oversize bag as I'd already ran out in horror fleeing back to the car, usually vowing to never shop with her again, though inevitably I did.
I was constantly fearing the house eventually being turned upside down by the police (not for prostitution,

as that was legal), but for the alarming amount of stolen goods appearing there. Lexi and Myrna, of course going way back together from the 'old school' (as they constantly reminded me) which must have been a school for LesbianGayBisexualTransgender criminality, had recently gotten one of their lags to show up with a van late at night. Together they'd taken a ride to one of Melbourne's new, flashy outer suburbs, clearing out a display home of all its contents. As we sat one night with Lexi mocking some old gay man on the telly, drenched in moisturizer and a salmon pink sweater over his shoulder, nursing a cat on his lap, Lexi unashamedly chirped,

"You see... it's seeing old guys like that which made me realise I'd get into drag, Girl. I was never going to turn out to be a sad old bastard like that...fuckin' look at it."

Well, I thought he seemed happy with himself enough as Big Ben chimed some guest none of us expected. Thinking, I might have forgotten to tell Lexi a client was coming, I offered to get the door as she raced to the room to make a quick "ready for action" transformation. I opened the door and there stood two men who immediately flashed their badges, identifying themselves as Russell Street CIB.

"Lexi Roper?" the burlier one asked.

"Does she look like Roper?" the other one asked as if he'd asked me if I was Charles Manson.

"Errr... I'll get her for you...come in..." I led them to the sofa where they quickly took out their notebooks, asking my name and what I was doing there. I lied and said I was just visiting. Thankfully, they didn't push further, only warning me that I should not "hang around" with people like Roper or I'd be tarred with the same brush and people might think I'd be just like her. Lexi knew straight away when she saw my face that it

BODYCAGE

was not an unannounced punter. I am sure she even knew why the police were there. As one handcuffed her the other sat lecturing me on the couch.

"Leave her alone, ya ugly bastard. She's a good kid," was the last I heard of Lexi as she marched to the police car parked tightly outside her front gate to the lock-up for the night.

With one of her contacts, I collected her the following day. Dishevelled, in a tight denim mini skirt and an all over stubble, we escorted her home.

"The pricks wouldn't even let me have a shave or my bloody makeup!" Poor Lexi... a broken travesty of a tranny. She never changed, but life around her was always a rollercoaster ride. Her girly antics were great a distraction at times, although I did always wonder why she was hell bent on making the whole world somehow *pay* for who and what she was. The time was flying by as the time of my first appointment with Professor Williams was upon me.

At his swanky Gynaecology clinic in the back streets of Richmond, I sat in the busy waiting room after checking in with the polite and understanding receptionist. Nervously reaching for a magazine, I took a discrete glance to see who I had for company... or even perhaps *what* I had for company was more apt. Noticing what could only be described as a middle-aged man, I almost gasped, with jaw dropping, to see he wore heavy makeup and a creamy mix'n'match twin set outfit the same as the one worn by the teenage girl sitting with him! The girl kept chatting to her 'twin set' companion as 'Dad', sometimes as 'Jenny' (why do so many of this variation call themselves 'Jenny' for God's sake?) who had sitting by him a youngish woman with a contentedly sleeping infant in her lap.

A few more of the similar ilk were seated around the room with the same types of garish, girly wigs somehow trying to soften, like a frame, the hard, masculine faces under whose heads the wigs were perched. It always reminds me of that other unusual dichotomy of the smaller the 'girl's' nose gets sawn down under facial feminisation surgery, the bigger they seem to want their boobs. Some direct correlation, I'd been told somewhere, that "the bigger the boobs" the more they'd buffer the pain and disguise who so many of these people really were- Like big airbags in a horror smash of a life... but with nipples.

The woman would smile softly at me, shaking her head with a roll of the eyes of disbelief when sure they were not looking, at the 'couple' by her side. It was easy to smile back and share her consternation as I too felt uncomfortable, perhaps even more so, after looking around further to see that the room was *full* of such 'misfits' equally as ill at ease in the room, trying to blend and disappear into the comfy chairs. Losing myself in back copies of "The Australian Women's Weekly", I dared not look up again as the silence chewed into me. The lady with the baby plopped herself into a seat closer, asking if I'd mind holding her child while she popped to the loo. She'd clearly seen my relief at having something to do for a while as I almost snatched the still nodding infant from her. Returning too soon, she popped the baby back on her lap as he slowly woke up to eagerly guzzle some fruit juice.

"Was he a good boy while mummy was away?"

"He was a little angel," I replied, "How much could he have done asleep for two minutes?"

She laughed, then asked quite stumping me,

"Are you getting help through the program too...to have one of your own?"

BODYCAGE

"Program?" I blurted, wondering if she too was on *THE* Program which the gender clinic's process was called, as my whole mind had suddenly gone blank.

"The In Vitro program... you know... to help you have a baby!" she explained, tapping gently on my thigh enquiringly as if I should have just *known* that. "The Professor is marvellous. We'd tried all over the country before we had success with little Troy so now we're trying for another."

Thinking how nice that must have been for her, there was no way I was going to explain that I had gynaecological problems she might not be ready to hear, I was spared any explanation as the receptionist called my name. I felt the icy glares of the 'not here for In Vitro' patients, as I smiled down at the woman and baby, wishing her luck on her next ride on the 'In Vitro-go-round'.

Almost dashing into the professor's office I shut the door with firm relief behind me. With a cordial greeting, the middle-aged, extremely proper gentleman put me immediately at ease as I took the seat in front of his huge desk. We immediately got started on the beginning of seemingly endless months of questions and examinations.

"So, Riannon... lovely name. Firstly I'd like you to tell me all about yourself and why you think our program would be of benefit to you." With pen and note book open at the ready, he sat back to listen as I took a very deep breath... pondering a reply.

"Well... where to start? I hope this doesn't sound too simplistic... but I am sure that I am one of those typical cases... you know of well... living in the wrong body."

Professor Williams smiled. Not a knowing or caring smile, but more of a 'well, I knew it' smile. "You mean - like a woman trapped in the body of a man, then... right?"

"Well... perhaps like that... but look at me...I can't really say I got the body of a man anyway to be trapped in, can I?! Really, does this look like the body of a man with a woman trapped in it?" I sat forward, almost pleading for understanding, stumbling and babbling on, trying not to feel disheartened by him saying "Oh, really?" and cocking his head as if to say "do tell".
Trying to be more specific and elaborate, I continued.
"What I mean is, that despite how I was born... with male genitalia... and being told of course that I was a boy... well, mmmm... I really think that... inside... I was developing the mind of a girl and preferred always the role and feelings of being female more than anything I could have *felt* was anything like male. Yes! That's what I'm trying to say... Does it make sense?"
"That sounds pretty familiar to me, Riannon. But, I'd like you to explain to me *how* you think a female might be thinking. And, how do you know that's what you're actually doing?" With pen poised to note my reply he sat back waiting as I pondered.
"I can't really honestly say, Professor, that I'm sure my thoughts are female or that I even really know how a woman may think." He cocked his head to one side...again raising his eyebrows. Wondering if I'd completely cocked this right up, I continued anyway,
"I really know of no other way to explain this further or if how I think may or may not be female, but I know for sure I don't think like any man I have known...and apart from this body...just take a look at my hands! Have you ever seen hands like this on any man?"
He actually leaned across his desk and picked up my hand. I honestly thought he was going to kiss it like the gentleman I thought he was, but he looked at it like a dead rat in a laboratory experiment.... up and down and all along.

BODYCAGE

"You're right, Riannon. They are actually about the most beautiful and feminine hands I have seen even on a biological woman, let alone someone in your position. And I will tell you something special. Can you see how much shorter your ring finger is than your index finger?" Holding his hand right up before my face, pointing to the finger which did not sport a wedding ring, he further enlightened me.

"Well, most men have a much longer ringer finger than the index finger... so it's interesting for me to note that about you." Interesting for me too and something for which I am forever grateful as they became a 'saving grace' many times! Finally, I felt I was getting somewhere, as Professor Williams explained that many transgender women were left-handed, even very ambidextrous of which I was both! Having written with both hands, though mainly my left, I thought it quite the norm that everyone just changed hands in class when one got tired of writing, much to the amusement of those who'd noticed. Apart from that, in swapping hands to write with, I noticed that it was just as easy for me to write backwards as well as forwards and was astounded to learn some intriguing facts about Leonardo Da Vinci along the way.

He too was ambidextrous and wrote in mirror writing... (backwards that is), which when looked at it a mirror seems correct. The most intriguing theory is the possibility that Da Vinci too may have been a transgender person with the main clue being that the Mona Lisa herself, bearing Da Vinci's own bone structure, is his portrait of his female self. In some of my readings I'd learnt too that he was at times on the wrong end of the law for sexual liaisons with other males... so perhaps this is a possibility. Intriguing too that some other societies whom had respected and found valid places in their worlds for transgender people had called us 'Twin Spirits', perhaps believing that both the male and the female resided in us at the same time, making us not creatures of abhorrence, but creatures with an assimilation or the privilege of seeing life from both sides. Perhaps true, and well understandable why many of these people held shamanic, magical places in these societies and were the ones chosen as go-betweens in disputes, usually between men and women, seeing the arguments from both unique perspectives.

"Riannon, I am sorry to appear doubtful of your explanations though. We just have to be very cautious about who we admit to the program. Many people who come to my office turn out to be little more than confused men. Be they gay men or otherwise... I'm sure you're aware of that. They are often thinking of seeking surgery for all the wrong reasons and if they slip through our screening it all ends in terrible disasters. It's a catastrophe when their lives fall apart after surgery, with so many of them committing suicide... the percentage is very high. So you can see how important it is that you are honest with us...and yourself." Now, those were words really did make of sense and I decided to make sure to be as honest as even embarrassingly possible.

After not too many years the Professor's words would be proven true...over and over. There were only ever a very small handful of people like myself whom I met, got to know, befriended or fell foul of, who really made it through their lives to be functional heterosexual women. The rest were lost to drug dependency, alcoholism, suicide *and* realising that they were attracted to women after all, settled for 'lesbian' relationships. Quite a lot of trouble to go right around in full circle on a gender merry-go-round to find out you're really a straight man after all! So the stats, I found were a good 70% hit the drugs or suicide and of the 30% left, 70% of those ended up with other women, biological or otherwise. "Know thyself... know thyself" - truly I'd have to take that very seriously!

So, promising I would be honest, I spared a thought for those confused ones who would have sat in this office before me. Those whom, if they'd only known themselves better and been a whole lot more honest, would have spared themselves and their loved ones so many agonies.

"That's why I came to the Program, Professor. I feel I am at last being very honest with myself and getting on with this. Hopefully, when all this is over, I can start my *real* life."

Nodding in agreement, Professor Williams seemed well pleased as this was obviously what he needed to hear.

Next followed a lot of personal questions about sexual experiences and how I felt about them. Going into all manner of details relating these experiences (of course to be as honest as I'd promised to be) I noticed the Professor had become quite flushed, squirming uncomfortably in his seat. Politely he informed me that the torrid details were not really required as he was merely trying to gauge my current sexual appetite in order to prescribe the right dosage of female hormones for me to start taking!

"You have enough material there already for a steamy novel, Riannon," he muttered in exasperation. Promising to send him a signed copy of my adventures both before and after becoming who I actually wanted to be, I was happy to take his list of appointments for further tests to come in several other departments, clutching with glee the prescription for the female hormone pills.

"What other tests are to be done, Professor?" Enthusiasm now bubbled forth.

"We'll be sending a schedule to you of appointments for the next few months in the post. Some are at the hospital, like the blood and urine tests. They'll help us understand more about your hormone levels and some idea of your chromosome condition. There'll also be psychiatric and psychological evaluations. Oh, and the hospital will also do a brain scan."

"Do you mean they are going to see if I've actually got a brain?" I joked... Really.

"Riannon, you really are delightfully scatty. No, they only need to take a reading of brain waves and patterns and we can determine a lot too from those."

I couldn't help wonder and feel quite amused that this man had associated my 'delightful scattiness' with my femininity, but clearly he did.

Before leaving he explained more about the prescribed hormone.

"It's called Premarin and the name comes from Pregnant Mare's Urine... Pre-Mar-Rin... which the hormone is derived from." I was almost sick!

"Does that mean that every time I hear the crack of a whip, I'll be off at a gallop?"

"Perhaps only high-spirited fillies like you, Riannon," he generously smiled his reply.

"OK, put five dollars on me for a win in the Melbourne Cup next year... it's the least I can do for you." I stuffed the paperwork into my bag, gathering myself to leave. The Professor added that the hormones may cause me to feel nauseated for a good few weeks, especially in the mornings, but promised that my body would take to it like a duck to water!

"On your next visit, Riannon, I'd like you to bring along a personal friend or acquaintance to interview. Perhaps someone you live or work with."

BODYCAGE

That would be great, I thought. I could bring along the lesbian I lived with or a violent criminal transvestite prostitute I answer phones for. Gee, what a picture of successful female heterosexuality that would present me being on the road to. I knew he'd hoped I could bring along a boyfriend, to demonstrate some measure of success on this path and show some degree at least of emotional support along the way. My next appointment with professor Williams would be weeks away yet and I knew at this point that anything could just happen. So, by time I'd get back to see him again, all the other tests and analyses would be back in his hands and reviewed. Everything could well be quite another story.

Anxiously, I headed from the surgery to the nearest pharmacy to fill my prescription. In my trembling hand were the keys to hope as the transformation was truly ready to start. The 'magic pills' I'd dreamt of long ago were to be mine at last. Hurrying to the tram stop I sat on the seat tearing open the packet, popping the first little yellow, oval-shaped pill into my mouth with a shudder. With eyes tightly closed I wished to open them again and find the transition already complete with a Pamela Anderson chest bursting forth like an air bag in a car crash sporting a complete set of female genitalia. Opening them again as the tram pulled up, I heard a giggle and a laugh as the doors opened and someone lumbered down the steps. It was 'Lurch', obviously making her way to the 'Girly Clinic' for an appointment with the Professor. She slightly caught my eye as I tried to squeeze on board with a couple of other passengers to shield me, hoping she'd not noticed I'd seen her. In my heart I wished her all the best of luck, hoping that the lady with the baby was not still there. If she was indeed already pregnant she'd be in danger of an on-the-spot miscarriage if she saw Lorraine walk in!

Feeling so reassured and on the road to the right help, the next appointments were eagerly awaited. With all the information together and assessed, I could prove who I really am. Soon, the nightmare would be over. Still bubbling with enthusiasm I could not wait to call Roula and tell her all my news.

BODYCAGE

CHAPTER FOUR

"That's great, Ri. I'm really happy for you and that the Professor was so encouraging with you. I had to wait nearly three months before he even put me on the 'mones. He wanted to wait 'til all my tests were done because I was so young. It was a horrible wait. All those personal questions were really upsetting as well." Roula's voice began to taper as she spoke... until it eventually sounded as distant as a whisper lost on the wind. Then I began to wonder if she was still on the line.
"Are you OK, Roula...are you *there?* You sound a bit tired..."
"Just a bit down, Girl. Am taking antidepressants now... they make me feel a bit faraway sometimes... sorry. I start to feel so helpless about it all sometimes and no-one seems to understand," she only just breathed on the tiniest breath into the phone.
"Well, I'll be around for a while yet, Roula... Don't worry...and I understand anyway," I offered, feeling at a loss to know what to say for the best really.
"It's just so hard with me being Greek 'n all that. Christ, I was my parent's only *son* and now look at what they've got. Can you imagine the shit they go through because of me being like this? It's almost unbearable at times to see Mum and Dad's pain. As if that's not bad enough, the psych assessors told me I might not be strong enough to even get through this bloody program." Her voice was now a struggle to make out apart from somewhere through the crumbling croak I heard her saying...
"Of course I am not *strong*... I am not a man... Men are strong... I know I am a girl and just want someone to hold me and remember I am just a girl." I knew she

was in tears as I now was myself, feeling nothing but her awful pain and exactly what she meant.

"I'm not *STRONG* Riannon... and I'm not a man... I've been through so much now and it's knocked me to the ground. Can't they see that?!"

With my heart aching all the more I could make out little further through her sobs, yet took on the anguish of someone whom to me was just a beautiful young woman with a whole new life to find and look forward to. Never could I have conceived of Roula being anything other than the girl I'd known her to be, as I struggled for anything to say to her.

"You know Roula, at least you have your family there with you, supporting you as best they can. It's the loneliest thing in the world when your own family has abandoned you. I can't begin to tell you how painful that is, especially as I gave all I could to mine. Now I appear as something unacceptable to them and they don't even want to know me... It's the same for a lot of us I suppose, so count your blessings, Girl. You're my friend you know and you all mean the world to me now... you're my family now."

With a little gust of liveliness she promised to be family for me too, asking me not to worry about her as I was a good mate. Thanking me for caring so much about her, she put down the phone with a promise to call me soon as she really was dozing off.

After not hearing back from Roula for a few days, it was surprise to hear her father's broken English on the other end of my phone late one afternoon. He had called to say that Roula had taken her life, all alone over the weekend in a cheap motel room in the city, at only nineteen years of age. He did not wish to invite me to the funeral, knowing that Roula would have been embarrassed as the law required her to be buried under her male name and the Greek Orthodox service would be conducted just the same. As distraught as I was it was some relief to know I would not have to have witnessed this last indignity, even in death, of this very dear friend.

I could not even imagine how these assessors had failed to see the inner and outer femininity of this dear, sweet angel as I anguished for days why they had not given her support and encouragement. I opted then to guard my every word with this Board and its Program about my own thoughts and circumstances lest I too be left rejected to deal with my own life hanging in limbo... a Twilight Zone between sexes... neither quite being one nor the other.

"I'll promise to get through this, even for you, Roula," I prayed to anything or anyone who might have listened. "I'll live out our hopes and dreams for both of us, I promise, my friend." I prayed too that, for whatever karmic reason, Roula's spirit now knew and enjoyed the value of being female where-ever she now was or perhaps somewhere she was already back among us- reborn, smiling contentedly in anticipation of life as a little princess with all the love and security she'd missed in this one.

1985

The first appointment on the agenda was for blood and urine tests. Also, a brain scan at the same medical centre on the same day. Those appointments went quite smoothly, apart from the nurse offering me a pan to pee in instead of a bottle with the ensuing embarrassment when I had to explain why I'd not need to sit on a bed pan to pee.

"Oh," she cupped her hand over her mouth, "I'm so sorry... I thought the request slip said 'transgender' and that you were a woman... err... going the *other* way! I didn't think for a moment that you were... already..." I cut her short to save a further mess and made a joke of being already 'there' where she thought I was going but didn't really want to be here, then bustled down the corridor for the brain scan. That went well too and they assured me that I did have a normal, healthy functioning brain after sticking all these K-Y jellied patches all over my head with wires attached to them. The technician in his white coat saw my concern, telling me that I should not worry-

"It's OK... you're not strapped in the electric chair. All we're going to do is shrink your brain and send you down to surgery to make your mouth bigger. I've heard that's the worst thing about the sex-change." Coming from an Australian bloke I found that funny enough, though I guess now anything so sexist would land him with a lawsuit!

As he filled in some information on my notes I asked him why it said 'transgender' on the slips, having not heard that term before. Thankfully, he gave me a sensible, matter of fact explanation which I am always happy to remind people of. Up until then I'd always just taken on board that term we mostly hear, 'transsexual'. As the technician explained anything termed 'sexual' has to do with who we have sex with or our sexuality. Clearly I was a little confused, so he went on-

"You know... A hetero*sexual* is sexually interested in the opposite sex. A homo*sexual* is interested in the same sex and a bi*sexual* ...well... has more chance of getting a date on a Saturday night! Nah... what I mean is... that's who they have sex with... So a TRANS*sexual*? Doesn't make sense, does it? Unless you're someone who has sex with 'trans'... like transport... a nice sexy bus or a hot train?"

"So why call us 'transsexuals' then?" I wondered.

BODYCAGE

"Because that's a term that just got commonly coined from about the 1950s and went into the vernacular. Trans means 'crossing', so you're really only crossing your gender from male to female and though some may change their sexuality, usually you are just changing your gender to be in line with your real sexuality. All clear?"

Actually it was, making lots of sense and I would only use 'transgender' from then on for that very reason. I wasn't 'transing' my sexuality, I was 'transing' my gender and much later realised why it was better to be rid of that term as the media always used it in negative connotations like some sort of sexual criminality. Any word with 'sexual' in it would always have the association of 'sex' and why would I want to be thought of that way in my personal identification? 'Transgender'... that's what I'd stick with and encourage anyone else to also.

Full enough with bizarre musings, the next appointment was to see a psychologist called Doctor Bowman and the psychiatric clinic. The doctor introduced himself, rather stoically I'd thought. Looking like a vicar, he did all he could to avoid eye contact and seemed himself uncomfortable with my being there. Seating me in a small room like a little cell, furnished only with a small, student style desk and a pen, he handed me a pile of papers which looked like a questionnaire. Still avoiding much conversation, he just bluntly asked me to start filling in the answers to the questions, then took me quite aback-

"Look my dear, I may as well save you the trouble and tell you right here to forget this whole business." My heart just jumped almost from my mouth then sank to the floor as everything seemed to go in slow, cold and distorted slow motion as he incredulously continued-

"Take a good look at yourself, woman! You have a completely feminine countenance and demeanour, your hands are way too feminine to pass as male and with that voice I really don't think a thousand operations can ever make you look like a man."

Not being sure if I'd sighed a gasp of relief or sheer disbelief, it was the greatest of pleasures to tell the Nutty Professor assigned to my case that I already was technically a man and that he too had been mistaken.

"But Doctor, I have no intentions of becoming a man at all. I'm already supposedly *being* one and not particularly happy this way."

"Oh God," he humbly replied, completely flustered and turning bright red. "I'm so sorry...I thought you were going...."

"The other way?! Yeah...right...ok, I've heard that once already today." Feeling I was getting an upper hand I just asked if we could get on with it as this was seeming like some sort of hideous farce as I wondered just what type of hands I had put my life into here. Leaving the room with his face still crimson, Doctor Bowman asked me to complete the two hundred or so questions, being a 100% honest with my responses.

The questions ranged from "Are you happy most of the time?" to "Do you ever think about having sex with your mother?" Speeding through and ticking madly away I needed little time to ponder a response and was quite sure that I'd never taken a second to consider a sexual encounter with my mother! With completed questionnaire in hand, I trotted across the hall to Doctor's office. Tapping on the door, he bruskly asked me in, looking up with a smirk.

"Ha...having difficulties already then?"

"Well, no... I've actually finished." I'd just about had enough of his attitude, so snapped back-

BODYCAGE

"Is there anything else you require of me today or can I leave you to *score* my test?"
"Actually, there's quite a lot more. You might as well sit down now and make yourself comfortable as you'll be here for quite a while." Reaching into his desk drawer, he pulled out a bulky folder. Opening it before me were those dreaded ink blots I'd heard of so many times. Loren had told me we needed to describe things we saw in them from a "girlie" perspective so my impressions could be analysed to show if my mind sees things in a male or female light.
 "Try and see something girly in them all, no matter what they look like. You'll be just fine....." Advice from Loren I thought I'd heed and hoped not to betray my dishonesty if anything did not look as girly as I could make out. Painfully aware of how my thoughts and impressions were now going to be judged, assessed, interpreted, the first ink blot was placed in front of me. And, there it was, in all its glory- a complete splattered renditions of female genitalia! There was no way he'd take into consideration that such a site was not uncommon to me as I'd been a nurse for years, so I was sure if I said it looked like a set of female reproductive equipment, he'd think I liked that type of thing and was inclined towards sexual interest in women. Knowing too that this Gender Program makes it very clear they are "not in the business of creating surgically constructed lesbians", I'd need to come up with something else quick. Feeling quite doomed I wondered what else to approximate to this ghastly image as I spewed out,
"It's an orchid... in a vase." No response from the good Doctor. Just earnestly scratching of notes in his book then flinging another before me. Beginning to wish I'd never discussed this with Loren and had the fear put in my head, I did remember she'd said to try to think

positive things about the ink blot images lest they think I am morbidly depressed. So, with a mind hardly thinking clearly at all, I gazed down to see a horridly demonic face staring out at me in "Hammer Horror" black and white on the desk.

"Oh, that's a cute little bunny. Yes, that's what that is. The Easter Bunny, think I can see his little eggs. Or a cartoon bunny. Might be Roger Rabbit." The doctor looked at me questioningly as my imagination scrambled trying to point out a cute little nose and floppy ears 'til he snatched it from me. The next one was flung under my own cute little nose and I was sure by now it would have to have been better than the last two. "Third time lucky. What could be worse than the demon bunny?" I'd thought. After a deep breath I was ready to gush about what I could see. Well, human entrails of course! It looked like Jack the Ripper's homicide photos from the 1880s had somehow landed in this doctor's office in Melbourne. There they were, spread all over the card- little kidney shapes, a convoluted colon, lungs and a heart with the major veins hanging out of it. Am sure it looked like an autopsy gone very badly wrong.

"It's the fish monger's shop window! Yes, I can see all the fresh seafood laid out, nicely decorated with bits of seaweed." Although I could barely see straight now with nervousness, I continued to blurt out almost anything whilst just wanting to die. Managing to explain that a detached floating ovary made a spectacular little soft-shelled crab, the psychiatrist looked up at me as if I was truly now quite insane. He showed me the last one...it clearly looked like a rabid bat and we both knew it. I said it was a butterfly. Game, set, match. Was I ruined?

"Okaaaay, all done there Riannon. Now I am going to show you a series of pictures and I am going to ask

you to make up a little short story about each of them, in your own words to explain to me what you feel might be going on." Holding the first picture before me I felt at first relieved not to have to make something up about the ink blots as this would be more obvious. I needed only think of girly stories with a positive theme. Almost excitedly expecting no problem at all the picture presented itself- a dying man lying in obvious agony on his deathbed with a priest standing over him, crucifix in hand, giving the last rites. The first thing I thought was that may as well be me now on the deathbed as I was truly finished, wanting only to escape this torment. Somehow though, I gathered some strength and told my fabulous tale-
"Well...this is quite a funny one, Doctor."
"Really?" His look told me he knew I'd lost it!
"Yes, this is my old neighbour, Mr Franklin who's just jumped into his new waterbed to find it had burst and began to leak all over.
"Well," ('gotcha now look on his face) the doctor asked, "what's the priest doing standing over him with a crucifix?"
"That's his flatmate, Daniel. He heard Mr Franklin shouting when he realised the water was leaking and rushed into the room. Daniel immediately found that very crucifix had punctured the waterbed earlier when Mr Franklin, a devout Catholic, lay upon it earlier to say his prayers in comfort ... So....."
"Alright, Riannon, that's enough. Really... Phew." Feeling sure this assessment was now well and truly finished, he still went on with one silly picture after the other as I garbled more and more ridiculous, incredulously inane stories before an exasperated Professor set me free on the world yet again.
 Being a tried and true glutton for punishment... Well with not really much else to do... I called Loren for a

chat about it all. Perhaps to find something to swap notes about or even glean some insight as to what to expect with the psychiatrist appointment soon to follow. So I asked if it was ok to come over.

"Sure, Girl. Get ya arse over. I've got a few girly things to do around the house today, but then we can lie out by the pool and talk."

Hanging up to let her get on with the 'girly things', I trail blazed in the heat to Loren's in my little denim shorts, huge sunglasses to hide behind, a big straw sun hat and a pair of plastic flip flop sandals. Looking like Jodie Foster in "Taxi Driver", I'd walked barely a couple of minutes up the St Kilda streets towards Loren's, than a stream of cars had shadowed me, circling like beasts stalking some prey... often passing several times to see if I'd notice them. Sometimes they'd flash their lights or give a little toot of the horn to see if I wanted to scurry over and do some 'business'. I knew enough about where I was walking to know they were curb crawlers looking for working girls and didn't want to catch their eye at all.

On such a beautiful, warm day, I wondered what they could be thinking to find themselves driving around inviting strangers into their cars for sex for a few dollars. Wondering too how their wives or girlfriends would feel if they knew their men were doing this behind their backs, a car pulled up way too close to me, almost blocking my path. Although really annoyed at this hindrance to my direct little march, I did look over to him as he leaned across to catch my attention from the passenger window and saw how unbelievably handsome he was. Walking briskly on, I just politely told him "No thank you... am just off to visit a friend down the road."

As he shrugged and shook his head to drive off, I looked back to see the baby seat strapped in the back of his car. Feeling a lump in my throat and a wrenching of my heart, I truly pitied his wife. Surely she must have been a pretty thing... and here he was, her adorable husband in his family car, about to risk catching a disease for quick, empty encounter with a total stranger. I felt truly sick with rage that men could behave like such a bunch of dogs or pigs, knowing fully that half the girls on these streets were not even 'girls' and so many already had AIDS which was why they could not work in the legal brothels (apart from the heavy drug habits of course). Pondering whether to take his registration number and somehow tell his wife, I realised the stream of crawlers was constant and where would I stop? Those men were fools and slaves to the sex drive, I knew that for sure and could hardly have cared what ghastly infections they picked up, but how I hurt for their women who'd have had no idea their men could have been bringing them home a death sentence. My concerns were wasted as I noticed him signal a skeleton in a bikini top and torn denim shorts standing in high heels in the driveway of an empty garage. "If only they knew... if only," I muttered to myself continuing on the way.

Trotting down the pathway at the side of Loren's house, I smelt the familiar odour of burning depilatory wax. "She must be doing her legs," I thought passing the bathroom window and a loud man's voice bellowed- *"Graaahhhh.. Hey YOU!! GRAAaaahhh."* Leaping back in horror against the garden wall, I looked up to see the sight which had terrorised me. A blackened-faced creature with thick-set hunched forward shoulders roared at me with menacing wild eyes. With hair slicked back and all greasy, I wondered if it was the Man in the Iron Mask until I recognised those devilish eyes as Loren's.

Rehana Incognito

Realising she'd achieved her goal of frightening me half to death, she continued to roar laughing. Through the fly-screen door on the back porch, she let me in as pall of acrid smoke belched into the pretty little garden, wafting over the swimming pool.
"What on earth are you doing Loren... with all that over your face? You look like the Tar Baby!" Heaving open the kitchen window gasping breath some air, I could hardly wait for her explanation.
"Well, I guess a *real woman* like you doesn't have the same problem as me do you? You know...my eyebrows.. I mean look at them... I have this little problem... They grow all the way down to my neck!" Throwing back her head with wild tosses of the hair, she roared that terrifying bellow of a laugh again.
"I can see you don't wax your face though do you, Girl... I bet you still have to *shave*."
"Actually Loren. I do neither. What little hair might appear on my top lip, I just go *pfffttt* and it blows away! So that takes up all of thirty seconds of my beauty routine. Sorry about yours!" Feeling like a good bitching gloat at my blessing in the facial hair stakes I figured to be in for a penny....
"And being a natural blonde I kind of like the soft, downy *peach fuzz on my cheeks* anyway."
"You're the most unnatural blonde I've ever met." Loren now seethed back, hacking away with her tweezers at those stray 'eyebrows' which had migrated somehow to her chin and under her neck.
"You look like a big bloke to me anyway and I bet you got gigged all the way here, didn't ya?" she venomously frothed.
It was hardly worth the mention that I could have earned a small fortune looking like a 'big bloke' on the way to hers, so I decided to let it rest. Such an argument seemed a pretty bizarre, undignified thing to

BODYCAGE

be discussing, having no idea why Loren wanted to communicate this way. A lot of it had to do with her seeming much wiser and further along in the program than I was...and to some extent she had reduced me to being that little kid, forever awestruck at the mighty knowledge and experience of my big sister, Karen, as I stalked around in her shadows. So, for the most part, Loren had now become a big sister to me with so much more to learn about the Board and the Program, and in all honesty there were a lot of good points about Loren to admire, so I let the conversation lead to the Gender Board.

"Ri, if you think you had trouble with that psychologist, you're in for a shock when you meet the Board's consultant psychiatrist, Dr Conolly. She is a HARD bitch and it's her decision in the end which gives the final approval whether you'll get surgery or not." Loren went on, plucking away. "Believe me, I know of girls who've been so broken by her, they've gone off and topped themselves. You better do *all* your homework, Girl, before you see her, that's for sure."

I thought so too, realising that homework would need to be done and I'd better find plenty study material. Loren went off to shower as her hairdresser was due to come by for a house call. I headed out to breathe more fresh air by the pool, picking up her parrot in its cage by the back door, to get some more air too and keep me company.

"What's your parrot's name, by the way Loren," I asked placing him under the big umbrella to shade him next to my lounge bed.

"It's Pincer... see that asbestos glove by the cage? Put that on and put your hand in the cage and you'll find out why." Noticing his wicked menacing look as my hand got near the cage to pick it up in the first place, I decided not to. Loren would often pack a big ceramic

Rehana Incognito

"bong" witch with heaps of dope and blow it into Pincer's face and get him to go a bit crazy, shrieking and calling out the unspeakable filth she'd taught him. Sadly, she 'fired up' Witchy-Poo one day as she sat watching TV, slowly blowing the smoke towards the helpless Sulphur-Crested White cockatoo's beak. Whilst glued to the news, she heard a thud as Pincer had fallen backwards from his perch, legs in the air... to shriek and curse no more. However...for the afternoon, he was happy to keep me company on the back lawn...making a few of Loren's strange, scary growling noises and coughs at me, or silently observing from his alien ornithological world. As I wondered what he made of us from this ancient mind, his pupils dilated and shrank, watching my every move.

Feeling way too cosy on the fabulous banana lounge, I closed my eyes to start a time travel journey...back and back as far as I could go to try and make sense of what I was embarking on. By Loren's lovely poolside, I tried to recall all I'd learnt in nursing school of early sexual development and the differences even between a male and female foetus. Thank God I listened and kept the information somewhere there, as it was all going to come in handy. I wondered about all those chemical signals- hormones, chromosomes and DNA involved in turning a tiny peanut of a foetus, which begins as a female prototype, into turning itself, if the signal is right, to become a little baby boy- completely. Dreamily, hazily, as I absorbed all the smells of heady Australian garden, I thought about the tiny little peanut, some weeks into pregnancy getting that signal to send out all the chemicals for the tiny little embryonic 'ovaries' to start their downward slide to evolve into testes. Then that tiny little set of neutral sex organs, with the miniscule clitoris and more female appearance, would get its little shot of chemicals to say "go male, go male" and hey presto, a willy! More importantly, I did also recall that a very big shot of male hormone was needed to change a whole brain to work as female, no matter how small the baby is really. The brain is folds and folds of matter and, in fact, quite large in comparison to the little sex organs which don't need a huge dose of chemical signal to change. Apart from that, those of us blessed with soft, feminine skin, and little or no facial hair development, can also be grateful for the fact that the skin is the biggest organ of all and may well have got even less of a male hormone hit!

A lot of that information, it horrified me to know, was determined from the study of brains of the gay and transgender people either murdered or worked to death in the Nazi concentration camps. A sobering thought for those of us who have it pretty easy now really, to remember all those who came before us, yet suffered horrifically through no fault other than some unfortunate situation well beyond the control of the average embryo! Although there are many reasons a woman or a man can be homosexual or bisexual, these same studies over-generally concluded that men were gay because they were the type who'd been born with female brains. Yes, for sure, I feel that is the truth in a lot of cases, but can only be proven after an autopsy. So most of us will have to wait for that to really know for certain!

All said and done, that explained a lot, including the fact that this mess up on a baby's chemical super highway, was often caused by trauma and stress of the mother early in the pregnancy. To think back to my parent's early stages of marriage with all the fighting I could recall, it wasn't 'til years later that I learnt my mother had indeed spent most of her pregnancy with me stressed out with my toddling big sister and chasing a husband who was forever vanishing off with other women! So, no matter the sociological reasons a boy might tend to feel he is better suited to living his life as a girl, the chemical ones are definitely often there too. In my case, I doubly didn't stand a chance in the masculinity stakes.

Of course there is a whole lot more and detailed information available about psychological and sociological reasons for gender and sexuality development and I'd recommend anyone to look into them deeply and understand it all more. The information about chemical, hormone and chromosomal reasons is there too and I am no expert on it, despite taking note of the basics, but at least now I knew why men have nipples- we are all the same at the beginning!

Squinting against the sunshine with a glance along from my chest to feet, I could see this body must hardly have received its blast of foetal testosterone at all. So, I knew the physical reasons possible for being a transgender person and took a lot of time to ponder the sociological ones, like absence of a male role model or over identification with the mother. Sometimes, it even pains me to know that many boys have just been made to feel terribly hurt in many ways about their physical self. To learn to hate themselves for being in whatever unfortunate condition, to be treated so cruelly, leaving them desperate to eradicate any memory at all of the person he was.

Truly, it was often more clear than not, that many people I'd known were victims of such tragic upbringings and backgrounds, seeking a salvation for who they were as a human being by inventing a new person to attract the 'love' of the sex who had hurt them the most. The damaged boy would obliterate even his own maleness, becoming the feminine 'lure' to attract the temporary comfort from the pain of his past.

BODYCAGE

The ones they would lure were those boys who'd *succeeded* in all their maleness with power, strength, control and admiration of those around them would be *made* to "love" them in a shallow veneer of an act of love, interpreted through sex . Over and over, they'd need to go out to seduce their victim, capturing him to make him pay the retribution for all those years of bullying and taunts by filling them up with those acts, as a blind substitute for standing in the pains of their past and learning to love and rediscover who they really are as men themselves. As somewhere I'd read, there is a hole in their souls... and it is penis-shaped, forever needing filling as the transient fix for a woe they can't yet look at!
 Of course those circumstances do indeed lead to some of the causes of homosexuality and a need to receive love from another male... and I could see how in extreme cases of this that homosexuality would suffice. In so much repressed rage at those who hurt them and a resentful hatred for women, easily getting the love and acceptance they'd missed out on, flying into gender reassignment is the ultimate hiding place from all the issues. Yet still, like a ball, pushed deep into a barrel of water, the harder you push it down the harder it will bounce back to the surface to whack you right in the face! It'll bloody well hurt too!! So, again- "Know thyself, *really* know thyself".
 So there I was, drifting off and going over and over all I knew of such things in my head, I felt sure that I'd armed myself with enough ammunition to take on anything Dr Conolly might shoot me down with. I'd also planned to get hold of as much library material and books in shops about the subject as possible when a sudden shock of icy water seared across my bare torso. Wrenching off my sunglasses and the big wide Jodie Foster straw hat, I squinted into the glare of the

sun before me, ready to take a piece out of Loren. However, peering back at me through the blinding glare was the form of a guy, smiling down, towering above with wavy blond hair and a laugh like liquid crystal he introduced himself.

"Oops, sorry about that...couldn't resist it. I knew you'd have to be Loren's friend anyway... she said she'd have company. Anyway... I'm Greg... come to do her hair... Is she around?"

"To be honest, I think she went for a shower to get ready for you... I think I might have been asleep for a while there. I'm Riannon by the way." I wondered if I was still asleep as my eyes adjusted that little bit more to see how gorgeous this Adonis apparition was hovering above me. Then just as quickly got to wondering why I bothered to think like that, as he was a hairdresser... so bound to be gay!

Loren had heard us chatting and swung open the screen door, bounding over in a tight little white tube dress, boobs spilling forth and hair wrapped in a big multicoloured beach towel. Wasting no time, she launched into her flirtatious repertoire, leaving both Greg and myself flushed with embarrassment. Yanking him from the garden seat he'd plonked on to chat, Loren hauled her prey back inside the house as Greg turned to mouth the word "help" as he was led away.

After about some forty five minutes, a dishevelled and agitated Greg almost tumbled from the back porch door as Loren had given him a break from her onslaught. He came over to sit by me again whilst Loren had taken to the hair dryer by herself, sitting in the kitchen with her head stuck between her legs waving her newly cut hair about like a giant ruddy mop doing the floor.

BODYCAGE

"She's quite a handful, isn't she Greg? Do you do get over here often for her house call?" I felt glad the hairdryer would drown this conversation.

"Yeah, I dread it though. She always tries to get a handful of me! But I play in a band and always need the extra cash for equipment and stuff...but am beginning to wonder if this visit's worth it. Anyway, it's either getting groped by her here or getting groped by gay guys at the salon down town. Hopefully I'll get out of the whole business soon... am sick of it."

Well, it seemed I was wrong about him being gay then. Although I'd heard there were straight hairdressers, I'd never actually met one and felt the chances would be quite remote! However, Greg clearly had no interest in Loren, so I felt no harm in trying to get to know him as he'd already made the moves with me. Still struggling for what to say to him, I eventually found some words.

"Do you play in your band or sing?"

"I play keyboards and write a lot of the music too. Would you like to come and see us play some time? We play most weekends."

I told him I'd love to and wished at that time I'd just given him my phone number but didn't want to seem too available and was concerned Loren would think it inappropriate for me to be seen as chatting up her hairdresser squeeze. Foolishly, I asked Greg to just get my number from Loren and let me know the next performance date and I'd be there. Appearing genuinely pleased that I'd come and see his band, I watched him bound off through the side gate of the house as I smiled to myself knowing for sure he was someone I'd enjoy seeing again.

The next couple of weeks I'd hung around the house more often than usual, looking at a phone which rarely rang, just hoping he'd call. Eventually, curiosity got the better of me as I called Loren to see if he'd asked for my number. She said he had not and I just thought "what a prick".

Feeling so disappointed as another weekend approached, I realised I should not have let my mind run so wild over Greg. At least I hadn't quite done my usual thing of naming the children and planning the theme for a spring wedding, invitations 'n all. With one final bash over my head with the stick of low self esteem, I wondered what possessed me anyway to think a gorgeous guy like Greg would want someone 'like me'. I was sure that Loren would have filled him in on the details that I was someone 'like that' too already in any case.

Lexi was at least sympathetic, suggesting that we go out and forget all about it... at dirty old Tangles.

"My old boyfriend, Russ, gets out today," yes... out of prison! "He's taking us out tonight with a couple of his mates, so throw ya glad rags on, Girl! They'll show ya a good time." The chance of a night out with Lexi and a bunch of criminals sounded more alluring than sitting home looking at a phone and a fun distraction. It would take my mind off fantasies and delusions about Greg for a while, so with bag of clothes and a little travel sack of makeup, I headed for Lexi's.

Russ was already there, answering the door with an enormous scotch in one hand... the bottle in the other. Clearly he was making up for lost drinking time, I'd thought. Lexi had just gone out to steal something new to wear for her special reunion with Russ so I was alone with someone leering and lurching at me with all the charm of Barry Humphries' slobbering 'Sir Les Patterson'. Mercifully, he suggested he take a shower and freshen up, as I headed to the "mug room" to look through the en suite for Lexi's 'Epilady' and give the little cactus hairs on my legs a quick whisk over. With

BODYCAGE

the whirring of the tiny little motor, propelling the spinning coil which ripped out the hairs with a wince now and then, I had not heard Russ walk into the room. Startled, I looked up to see him swaying in the doorway. With muscles rippling, after months inside, his body didn't look half bad. With only a towel tightly wound around his waist, he fixed his gaze on my now spotted legs with all the tiny bumps of the hair ripping session, tracing a line from toes to thigh.

 Flicking the switch of the Epilady off, I rolled my shorts back quickly down to cover my thigh. Having not given thought to the fact that I was alone in a house with a guy who had just been released from prison, it seemed he was giving it plenty of thought! His intentions were clear as he sat by the bed with me feeling just frozen, realising there was not much I could do if this got out of hand. Lexi would not have liked this at all, I'd thought and would probably have hurt me a lot more than he could, so I opted for my best shot, pleading-

"Look Russ. I think you're a great-looking guy, but this is going to put me in a bit of a spot with Lexi you know... So please don't put me in this position. She's a really good *mate*... you know?" 'Good mate'... they seemed to be the words which worked, remembering something about honour between crims and the bonds of friendship, I sighed a big 'phew' and was glad to have thought of it.

"Yer a good kid, Riannon. Any other bitch would have been down swingin' on a piece of this thing in a heartbeat." He pulled back the towel over that 'thing' as I took a quick glance and thought I probably would have too were it not for Lexi. Feeling glad that he'd left the room, the pain of the myriad bee stings on my legs was welcome in comparison to the thought of what Lexi would have made of me. So I stayed in the room, tampering with makeup 'til she returned.

Rehana Incognito

After dinner together at Pizza Bella Roma on Fitzroy St, St Kilda with the extra couple of thugs who'd joined us, we walked into Tangles at nearly midnight. The place was full with every drag queen making a beeline to descend upon the boys, which was a relief to me as I was glad to be rid of them! Not being noticed, slipping from their company, I glanced over from time to time to notice the bevy of beauties from the cabaret show had clustered around them like a pack of gangster's molls, which undoubtedly a few of them would become. Those guys had been in prison long enough not to even care about the biological condition of these 'girls' either, perhaps seeing them too as some kind of 'renegade' women or 'gender outlaws,' I'd once hear described, to make them bad enough or risqué partners for them to be with. To me I just figured they saw themselves all as 'bad boys'...being as naughty as they could together, whilst making the whole world pay! As far as I was concerned they deserved each other.

Jostling through a crowded sea of hungry eyes, I noticed someone barging his way through the crowd, waving madly towards me. It was Greg!

"Hey, Riannon! I hoped you'd be here." He reached out and placed his hand on my waist, pulling me towards him and away from the curious stares. "I asked Loren for your number last week but she said I'd have to go find you myself here...so here I am!"

"Well, I haven't really been here for weeks actually. I hate this place. To be honest I was feeling a bit let down when you never called... I'd hoped you would call...So my friends took me out for a laugh." I was still tongue tied, trying to talk coherently.

"I can see why you'd hate it...It's a freak show! Anyway, it's great to see you... Need a drink?"

I needed a cup of tea, a tranquiliser and a lie down, but his hug was just as good a tonic with its warmth

BODYCAGE

and sincerity and everything about him made me feel cared for and special. I could hardly believe that I had found him again (or he found me) or that Loren would be so selfish and mean. I vowed never to care less about how anyone like Loren felt from now on... that was just plain nasty. Greg and I both decided she was a bitch not to have given him my number and danced the night away, as the carnival flowed around us until it started to look decidedly *sick*.

Greg was pleased when I said I wanted to get out of there as he'd only come to look for me. Funnily enough, I'd only come to forget about him. I didn't spare a thought back then to realise that when you stop looking for something, searching and fretting over it, getting on with your life- it comes! There was no point in either of us staying, so I accepted his offer to drive me home where we sat on the couch watching MTV almost to dawn. Barely able to keep my eyes open, I felt bad asking him to go home.

"It's been a great night, Greg...thanks. I've really appreciated your company but I've got to get some sleep." I really didn't want him to go and asked if he'd like to tuck me into bed. He said nothing but stood up, reaching for my hand, drawing me to my feet. I don't think I could even feel those feet, kind of floating to my bedroom, slipping off my clothes as he looked away, down to that ever-embalming cover and support of the panty girdle! I dived in and snuggled under the sheets.

The long goodnight kiss seemed to go on forever as I wanted it to, although almost falling asleep. As I nearly drifted completely away, Greg slipped from the bed, promising to call in the 'morning' to see if I was up for going to the beach. As he started the car, I sat up and peeped out of the curtains to watch him disappear into the dawn. Nestling my head back into the pillow, I thanked God to have found him and enjoyed the warmth of his closeness.

With the phone ringing next to my head after the deepest sleep, I still thought it all a dream except to hear Greg's voice on the line.

"Hi there. it's me... are you up? It's a great day out there so I hope you're still up for the beach."

Groggily, I said that I was...kind of awake...and would *love* a day at the beach. Making my way to the bathroom, the thought of what I'd need to go through to appear in a swim suit soon cleared my head. A couple of tugs and delicate placing of surgical tape, hid all trace of the slight 'imperfection' to the full beach bunny look. Slipping into a very bright yellow one piece swimsuit, I turned to look in the full length mirror, tying a Balinese batik sarong in a huge knot on my hip and plenty of leg and thigh out the side. Although something I always hated, I gazed up to see how it looked, no longer ashamed or afraid of what I'd see, I swept a gaze from my feet to face. In the many weeks which had passed, I hardly knew the svelte, sexy blonde peering from the mirror was me. With curves accentuated in all the right places and an ever increasing cleavage, the sight was almost beyond belief.

Wanting to ask "who are you?", she looked out and shone her reply... "I am you! Don't you remember me? I've lived in your mind all your life." And it was me, I touched me... running and patting my hands all over and through my hair. I started to 'remember' for a while and was off to the beach *on a date* with this gorgeous guy.

Spending the whole day together at South Melbourne Beach, laughing and swimming, sailing across the bay on a windsurfer and painfully, slowly rubbing sunscreen into each other, the day flew by just way too quickly. Even though I was four years older than Greg, I still felt like a teenager and Greg seemed quite a man of the world to me. I felt like a silly teenage girl, with little experience out on her first date, which in view of the circumstances, I suppose I was. Arriving home at sunset we found a note from Tracey to say she'd gone for the weekend so I asked Greg if he'd like to stay over. Sunburnt and washed out, he joined me in bed with just one sheet over us in the heat. Kissing and cuddling through the night I felt both our frustrations that there was more we wanted to be doing but neither of us were sure what that could even be anyway. As fate would have it... we'd have the next four years together to find out.

Within a month of dating and meeting Greg's lovely family, we decided to take a little apartment together on Toorak Road, Toorak... about the classiest address in Melbourne. How I loved the little flat, not caring that it was so tiny. I just enjoyed being able to say that I lived in *Toorak* with my *boyfriend* ! Life for us there was usually bliss, as Greg went to work in the day, played and rehearsed for the band most nights and I studied my old catering books, planning endless menus for when I took my job when Felicity's restaurant opened. We made a cosy home and delighted in coming back to find each other late at night and disappear into a heavenly, dreamy sleep in eachother's arms.

Even forming a sex life, I could see that Greg quickly became frustrated that I was not yet fully female. I still slept in the security bond of the panty girdle or sometimes even my jeans. Even in the shower I'd wear that stupid tight girdle in case he walked in on me and I started to fear he might slip away from me. Eventually, I found the courage to try and talk to him about it as I lay in bed, only wearing the tight jeans as he sprawled naked with one leg over mine, I fumbled out the words.

Rehana Incognito

"Greg, I know all this must feel crazy to you too... and frustrating. And I know you have women approaching you all the time at work... or anywhere... I notice when they do... and I feel helpless cos I can't compete with that. I worry that you might feel you're missing too much by being with me and start to resent that I cant give you everything yet. Really...I think that if you need... that... well, I'll understand." I'd started to cry and choked out the rest.

"But...please don't leave me right away. Really, I need you in my life..." I waited for him then to agree as I hung my head down and tucked it into his chest.

"Woman, you must be outa ya mind." He pulled my head up to look at him, with tears too now rolling from the corners of his eyes. "I couldn't think of leaving you just because of that. Yes, sometimes it's frustrating but there's more to a relationship than that.

Pulling the quilt over my shoulders, Greg dabbed at my tears with a handful of sheet. "What we have right now is irreplaceable... don't forget that. But I'd be lying if said I don't hope you have your surgery really sooner than later and we can just get on with a normal life."

And there it was again- that *normal* life I was pining for and always trying to find or make. When would things ever be normal or at least what I thought normal might have been?! The question had certainly been posed, loudly and clearly, so I guess the scene was being set and the players lined up to show me the answer to what I'd asked. Our vision of a perceived life of normalcy was beginning to unfold. Up 'til then I'd only dreamed of a prince indeed, holding me safe and secure in his arms and his heart, feeling I could never have loved him more. He was perfection to me, in every way... I wanted to be the embodiment of perfection for him too- As soon as I could be. How could I begin to repay this true and guiltless heart in a guy so young for his strength, support and loyalty?

I had heard of surgeons in Sydney who would perform reassignment surgery, waiving the two year period necessary in Victoria if one could be psychologically assessed as being female in New South Wales. After making enquiries with other 'girls about town', I eventually had the number for a plastic surgeon in Sydney. Calling him immediately, an appointment was made to see him in days. Dr Howell had arranged my visit to him as soon as I had seen the affiliated psychiatrist to assess me for recommendation...or not. Flying to Sydney and making my way to the psychiatrist's office was a blur. This imposing, middle aged giant turned out to be as friendly as an overstuffed sofa and, after one and half hours of intense probing and discussion, the gentleman sat back with a beaming smile across his glasses to announce his verdict.

"Riannon, you have shown yourself to be a perfect candidate for this surgery. Actually, I don't know how you made it this far with so much resilience. I am sure you'll have the strength to make it through any harder times to come after your surgery and it's a pleasure to say I will recommend you."

I felt like I'd won the lottery as he went on...

"It won't all be easy going...am sure you know that... but you are one person I am sure could have managed to go through all this years ago. You're going to do just fine."

"Don't worry. I know... It's not like going to the dentist to have a tooth pulled!" I took another huge sigh of relief to have found someone else who knew who I really was in my heart and soul. I had actually enjoyed his assessment as the thoroughness of it all and knowing I was understood and supported in my honesty was a comfort. Now tears of relief tumbled over my cheeks. In such a short time this man had clearly seen me for who I was. Off he was about to launch me on the road to release from this cage of a body...just like that, so simple! No further need to tear my mind to shreds with the program in Melbourne. For God's sake, as he'd said... I was ready for this years ago so there was no need for me to prolong this torture any further.

Dazed, I descended into the station, disappearing into the bowels of Sydney to make my way to the offices of the good Dr Howell. Hurtling through the tunnels, station after station passed, as with the clickety clack of the train, I felt like I too was on the move to somewhere at a deeper level. I was going somewhere... somewhere I *needed* to be, far away from the trap of this body I lived in. Ominously, I noticed the same stations had passed certainly more than once as I came round with a start. I was on the wrong line...it was the City Circle line!

Alighting from one confusing roundabout to another, I made my way up to the surface, jostling through the crowds along Elizabeth St, to arrive at Dr Howell's building flustered and a little late. Dr Howell somehow reminded me of all those scary doctors in horror films... like Dr Jekyll who'd almost become Mr Hyde, complete with the uni-brow and hairy hands! Somewhat cold and distant, his raven-headed body appeared listless and pale. Speaking of his surgical procedure, now he knew I was ready for his slab, I felt reminded of the crazed Dr Frankenstein ranting about his beloved creation. He thoroughly chilled me, touching and prodding me with the now familiar examination and just as embarrassing. What could I do but lie there on his sticky vinyl examination table, escaping again into dreams, pretending the indignities were not happening to me.

BODYCAGE

Yes, I wondered all about it... with Frankenstein still on my mind, wondering who on earth had written it-
"Genteel women are, literally speaking, slaves to their bodies. They are taught from infancy that beauty is the woman's sceptre. The mind shapes itself to the body, and, roaming around in its cage, seeks only to adorn its prison." Wincing as the doctor's cold fingers prodded from side to side at the future excavation site of my designer vagina, he did remark that there was an interesting alignment of the muscles there and it would make things much easier for him to work on me. He promised to do his very best. It was then I remembered it was indeed Mary Wollstonecraft who'd written those words of the women in their prisons in 1772, in the novel "Frankenstein"!

Visions of strippers and go-go dancers of the sixties seen on TV shows and in movies, played out on a stage in my mind, performing in their cages for the pleasure of their 'captors'. Women dancing in cages... or just locked in them for whatever cruel purpose reminded me of the unpleasant history of the word 'pornography'. 'Porneia' were captives of Ancient Greek armies, kept bound, caged and accessible for all manner of sexual degradation to satisfy the troops far from their own lovers, or merely to degrade and humiliate the vanquished. This ugly, brutal and unjust agony of women, and undoubtedly children, wove a thread through me with many others. It formed a vile, choking dirty shroud I would wrap tightly around myself, hanging it for all to see on the walls of my life.

"Everything should go just right, my dear. Go back to Melbourne and let us know when a time is suitable for you to take a week or so in hospital for your surgery and remember to take three weeks off your hormones to reduce the risk of any blood clots. We'll make all the arrangements for your hospital stay." After another soulless, cold handshake and a brochure with all the costs for the surgery, anaesthetist and hospital stay, I scurried from his office. In my rush I took a glance across the colourless silent waiting room. One by one I clocked them sitting along the wall like a line up of the Easter Island Statues only not as soft, I'd thought- Hard, glowering faces of a bizarre assortment of feminine-clad parodies of women glowered back at me. Feeling truly that they despised the sight of me, I was grateful to pull the door tightly closed behind the waiting zombie-like Frankenstein's Brides!

After sleeping solidly for one hour on the brief flight back to Melbourne, Greg seemed like a vision from Heaven waiting for me at the arrivals gate at Tullamarine.

"Well," he asked "what's it to be then?" He held out is arms to catch me and whirl me around. Glowing with happiness that the end was in sight I let him stew...

Passers-by were starting to stare, as Greg pleaded that I tell him and I whispered up into his ear,

"Well, everything's going to be just fine, Greg....it's nearly all over. We'll soon have a nice new vagina of our very own!" We squeezed together in further delight as I told Greg the passers-by must have thought we'd just become engaged or announced we were having a nice new baby of our very own.

Greg saw the hilarity in that too,

"If that were the case it wouldn't have just been me here waiting for you... it'd have been the Guinness Book of Records ready for the next miracle birth." I didn't think the world was quite ready for that one yet!

A few months more of hard work from both of us would be needed to come up with the money for the surgery and Greg was indeed willing to contribute all he could. At first I felt a little uncomfortable about his offering to contribute towards the surgery, until he cleared up his motive in his inimitably Aussie guy way, "Hell, Love...I don't mind helping you out at all. Why should you have to pay for it? It's not your fault. Besides, I'm the one who's going to be using the bloody thing, right?!" He was really someone to be so proud of- innocent in his desire to express, in the best way he knew, his true masculine strengths and spirit. I owed him the world.

Although we both resumed our routine lives, I still decided to keep attending the remaining appointments with the Victorian Gender Program. Guidance and certainty were still needed, to be sure that matters were running in some sort of order throughout the transition. Assurance that I was doing the right thing was also needed. Besides, if anything were to go seriously wrong after the surgery, I wanted to be sure that my case was familiar to all the right people and help might be available should I need it. Feeling now so confident that Dr Conolly would not be an intimidation with my alternative plan, I kept my appointment with her.

Pressing the doorbell of her elegant South Melbourne Mock Tudor villa, a dreamy chime echoed through the lovely front garden and along the hallway from behind the big black castle-style door. How comforting it sounded I'd thought, now almost relishing the opportunity and challenge of having this lady pick my mind apart. Almost reeling back in astonishment as the door heaved open, my gaze swept up...and UP.... to meet the smirk of the tallest woman I'd seen on earth. A huge ungainly hand reached out to clasp mine as I turned scarlet wondering if Herman Munster had escaped from Hollywood and was moonlighting in drag as a Melbourne psychiatrist.

Rehana Incognito

Could this possibly be a real woman? Had the Board actually appointed a transgender psychiatrist to assess us? Speechlessly, I tagged along behind her, scrutinizing her every move and gesture. Who was assessing whom here? Searching for signs to justify my suspicions, I noticed that her voice was surely quite deep, but then again, she was a *big* woman so would hardly have expected her to sound like Minnie Mouse. Her skin was soft enough. No trace of that subtle beard line waiting to sprout from just below the epidermis, or the telltale scars of electrolysis along the same line. Pictures of sweet children adorned the walls so I enquired if they might be hers.

"No, there not," she sharply snapped back, "they're my nieces and nephews."

Realising she had probably guessed the nature of my enquiry, I felt confident now that I'd gained some superior ground during this little encounter. She continued,

"So, my Dear, tell me exactly why it is you want to be a woman." She was clearly wasting no time in getting to the point and to me. Starting to think that she actually looked more like Dustin Hoffman's 'Tootsie' by now, it was hard to keep focused on her question. Peeping over her little half moon specs, tapping her huge fingers against the desk, she condescendingly leaned back for my reply.

"Well Doctor, at the risk of sounding clichéd... and very by-the-book, I can only explain that I feel like I already *am* a woman... now. All I want to do is get what I consider to be unfortunate obstacles out of the way... so to speak... then get on with my life, legally female of course!" Leaning back now myself, I awaited her retort.

"Oh...but Dear...that does sound very by-the-book. You may well have done what the others who sit there way too often do- Just read a whole lot of literature on the

BODYCAGE

subject of gender Dysphoria and rattle off exactly what you think I want to hear. We have to be so very careful with that type of thing with our patients as we're often deceived by some marvellous Academy Award performances from you girls. Then they get their approval for surgery and become mentally unstable, trying their best to blame us for their own poor self-awareness. Besides, what on earth makes you think that, despite your *unfortunate obstacles*, you are really a woman at all?"

"I can only say, Dr Conolly, what I've said before. I just *know* that I do not look like or think like any *man* I've ever seen or known and haven't the slightest desire to." By now I was feeling that I was being assaulted as well as insulted. I felt like a mouse, cornered and tormented by this twisted Alice in Wonderland's 'Cheshire Cat' as her smirk again slapped at my bewildered gaze.

"Riannon, I've actually reviewed your assessments in detail. Professor Williams and Doctor Bowman are very pleased with their evaluations of you. They have both noted that your physical attributes are definitely more feminine than masculine... and those I can certainly see." She peered over her glasses again like I was naked.

"Yes," I replied, quoting Professor Williams' remark that we're not all T-Model Fords. "They both told me that too." Dr Conolly had indeed been toying with me like a cat and her mouse. Trying my patience, she gauged every flicker of my eyes and uneasy squirm in the comfortably padded Chippendale chair. Pushing sensitive buttons she tried to illicit the appropriate masculine or feminine reactions. Thankfully, I'd remained calm and just bitchy enough for it to be seen as that, remaining in the boundaries of the feminine. I recalled all along the story of a transgirl called Marilyn, who, when also backed into such corners right there, decided to put her fist through the sturdy wall panelling of the consultation room. Quite a feminine touch that was...and the only thing she got through was the wall itself.

Doctor went on,

"He has noted that, in view of your physical characteristics, your transition and post-operative life changes should be relatively easy. That certainly is a blessing." Never up 'til then had I considered this body to have been a blessing, having really only ever seen it as leading to humiliation and unfulfilled desires. All those years of hating and shame of it... when really it was waiting, all along, like on the sidelines, to become the gift it should be. I'd made a note right there in that room to try and remember all the times that many things could seem like tortuous tests or burdens but really be blessings in disguise. I'd *try* to remember to find them, watch for them, but things were soon to take way too many twists and turns and way too fast for me to notice much of anything. However, I still took the time to feel sorry for all those people who may well have been like myself, or felt that they might have been, yet let down by bodies which were more masculine ever to pass as female in any circumstances other than a blackout.

The upheaval this change would bring in life is an ordeal from every point of view and I could hardly imagine how arduous and disappointing a path it was for those whose bodies had masculinised far more than mine ever did. Dr Conolly wasted no further time letting me know just how bad it was for them.

"It has helped a lot to see how you look and are comfortable in your skin, Riannon. So many transgender girls have convinced us in the past of their desire for sex-change surgery and that they would

BODYCAGE

cope. Even with their totally male voices, excessively hairy faces and masculine bodies, they'd try to convince us. However, their lives are most of the time just tragic failures...with no-one accepting them for who they believe they are at all... and making nothing but tragic failures of their lives."

I nodded in agreement, having seen and met so many of them already, wondering which ones were coming along the assembly line next to run away from their problems in a mask of makeup and a hiding place behind a pile of skirts. Dr Conolly was clearly expressing her compassion and concern, so perhaps I'd judged her wrong.

"After convincing themselves that surgery was the final stage in their *cure*, it is then a constant torment to be reminded by their appearance of features of themselves they just cannot really change. Society can be cruel, Riannon. Children are merciless when they notice... You'd know the statistics of how many of these girls commit suicide and am sure you now know why. It's my dearest wish that all these people would look deeper into themselves and determine who and what they really are before making irreversible decisions." I could only nod quietly in agreement... thanking God all the while that I wasn't so cursed to be one of them.

In passing years, ample opportunity was certainly afforded to observe the tragic messes made in the lives of people who believed their whole world would change like a magic wand by mutilating their bodies to become something deep down they knew they truly never were nor could be. Then the doctor floored me again.

"As for the psychologist, though, there is some trepidation in his report. There are aspects to your personality he had described in terms of leaning towards the masculine side." Giving my head a shuddering shake of incomprehension, I covered my mouth to hold back a gasp. "How do you feel about that?"

Not knowing what to *feel* exactly, I had no idea what aspects of my personality she meant. My over-romanticising mind could only get to thinking about my love for reading all the Linda Goodman astrology books, trawling for answers and clues in everything and wished I could have just told her, "Hey, I am an Aries woman, by-the-book. We're supposed to be strong, decisive and arrogant bitches, we're ruled by Mars...the God of War. Does that make me a *man*?" Though I knew for sure I'd be struck off and put to the bottom of the heap. So I simply sat for a moment feeling like I'd been whacked in the face with a wet sand-shoe.

"All I can say is, I think I've developed a lot of strong... survival.... qualities in my life... having made a lot of hard decisions and a way for myself somehow. Each time I got through something, I felt a little stronger. Perhaps those strengths, and a good sense of humour, did give me an air of armour that most biological women probably don't have. And after all... I am *not* a biological woman...I have a bit of history and experiences of life biological women don't get to experience! Of course they are going to make me think a little differently... Aren't they?" Dr Conolly gave a barely discernable nod of agreement, confirming she'd further noted something she *needed* to hear from me.

Getting back to my astrological musings, I remembered my Aries mother and all that fire and strength I found at times in her when she was fully aflame.

"And coming to think of it, having learned most of my character and personality from my mother, no-one could say *she* wasn't a woman deserving to be so!"

BODYCAGE

Perhaps, I'd defended my mother and my past enough for now as I wondered whether to announce that their program would not be necessary for me anyway. I could have gone soon enough to Sydney and have the surgery without their approval, yet at my own financial cost. However, Dr Conolly continued,
"I feel you're certainly going to need those strengths, Riannon. If you wish to proceed, these assessments clearly define your identity as more feminine and your psychology too." The interview then merged into a blur of matter of fact, familiar questions which I could hardly now recall... possibly as I'd *like* to forget and obliterate forever. Dr Conolly finally waved me off down her cobbled garden path, after what seemed like a whole day had passed in there. With a promise to speak favourably to the Board on my behalf at its next meeting, she hauled the big door shut as this little Dorothy skipped down her Yellow Brick Road, thinking all the flowers in the garden had taken on somewhat brighter, glowingly iridescent hues. I made my way straight to Loren's to tell her all about it, even though she hadn't yet forgiven me for stealing her hairdresser!

Loud music shuddered with thuds against the front door as I pressed my face against the glass to try and make out through the opaqueness if she was coming to answer the doorbell. Suddenly an ungainly form took shape in the hallway thundering towards me, stomping along with thumps to the music. A gravelly voice boomed out once again the words to the song along the way...

"I was born to be laughed at,
stepped on
and treated like dirt.
Cos I was born a womaaaaaaan,
I'm glad it happened that way."

The door flew open and it was no surprise to see that it was *not* Tammy Wynette... but Loren.
"Oh hi Girrrrrl, Come on in. How'd your appointment with Dr Cunnilingus go?" Leaping through the door before the neighbours in the adjoining duplex might hear any more, I followed her stocky frame in the hot pink body tube with bubble-gum matching strappy high heels.
"Loren, do you think Dr Conolly is... you know... one of us?" I ventured to ask, feeling sure she of all people would know.
"Ri, do you realise you got to be the stupidest queen I ever met? She's a bloody big *DYKE*, Love. Like you... Here, lick this!" Hoisting up the tiny bit of skirt covering her panties she shoved her crotch into my face as I gagged and spat, falling into the couch. She merely roared her usual laugh, though hoarsely bringing on a coughing fit, leaving me wondering how she could have such feminine voice yet never for a moment alter that manly, rough cough!
"That's why she hates us...didn't you get it? Those dykes all do. We go and get lopped off the very thing those bitches wish they had... How bitter do you think *they* must get?!"
"Well, I didn't think she was bitter at all. Just being very cautious about who they let through." I felt a bit smug to let her know that I just might have been referring to her... without really saying much more.
"Ri, yer fucked, Girl. Absolutely fucked."
In a way she was right, about the lesbian ladies anyway, as I was to encounter a lot of hostility with them. Some were cruel to the extreme and very heartless... whatever their reasons. Once, a lesbian had picked the wrong tranny to start on in a gay bar with Lexi over Christmas. Whilst using the bathroom we turned to see a boiler-suited lesbian with a huge

beer belly, like a greasy mechanic in a garage, clutching her 'tinny' leering back and forth at us. With a mighty growl she lunged at Lexi telling her she should be using the men's loo. A pretty young girl dressed as a fairy skipped from a cubicle and tiptoed up to the lesbian's face to say,
"I feel a lot more comfortable with them being in here than I do with *you*! You should be using the bloody men's room." The lesbian sneered at us all, which was enough to have Lexi see red and was all it took to kick her off.
 By the scruff of the neck, the lesbian's face was hurled into the mirror and splattered with her hair wrenched back, nose bleeding and a frothing tinny spinning on the floor. Heaving the messed up face up to the mirror, Lexi politely enquired-
"There ya go, Sweetheart. Now do ya reckon you got something to laugh about...? Take a good fuckin' look at yerself." Lexi dusted herself off as 'King Kong with a clitoris' sunk to the floor to wallow in her spilt beer. Lexi spent the rest of the night dancing with the 'fairy'. We never saw the lesbian again.

CHAPTER FIVE

Felicity's period-themed Victorian tea rooms, aptly named "Victoriana", opened with great fanfare and celebration with even a huge searchlight swathing the skies over East Melbourne announcing its fabulous arrival on Victoria Parade, right next to the busy Dallas Brooks Hall to attract the right type of theatre crowd... we'd hoped. Melbourne's glitterati of gay media celebs, theatre and TV stars, including some newspaper and magazine people, enjoyed the upstairs-downstairs ambience of the authenticly-styled parlours of fine dining and luxury. I ran from the kitchen now and then to catch a glimpse of anyone famous 'til my feet were well swollen.

As laughter and merriment tormented me from above, down below my busy kitchen started to look like I was going down with the Titanic. The bathrooms upstairs had somehow flooded and I was now working and wading in an above ankle-deep sewer, trying to get out hot canapés and hors d'oeuvres. As the ensuing health hazard threatened to ruin the night, and probably electrocute both myself and my little Italian helper boy, who I called 'Manuel' because of his poor English (and the whole place reminded me of "Fawlty Towers" anyway), I persevered. Still, we got through it all, and in the wee hours, as most people had well and truly left, I went upstairs to join whoever was left, as Felicity took centre stage with tales of her encounters and antics on the Far East's strip circuit in the 1970s.

She would truly mesmerize us all with her accounts of life as a 'reassigned woman' as I filled my mind, pondering how my own might be. It was better to hear about Felicity's life of glamour and excitement, boyfriends and travel and all the lovelier things I could barely imagine, than be stuck below worrying if I'd die

BODYCAGE

on the operating table or wake up with a colostomy bag plugged into my intestines as I usually did! Perhaps I may even have woken from surgery to find my feet had been burnt to lumps of coal as one unfortunate girl did on a cheap sex swap surgery trip to Egypt. Surgical lights in the operating theatre had been held too close to her feet as her legs were held high in the stirrups during her transformation. Always beware of having your genitals created in ghastly hospitals with dodgy surgeons in equally dodgy countries! You could end up looking like a super model with black hooves for feet.

Often, though, I had to wonder if Lady B's stories could all have been true, they enthralled me, filling my head with all manner of flights of fancy. If they are true, that's surely got to be a book worth looking out for... were she to ever write one. As it stood, Felicity was working with a crew on an adult board game, and after all these years, I've been really happy to see it for sale on certain late night TV channels, so was really happy to race to an adult book shop seeing it proudly sat, with all manner of sex toys, on a shelf with her name on the box! Still I listened, totally glued to every word of her tales on her 'tour of duty' and madcap mayhem in the sleaziest strip clubs or extravagantly glamorous cabaret theatres of Korea, Singapore and Hong Kong too.

"Darlings," she felt comfortable enough to share with her closest gay friends and Basil Fawlty of a Maitre'D and business partner, "I had to share the tiniest change room with those Korean acts and the whole place stunk of kimchee. There was hardly any light and I had to put my makeup on practically in the dark. God knows what the hell I must have looked like by time I got on stage. Those dirty little bastards couldn't have cared less anyway... couldn't keep their eyes off my bloody tits!" She gave them both an almighty bounce to make the point. They were actually by now quite pendulous after so many years of putting on weight and I felt sure she'd knock herself out with them if she ever had to run for a tram and get hit in the face!

"Look at them," she churlishly laughed, waving them up and down, "I don't even know where the silicone implant is anymore...Probably absorbed into my bloodstream by now! No wonder people say I am so plastic." Holding a delighted court she went on....

"I had the worst experiences of my life in that hole. I remember catching a glimpse of the Snake Dancer in the mirror one night, when I could see, and was doing my makeup. There she was wrapping a big roll of masking tape around the snake's snout... and its rear end! The bloody thing had gone and died and she didn't want it oozing muck in her act- playing with the snake... doing dirty, tantalising things with it." I'd guessed the show had to go on... even in Korea... and listened more.

"She certainly put on quite a show... Covered in little elastoplasts from the numerous nips from her other little snakes, all over, she ended as usual in her grande finale, spinning around, whirling the snake corpse above her head. In her final, frantic crescendo, the snake was thrust between her legs in mock ecstasy before one almighty vigorous twirl above her head. Snake Lady had been oblivious to the groans and cries from the front row audience as bits of snake guts and crap were being catapulted over them in a big stinking shower. The tape had slipped off from both ends!"

Lady B said she felt no pity for the 'dirty buggers in the front row' who'd have to go home and tell their wives how they got covered in a snake's entrails and now having us all agog as one story led to the next. Spellbound, I took in the next one.

BODYCAGE

"And... worst of all," she'd draped herself over the Baby Grande as some elderly guy hammered *boom boom* on the keys every time she delivered a riotous punch line,
"Boy, I'll never forget it. I was dancing through the crowd, nearly down to just the g-string, and getting guys to take turns clipping off the stocking hold ups so they could slip me a tip... I came across a guy in specs. I loved to take them off and give them a buff and polish with my boobs before putting them back on them. They loved that, so I pulled this guy's glasses off as the spotlight danced across us, only to have him start to shriek and clutch at his face. His friends were screaming too... why I had no idea... As I looked down to buff my trophy and see that it was a prosthesis nose attached to his glasses! I screamed when I realised and screamed again when I saw this guy was franticly trying to cover a gaping hole in his face where his nose should have been. Quite an exit I made after that one, my Lovies." *Boom boom.*

The whole place stayed in fits of laughter, which usually remained the case where-ever Felicity was, at least until she'd eventually tired herself out. She caught my eye as I tallied the cash register, with the sun already shining through the stained glass of the front door, sending a warm smile as her dwindling audience recomposed themselves. Smiling back, I had to grin and wonder again how much of it really happened and if it was all an extravagant mask to cover some 'tears of clown'.

With her crowd still charged from the stories one night, as we were able to close up early and take up the leftover's invitation to join them racing out to St Kilda to see the much talked of new show at Tangles. With Greg away on a country tour with the band, I felt like taking some time to myself and having a laugh, out with Felicity. Waltzing into Tangles, the first people I'd meet at the bar would have to be Lexi and Loren, like Heckle and Jeckle, the cartoon crows, they stood perched at the bar scowling down at everyone. Formidable enough they were on their own, it was a sobering sight to see the two of them together... seething. Lexi now had her nose out of joint that I couldn't do the phones for her anymore with the Victoriana doing so well and Loren would just be a bitch for the sake of having a comparable bitching partner to work with. Waiting for whoever would be the first to come out with the nastiest, sarcastic comment didn't take long. Loren took the first swipe.

"Hey, Girl... How's life as a real woman going? Still got your *straight* little job and straight little affair with Greg going on?"

"You know, Loren. I thought you'd gotten over the fact that maybe Greg just didn't really fancy you. That's life, Love! You know, one man's meat's another man's *poison*." And by now she surely was poison. "Besides, you might land yourself a straight job too if you didn't act like a demented drag queen every time a pair of trousers went by with the essential weapon contained within." Now expected a glass to fly at me, Lexi saved the spat from getting any uglier.

"Now ladies, we didn't come here to get into an argument did we?" she hissed under her breath, eyeballing towards a couple of guys to her side. "We're all here to have a *nice* time while these footballers are in from the country tonight, aren't we?" The place did seem a little fuller than usual with good-looking guys and Lexi had spotted a group of them watching us (hence her ploy to pull Loren into line before anything too unladylike might have occurred!) Lexi and Loren, like two little puppies who'd just found their toys, sprang immediately to their game. There was money to be made, and if not, a possible good lay to pass the night away. The lady game had started as all the components of the game came out to be played all the way to the bedroom. Like Black Widow spiders, they'd lure their prey by all the trappings of femininity before being eaten alive, or more often than not, it was "Bend over honey, ladies first...and a ride there's going to deserve a ride back!" It sickened me that those guys were so easy and how little it took to lead them astray like they'd become totally lobotomised Stepford shags.

One by one I'd watch those macho footy heroes as they stood transfixed, eyes glued to the showgirl's every move and gesture as they parodied and impersonated femininity. It's easier still to see now, how in the heat of those moments, these men could easily forget they were stumbling straight into an encounter with technically and performance-wise...another man! Each of these footballers would barely hesitate to make a move on any of those performers... as soon as their pals were out of sight to see them do it. It was laughable really, to be so discretely asked for our numbers or to step outside for a bit of fun. I wondered why they'd bothered with the discretion, as they were all at it! I wondered too if all these so called macho, sports guys really only played sport to have contact with other guys!

They weren't fooling me, I knew their game. They wouldn't be taking my number *or* take me outside for fun with a couple of 'straight' guys and their mates, only hoping to fulfill what they really were often after - coming casually into contact with *eachother...* with me in the middle as a buffering excuse. This world was looking sicker by the moment as I wondered if their wives or girlfriends knew and did anyone care? And what about all those bloody romance and fairy stories I'd read... what was that all about? Had the real princes of the world taken the night off? And now I'd hoped one day that Walt Disney and the Brothers Grimm would pay for all this delusion they'd left me with!

 Eventually Felicity had called me over to join a couple of the better-mannered ones for a drink as they seemed to be intent on putting down the showgirls... snickering and mocking right throughout the show. It soon dawned, as they made comments like "Look at the sick bunch of freaks in the Aids Parade", that they hadn't realised Felicity and I were something akin ourselves! Two of them had their arms draped over me, swigging at their cans of beer, another stood leering in front telling me how lovely he thought I was. All I needed was for Loren to walk past right then and give the game away and find myself killed! So, there I stood, trying to squirm away from them- 'The Three Men and a Little Tranny'.

 Squeezing through the throng at the bar yet again, I spotted 'Lurch' Lorraine swaying precariously from side to side with a crazed grin on her face, staring into nothingness imagining a conversation with someone invisible, in a pool of stinking pee which had blackened a big wet patch from the crotch of her jeans to her knees. I never saw Lurch again, though Shantelle told me (before she was found dead on her sofa after a heavy night of drinking) that Lurch had found love in the form of a bisexual Satanist from 'up bush' in Wonthaggi. Charming, I'd thought, not even daring to ponder if 'like' really does find 'like'... Or possibly it could even be true that we attract exactly in a relationship a reflection of just *what* we believe ourselves to be!

 No, such knowledge was far from my understanding, having not even heard of the insightful works of Harville Hendrix about psychologies behind relationships. Nor had I read anything yet by Robin

BODYCAGE

Norwood, like 'Women Who Love Too Much'... but I sure did later, and can thoroughly recommend their works to anyone who might be still asking "Why? Oh why the bloody hell, why do we do some of the stupidest things for love?!"

The showgirls began their finale for part one, as the six Amazons in high heels, spun around the stage with hands joined in a central star worthy of an Ethel Merman aquatic spectacular. Huge plumes of large pink feathers billowed across the stage behind them as their long painted fingernails sparkled to the crowd with undulations of girly hand gestures. Merely in a glimpse of those huge over-made-up eyes, the shimmering glossy lips, the feathers and all the raucous noise, the girls seemed transformed to a flock of gaily-coloured parrots, raucously screeching, squawking and clawing through their flock. No-one noticed a shaken white dove slip from the grasp of the predators, as the "Dream Girls" number started.

"Round and around and around we go.
Where we'll stop
nobody knows.
Successsssss... we got success......"

Where they'd stop...I think I did know!

Making it to the bar in time to find the star of the show refreshing herself, I noticed she stood alone. Delores De Longe was one of the most beautiful *women* I'd ever seen, let alone trans. Unfortunately, her romantic attractions had mainly led to involvements with the roughest, most violent of men. Her face had been pulverised so many times that she was virtually in a constant state of reconstruction and an ever-concealing layer of pan-stick medicated cover foundation for the black eyes! At least she had the sense to blame herself. She fully understood that she'd seduced these men, who'd thought themselves to be heterosexual, into performing sex acts which had never really crossed their minds. Of course she realised then why they'd felt robbed of their own masculinity and take it out on her for twisting them to this extent and lashing out their hatred for homosexuality in others, and now in themselves, on her. Still, despite her awareness of that simple concept... she would keep on doing it again and again.

Delores kindly offered to buy me a drink, which I graciously accepted. In fact, she proceeded to buy me lots of drinks, to the extent that I'd drank them all, not noticing her hand had slipped down my back and now rested cosily on my bum! When I startled and looked down at the hand so she could notice I'd seen it, I mentioned that I'd really thought she was only into guys.

"Well," she replied..."you know...an arse is an arse to me." Like the drunken country blokes with their beer cans, she too leered at me, giving my bum a hefty thwack. Perhaps she thought she'd take a break from violence tonight and find a more compliant date, but there could never have been enough alcohol for me to want to try that one! Things seemed bad and confusing at times, but I was nowhere near ready for that... and Delores certainly did not like the knock-back as she menaced at me.

"That footy crowd from up bush didn't know you're one of the girls did they?" she kind of sneered. "I saw them dancing with you too and I know they never dance with any of us in front of their mates."

"Well, they didn't ask, Deli, so I didn't really see a need to tell them." I expected her to storm off and tell them herself out of pure spite. Instead she stood back and swept her eyes up and down me like a searchlight.

"You're not wearing any makeup tonight are you?"

BODYCAGE

"No, I just came straight from work... in and out of a hot kitchen all night. Sometimes I've got to run and let guests in at the front door and last time I wore too much it had melted down. I looked like a Kabuki clown from a Japanese horror movie." I whooshed down the drink, but she wasn't yet finished.

"Oh right, I heard you're working at Lady Layby's little folly... But isn't it about time you got real like the rest of us and started using that body to make some decent money while you got it? I don't mean in the shows or anything...the money's crap... But can't you work with Lexi or get yourself into a parlour or something?"

She may not have liked my reply and it may have seemed like a dig... but all the same,

"I don't think it is *decent* money to be doing that, Deli. I'd find it pretty repulsive actually and am pretty happy doing what I am doing... although the money's slow. I'm saving to pay for my own surgery."

"Well, you'll regret that too, you'll see. When they lose their balls they lose their fuckin brains too... and their boyfriend's," she sneered again.

"My boyfriend didn't get together with me for that, Deli... So it's not making a lot of difference! He's the one who needs me getting it over and done with as soon as possible... So I will!"

"I still think you're a fool. You should make as much money out of the bastards as you can, Love. Look at 'em... They're just a pack of rats out there lying and cheating where-ever they can. If they want to spend their money, let it be on you. Do it while you can." Her thoughtful advice continued.

"Deli, I got nothing against working girls...but I don't think I could have sex with someone I wasn't romantically attached to really. Or not even *attracted* to! Anyway, I'd faint if all he wanted was 'down there'." I nodded to below my waist. "I've peeped in on Lexi through the keyhole, so God no... That's really not my type of thing! My relationship means the world to me and I wouldn't give that up or jeopardise it for anything now." So it was true. I really was Pollyanna with a penis.

An Eartha Kitt song had begun to play as Shari took the stage for her final, sultry number, slinking out in skin-tight faux leopard, playing seductively with a long black tail. Lip-syncing the words, she reclined pouting, scissoring her legs up and down with exaggerated spreads as Eartha purred and growled,

"If you want me
you better show it.
If I've got what
you desire...."

A leg lifted again unbelievably high as a big gasp came from the crowd... and a few woops. I almost dropped my drink, shooting my gaze to Shari on the stage, on her back, leg scissored in the air as one of her testicles had popped completely out of the tight g-string for all the world to see. Shari had not yet noticed.

"Hey mate," one of the country guys yelled. "One of yer balls is hangin' out!" Quite a show stopper that was! I turned to Deli in horror.

"He's quite the charmer isn't he? How do you put up with those guys when they heckle like that?"

"They don't bother me, Love. He'll be one of the first after the show hanging around the change room trying to swing off both her balls. It's always the one with the loudest mouth trying to prove something to his mates who comes crawling after us when they're not around. You know, when I look down from up there and see a heckler, I always know he's the one most insecure about his sexuality. He yells cos he can't handle the fact that we got him... hooked. We turn them on and there's nothing they can do about it, so he lashes out.

BODYCAGE

That's the one who'll be lining up at the end of the night when his mates are gone begging me to take him home or in the change room and fuck him senseless."

I felt Delores was probably right, thinking back to Lexi's story about when she was my age. The police had picked her up when she had to work the streets of St Kilda in drag. When they'd realised what she was, they'd often get her to perform oral sex on them all. Before legislation of the sex industry in Victoria it was common enough for the police to enjoy the humiliation of any sex worker they arrested. The story was the same anywhere and her ordeal was often not over as she was many times stripped naked and photographed, also for a laugh. As a farewell gesture on one such arrest, Lexi was shut inside a big metal locker, pulled to a long flight of stairs and rolled down, screaming from inside all the way to the bottom. Yes, they were the *real* men I guessed, trying hard to prove their point... to each other. Lexi still had the scars, some covered now in tattoos, and, needless to say, has a pathological hatred for the police. It explained a lot why so many at that time were attracted to a lifestyle far removed from anything like law and order in a world where everything seemed turned upside down.

Deli offered me a ride home after closing time if I was willing to wait around for a few minutes. To save the dollars I took the offer as she said the bouncer's would keep me entertained 'til she was changed and ready. Standing by the exit with them, we did have a little giggle at the spilling out parade, stumbling out into the daylight as the Sun peeped over the waters of Port Philip Bay. Trying to keep a straight face, we watched the punters leave with an array of tranny hookers and drag queens on their arms, keeping up a bizarre pretence that they somehow felt they were going home with women! Watching a couple of my 'luckier' friends

who'd already had their surgery leave with their prized pick-ups for the night, I envied them now, free from their cages, believing that their new lovers would probably never have known they were anything other than how they looked now. How I impatiently wished for that freedom.
"Thank God you don't have to face that every night, Love." One of the bouncers laughed into my ear as every combination of sexual disorientation now trickled by.
"You're not wrong, I'd have no faith left in the world at all," I said, wandering back into the almost totally deserted club to look for Deli. Finding the darkened corridor, leading to the backstage change room, I tripped my way over props and racks of costumes to eventually find the change room door. No sign of Miss Delores de Longe. Finding another door, I thought might be a janitor's cupboard, I threw it open to check anyway, flicking on the light. Two horrified faces darted up to meet my eyes as I stood frozen.
"Christ, Girl," Deli gasped. "I thought that door was locked." And there, bent over a sluice sink full of mops with trousers around his ankles, was the loud-mouthed 'yer ball's are out' heckler skewered by Deli like a pig on a spit. He shot across the room as I shot as quickly out the door thinking- Get me out...OUT...OUT!
I left Tangles alone for a long time after that and was glad that Greg had fewer country gigs now and would be home in Melbourne a lot more often to enjoy what I'd made of the nearest thing to a normal life I'd ever dreamt of. After so recently surviving the carnival of insanity at Tangles and all those ghastly images in my mind, I began to wonder if the world would ever understand and accept people like me. Or at least would the people of Australia? With so much of that macho, misogyny to face, what hope could there be

there? Even in Russia and China, I knew that transgender women had been given equal female rights, but in Australia it would have been a criminal act for me to marry... a man! Even after surgery.

How, I wondered, could anyone take us seriously when our main visible presence were over- made-up parodies of women in drag shows and transvestite street walkers servicing the seedier side of life in dirty, dark alleys? Those illusions of the feminine, parading on stages, offered only a caricatured image to tease and entice sexual encounters with men who'd surrendered their souls to the power of testosterone. Only then, after they'd sickened their gullible minds, would the deception dawn on them. The trappings of femininity would finally be found on the floor near a bed in the morning... often enough, not only the clothes, but the wigs as well. There on the bed lay another naked man, with smeared stains of lipstick, blurs of eye liner and fading make up, exposing his very own eager-for-gratification manhood, lying in scruffy sheets scattered with broken off bits of stick-on painted nails... like rose petals on the wedding bed of an unhealthy marriage!

Did those men really ever wonder what happened to their 'Dream Girl' through the night, turning out to be nothing but the smudged image of brightly coloured paints left on a pillow slip? A messy pile of man-made fibres lies on the floor having long-since fallen off, relinquishing its illusory duty, masquerading as a woman's hair. No wonder Deli's face was a regular bloodbath. Cuddling up in my own bed with Greg on a Sunday morning, with the paper exploded all about us, felt unbelievably normal!

Realising that the whole Tangles scene and time spent at Lexi's served only as something to play with my head, as those who enjoyed that life saw me as some kind of outcast myself, my reservations about Tangles were soon confirmed. Flicking through the pages as Greg nodded back to sleep an article glared out at me,

"TRANSSEXUAL FOUND DEAD ON BANKS OF YARRA"

"Greg, wake up," I tapped my nails against his shoulder. "Look at this!". Not quite believing what I read and how cruelly it had been reported, I wafted the paper in his face. "Oh, my God...it was that poor old thing that used to get up and dance by herself in Tangles. I only saw her a couple of weeks ago in that little spangly dress it says she was found in. She talked to me for a while in the loo. Look, Greg...it says she was found dead on the banks of the river."

Greg, stirred and moaned, not even wanting to open his eyes for a glimpse. "Look, Love," he murmured, "I don't know why you bothered going to that hole anyway, let alone talking to those bloody freaks."

"But the poor old thing was harmless, Greg... She'd only had her op last year and said she thought the doctors had only used her to practise technique on. They called her 'Silverfish' at the club. you know. those little silver cockroaches? How awful.. remember her?... she always wore her those tight little sparkly outfits and g-strings with all her bits hanging out the side. Am sure you were laughing at her too the night I met up with you. I told you I thought it was the highlight of her life to be out there on the dance floor, starring in her own show at last, remember?" I now dug him deeper in the ribs. No response so I ranted on.

"I think this is really awful. She had told me in the loo that she thought she'd be going home with a couple of footy players and was so thrilled to be getting a chance to use her equipment. She said she was Sweet Sixty and never been fucked."

BODYCAGE

"Well," Greg finally stirred, turning over, "she's fucked now isn't she. Can I get some bloody rest? It's Sunday morning for Christ's sake and how'd she end up in the Yarra anyway?" He'd woken up more and groped one of my breasts, ready to start his Sunday as any Aussie male would love.
"It says here that a the wigless, bald-headed body was found battered and bruised after having floated in the Yarra some 48 hours." They had assumed it was suicide and she'd probably been battered against pylons after jumping from a bridge. "Oh, no, look at this... they had to mention that her bra had been stuffed with nylon stockings stuffed with budgie seed and it had started to sprout after two days in the water!"
"Amazing," Greg laughed, "I didn't think anything still grew in the bloody Yarra. It's dirty enough without filthy old dead drag queens floating 'round in it."
He was about to sustain a clip 'round the ear himself for his callous insensitivity when he was saved by the phone ringing. I leaned over, depriving him of the object of his Sunday morning pleasure, only to hear the voice of Loren on the line.
"Girl, have you heard about Silverfish in the papers yet?" Genuinely thinking she was as sorry as I was, I replied,
"Yes...just seen it actually and was talking to Greg about it. He thought the Yarra was polluted enough without the likes of *us* in it." I glared at him and he huffed back, rolling his eyes like I was being quite silly. "I'm surprised you're up so early to have even read it yourself."
"Haven't been to bed yet, Girl. Just got home from some trade's house I picked up last night and had to flee before his wife got in from night shift somewhere. Good that was tough to get away, he was stuck to my dick like a leach all night...."

"Alright, Loren. Alright, I got the picture. Do you have to speak so loud? Greg's right next to me here and don't want him listening to that stuff...ok?"

"Oh, he aches to hear about our girly antics," she laughed now maniacally.

"No he doesn't and they're your antics...not mine! Is that all you wanted to tell me anyway?"

"Just wanted to tell you about the Silverfish story and have a little girly chat as I'm not tired yet, as you'd expect a man my age shouldn't be." She goaded me, trying her best to push the buttons.

"Honestly, Loren. I can't believe you think that way and do that stuff with guys." I was about to hang up...but hesitated to let her have the last word again.

"Ri, I've told you before...the men like it! And anyway. a ride there deserves a ride back so I give 'em one." More maniacal laughter down the line.

"Will you stop that?! I'm really quite upset about Silverfish cos I really liked her. She was just a harmless old thing." This was pointless.

"Well...I feel sorry too," Finally, I thought, some human compassion. "Feel sorry for the poor guy who found her. Imagine walking your dog along the river and finding that bloody sad old bloke's corpse, with no dick and birdseed sprouting out of his chest? And an ugly old bald head too... must've looked *real* pretty!" Compassion? Not a hope.

"Loren, I think you're a heartless bitch. It was probably the only happiness she ever had, thinking she was going home with those footballers and finally get a bit of affection." I stepped out of bed, pulling on my dressing gown as Loren fished with her coup de grace.

"Yeah, well I heard about it all last night. Some of the girls saw her leave the club with some of the footy guys, She must've thought all her Christmases had come at once... flying along St Kilda road like Lucy

BODYCAGE

Jordan with the warm wind in her hair....dreaming of a thousand lovers," she sang in a pretty good imitation of Marianne Faithful. "Ha, those guys must have got a real laugh, giving her plenty of tease and leading her on before sending her for a little dip off the bridge. Oh well... boys will be boys. I reckon they were pissed off cos she didn't have a cock for them."

"Loren. *THEY KILLED HER*! You're such a heartless bitch. I know they did it just for *sport* to try and prove something to themselves, and don't think it's funny someone's lost their life. So what kind of *men* do you think they are to treat another human being like that? I don't think they're men at all... I think they are animals...and that's an insult to *animals* !"

Down the line Loren had burst again into song. This time bass baritone to be more offensive, of course...

"I was born to be laughed at
stepped on
and treated like dirrrrrrrrt.
'cos I was born a womaaaaaaaaan.
I'm glad it happened that waaaaaayyyyy. Ri, yer fucked, Love... see ya." Click.

Rehana Incognito

BODYCAGE

PART THREE

Rehana Incognito

BODYCAGE

CHAPTER ONE

1986

In a half light between dead of night and daybreak, Greg stirred slightly and woke me with his murmur. Waking just that little more as the first rays of light had streaked across our faces on a chilly autumn dawn, I clearly heard his words-

"I don't know what's real and what's not real anymore...." He was pleading to a listener in a private world I could only imagine. Feeling so grateful to have him lying there, close to me, I gently stroked his head to comfort him. I was anguished with the knowledge that it was the state I was in, which at the back of his mind, was now playing in his dreams and making me feel the guilt for my effect on him. I was the cause of his confusion although he'd never made me feel anything but pride in who I was to him. Now I wondered how he, so young, brave and caring, could be processing my situation... and how difficult it must be for him. How bizarre, I thought it must be to be in love with a woman he sees in his heart and soul as such, yet stuck in my position. He even had endured hours of interviews and embarrassing questions, month after a month with the Gender Board with me.

Still, I watched him sleep on, sending through the stillness all my honour and appreciation for what he was doing, my pride and admiration that he'd stood by me through all this. Speaking in my half dream, hopefully through to his, I told him when I think of how crazy my life must seem, with all my weird friends included, I sometimes wonder too what's real and what's not real. How I wished I could fly into his dream right then... and share with him mine.

Greg dressed and showered quickly for work before slipping beneath the covers for one last cuddle before leaving. I wanted to ask about his troubled dream, but thanked him for being in my life.

"I love you so much, Greg... you know that don't you?"

"I luv ya too, hon and I'll be missin' ya all day."

He was out the door and I fell back asleep, knowing I would miss him too. He'd call during the day...he always did, just to see how my day was going and if I really did miss him. I wanted that sleep now to go on forever... or at least until a time when I would awaken to find this mess over with. Hours passed until the phone chirped and I reached over, then back, not wanting to answer it and go back to oblivion. Then, realising the time, I thought it might be Greg and picked up the phone, mumbling a dozy- hello?

"Hi Riannon....Guess who this is?" That voice had me stumped, actually wondering how Kermit the Frog and Freddy Kruger had managed to produce a love child... and how did it get my number?!

"Emmmm.. I dunno. Who's calling, sorry?" Now I was all ears, wondering if I was still dreaming myself.

"It's me, Deena, remember?" the mystery voice squawked.

"I talked to you at Tangles a few times. Lexi gave me your number because she told me you're having a sex-change operation too." On and on she croaked in that voice which modulated then lost pitch with every second syllable. Way too much for me before my first cup of tea!

"Oh...Deena...yeah, I remember now. Sorry, I thought you just like to dress up... Like on the weekends and stuff. Don't you think this is a big move to suddenly decide you're going to be a woman?" Surely I must really be dreaming I thought. No-one could possibly be starting their day like this.

"Yes, I know there's a lot to learn about it, but that's why Lexi said to call you. She said you were really nice

BODYCAGE

and understanding about it all. So *here I am* !!" And there I was...about to become the Mother Teresa of the Gender Dysphoric, dispensing advice and wisdom about what you'd need to *learn* to become a woman! This had to be one of Lexi's wind-ups for sure as Deena had the physique of a bear and the body hair to match. How could I be responsible for encouraging *this*?

Her next utterance saw me crashing back into the pillows, praying to be rendered unconscious and not be dealing with this at all.

"I'm wondering if you'd help me out with a full body wax?"

"What do you mean full body wax? I don't know anything about body waxing and rarely enough waxed my own legs... getting in enough of a sticky mess with that. Perhaps it's something you could learn your own technique for, Deena."

"Well, I'm already almost through it...sort of. Well, I've done most of my legs...and chest." Now I was stifling gasps in disbelief as she told me she only needed help to do her back and shoulders! What could I possibly say?

"Sounds like you're well on your way to womanhood there then, Girl." Anyone who had already endure that much depilatory pain deserved some consideration and sympathy I felt, so, martyr that I am, made the offer-

"Bring your wax pots and come over after lunch. We'll have a laugh and get your whole body as smooth as a baby's bum. I'll also fill you in about all you need to know about doctors and stuff. Do you want to take down my address?"

"No, Lexi already gave it to me. Thanks." Thanks Lexi too! I bet she thought Deena would just knock on my door and scare the life out of Greg.

Rehana Incognito

Hours passed with still no sign of Deena as I started to feel a bit edgy, wondering if Greg might come home early to find his home had become the House of Hair Removal on Toorak Rd- Look for the big pair of hairy legs, lit in neon, flashing and scissoring back and forth over a little block of flats near the shops. Thankfully, the doorbell eventually rang. Flinging open the door, I saw no-one there, until from one side, a huge whiskery face covered in welts and bumps popped around to greet me. It was the 'woman' behind the voice. Certainly not Kermit the Frog, but perhaps I thought she could be a dead ringer for Oscar the Grouch's sister.

Apart from the red welts, bits of wax remained stuck in patches here and there, with the hundreds of hard-to-rip-out hairs still in situ. Wearing a streak of badly applied red lipstick, men's jeans, a t-shirt and more bits of wax on her neck, I noticed her left arm was completely bandaged. Spattered in purple mercurcome, seeping through the bandages and gauze netting, I pulled her by the good arm quickly through the front door lest my neighbours set eyes on her.

"Girl, am so sorry I'm late. My car got hit by a tram on the way over. Sliced the bloody thing nearly clean in half. You should have seen the mess. Completely the driver's fault though... he shot through a red light as I was turning off St Kilda Road."

In a daze myself is at her on the couch, listening aghast as her story continued.

"Just spent the last couple of hours in Prince Albert's Hospital, getting myself patched up in the emergency room. But don't worry, I'm insured and I managed to save the wax pots from the car before they towed it away."

BODYCAGE

"Well, that's saved the day then, Deena, hasn't it?" My mouth still agape, I staggered into the kitchen to heat up the wax pots and prepare some tea.

"My God... your arm looks a mess though. That must have hurt," I called from my little kitchenette.

"Yeah, I suppose it did, but all could think while they bandaged me up was what a great pair of fish-net tights that gauze netting would make. Took my mind right off it." Only a true, die hard transvestite could have been thinking about dressing up whilst practically a piece of road kill, I thought. Thankfully, the phone rang before I could make that comment. It was Greg.

"Hi Darlin'...Just rang to see how my little Bunny's day's goin'. I'm just getting ready to finish up here then heading home."

"Take your time, Greg... I just have a friend here at the moment and I'm helping her wax her back." Not even pausing to think for a moment what I'd just said, Greg nearly yelled down the phone,

"*Love*... did you just say you were waxing your friend's back?"

"Oh, I think I did, Sweetheart. I must be half asleep again... or it might be the hormones... I meant her legs. This might take a bit of time though, so don't rush home and I'll see you later." Replacing the receiver, I felt dreadful to have lied but just didn't want to add more to his confusion and have another night of his fitful sleep with disturbing dreams. I shook my head in disbelief at the now almost naked, giant fur ball, spread-eagled on a sheet across my living room floor. How crazed was my life now becoming that this would become part of my daily routine?

"Thanks for helping me out with this, Ri. It's really sweet of you," she lifted her head to say. Like a zombie, I wandered back to the stove to stir the putrid pot of inky black wax, tearing strips of cloth to begin this tortuous procedure.

"Deena, are you sure *really* sure this is what you want to? I mean... it's tough enough without having to remove kilos of unwanted hair every month, on top of everything else." Wrenching the first strip of wax from across her shoulders, I shuddered myself... noticing she didn't even flinch.

"Yes, of course this is really what I want to do. Been on the 'mones now for about four months... Bought them off a queen who got rejected by the Board and got quite a set of knockers now. Look."

 Rolling over like a big she-wolf, quite a healthy chest was revealed, showing an onslaught of oestrogen had indeed taken effect. She then told me she'd been knocking them back like Smarties without any medical supervision or advice, not even caring as I let her know how dangerously foolhardy that was. There had to be something grotesquely surreal though, about a large pair of nipples set amidst two swollen breasts covered in hairs... which had been hacked at badly with a razor! As hirsute hooters really played with my psyche, I decided that hairy breasts really belonged on a female gorilla... or the nearest relative thereof.

"How can I get around in summer in little off-the-shoulder numbers with all this lot on me? I wanna flash a bit of leg too, especially when I learn to walk properly... like you. You gotta show me how you do that. I mean, Girl... How *do* you walk like that? You're like a bloody big cat."

"Just pretend you already got a pussy between your legs, OK? Then the rest of your body might follow. But you're not listening to me, Deena. I'm trying to tell you that it's not an easy road to travel, changing your sex just like that! The process itself is an ordeal and, even after the surgery, there are no guarantees. The suicide rate is very high afterwards... you know that don't you?" I sat on her back to get some more muscle behind my strip-ripping.

"Yeah, I know it's all weird and really tough. I read about it though and think I've kept pretty up-to-date on it all really. Actually, I just read in a magazine about these drags in Pakistan... they're called Hydrants. Have you heard about them?"

"Yes Deena, I have...and I think you mean Hijras... they are in India too."

"Yes... that's them. They go out in the community and do little song and dance shows at weddings and stuff. They even get plenty of sex with the men because the women there can't.... Well, not unless they marry them. Their life must be incredible...Sooooo lucky!"

"Sounds like the girls at Tangles if you ask me... but they don't have to do it to get food on the table. The Hijra do, and are often made to be that way by their families to bring home extra money." I let the wax strips go on wider to pull out more hair in one go.... *Rrrrrrrip*, and still she didn't flinch.

"What makes you think dressing up as a woman and having to have sex with men who'd only use you cos they can't get the real thing, is such a big achievement anyway, Deena? The men who use the Hijra at least have their excuse as they need sex and can't just go out and marry for it. I wonder what the guys sniffing around Tangles and paying people like Lexi use for an excuse." Claiming to be devotees of the Cult of Hermaphrodite would hardly have cut it.

"You're right. I think they're dogs too, but I don't care, I wouldn't mind being their bitch for a while. It's alright for you... you have Greg every night. Oh, by the way, would you mind calling me Kylie from now on? I've decided to use Kylie's name 'cos I really love her... She's my idol and I want to be just like her." Honey, I thought, there's not a million operations you could have to make you look like her, but replied all the same that I'd call her Kylie, perhaps slipping now and then as I was just getting to know 'Deena'!

"Ok....*Kylie*," it was like talking to multiple personalities being channelled through a psychic,

"What do you think is going to change so much about your life if you have this operation too?"

"Well, the sex of course! Why else do you think I would do it?! I'm gonna buy a camper van, stick a red light in the window and screw my way around Australia with the cutest guys I can find and make money all the way too." In the condition she was in, she'd be grateful for one dollar and I thought she'd be better off buying a caravan, joining a circus and working as the Bearded Woman. But then again, I may be wrong, having after all, seen enough guys pay to have sex with Lexi Roper.

"At least I'll get my new equipment broken in, Riannon... hey...?"

"Hmmmm... you should be so lucky... lucky lucky lucky. Sounds like you're going to get it worn out. You'll end up having to go back in and getting a re-tread like a worn out old tyre."

She squirmed in ecstasy at the thought of all those lovers coming her way. "I'm going to have a gorgeous boyfriend too... and work as a hooker on the side. Yeah, that's what I'm going to do. Gimme cock 'til I drop!" Her eyes glazed over, rolling back like a shark about to clench those jaws closed on its prey.

"You know Kylie...you might just really be having sex 'on the side' too... if your operation gets messed up." I decided to test her mettle a bit.

"Whadda ya mean?" She turned sharply, looking over her shoulder.

"You could wake up with a colostomy bag attached to your side and a completely unusable vagina. It does happen, I was told... quite a lot. Didn't you know?" Although, knowing her, she'd be lucky enough to be given a womb and ovaries thrown in too. She said she wouldn't mind a colostomy bag as long as she could get the hat and gloves to match!

After some two hours, perched on Kylie's back and wobbly chest, ripping off strips of hairy wax which came away looking like scrubbing brushes, I was close to insane. Listening to her psychotic babble about planned sexual exploits, dresses and makeup was maddening. Not to mention her constant croaking of Kylie Minogue and Madonna songs to punctuate what she was saying at any opportunity. She'd spent the previous evening skulking through an all-male gay sauna and spa with boobs tightly bound in bandages under a bulky sweat top. In a quiet corner of the complex she'd slipped off the bandage to submerge beneath the heady, foamy waters of a hot tub, just her head and shoulders above the surface to lure any possible partner into the tank for a fumble. Now and again some had joined her, groping around in the stinky chlorine until they'd flee in horror, like coming across a plague victim, as they noticed the knockers bouncing in the froth. Kylie was determined to leave all that behind.

Feeling glad when she finally left, I wondered what happened to the days when gay guys just dressed up as their favourite diva, putting on a smutty little show in their local bars, not rushing off to see a team to have their genitals transformed to match idols they had determined to be suitable *images* of womanhood.

All the more, that moment, I accepted the Board's harsh criteria for fulfilling the conditions for approval for 'reassignment'. Their intention was purely to weed out those who were undertaking this procedure for all the wrong reasons, hence sparing heartache and turmoil when they realise they have mutilated both their bodies and lives. As it was put to me however, the fact remains that anyone can seek out enough information about gender reassignment to bluff themselves through telling all the 'right' answers. Many enough biographies are there to extol the joys of successful changes, yet those who become the suicide statistics afterwards have left no such legacy of all that went wrong in their devastated lives.

Looking at Kylie and the many others like 'her', I wanted to be sure that I knew *myself* too. I wanted absolute certainty that perhaps I too was not deluding myself in taking this path in life... and could I imagine any way to continue through my life *without* taking it? Staring at my body again in a full length mirror, I anguished, wondering what else I *could* even be. All the material and biographies I had read told me I was no different from anyone else taking this step with sincerity. In fact, in so many ways, I was far more fortunate than most. Seeing no way I could (or even would) want to go through this world trying to be anything like a man, equally as much I'd never accept living as a woman, yet not be surgically complete. With the blessing already of an attractive, lithesome body and the bone structure of an attractive Scandinavian blonde, I felt my body had previously been a curse with no purpose to carry me through as male. Feeling somewhat sad for Kylie, with her knobbly big hands and hirsutism, I thanked God for those natural characteristics which affirmed clues and confidence that I was headed in the right direction.

Still I felt impatient about not totally matching up to the image for which I was extremely grateful, as the strain on Greg played too much on my mind. I wanted the surgery over and done with to get on with the ever-dreamed-of *normal* life.

BODYCAGE

CHAPTER TWO

Immediately, I called Professor Williams for an appointment to tell him I wanted to go to Sydney as soon as possible for Dr Howell to do the surgery. The bank had just extended my credit card limit to a healthy $5000, so the temptation to get my 'Visa Card vagina' was almost too much. The Gender Clinic accepted the urgency and soon enough was standing before receptionist where a petite, red-headed girl of about 22 years old stood sobbing before her.
"I don't know what the hell that surgeon thinks he has done to me. It's a bloody mess down there. It looks like Safeway's fucking *meat department* ... and there's nothing I can do about it! He's ruined my life."
The girl looked so beautiful, quite like a model really, willowy and pale, just stepping from "Vogue" magazine perhaps. Truly I pitied her... to have come so far on her journey, with all the same assets as myself only to have her life messed up by bad surgery. And it was true, there was nothing she could have done about it, as she'd have signed a waiver prior to her surgery that no responsibility would be taken for anything which went wrong or the results. Glancing to her side, I wondered if there was a dreaded colostomy bag stuck on there too... thankfully, there wasn't. Now, filled with dread, I realised I'd soon possibly be heading for the same situation.
After catching my gaze, the girl simply walked, without another word, from the office. My head reeled at the thought of this Russian roulette with my own body... but what was the alternative? I felt like a freak *now*, neither being in one world nor the other and it hardly occurred to me that I may well have been living in both! Should I forget the whole thing, panic and run out the door too, learn to act like a man and try to make myself

look more like one? Then what - to be gay and have no interest in anything to do with that? I'd be pathetically left alone to turn into some effeminate, lonely old man drenched in moisturiser with a coral pink cardigan draped over my shoulders, nursing his cat. Hell, I am allergic to cats and also realised that way too many dreams waited to be fulfilled, and not on my own!

So, I'd risk the surgery and do my best with it, no matter what the results, to live as best I can in the only role I could imagine or wish for. That, it seemed, was the crux of all I wanted, no matter the risk. Finishing the job, I was already so near to successfully completing, was what I'd decided to do, knowing I'd never really be at peace... forever wondering, had I not at least tried.

Professor Williams gave me the look that I had done something terribly naughty and bade me sit down.

"Professor, I'm not going to ask for preferential treatment from you and your department, but I don't think I can stand much more of this waiting. I know you have to be thorough with the assessments, but for goodness sake I am fulfilling more of the requirements than most. I can't live in Limbo Land for one more year, just so your department can be sure. I am sure! I mean...*look at me...* I'm hardly going to decide at this stage that I could go back to anything like functioning as a man and regretting anything, am I?" Hoping he could see how exasperated I'd become, I grimaced as he replied.

"Well, Riannon, we do have to be absolutely sure that you are making the right decision and are ready. That's why we feel it should always be a two year period...and that *is* the rule... I am sorry." Shuffling papers on his desk, he clearly indicated my audience was over. I felt like I was drowning as he prepared to dismiss me and

BODYCAGE

anger rose like a bomb about explode. Yet, it came out in the form of words.
"OK, in that case, Professor, I'm sorry too because I have already been assessed and approved for surgery in Sydney." Fiery words indeed, with all the charge and threat I wanted from them. "And I have had enough of you people anyway, playing God with my life." Too often I'd seen the most dubious of characters working as prostitutes and presenting gay men as their boyfriends to dupe this Board with their deceptions for approval for surgery and many others, for the wrong reasons, getting away with it. I wasn't going to put my life on hold any longer because of the actions of a bunch of con artists who'd messed up their own lives with dishonesty.

Astonishingly the professor promised then to call a meeting of the Board in which I could present my case. Calling his bluff and finding such acquiescence seemed all too easy, as three weeks later I was making my way through another dismally cold winter morning along the wind-lashed streets of Melbourne. After trekking through the rambling sprawl of the Royal Women's Hospital, I found the door to the meeting room where the Board awaited me. Although a much-anticipated sight to see them all seated there like the Spanish Inquisition, I knew they'd put me through an ordeal to prove to them all why I'd want to become a woman.

A few minutes part as 9 A.M approached. On the dot, a huge shadowy figure lurched toward the door, its outline become clearer as it reached the frosted glass. As my heart pounded the door flew open and there stood Dr Conolly, stepping out to offer a comforting smile and a gentle pat on the back. Guiding me sullenly to a seat at the head of a very large boardroom table, I'd nervously clattered into the seat, almost knocking the thing over.

Taking a moment to survey my surrounds, I felt like Marie Antoinette, shaking timidly as she'd nervously reached the scaffold to face her inevitable decapitation. The poor woman, in absolute terror, had accidentally stepped on her executioner's foot, which I now could well understand, feeling it so sad that her last words should have been- "Monsieur, I beg your pardon." How gracious she was until the end after such a slight accident, even to someone about to remove her head from her body. I decided to be just as noble and fine an example of dignity and keep my head, holding it high.... myself!

Gazing slowly up as the 'head' of the table, I surveyed the room to see who I had for company. The chairs, the table and faces seemed to go on forever. Each person seated had a pen and notebook before them. Weak morning light streamed in through the enormous windows across the room, leaving lines like bars across me from the Venetian blinds, spotlighted in the chair. Still feeling marked like a bird in a cage, Professor Williams 'ahemmed' himself to draw attention to the beginning of the proceedings.

The 'panel' assembled consisted of surgeons, students, psychiatrists, law representatives, nurses and I think the girl who pushed the refreshments trolley through the wards as well. Some of them were familiar faces, some of course were not, as I felt they could have just given me approval there and then, whipping me onto the boardroom table, getting me off on an assembly line to completion straight away. Thinking this was going to be about the most embarrassing thing in my life, I was sure there was a film crew there with spotlights too and I'd be featured on "Sixty

BODYCAGE

Minutes" or "Australia's Most Wanted" by the weekend. Then again, perhaps I was just overwhelmed.

"These people are all associated with the Program in one way or other, Riannon," Professor William's voice echoed through the room, assuring me. "We'd like you to feel comfortable and just answer all their questions as honestly and concisely as you can." Handing the floor to Dr Conolly, she leaned in my direction.

"I'd like to ask you, Riannon. Do you think if you were stranded alone on a desert island, that you would still prefer to be surgically female?" Well that was a show-stopping starter, I thought... and quite an unexpected shocker. Fixing her gaze intensely on me, she poised her pen in readiness for my response. It did not take much thinking about as I blurted,

"Of course I'd like to be completely surgically female. I might get rescued... by the Navy! The cast of thousands scribbled down my answer and I am sure I heard a few giggles, feeling for sure I'd won the nurses' votes. The senior members simply looked sternly my way.

Feeling I'd totally blown my chances, I just *knew* they'd thought I was like the others who'd come only with the hope that the operation could open an entirely limitless world of sexual conquest, like taking on the entire Pacific Fleet. Struggling to do my best with the rest of this interrogation, the time dragged on for what seemed like hours. The questions were often mundane and some designed to clearly annoy me. However, surprisingly enough, all of the specialists I'd already dealt with spoke highly in my favour, particularly Dr Conolly for which I'll always be grateful.

Leaving this auditorium on my dismissal, I made a promise to all assembled to give my best effort as a fine new 'reassigned woman'... if set loose upon the community. Almost running blindly through the maze of the hospital corridors, I scrambled to the exit, tightly pulling my coat against the cold around me. A gentleman held the door open as I smiled back, knowing that was how I liked things to be and how, if I had not proceeded, only doors would have closed well and truly for the likes of me. Hoping my case had been presented as well as I could manage, perhaps despite any blunders, they would have seen things 'my way'. Professor Williams had said that the final decision would reach me by post in the next few days.

I became the Phantom of the Post Box, waiting every day for the postman to come pedalling down the road, almost snatching letters from him before they got to the slots. The days past agonisingly slowly. This little crowd of people had total authority in deciding whether I'd have any future which promised any degree of normalcy or decency. Their decision alone would mean the difference between expressing my life as the person I knew I was and wanted to be more of... or reliving the nightmare which began each time I woke up. As the joy of life increased with each moment of being together with Greg, I knew there was no way for me to remain halfway across the road I needed to cross, with one foot in both worlds but no real place in either.

Perhaps, I'd thought in another time and culture, I might have been an American Indian 'Berdache'. Those who had been born like myself, that is for sure, yet with nothing like, of course, the hope for any medical support or intervention. They certainly didn't need it, nor the 'Mahoos' of Polynesian culture who had the same respect and place in their worlds, often privileged to the shamanic worlds of magic and healing, accepted and integrated in societies which saw them as 'Twin Spirit' people, whole and complete as they were. If it ever existed with my own race it must

BODYCAGE

have been countless generations ago. Since then all manner of dogma, religions and their condemnations had come along, leaving us only as outcastes, unacceptable and for the most part either driven to end our own lives or having them taken from us by whatever unfortunate means. That was their abysmally painful journey in *their* world, but mine was a world where people knew of talented gifts of surgery and unravelling the clues of chemicals in our bodies, showing another path and solution to what must have seemed to those less fortunate... a hideous injustice. With them and *for* them in my heart... I had to be passed.

Refusing now to even contemplate rejection from the Board, I lost myself in work at the tea rooms. There, I'd stay back 'til almost dawn, scrubbing the bottoms of pots or endlessly rearranging the stock in the pantry, fridges and freezers. Eventually, with a mind completely anaesthetised, sleep would afford temporary sanctuary from the haunting spectre of dread. Cocooned safely under the covers, lying safely in his embrace, it was for Greg alone right then I wanted to be whole and complete, repaying all his support and loyalty.

At the end of August, 1986, the letter finally appeared in the letterbox. I couldn't bear to open it alone, stuffing it into my bag and jumped on the tram to Greg's work in the city. Trembling with excitement, I tapped on the window to catch Greg's attention. Waiving the letter marked Department of Obstetrics and Gynaecology, I mouthed the words "It's here...See you at the juice bar for lunch?" pointing across the road at our little spot. Not about to wait for lunch, Greg threw a towel over the head of a semi-shampooed matron, running out the door to drag me off my feet along Collins St to the juice

bar. There we snuggled into a booth, with his arms tightly around me, I clawed open the envelope to read,
"With the confidence of the entire Board, we recommend that you be approved for Gender Reassignment surgery at the earliest convenience."

For ages we sat there, quite blank, dabbing tears from each other's eyes as the fruit and vegie juice settled to sediment at the bottom of our untouched glasses.

The letter from the Board contained a whole heap of legal forms which needed to be signed by lawyers, to which Greg again eagerly dragged me through the streets. These forms were witnessed and signed to state that I was of sound mind and gave complete authority for a surgeon to perform, in detail, what needed to be done to make me functionally female. The completed medico-legal form could be presented to any surgeon I chose myself or appointed by the Board. Having voluntarily jumped the two year period required to qualify for Medicare's government funds to pay for my surgery, Felicity gave me the details of a good plastic surgeon who specialised in gender reassignment, whom I'd need to pay myself.

Further easing my mind, Felicity introduced me to two other friends who were 'created' by Dr Abrams and were keen to show off the skilled craftsmanship. Apart from the convincing external appearance of the work, they showed me they had plenty of satisfactory depth, providing I wasn't considering taking on a horse, and that they both had very pleasurable sensation, capable of reaching climax. Although, they too reminded me, there were no guarantees of any sensual response after surgery, the deluxe model designer vagina was definitely for me! I chose to see Dr Abrams.

The doctor's secretary chirpily arranged a consultation appointment almost immediately. Every cog in the wheels of a process to take my body, rearranging

BODYCAGE

things here and there... changing every facet of my existence, began to click into place. It did actually feel like stepping into an assembly line machine. One which would convey me along through its portals, adding bits here and taking away bits there, to churn me out the other side, brand-spanking new and a date of manufacture, without a warranty, stamped on my behind. There was to be no turning back in fear, giving up the challenge or the dream, as I'd stepped onto a convey belt mechanism of metamorphosis.

Arriving at the doctor's suites it was a relief to be greeted by his motherly nurse. I'd recognised her as having smiled sympathetically and encouragingly at the auditorium room at the Women's Hospital, when the Board gave its verdict of me. How could I have forgotten the matronly vision with the perfect beehive of red hair, in her crisp starched, mauve uniform, smiling the same as she was now at the surgery? The image of proficiency clasped my hand with such care and tenderness that it felt overwhelming to be so gently led into the sweet, nurturing, feminine world.

"Hello Riannon, Love. I'm Cecilia." Her older generation raw Australian accent made me smile as comfortably as when I'd been greeted by of some of my school friends grandmothers. "I knew you'd make it through with flying colours! When I heard that quip about being rescued by the Navy, I knew you had to be a woman... I'd thought the same answer myself!"

"Am glad you didn't think I was just a tart then!" I clasped her hand tightly back.

"No, Riannon... You know it's not your fault you weren't born a woman...but at least anyone can see that you are a lady. And there's a lot to be said for that in this world." Feeling very flattered that she'd noticed such a thing, I thanked her for having taken time in her training about transgender cases to come to the hospital that day. Having already met several of us and cared for them both pre and post-operatively, she was very comfortable and familiar with the whole routine... even if I were not.

Doctor Abrams, in the manner of a debonair movie star, put me also immediately at ease. If anything, he made the whole procedure seem as simple as having a tooth out! My tall, handsome Ashkenazi Adonis was incredibly caring, punctuating his guidance with the gentlest reaffirming touches. Even the most embarrassing details of the procedure I'd been hesitant to broach, he'd already preambled, explaining them in a delicate manner with charm, humour, consideration and respect. Feeling almost ashamed, I blurted out the one question I could not get from my mind, plaguing me with concern, gnawing constantly.

"Doctor, I was wondering...if during any of your surgeries... you have ever... errrmm... Well, have you ever caused an injury that required a patient to end up with a colostomy bag?"

"You've obviously heard of some of the horror stories, Riannon. And that is a very real *possibility* during surgery... I have to be honest about that. As you know there are a lot of things which can go wrong, but as yet, rest assured, I have never had this complication with any of my work." Moving measuredly from his seat in front of me, he walked around the desk, sitting on it by my side. With a gentle hand resting firmly on my arm, he promised that if anything did go wrong, he'd have the best specialists on standby.

"Just meeting you today, Riannon... and reading through your notes, I can assure you that it means as much to me to do my best to help make your life complete."

I sighed a big relieved smile again, asking if he did cut my bowel by accident that any new colostomy bag should be a designer one with matching gloves, then I'd not feel so bad! He told me I was a dreadful woman for saying that, but had a good laugh all the same!

"You're such a warm person, Riannon, with a body that is in fantastic shape for any woman. It will be a pleasure for me to help put everything together, the way it should be. You'll have a great life ahead of you... I'm sure." I was on the conveyor belt, and that man was so smooth he could have strapped me to a belt in a saw mill... I'd still have sailed off confidently trusting him.

Calling big sister, Karen a few days prior to surgery was a necessity I'd dreaded as the hospital need a contact of next of kin in case of the dreaded worst case scenario in hospital. Even though she'd made her opinion of this path well clear to me already, I thought it best to let her know what was going on. Also, as the only link now with my family she was at least begrudgingly communicative though mainly as I'd often send money to help with her son and new baby daughter.

"Well, Ian... I think you should pray to the Lord for forgiveness." Well, that stumped me as she explained she'd found her version of spirituality in an evangelical church and proceeded to dispense her understanding, God-fearing advice. "God made you a *man*, Ian, and what you're doing is sinful. You should stay a man, meet a nice girl and settle down and have kids or something."

"Karen, if God made me a man, He certainly did a pretty weird job of it. And would you mind not calling me *'IAN'* ! It feels ridiculous, and by the way, why are you so intent now on calling me a *man* ? You used to call me nothing but names when we were kids and I was supposed to be your *brother*. You tried to make me feel as much like a freak as possible. So what the hell type of cruel, unfair trick would it be to have me marry a woman and expect that to be a worthwhile expression of God's will for me?! Some *husband* I'd be able to make.". I could not believe that I was spending forty cents a minute to listen to this abuse.

"It's just evil what you're doing, I know it's not what God wants. People who do things like this are all sick!" Wondering how she thought she knew what God wanted or not, I let her rail. "You hear of these people all the time, dirty homosexuals and child molesters... all of 'em. They should all be taken out in the desert and shot 'n buried." The rant would have gone on forever and ever, Amen, had I not given her *my* shot.

"God often gives us a cross to bear too, Karen, perhaps to learn about ourselves and other people. This is the cross I have to bear and besides, He also gives people intelligence to use medical technology and their skills to fix these types of problems to help people improve their lives. I for one will appreciate that gift and know for sure that Dr Abrams is very gifted in what he does and realises *he'll* help me live the life I want to live. Not to live the hypocrisy you're asking me to live!"

"Doctor *ABRAMS*, huh... Jewish, of course, that figures. You'll be sorry you're letting these people make money out of your misery, Ian... you'll see."

The milk of her version of Christian kindness was now too much to bear. I didn't want to further incense matters by telling her my surgery was being done in Masada Hospital in an affluent Jewish suburb, wondering how well she knew about the fortress of Masada. There the Jewish people had held out to the last before ending their own lives rather than face a hellish retribution from the Roman army for their uprising some two thousand years ago. Masada Hospital now seemed all the more a fortuitous omen

BODYCAGE

than a scary medical ordeal. Asking if she'd mentioned anything about this to my mother, as I thought of her often, going through all this without her knowing or support, her cold reply was devastating.

"Mum said she thinks it would be better if you died on the operating table."

"Tell Mum not to blame herself please, that's all I ask. It wasn't her fault I turned out this way. I'll call when it's all over."

Flicking through a magazine a week or so later, I came across a prayer for the day which stood out as a kind of 'equal opportunities' decree from God Himself about us all. Cutting it out, I simply popped it into an envelope addressed to Karen, hoping she'd understand when she read the words quoted in terms familiar to her now, from the Book of Galatians 3:28,

"In Him the distinctions between Jew and Gentile, slave and free man, male and female, disappear; you are all one in Christ Jesus."

Those words of advice will stay with me and be shared with anyone who looks for excuses to focus on perceived differences or betterness of one of us over the other on a planet we all share... and I remain truly grateful for them. It may seem obscure that such thoughts were being pondered and questioned in my mind, but being about to undergo a change so profound in myself physically, brought up consequences in my spirit and soul equally as much. The spirit and soul needed to know and be assured too that this decision was right and justifiable by anything we could call God, the Universal Mind, the Absolute or our special Mother-Father Creator. The event of stepping from one world to the next challenged me as much as facing thoughts of death itself... and what may or may not come after that!

Rehana Incognito

With my sister's 'warm wishes' still ringing in my ears, the morning of the 21st of September seemed to be moving in slow motion. Having hardly slept at all with anxiety about this day unfolding, I just lay quietly watching Greg still fast asleep, thanking God that *he* was there for me. He'd taken the day off work to take me to the hospital and be there for what time I'd need him. Streaks of sunlight filled the car as it flashed through all the trees on the avenues to the hospital, as I admired them all slowly coming into their full spring bloom. I too was off to be born in a spring from a long, bad dreamy sleep which was mostly cold and dark, very dirty at times and a struggle to break through the surface! In a kind of dread, I knew I was off for a type of rebirth, but knew on that day, part of who I was would die. Suddenly feeling an overwhelming sadness for a lonely little, confused boy who never really felt he was, I clutched my little overnight bag of hospital goodies.

Struggling for something to stop any tears, I looked into the bag at my sensible nightie and recalled a story of one girl's operation. She'd swished through the corridors in a see-thru negligee, setting a trail of heart monitors beeping in her wake, as one by one elderly men and heart patients clutched at their chests! Greg looked over and laughed nervously too.

"What are you laughing about, Bunny-Buns? I'm scared to death and it's you who's having the operation! Can't even think what to say really." Greg turned the car into the long driveway up to the hospital. "Don't worry, just think of Dr Abrams as a nice friendly rabbi performing a pretty radical circumcision." Giving Greg a vicious look, I told him I had no idea he could be so sick and remembered not even feeling my legs as I walked to the Admissions desk.

BODYCAGE

Thankfully, it was Cecilia who came to take me to my little private suite.

"I'll be here for you every day, Honey... Don't go getting worried about a thing, alright?" Putting me instantly at ease, she took my bag, helping me feel at home in the room. After taking a shower and scrubbing myself all over with the antiseptic wash, I put on the surgical gown, popped my hair into the little green paper cap and climbed into bed to eagerly await the pre med injection. With Greg sitting quietly by the bedside, the time ticked by as the medication took effect. Greg looked ever-impatiently at the clock, holding tightly to my hand. Meanwhile I was singing some song to myself, slipping in and out of awareness of night and day, awake or asleep...

"Girl.... you'll be a woman....soon..." Who the heck sang that? I fell asleep again, then woke as quickly to look over at Greg, seeing his concern at my acting strangely.

"I know, Greg... I just want it all over as soon as possible too. Thanks for being here." I was getting weepy and more emotional, barely able to think straight or stay awake as the medication had taken further effect. "If anything happens to me... remember, I love you very, *very* much." He kissed me goodbye as an orderly had slipped me onto a trolley, waving all the way down the corridor until I turned from his sight. Intermittently watching and counting the lights on the ceiling and looking into the eyes of the orderly, who just kept smiling back, I soon was parked up in the operating theatre. Recognising Doctor Abrams eyes twinkling at me from over his surgical mask, he leaned over.

"Are you alright, Riannon? Won't be long now and you'll be back tucked up in your bed... and it'll be all over."

Rehana Incognito

Not sure if my mouth was moving or not, I slurred that I hoped he'd do his best for me while I slept.

"Of course I will... Now I am going to give you this little shot... and I'd just like you to count from ten back to...."

Next I was aware of people moving about my bed and I was trying to think of ten, nine, eight... before realising I was not in the theatre, I was back in my room! Peeping through one eye, I noticed it was pitch dark outside. Hours had past and my head was being turned away from the window.

"Come on, Sweetie, don't fall back asleep. Try and wake up now...It's all over. You did really well and you're back in your own room." Cecilia appeared to take form by my side like she'd been teleported in Star trek. Trying to mutter that question which needed to be asked, my lips were moving, yet nothing intelligible came out.

"You're still a bit groggy, Hon..." Cecilia leaned close to my head. "I can't make out what you're trying to say... try it again..." Quickly registering that Greg was in the room, I started to come more alive, running my hands frantically over my abdomen, I gasped,

"*Ith* there a *colothtomy* bag?"

"No, Darling," Cecilia laughed with Greg grinning along with her. "Everything went so smoothly."

"Oh... great," I again murmured groggily, realising the time was late. "Have I missed Dynasty?"

I must have truly been medicated to the hilt. They had actually sat me up to watch Dynasty apparently, though I have no recollection of having done so! I recalled opening my eyes again a couple of times to see Greg's head lying on the pillow next to mine. Now and then he'd gotten up to soak a cloth, dabbing my head through the night as my temperature soared.

Somewhere through that night, I'd awoken to find Greg had gone and a nurse with short, cropped hair was

BODYCAGE

roughly taking my temperature, pulse and respirations, prodding and moving me like a rag doll. Asking what time it was she brashly replied it was 4 A.M. Turning away, I wished to see Cecilia's smiling face, knowing it was not long 'til dawn and her motherly care would be there in the morning. Closing my eyes again in exhaustion, I sank back into the pillow, deliriously wondering what the new day would bring.

Surely, at seven am, Cecilia breezed into my room like a mini whirlwind, fussing about me and seeing I was comfortable. Thanking her for all she'd done, I mentioned the manner of the nurse through the night.

"Oh...that bitch," Cecilia shocked me, "I had to give her a piece of my mind this morning at handover. You let me know if she's less than congenial with you again. I'll soon have her sent to another ward."

"She didn't really bother me, Cecilia. It was just her manner... she just didn't seem to want me there and was a bit abrupt." I felt bad that I may have gotten her into trouble, but as an ex nurse myself I knew how to be gentle and kind with a patient, even if they were dead!

"What did you give her a piece of your mind for though?"

Cecilia propped about three pillows behind me after giving them a good pounding to fluff them up as she told me about the incident with the other nurse.

"Well, as I left you last night at the end of my shift, I was letting the night staff know about your condition when that cow said 'oh, yeah...what does *IT* look like?'. I was furious and told her you're not an 'it' and you look a lot more feminine than she ever will! That shut her up."

"Oh well, I've had worse, Cecilia. You can't please everyone I suppose." Hell, I felt like I'd been run over by a tank.

Rehana Incognito

"Never you mind about it, Ri. Don't concern yourself... you just get plenty of rest... you're going to need it." Wisely telling me to go back to sleep if I really wanted to, I did... thinking what a rotten cow that nurse was and hoping that such events would be few and far between now that my surgery was over. Cecilia busied herself, adjusting drip tubes winding out from under the sheets from God knows where as I slipped off again...and again.

On my next more alert awakening, Cecilia asked if I'd like to take a look at my new 'water works'. Peeling the sheets gently back over the little tent frame which had been placed to keep the bedding off my middle, she propped me up a little more, holding a large mirror between my legs. Before having a chance to say that I was still feeling very nauseated and not quite prepared to actually *look* at it, I remembered the words of April Ashley in her wonderful 'Odyssey'. She'd looked down after surgery and thought it looked like a cross between a patchwork quilt and a pound of chopped liver.

"It's alright, Love... Don't worry... looks like any other woman's piece of equipment that's just given birth and had an episiotomy. We always like the girls to look straight away to accept the fact that it is now there." Cecilia said they'd learnt such things through trial and error, telling me that one of the first girls done there had waited a while to look and must have been one of those who'd slipped through the assessment process.

"When we finally got to show her what was now there, I guess she only saw what *wasn't* there and went running through the hospital screaming 'they've cut my dick off. They've cut my bloody dick off!' My God, it was awful.... Didn't know what to do, Riannon. We didn't want that happening again. So, there you go, Sweetheart..." She stood gleefully behind the mirror bidding me look down. "Isn't that lovely?!" Seeing my face looking frail and washed out, I gazed over the curves of my breasts, down to the bare abdomen, past the curvy hips and proudly beheld my new genitalia.

"It's better than what I saw there last time I looked, Cecilia." It was an ordeal to have sat up, straining to look down there, all that conversation... and seeing the fine workmanship of Dr Abrams for the first time, with tubing coming out of my urethra, all bruised and oozing. Passing out once again, I crashed back into the pillow.

Rule Number One Of Sex-changing-

1. If You Like Using What You Already Have For Anything Other Than Peeing, Don't Go Cutting The Bloody Thing Off!

You'll run screaming through a hospital ward, upsetting nice people. Furthermore, if you don't ruin your life and others'... there and then, you soon enough will. If you enjoy what you got between your legs and found someone to enjoy it with you- Keep it there and don't waste the Health Service's time and finances... or your own. You've been nicely warned and, believe me, Mother Nature doesn't make *that* many 'mistakes' either with gangs of men all over the world who really *should* be women. Chances are those haunting, tormenting problems are deeply psychological and sociological ones, which can be corrected and helped, with great difficulty and unlimited professionalism, yet better than dealing with the carnage and embarrassing mess of having mutilated a body to fly off in a rocket to a planet you can't really survive on. It's *that* life-changing.

It would be capricious to say I woke up after hours of blissful sleep moaning like a movie star- *"at last I'm a woman."* If indeed I were feeling anything like a woman it would have been Frankenstein's Bride. With more drips and tubing hanging out of my arms, the catheter draining into a bag of urine by my side, and a stench of the anaesthetic still in my lungs, such privileged delusions were banished. In fact, being pumped up with so much Pethadine, the next twenty four hours was a blur of bizarre dreamy visions in my sleep and equally as bizarre when thinking I was awake. If only I could have put them to paper at the time they would have made for a whole series of shows for the Twilight Zone. One minute a nurse had become Chrystal Carrington in "Dynasty", the next she'd turn around and was one of the lizard people from Teri Tinsel's drug induced hallucinations!

Greg was by my side at lunchtime, having bounded into the room with a big bunch of flowers, sitting quietly holding my hand, forever at his task of soaking the cloth and mopping my sweaty, streaming head. Lots more flowers duly arrived along with some nice cards which Greg dutifully read. "Welcome To Our World" the waitresses from Victoriana had written on their lovely card called "Congratulations- It's A Girl". They'd written that they missed me and hoped I'd be back at work soon. I didn't... only wanted to sleep! Greg sat me up to smell the flowers as the nausea of the anaesthetic rose from my lungs again. The room began to spin and a spray of vomit spattered all over the lovely flowers. Welcome indeed.

Frankenstein's Bride made a quicker recovery and healing than expected. Doctor Abrams had popped in to see me in the morning every day. He was pleased on my seventh day after surgery enough to allow me to go home. Knowing of my own past nursing experience, he made me promise to take it easy, allowing me to perform some of the little post operative care procedures by myself. Cecilia helped me pack my overnight bag, placed in the lovely cards, the stuffed

BODYCAGE

animals and prepared the little after care survival kit. Greg would be at work until early evening, so I'd go home and be his surprise when he came back to shower before coming to see me in hospital. Masada staff had called a cab and, as I hugged Cecilia goodbye with the promise to stay in touch, she gently walked me unsteadily to the cab and bundled me off.

With the morning sun streaming through the taxi window, I smiled as it bathed me in my newness, though I'd still felt abnormally hot, winding it down. The trees sped fast as the cool breeze comforted me, laden with their full open spring blossoms. Joining them in their opening too, I wondered at the prospect of my new life and promises of things to come. Sitting back, exhausted in the soft seat, I began to fade now... feeling myself now like Lucy Jordan in the ballad... She *"rode along through Paris with the warm wind in her hair.*

To her white suburban bedroom in a white suburban town...
dreamin' of a thousand lovers,
as she lay beneath the covers, singing nursery rhymes, she'd memorised in her daddy's easy chair."

Was I lying beneath covers? I wondered myself... Was this a lie or a cover?
Or would I soon *'run naked, through the shady streets... screamin' all the wayyyyyyy'* ? Who knows! I was nearly home with my exhausted body, feeling all the while gratefully exhilarated to be born again with the hope of making every dream come true. Dr Abram's Reassigned Woman Number 14 had been launched on the world... and *Pollyanna* had a pussy.

After another passing out on my own bed for two or three hours, I set out to the bathroom, attempting my own post-operative surgical care by trying the prescribed daily saline rinse. Into a quarter-filled tub I sprinkled half a kilo of sea salt. Submerging beneath the little waves, I lay back wafting the water gently inside me to cleanse and assist with the healing. A silastic rubber piece of tubing with tiny drainage holes had been inserted as far as it could go into my vagina to keep it spaced, making it easier for me to keep it clean and hold everything in place where it needed to be. A tiny cloud of blood drifted out as I peered down. Breathing a huge sigh of relief to see what was now there, even with the little cloud of blood, I lay back weary still from the whole ordeal, dreaming on, bathed in my salty ocean of amniotic fluid.

"Bunny? Is that you?" was the next thing I heard, calling at me from the living room. He ran through the apartment, realising the lights were all on and the radio was playing. Standing haltingly at the bathroom door as he always had been used to doing in the past, he was glad when I called out that I'd come home early to surprise him.

"Great, hon! Hurry up, I can't wait to hug you. I'm gonna get a beer outa the fridge...wanna celebrate? He was about to walk away.

"Sweetheart," my voice echoed as I sat up in the bath now wide awake. "You don't need to be standing out there anymore you know. I've got nothing I want to hide from you now.

Stepping shyly around the corner into my candle-lit cave of creation, he stood in the doorway staring in wonderment. Gazing up, I smiled with my hair bundled up in a ponytail on top of my head, lying in the saline sanctum of a warm womb, as Greg walked hesitantly to the side of the bath, kneeling down to let our arms find each other.

"You look so beautiful, Riannon and I'm so proud of you." He stroked along the length of my legs as tears streaked down both our faces. There he held me for

BODYCAGE

the first time... naked... as the day I was born! Not needing a slap on the arse this time either, I was already breathing... quite heavily, as we held our pose for what seemed an eternity or at least 'til the water got too cold. Greg helped me to stand, reaching for the biggest, fluffy white bath towel. Although I'd lost several litres of blood during surgery and some 10 kilos working out to be fit enough for surgery, I still felt like Botticelli's painting of the Birth of Venus come to life, stepping from my huge shell to scatter my love though the world!

As Greg held the towel open invitingly, I stood before him, proud and free, then was gently dabbed down before he tucked me into bed. Greg removed his clothes, jumping in beside me... drawing himself close. We dozed off quickly and easily together as the room darkened. Slowly, noises of people passing our window on their way home from work faded as the rattles of passing trams became more and more infrequent 'til all was still. Passing in and out of consciousness throughout that night, I felt that nothing else existed in the whole world but this man and myself, entwined together feeling as one as our very own breath.

CHAPTER THREE

The morning noises from the street outside, slowly brought me around. The trams shuddered by with Felicity's words forming themselves partly in the other dimension of consciousness between the worlds of night and day- 'Men are like trams, Riannon. If you miss one then another comes along soon after. Sometimes you get on and take a short ride and sometimes you stay on all the way to the terminus'. Her maternal advice and words of wisdom ricocheted through my head with the early morning traffic passing the bedroom window. Life resumed its normal routine for me, though restricted to around the house. For several days the only sojourn I could make was as far as the corner delicatessen without blacking out, whilst Greg enjoyed taking care of our every need including the unremarkable breaking in of the man-made virgin I'd become. It seemed an awkward, clumsy event with little pleasure involved on my part and a feeling that I had something totally alien now happening inside me. After speaking with most of my straight girlfriends and learning so much more, that wasn't such a bad thing and rather quite the norm with most girls' first time!

By Christmas 1986, I had settled in to work again as seasonal parties and entertainment at the Victoriana took so much of my time. I was grateful that we now opened on Sundays for afternoon Devonshire Teas, gratefully taking the extra shifts to help get those credit card payments quickly down. The Victoriana had become popular with the endlessly disgorging busloads of Japanese tourists who were always good for a laugh and a chance to improve my Japanese. The temperature extremes had abated as my body settled in to its final form in every way, matching an image in the mirror which I could never have believed.

BODYCAGE

Confidence increased with every step I took, that all about me was how it should be, relishing taking a shower at the local swimming pool, totally naked like any other woman without a second thought. Slinking through the steamy change rooms I felt like one of the girls in Malcolm McClaren's video of "Madame Butterfly". Yet, several times, as my body grew stronger and fitter, swimming up and down those lanes I cried so much I am sure I flooded the pool. Not really knowing why I was crying, I only felt relieved that my eyes, being red with the chlorine, would not have betrayed my weakness.

On the warm, sticky Christmas Eve we all gathered in the kitchen at Greg's mother's. Aunts and cousins helped as we organised the carnage left behind by the some fifteen or so children and a barbeque banquet buffet. Bundling some of the wonderful gifts we had been given for our new, bigger flat into a huge bag which Greg's brother held open for me, their mother's voice called out,

"Ian!"... A poison-tipped arrow may as well have shot through my insides from across the patio as we both looked up in that direction, equally both almost replying! Mercifully, Ian... Greg's brother, shouted back "Yes?" before I could. Granting his mother's request, he despatched more 'tinnies' out of the 'esky' for the men in the back yard, standing around the barbeque like a bunch of scientists controlling events in a nuclear reactor. That was a close call, and I'd have to watch out for that one in future. Greg stood by the sink, stifling snickers, as he had endured a similar experience when Karen had called our flat asking to speak to an 'Ian'. Greg had said there was no Ian there but he had a brother called Ian to which Karen had replied she had too and this was his number. Up until then Greg had never asked nor even wanted to know, but thanks to Karen and her attitude, he did... and we both found it an amusing coincidence all the same.

 The patio door squeaked open as Greg's Aunt Connie came in to say goodbye with her children to whom she'd seen I'd taken a great liking, remembering presents for them all. Telling us how glad she was to see we were together and seemed to be going strong, I was gob-smacked again as she asked if we planned to start a family too.

"Greg's all the baby I can cope with right now, Connie...aren't you, Darling?" He snickered, sidling up to escort me out to say goodnight to the leftover men folk in the garden.

"She's such a lovely girl, isn't she Sheryl?!" I heard Greg's blue-rinsed grandmother say to a chorus of "yeah, she's bloody lovely" from a few of the guys. Feeling all the while comforted to find acceptance with a wonderful family in a suburban Australian dreamscape, which I could barely have dared imagine in my own family life, the thought gnawed in the back of my mind that one day they'd all know the other me. My dark, secret, guilty past would be exposed... and, like an impostor at a regal celebrity ball, I'd be unceremoniously ejected! Although I enjoyed them all immensely (and swear to this day that the character of Kath, in the Australian TV comedy "Kath and Kim", was based on the life of Greg's mother), it was always a relief to leave their company lest I inadvertently let anything slip. Trying ever more ardently to remember, when people asked about my childhood, to always say "when I was a child" and not to slip as I used to nearly do, completely giving myself away saying "when I was a little boy." It never felt right to say "when I was a young girl" or whatever... because I was not... and it only seemed deceptive for me to say it. For the sake of my own conscience and integrity, I stuck to "when I

BODYCAGE

was a child" but, if anyone referred to me as a girl when little, of course did not correct them!

Greg must have picked up on my love for children over Christmas, noticing how much I enjoyed them. He'd come home soon after with a little puppy for me, only a few weeks old, still needing to be fed through the night as his mother had birthed too many and one less puppy to feed would make it easier for her. Greg promised he'd fix all the feeding with the meat as the puppy grew, knowing well I'd not cope with that. I'd wished he'd gotten me something like a tiny little Chihuahua that could live on a tin of tuna for a month, sparing me the revulsion of meat! However, Greg had taken the little German Shepherd, Labrador cross from one of his band mates, bringing him home on a day his favourite football team, Essendon ("The Bombers") had won their game, so we called him Bomber.

Bomber became my pride and joy, coming everywhere with me in my huge shopping basket, even sitting on the counter as I did the banking with no-one even minding when he pee-ed all over their 'deposit' slips, as he was so cute. He became known everywhere as my little baby, propped up from my basket so he could sniff from the window on the tram with everyone wanting to start conversations because of him. Soon not a shopkeeper or tramp outside a pub did not know us... in fact we knew everyone in my whole neighbourhood.

As if Bomber were not enough to keep me busy, Greg set up an enormous fish tank, full of every tropical fish imaginable, spending a fortune sometimes on just one fish which would often have dropped dead the next day. Telling him I'd have been just as happy with a goldfish you could keep in a bucket of pee for a week and it would live, I could only shake my head in exasperation as the aquatic world took over our living room. Fish tank completed, Greg came home yet again with big cage and the cutest little yellow budgie forlornly huddled in a corner of it.

"Got sick of you ranting all the time to Bomber... thought I'd get you something that might talk back to you one day." He proudly placed the little parakeet on the coffee table. Naming him Pepsi, as he gave me such a lift, I promised not to cook a chicken in his presence, though admittedly almost fricasseed *him* as he once flew into a chip pan, dive-bombing around the flat. Fortunately, I was speedy with the spatula, yet still could not bear the thought of him in his cage all the time except to go for his snacks or to sleep... So he remained a free-range parakeet most of the time. Having completely filled the flat with all manner of household plants and balcony like a small commercial herb farm, I realised soon I'd been trying to create my own little Paradise world of a Garden of Eden... much as I'd done as a child though never really quite succeeded.

"Christ, Ri... when are you going to ease up on these indoor plants?" Greg, ducked under the biggest Monstera Deliciosa I'd ever seen, having dragged it home from a car boot sale for $20 one Sunday morning.

"I'm gonna need a bloody machete to get through my own house one day."

"I'll stop when I've bought a Triffid and it's eaten you...OK?!" I realised then we'd soon need a house... and more importantly, a garden. We could have more animals, more birds and more plants- I'd be in Heaven, albeit an outer Melbourne suburban one which is all we might afford. The only drawback to that was we were actually quite *poor* ! We spent most of our money on pets and plant life, rent, running a car and paying off my womanhood! Lady Bancroft, Star of South East

BODYCAGE

Asia's Strip Scene Circuit, had the most perfect solution.

Rehana Incognito

BODYCAGE

PART FOUR

Rehana Incognito

BODYCAGE

CHAPTER ONE

"Honey, with a body like yours," cooed Lady B across a champagne glass which seemed perpetually replenished. "You gotta get out there and make money out of the bloody thing... one way or another." She reclined on her sumptuous chaise-longue, alluring 'come hithering' to Greg and myself, somehow demonstrating her point. Although she now had a body which looked well as if it had born several children, I could hardly help but think she looked like an x-rated, younger version of Barbara Cartland lying there dispensing advice to the lost and lovelorn. A dazzling presentation of all her memorabilia of promotional pictures and photos from her days on the circuit made the possibilities clearer and tempting to me. A lifetime of a body which brought nothing but shame, frustration and imprisonment to me had left its mark. Would people really *pay* to see *me* peeling my kit off slowly on stage in foreign countries... or anywhere?

Gripped by doubts once again, I grappled for excuses.
"I could never get away with something like that, Lady B. I got the memory of a goldfish... I'd never learn routines and stuff. I'm OK with my little job at the restaurant and what would you do there without me?" I could have gone on and on with the avalanche of doubts and excuses not to have to spread my wings to improve my situation.

"Riannon... you're fucking nuts. How much intelligence do you think it takes to learn to be a professional stripper? Have you ever tried to have a conversation with one of those girls? For Christ's sake they couldn't understand a conversation with more than two or three sentences in it... And I bloody well did it, didn't I!" Felicity told me I had the grace and countenance of a big cat, walking around her restaurant like a panther on the prowl and everyone had noticed, remarking on way too many occasions that they wondered why I was working there. She said I'd walked upstairs to enter the dining room many a time when the last kitchen orders had come through with some noticeable stirrings and woops when people had thought I *was* the stripper, booked for a party or whatever. I had actually noticed and laughed it off.

"Every guy in the place has their tongue hanging out of their heads with you slinking around in there, Riannon. I was going to suggest ages ago that you might as well get paid for it. I've seen and learnt so much from travelling around and it's got me to where I am now. I'd be selfish to want to keep you in my kitchen and never experience it." Lady B, jumped from her repose, bumping and grinding across her parlour in a sudden demonstration of her skills. Thinking she had some pretty good moves, I kind of realised she'd mainly just given one huge shimmery shake and it was the whiplash which kept her still swaying! Who knows, but Greg had certainly been captivated.

"You can do it, Love," he beamed, nodding with increasing fervour. "You've got one of the best bodies I've ever seen and are smart...and quick. You'll pick it up in no time, won't she?" He and Lady B seemed to have some conspiratorial deal going on as he promised to work with me on a double act performance with Lady B as our instructor and choreographer. Like Pepsi flying from his cage, this little golden bird flew straight into the chip pan.

Lady B agreed that I'd probably be a nervous wreck for sure, as my own boyfriend promised to use all his experience as a stage performer with his band to help me get comfortable with stripping my clothes off for total strangers in faraway lands! Agreeing that it would be a great way for us to see some of the world, have

BODYCAGE

fun and get our debts out of the way with more to spare... Lady B arranged times for us to come by and begin our training.

Drilling us like an army sergeant for weeks, she'd circle around us with a huge cane, whacking me into the correct pose or posture. Feeling confused enough about how to suggestively remove a garter belt and stockings without trembling at the thwack of a cane for an out of place nuance, I persisted. She'd drilled us well as I'd do clandestine little strips at the gym, at the swimming pool or fall asleep stripping off my clothes to any music still playing in my head or by the bedside until confidently convincing myself that I was, though quite terrified, now a stripper.

With Greg in a state of constant arousal at having a live-in stripper performing for him daily, nightly or whenever we got a chance, two months flew by. Greg had a much better memory for the routines and had collected all our show music to splice together for our routines. He'd worked out lots of little signals and clues to help me remember the routine, lest I forget... which often I did, so felt confident to have him by my side at least. Our opening number, we'd decided was a kind of tribute to my musical heroine, the great diva queen of androgynous drama, Annie Lennox. In a kind of Sado-Maso routine we'd decided to open with "Love Is a Stranger"...

"Love is a stranger in an open car
to tempt you in and drive you far away..."

I still nearly pee when I hear it to this day, reminding me of the sudden stage fright when it came on! I'd be dancing alone, in my own little world to the song showing me on my own, dreaming of the love to tempt me in and drive me far away.

"and I want you
and I want you....

and I want you, something sad obsession."
 Greg would appear next, the archetypal 'stranger', joining me in some tight, black leather gear and a mysterious, masterly mask straight from a dungeon, ready to 'touch me and tease me as we stumbled into daybreak'...as the song said! After playing around with that for a few minutes, the song went into yet another Annie number with George Orwell's "1984"-themed "Sex Crime". To that increasingly intense and dramatic piece, we managed our twirls and simple acrobatics as I got down to a red, black-laced corset and long, silky black, slit-to-the-thigh pencil skirt which he gleefully ripped off. Playing out some forbidden crime to be doing what we were doing, the next part of the routine was to the Dark Diva herself- Grace Jones and her song 'Suffer'. Greg had to give me two great simulated slaps in the face as the man in the song said,
"Take that..." whack,arrgghh
and that...." whack, owww. My Velcro corset had been ripped off and flung aside as I tossed my head back twice. Feigning the slaps had hit me hard, thrusting out my chest in a mighty heave, I arched back on my knees.
 I wanted to finish the routine with another Grace Jones song which bizarrely had followed the inadvertent 'theme' we'd choreographed for our show. The song I wanted was called "Saved". Being truly borderline retarded with any complex routines, we decided not to push that particular show any further lest I fluff it all up. So "Saved" (*"I'm no longer depraved... Look at me... I'm just a simple girl."*), was not to be. Acting out my 'salvation' from the strangeness of love, feeling complicit in a crime and all the suffering of what I'd taken love for, as our art well and truly imitated our lives, would be for a whole other show! For this show, reaching the finale of twirls around Greg, who hoisted

BODYCAGE

one of my legs over his thigh, I fell back clipping off the hook and eye of my knickers to be left in a flesh-coloured, tiny G-string. Feeling as nakedly ashamed as Adam and Eve entering disgrace and outcasting in the Garden of Eden, we skipped merrily off together as our music faded out.

CHAPTER TWO

1987

Lady B hastily arranged publicity shots, more costumes, putting us in touch with her previous agent then resident in Hong Kong. He too-gratefully, I'd thought, accepted us coming straight away for bookings in Hong Kong, Japan, Taiwan and Korea. With our car and belongings in storage and Bomber and Pepsi packed off to stay with "nana and pop" for a few months we flew off, aspiring to make fortunes in the Orient. Stopping over in Bangkok, I locked myself in the hotel room, barricading the door with a chair to rest from the trip. I didn't mind Greg going out with a bunch if Aussies he'd met on the plane as I was terrified, which was pathetic really as Bangkok is about the safest city for anyone to be in. However, with all the crowds and feeling too many stares at the tall, blue-eyed blonde, I was too edgy to go out playing tourists. I *did* mind when Greg got back, explaining he'd spent all night trawling from bar to bar with them watching such weird shows advertised on billboards outside bars like-
20:30 Woman with boy.
20:35 Boy with boy.
22:00 Woman with dog,
22:05 Boy with dog.... etc, etc.
Ping pong balls had flown all over the place of course to the Aussies' delight... and my disgust (I'd only ever thought that to be a tall, traveller's tale!)

Wondering how many of them might have been girls 'like me', I felt inspired to kick off a bit more with Greg.
"I can't believe you'd look at anything that disgusting Greg. It's filthy, degrading and sick." He knew not to try and crawl into the bed near me.
"Ahhh, Love... you don't understand. Men like that type of thing and it's the only work these girls can get. It

supports their whole families. You ought to be grateful anyway...'cos I only *looked*. Most men would do a lot more if their girlfriends weren't around." To Greg's disgust, he was left to set up camp on the sofa alone after that! Wondering how they could call themselves *men,* leaving women to a lifestyle of degrading themselves that way to make a living, I wondered where strength was in men to protect and provide for those more vulnerable. Where were princes and warriors and wizards who'd use all those qualities I'd expected men to *be* and to *have*? I didn't appreciate enough then that one of them snored blissfully on the sofa as I lay steaming about all the injustices done by his brothers in arms.

Felicity's grossly overweight, sweaty agent, Jeremy met us at Kai Tak airport on a heavily humid, smelly Hong Kong afternoon. Flapping effeminately, he was the stereotypical moustachioed, leather-queen type but extremely outrageous, flirting with any young Chinese lad who stopped to gawk. Our cab wound its way through clambering, crowded and noisy back streets to a decrepit-looking, rickety high rise Kowloon chicken coop just off the busy thoroughfare of Nathan Rd. Really handy for shops! After a final flirt with a mortified Chinese taxi driver and having uttered every Cantonese obscenity Jeremy knew, we exploded onto the footpath.

"Who gives a damn about that little bastard? I know he wanted me... they all do." Jeremy believed his every word. "They're just too closeted to say so, but Chinese boys are like Chinese food. You have one then five minutes later you could do with another." He threw the fare at the driver, uttering something unrecognisable but guttural enough to see he'd insulted the driver who quickly sped off. Greg and I lumbered our baggage up seven flights of stairs as there was no lift, passing a weird, obscure array of little Oriental businesses operating from every floor and doorway as the heat and humidity left us feeling we were walking slowly through the bottom of an overheated swimming pool.

We'd had little time to pass out on a bunk bed in our room, clearly designed for a Cantonese Lilliputian dwarf and a quick cold shower each, before Jeremy dragged us into the station. Whisked away in a flashy tube 'Hong Kong side' to club UA (Universal Artists... wow!), we were off for a dress run through of our show. UA was thankfully just a short walk from the station but even in that short distance I felt uncomfortably awkward at the constant stares and gaping of the crowds in the street, wishing to make myself invisible. I'd noticed in the tube, that over a sea of black-headed people it was only really Greg and I who stood out above the lot. Jeremy's outrageously flamboyant behaviour was an affront to all we passed but equally as confrontational to Greg with whom Jeremy wasted no time in trying to flirt with too!

"Why not, Greg? You've been sexually involved with Riannon for long enough now haven't you? It's no difference with a guy like me than with her... you know."

Greg had turned white and my blood had gone cold as we stood stopped in our tracks. "She just has a pair of tits and a plastic pussy, so that makes you already gay really, doesn't it?!" ... as if I had actually in fact turned invisible! Entering the lift to the fifth floor to the UA, I was truly aghast, defensively having the nerve to speak up against this assault.

"Greg has only ever known me and seen me like any *normal* woman, Jeremy. And I think there's a *huge* difference between you and me!" Expecting to be told to get on the next plane back to Melbourne, I looked

over to Greg with his mouth agape in disbelief, coming further to the defence.
"Look, mate..." Greg looked him straight in the eye, "I'm straight...*she's* the *woman* I am with...and that's it."
Ding, the doors opened on the fifth floor of a fairly plain office-type building. Wandering slowly down a grey corridor, we followed signs pointing to "Club UA". Not expecting by now anything too glamorous for our stage debut, we kept an open mind about it. Danny Chan, in a sharp business suit and kind of bouffant hair reminded me of the 'Dear Leader', Kim Il Song of North Korea, was introduced as the club manager. Giving us a warm welcome to his club, he too seemed over-grateful to have us there. Gazing around the club our eyes soon adjusted to the dim lighting, discerning that the place was actually a dive! Greg leaned over after knocking his head on a low-hanging, inverted paint tin light shade which had been punctured with holes for a cheap mirror ball effect of dotted lights on the shabby walls.
"This place is real fucking glamorous," he whispered holding up a grubby-looking glass set on the red and white checked, tatty plastic table cloth. "What the hell look do you think they're going for here?"
Peering up at the ceiling, I realised it was draped in real fishing nets which I'd thought, by the smell of the place, may actually still have contained rotting fish. With the state of the crumbling ceiling it was clear that the nets were there for practical reasons- to catch the bits of falling plaster before they landed in the middle of someone's meal or drink... or bring the roof down in the middle of someone's fabulous UA show!
"Dunno, Greg... I thought, with the checked table cloths, the tin lamp shades and nets and stuff it might be a poor rendition of a Tex-Mex seafood place. But maybe you're right... it's just a dive." Greg hurtled our

costume bag into the least cluttered corner of the change room which did double duty as a janitor's closet. Handing me a glass of beer from Mr Chan, Greg downed his in one eager gulp.
"I don't know what I've gotten us into here, Buns... and I don't trust that old faggot, Jeremy. I know you're nervous enough without having to perform in *this* place."
"Don't worry," I gave him a reassuring stroke, grateful for his concern, "let's just make the most of it...we're here now. It's only our first try at this so I guess we can just use it as practise and experience to see how we do." I lied through my teeth, just wanting to head straight for the airport and *home.*
"It's not that bad... really." My voice now wavered. Clearly Greg could see I was almost disappointed to the point of tears as I pushed aside jumbles of costumes and junk, to make way for the clothes we'd removed to get into our costumes. From out of the cluttered pile a *rat* skimmed over our clothes, shooting across my hand then disappearing just as quickly behind a wall.
 I must have fortunately passed out backwards onto Greg as Jeremy burst in, having heard a scream of which I'd had no recollection. Jeremy fussed about unconvincingly trying to professionally reassure us that we'd soon get used to the rats as rotting food was everywhere... as were the rats.
"Greg..." I now pleaded, trying to put my baggage back together, feeling just like my mother on arrival at Wittenoom all those years ago. "I want to go home... Get me out of here...now! Jeremy, this is *not* going to work." My pleading was not going to work either as two Chinese girls and a male dancer joined us in the closet, laughing hysterically at the whole thing. They were so kind and good-natured about it that gradually I

BODYCAGE

began to relax, accepting that sharing a change room with a rat might actually be an insignificant matter, all things considered. Another drink or two materialised before us giving me the courage to accept that I might be standing in a dark and dirty place right there, but I'd better find it in me to present the great show we'd worked so hard on shining forth with. Time to bloom in that dirt where I'd found myself planted!

The new friends had made us feel so at home that Greg and I decided if they could '*bare*' it, we could too. So I got myself prepared to bare it all too, well almost all. Easing my nervousness, the Chinese trio went on first to show off their new balletic, not-so-revealing strip show for the season complimenting the Australian 'stars'.

Greg and I stood stiffly like soldiers on parade as the trio tumbled back into the change room past us at the door waiting to hear our names announced. Edgily primed on adrenaline I recall hearing our music start... the "Love is a Stranger" segment. But my feet would not move to take me out onto the stage on the beat which should have taken me halfway across it! With a sharp shove from Greg, I was jettisoned out the door as auto-stripper piloted me numbly alone through the start of the routine.

In the crowd I could make out many other performers, all the bar staff, Danny Chan, Jeremy and even the cleaner-come-toilet-attendant. Robotically I went through it, absolutely relieved and grateful when Greg thundered out confidently to join me, dancing out his role as my punishing, controlling redeemer in all his studded leather finery! 'Captured and surrendered' to Greg by the end of the show, I lowered my leg from its pose over his thigh. Clasping his hand with a quick flourished bow we fled off together again with that feeling of Adam and Eve, exposed and vulnerable in our erroneous ways, dashing through a raging tempestuous storm which may well have just been the claps and foot stomping of our adoring new fans! It had to be, I'd thought, better than the wicked stick-wielding drillings of Lady B when Deena/Kylie had come along to peruse our act, calling out all the time- "Come of Greg... show us yer dick for fuck's sake!" Yep, she's a real *LayDEE* !

The club began to quickly fill as Mr Chan and Jeremy had both assured us our act was fine and looked great on stage. By 11 P.M the place was full and I could see why it was dimly lit, apart from camouflaging the shabbiness. All the patrons were men, some nervously clutching dirty magazines which they must have been spending some time riveted to before heading out to see some of their fantasies in the flesh. Occasionally they'd sneak further peeps at the magazines, nervously gazing around to see if anyone had noticed. Jeremy said they'd buy the magazines and get so worked up that they came to clubs like that as it was the nearest most would get to ever seeing anything like their dreams come true.

"Great, Jeremy," I sunk into my chair. "All that training in classical exotic striptease and now I am just a cheap thrill for these guys. I hope they realise the g-string doesn't come off in our show!"

"That's up to you," Jeremy wryly replied. "But remember, Riannon... if you do decide to do 'full show', they pay an extra $200."

"That's not even fifty Aussie bucks, Jeremy. They could never pay me enough to let them see me totally naked."

"Dahhrrrling, you'll soon change, you'll see." He folded his arms like he'd already had me all so worked out as Greg ended that conversation.

"Not while I'm around she won't be."

BODYCAGE

On our signal to head for the change room to prepare for the first proper show, butterflies hit my stomach feeling more like big hairy, deranged bats from hell. Hardly remembering which part of my costume went where, Greg came to the rescue, putting me together. The trio breezed through on cue, bouncing and giggling around, getting a really good eyeful of Greg standing in is little black crotch-hugger, jock strap g-string as he put the rest of his costume on. Annie Lennox music started again for all my world like the executioner's drum roll.
"Don't worry, Darlin'," Greg saw my mood change. "You're only out there on your own a couple of minutes and I'll be right here watching you 'til I come out. With a farewell hug, I tried to step forward on the right beat, missing it yet again as Greg gave the familiar shove, activating my circuits to performing mode! Catapulted onto the stage, auto-stripper kicked in again with some of Felicity's tips about playing up to admiring eyes in the crowd. Beckoning 20 and 50 dollar bills seemed to flutter everywhere as I made my way to gyrate before those who had the notes. Felicity's tip of the day from my last rehearsal came straight to mind. She'd suggested I put a finger dipped in fish paste up myself for that "authentic smell to drive the punters wild" as I danced anywhere near their faces in our show. She promised it would be great for tips as they'd truly loved that. Personally I'd already decided on a liberal dousing of tropical flavoured body oils! One by one they stuffed my stockings and garter belt with cash with a few making it into the cups of my corset. Not remembering a thing again, I was back in the change room plucking a $50 bill from the G-string up the crack of my arse before even knowing what had happened!
Following many more performance nights at the UA, I was perfectly relaxed as the shows ran flawlessly. With

Rehana Incognito

Greg proud of my effort, overcoming stage fright, Jeremy was satisfied we'd made the grade, Mr Chan was pleased he had more Westerners performing... and the rat kept his vigil spying us surreptitiously from his corner every night. We worked hard, three shows a night, four nights per week, zipping around Hong Kong and Kowloon by day seeing all the sights, finding it all very romantic until pay day came along.

Jeremy had told us we needn't pay rent at his place until our first month's pay at which point he told us he required most of it for our little shoebox room without even a window. Right there we knew we began to smell the biggest, stinking rat in Hong Kong. Realising, after we'd paid this 'extortion fee' to stay in the room, we knew there would not be enough money left to get through to the next pay day. Our hearts sank as Jeremy sharply suggested that, as I had a British passport, I could find an extra job in a bar. Calling Felicity in a panic, I was grateful that she gave me the number of a previous employer in a bar just behind the Holiday Inn on Nathan Road and quickly dialled the number.

A very caring and kind, classy English lady called Pat gave me instructions to Hankow Road, just a few minutes from our hideous block, to find "Bottoms Up" bar situated down the stairs in a large basement. Seeing the name on the sign above the door, I half wondered what the significance was of the neatly-arranged rows of peaches printed in black and white on the sign could mean. Greg and I made it into an almost twilight cavern, drawing back a heavy velvet curtain where a neatly-suited Chinese sentry of a doorman stoically bade us to wait as he went to announce us to Pat. Peering further into the bar we noticed what seemed to be a couple of different, very large booths. Each was an exotic dreamscape, themed

BODYCAGE

individually with separate, sumptuous colour schemes, fabrics and furnishings. In the centre of each of these cosy nooks, stood a circular bar with a central stool upon which sat draped over cushions, *topless* barmaids... looking bored to the back teeth at the lack of business at this early hour. The robotic sentry asked us to sit at a bar of our choice, order a drink... and Pat would be there shortly.

Hesitantly, we peeped into the room in front where a middle-aged Chinese woman sat in a black lace shawl, delicately placed on her breasts with just enough exposure of nipples to tantalise her guests, keeping the blast of the overhead air-con from freezing them like bullets! She was semi-reclined on an enormous cushion, swinging back and forth to pass the odd drink, fidgeting with cassette tapes at her little deck. Champagne-pink lighting around the purplish bar lit her skin flatteringly, giving it an illusory glow of a woman years younger. Only a couple of indifferent 'Grey Ghost' businessmen sat at her bar, engrossed in papers and forms. The woman in the opposite booth had no such saving grace of flattering lighting.

Clearly in her late forties, the very drunken Irish woman held more of an audience with a few local Cantonese men pretty much riveted to her near naked, scrawny form even though her dry, streaky breasts hung like strips of bacon, wearing a face which had clearly seen too much heartache, weathering and stress to be anything like pretty. She almost slid from her perch on the stool as the local men prepared to leave, hurling a rapid fire stream of fluent Cantonese abuse at them for not leaving a tip or buying her a $HK38 'Ladies drink'. That was the bar for us... and we took our seat. Ordering our now regular Long Island Iced Teas, we made a little conversation with the barmaid who introduced herself as Fidelma. She'd

Rehana Incognito

lived in Hong Kong some twenty or so years, married and divorced a Cantonese businessman and left in the lurch to "have to sit there letting these little bastards look at her tits to look after her two kids". Clamouring over her bar, she clumsily made an exit for the loo, taking a break to freshen up. As she noticed Pat's office door had opened, she made her way to meet us.

Immaculate and smartly groomed with long, thick black hair styled like a 1940s movie star, Pat was a middle-aged, very posh spoken ex-pat English woman who had lived in Hong Kong since the Korean War. With a genuinely warm and welcoming smile she sat by our sides, delicately placing her translucent cup of steaming jasmine tea on the bar, her tiny porcelain hands gave the gentlest of handshakes.

"I see you've met our Fidelma then," she chimed in that delightfully sweet, comforting Home Counties accent. "We're so grateful for Western women here that we tend to overlook little details like that, My Loves. We just let her take as many complimentary drinks as she likes and when she slides under the bar her shift's over for the night."

With a little sniff of a laugh I promised not to give any such problem, explaining that I had no experience with work like *this* before and happily presented my reference for managerial and catering work at the Victoriana Tea Rooms.

"No need for me even to look at that, Riannon. Felicity is a dear friend and anyone she recommends to me is welcome here. There's nothing too difficult for you to learn about this job, it's pretty straightforward. You don't even need to handle the cash. The waiters are around the bars and will present the bar bills, take them to the office and bring back change and all. You just sit in your booth, keep looking pretty, chat to guys and keep them laughing and happy. Take their drink

orders and present them to them... and play whatever of your favourite music you like all night. Sound good?"
"Sounds perfect to me... are you OK with it Greg?" He nodded that he was as Pat told us boyfriends could not come and sit at the bar during my shifts as it had understandably caused problems in the past due to the fact that girlfriends were of course sitting practically naked with strange men ogling their breasts and making passes. Pat, it seemed was terribly sincere, managing to maintain the reputation of running one of the few bars in Hong Kong which was not involved in extorting exorbitant hidden charges for unknowingly purchased 'Ladies Drinks' for unsolicited female company, or even being charged for some unrequested hooker sitting next to him. Pat's reputation rested on none of that at Bottoms Up.
"There's just one thing I was wondering Pat. Why the crate of peaches on the 'Bottoms Up' sign out in the street? And look, you got them all over your drink coasters too." Pat looked extremely confused then laughed in a kind of exasperation.
"Greg, run upstairs and take a look at that sign and come back and tell your girlfriend what those 'peaches' are." Greg dashed up the stairs to return in a flash, slowly shaking his head as if I were quite mad in anticipation.
"They're *arses*, Riannon... not peaches. A bloody bunch of all different arses!" He slapped his head in disbelief.
"Oops," I whispered over to him... "I told you I was useless with those ink blot tests, didn't I? Did any of those bums look like mine?" He promised we could both check for my arse look-a-like on the way out. There was just the one by the way!
As if she'd heard my whisper, Pat quickly explained that no *man* would ever have mistaken that assembly

of backsides as a fruit display... and that I would get sick of them asking to check to see if one of them was mine in the pictures. She also asked if we had seen or heard of Bottoms Up before anywhere. As we were sure we had not, she told us to rent a copy of the Bond film "The Man With The Golden Gun". We did and there we saw the bar where I was to sit as 'boobs in the basement' wearing only g-strings alternating to hip scarves, to chain belts and a thousand different pairs of interestingly exotic knickers, serving drinks, telling dirty jokes and playing nice music on the nights I wasn't dancing with Greg as Universal Artists!

Tunnel-visioned Chinese men would gabble away whilst riveted to my chest... unless they were alone. Otherwise they'd just slowly sip an overpriced drink they'd make last three hours before drifting off home to their wives in high-rise hen-houses as tourist ghosted in later in the evening. Remaining the consummate hostess, I laughed and bantered with the heat-weary tourists. US sailors on leave would spar with British navy personnel stationed in Hong Kong or floods of expats and local businessmen needing to see something of a Western woman in a sea of Oriental faces, black hair and probably not the most ample-bosomed ladies on the planet, were always good company. So long as they never tried to demean me for my job or reach across for a grab, things felt quite naturally comfortable to me. Having grown up with topless bathing and never having developed any stigma about my breasts being bare it felt mostly wonderful to be an object of admiration, though it never really sunk in. It was only when they just stared into them instead of noticing my face that I felt a tiny twinge of wondering if they thought I was some dirty piece of meat or was I appreciated like a fine statue in a museum?

BODYCAGE

Kidding myself it was surely the latter, I danced along to the music as best I could in limited space, learning to lean deeply across to pass drinks, presenting a sensuous angle for adoring eyes with a perky little upward bum thrust if I bent over. By the end of my shifts, I could barely stuff more $20 and $50 bills into the huge "Pat's Typhoon" cocktail balloon of a glass. Anyone who'd drunk just a little too much, stepping way out of line with me or the other girls quickly learned that those penguin-suited, wily Oriental waiters were all security and martial arts trained. In the blink of an eye any poorly-behaved foreigner would find himself on a quick tour of the back alleys of Kowloon which were not an attractive view from being kicked to the ground. As Greg had come to escort me safely back in the early morning hours after spending his nights watching TV or finding other Aussie men to hang out with, he got to know Pat quite well.

Pat clearly adored him, and indeed us both, in a very maternal way, allowing him to come that little bit earlier now and then to sit quietly at my bar for a drink as I finished shift... as long as he did not make it known to my guests that I was his girlfriend. Despite Pat's good intention, her wisdom and experience were actually well founded. With every man who flirted, buying me a 'Ladies Drink' or leaving a huge tip, Greg had seethed to himself that these were potential rivals and I could clearly see he was on the edge of striking out at them on several occasions. I could not blame him, having taken on a very mature role already in his life, yet knowing now where he *really* was, I'd have called him a boy... with all the emotional instability which came with the generation.

Sitting in front of the mirror in our change room at the rear of Pat's office, Greg watched me clad myself back into my civvies with increasing relief as each item went on, right down to the sensible sneakers to give my feet a break from the towering high heels. Step by step I was becoming his 'Bunny' again- The one he'd met, respected and fallen in love with, becoming more and more respectable and acceptable until even the long, false eyelashes were ripped off and stashed in their plastic box. I knew exactly what he was feeling, yet thoughtlessly blurted that I felt it would be better if he didn't pick me up at the bar anymore... to avoid putting himself through seeing me at work there.

Dejectedly gazing up to question my reflection he pleaded that I tell him I wasn't trying to break up with him.

"Don't you want me anymore, Bunny... Is that it?" He could see me every night being more open, communicating in ways I did not with him and being grandly compensated for it. To me it was simply work, though I did enjoy being able to talk with a lot of other English people and appreciated, after all I had been through, that these men actually found me of interest and worth. I too, found speaking to lots of men who'd led vastly different lives of exotic, worldly experience a fascination as well, all the while wanting to know more and wondering what I might be missing.

"I don't want you to take it that way, *Greg*. Of course I still want you...it's just uncomfortable for me to do the best I can in this job with you sitting there watching everything I do and listening to every word I say. That's what they're paying me for, Greg... and that's what *we're* living on." Turning to lean and hug him, he shockingly thrust me away, storming off alone into the hot, sticky night. Looking up to see him leave, I noticed Pat was standing there the whole time, having heard all we said.

"It's tough, Riannon," she fanned herself as perspiration dripped down her cheeks and neck then

into her cleavage. "You need to be in a good frame of mind to make these guys feel relaxed for their little piece of escapism... make them feel special."
"You're right... I know. I won't let him back before closing time again... It just makes me feel so guilty that this has hurt him so much." Pat gently rested her hand on my shoulder with a loving and understanding smile in the mirror as I gathered up my makeup and cassettes. Hurrying home through the smelly, humid streets, thunder clapped like the sound of an atom bomb as all of Niagara Falls seemed to have tumbled upon me. Still drenched, I'd crawled into bed next to Greg as he rolled to the wall, pretending to be asleep. Lying awake for hours, feeling like a total bitch, I listened to the rain before nodding off... thinking of the lovely card from the girls at Victoriana-
"Welcome to our world....."
"We can go straight back to Australia if this is too much for you, Greg." Was all I could manage to murmur as soon as I noticed he'd stirred.
"I'll be O.K. ... I think you're right though... that I just don't need to be seeing it and it won't get to me. At least I know that you won't let them take you out of the bar and you'll be there when I come for you." Without a kiss or hug, he slung a towel around his waist to head for the bathroom, closing our door firmly behind.
He was right to be concerned, having met the other girls who worked behind the bar. The 'menu' at the bars where we were sat mentioned the prices of all the drinks, including the ridiculous 'Ladies Drinks' for the bar maid or for any 'hostess' girl who used the bar to pick up clients to take out. Greg knew what it meant where it mentioned our 'Buy Out' fee of $HK500 to compensate the bar were I to go absent. Then it would be up to me to command an even higher fee from him for whatever else happened between us. I always just

said they couldn't do 'Buy Out' with me as I was attached. No problem of course as the bar usually had a few working girls plying their trade from Bottoms Up.

One Chinese girl had moved to Hong Kong from Beijing and didn't speak a work of Cantonese, as I noticed her isolation from any local people in the bar whether they were working girls themselves or one of the patrons. Also, it was clear that they had noticed well before I did that she was not the type of girl who had been born one either. It kind of amazed me that Chinese people could always tell a fellow Oriental was transgender, yet my Grey Ghosts compatriots seldom realised at all! Jessica reminded me of some forlorn, fallen, though kind of raucous empress. Watching her swing into action, generally extremely drunkenly, she slowly... snake-like... mesmerised her prospective quarry with exaggerated 'China Doll' antics. Giggling coyly, she'd play at demure, overtly pathetic compliancy until her 'squeeze' was completely fallen himself and ready to negotiate the rest of the proceedings for an hour or more of Jessica's private performances. Coiled around him like a gaily attired, perfumed anaconda about to swallow a pig whole, she'd lead them willingly away, one after another, 'til the bar had shut.

One night when business was slow for Jessica, she'd knocked back vodka after vodka between intermittent giggles and girly antics, followed by her staring off into some unknown distance before launching into those cat-screeching Chinese opera sounds, usually accompanied by rhythms of my Grace Jones tapes. Perhaps it helped her cope I'd thought. As she got more boisterous and desperate for a 'case' to go out on, she was getting the wariest looks, as one by one, guys slid away from her... except for one American, almost as drunk as she was. A ghastly, weather-

BODYCAGE

beaten Australian farmer, who'd bored me all night with talk of his vile life on a cattle ranch in the North West, listened in as she snared the American to buy her favours. He slid across to a stool by me, writhing around to dear old Grace Jones, sipping my exotic, expensive drink which was really a glass of coloured water.

"She's a bloody fella, Love," he breathed out of his fumes at me, stopping mid gyration and almost spitting my drink.

"Reckon I ought to tell that poor bastard he's about to blow five hundred bucks on a bloke?"

After my own brief life had finished flashing wildly before me, I leaned back over to whisper to him...

"Better not, Hon... perhaps the gentleman likes that type of *lady*, this is Hong Kong after all... Something for everyone.... And you could just ruin his whole night if you make a scene about it," I retorted.

"Oh, yeah...you're right, Love...bloody too right. Each to their own ya reckon?"

"Yeah... each to their own." And why wouldn't you just piss off and burst into flames somewhere too, I thought.

"Aghh, I think it's pretty sick anyway, if you ask me... the lot of 'em," he growled and snarled as Jessica and her punter staggered out of my little golden cavern.

"Well, diff'rent strokes and all that, hey... and I don't think anyone *did* ask you!" I just wanted him to go, half expecting a drink to come hurtling at my face. He simply lumbered himself unsteadily up, taking all his phobias to the next booth where the beautiful, American black Velvet waited for him at her bar. She had a mouth on her to put him right in his place. It wasn't long before she'd sent him off too, scurrying up the stairs.

Rehana Incognito

The long nights, working two jobs in smoky bars and clubs with the incessant heat, took more of a toll on me as every day passed. Mostly Greg and I would walk home in silence like Hansel and Gretel through the scary woods to step into a shower together in the soft light of a candle, just soaping each other down as we'd watch the day and its heaviness swirl down the drain with the suds. Now I'd smell heavily the alcohol on his breath too as he'd spend most of his nights with other Aussie guys trawling the bars in Wan Chai on the nights I was working at the bar. Still soaking after a cold shower we climbed into bed a few weeks later with Greg feeling frisky and me just lying there with that air-con madly rattling as all the faces which leered at me in the bar spun round in my mind. His boozy breath mixed with the unbearable heat was driving me nuts. In irritation I turned my head to dodge his kisses, sliding slightly from him.

"I can't, Greg...not tonight." Was this a weird welcome to the female reality... and was I having fun yet? With a huffy sneer he pushed me away, turning his back on me again to sleep facing the wall. Now staring at the ceiling, feeling totally alone... wondering what restlessness questioned if this was all there was, I desperately wanted *something* more, not knowing exactly what nor being able to grasp a hold of some deep, aching dissatisfaction. The thought of making love with Greg after weeks of acting as appetiser meat, and the relentless drain of energy as the same guys left me feeling like nothing more than a living shop window mannequin, was far from my mind or needs.

Greg had a body like Michelangelo's David, that was for sure. After years of training in ice-hockey, surfing and several martial arts, to see such perfection lying there... wanting me, felt criminal. Even with all his tenderness and wonderful loving... more and more I realised it was not enough... Something *was* missing. Turning away from him sexually now, our communication dwindled to hardly speaking except to discuss what was necessary to work, as we began to socialise separately too. Worst of all, I could not even bring myself to cook for him anymore either. Venturing out alone, I discovered markets with hidden surprises and endless supplies of vegetarian meals I could enjoy without the need to sit and make uncomfortable conversation with Greg... at a time we just slipped apart. Greg had discovered the likes McDonalds and Burger King and pretty quickly the pimples to go with it.

Beating myself with guilt about this, I wondered if he was getting enough nutrition, hoping he'd not go completely to seed too, morphing into a lump of lard flinging me about on stage. In words he took to be a veiled challenge, I suggested the spots might clear up if he used some of his spare time to go buy healthy foods and learn to cook for himself. "Men Are From Mars, Women Are From Venus" had not hit the shelves yet. Had it been, I'd not have read it... feeling quite sure that I already *was* the 'Battle of the Sexes'. So, as the face of rage welled up before me, I quite expected fire from his eye sockets, waiting for all hell to break loose and little experience to know what I'd just triggered or how to make it better. His fist clenched and slammed, thankfully, into the wall!

Shovelling blame straight back onto him, more ill-thought-out gibberish added fuel to the flames.

"Well, that's going to make it *real* comfortable to work together tonight now, isn't it?!" Picking up my costume bag, I made for the front door.

"I'll see you at UA... and there's a vegetarian snack bar just behind the Holiday Inn called Bodhi. Grab something sensible to eat there on your way to the MTR."

Rehana Incognito

"Fuck you... fucking bitch...!" Was the last I heard from him, closing the door. Standing outside on the landing before heading down the stairway, I stood frozen, feeling like a mother not fit to care for a child. Is that what I'd become? I didn't want to *be* that, so clopped my way down the stairs, stilling myself for what the night might bring, scowling at any man who leered at me traipsing through the MTR for my train.

 The Chinese dancers at UA were flogging off heaps of jewellery in the change room for me as I began to panic that Greg had not arrived. About to give up, heading for a phone to call Jeremy's flat, the door opened and there he was... with Jeremy and a very tall, middle aged blonde woman. Jeremy introduced her as "Delilah from Australia too", though she'd been living for years in Thailand. Greg seemed to have already met her, plonking her heavy costume bag in what space he could find, before starting to strip off and ready himself. Asking Delilah if she'd worked here before, in her husky, down-to-earth Aussie tones, she told me she'd worked in this very club for years, all over Asia and was also a good friend of Felicity's from years back. It was no great skill to put two and two together and realise Deliah too was a 'sister' and I actually felt grateful that this very *big,* experienced sister was going to move into Jeremy's other spare closet too. With jewel-encrusted fingers and dagger-long red nails, her thigh-length mass of blonde hair evoked an image of a Celtic warrior princess. Fierce indeed, to say the least, her voice boomed forth as I felt the exhilaration of a friend at last 'like myself' with whom to swap notes...or perhaps, commiserate! I really liked her forthrightness and attitude as she turned to Jeremy.

"It'll be nice to stay with you for a while. At least until Jeremy gets me a better gig than the last episode he

sent me off on," she snarled at him, rolling her eyes and turning her head as he turned sheepishly to go.
"Now now, Lilah... Don't go giving the kids a bad impression. They're off to Korea shortly and I've promised they'll be in excellent hands." He squirmed, glaring at her. I could hardly wait to get her alone and learn more, aware enough that there was more to Jeremy's ethics, or lack thereof, than I'd already seen.

Delilah's little show came on after ours, so Greg and I sat at our discrete little table with Jeremy to enjoy. With 100% energy and enthusiasm, her strip went along like clockwork. In fact, I am sure she could have done it in her sleep, as every move fit like cogs in a well-driven-in machine. Uplifting music with skilful, exotic movement held the room spellbound. Sadly though, despite the professionalism, with embarrassment on my part and clearly on Delilah's, she had the body of a matronly mother. Splayed on the floor to flip her legs high, cellulite literally cascaded like overflowing cottage cheese pouring over her. Combined with her breasts which looked like to saggy socks with cricket balls lying in the bottom, it was kind of a grotesquely repulsive sight. The audience, however, went wild as I felt truly relieved for her. Catching my eye as she skipped from the stage, with something like saddlebags hanging out of a shiny sequinned g-string, I smiled approvingly that she'd still got it, raising my hands in an appreciative clap.

Greg disappeared when his second show was done at, off to catch the drunken Aussies, I'd guessed... yet not questioning. Delilah came back to Jeremy's. Throwing her kit through the bedroom door, pulling it shut, she turned suggesting we head straight out as the 'night was young' for some girly time in Kowloon! Perfect. I didn't need to wait long for note swapping with her and relished the thought of her company after so long with just Greg and hit-ons at work.

Perching ourselves at the bar at the Holiday Inn, where we'd decided it would be pleasant to talk, have a drink and maybe find one of those Oriental dream boy lovers she was only into, Delilah's face was drenched in sweat from the humid walk. Reaching into her bag for a powder compact to blot the glow, I followed the plummet of string of condoms dropping to the floor. She hadn't noticed at all, as I did my best Playboy Bunny Dip to pick them discretely up. A gang of businessmen observing from further along the bar *did* notice, finding themselves now riveted to the scene. Embarrassedly asking if she'd missed anything there, I plonked them back in her bag.

"Oh, Lovey... it pays to advertise, you know! She growled a little louder in the businessmen's direction. It was the red flag before the bulls as they charged. Sitting back speechlessly, I watched 'Lilah work the lot of them. Within seconds, she'd negotiated a price, taken their room numbers and arranged a time to pay them a 'visit'. Making it clear that I wasn't in the deal, Deliah scrutinized me like bacteria under a microscope.

"Lovey... are you mad? How the fuck do you survive here if you're not doing punters now and then? It's quick, it's easy and over in minutes. They'll be snoring and happy before you even get in the lift and back to the bar."

"Hmmm...I'm sure it is... but I couldn't imagine having sex with someone I didn't love."

She giggled, "Oh, Lovey... you're fucked!" Now, I'd heard that before, wondering if I was the only one, in the little world of '*Trans*' People, who felt this way about just allowing easy access to my body with total strangers.

BODYCAGE

"Well...not tonight, I won't be!" I mused, ending that conversation. Downing several more Mai-Tais and Long Island Iced Teas, drinks streamed down the bar from the punters like a conveyor belt. Lilah disappeared several times, leaving me to the barrage of interest at the bar, making pathetic conversation as far removed as I could muster from anything that might have let them thought I was working the bar myself! Finally, her hefty feminine sway on her high heels had turned to an ungainly swagger as she struggled to close her purse, stuffed with hundreds of dollars.

Not content with her earning the dollars and bit of fun with the strangers, what she really needed was to find her 'lover'. Having arrived in Hong Kong after a relationship with a Thai boyfriend had fallen apart, her driving goal, like a salmon swimming upstream to die, was to replace him immediately with another. Falling arm in arm through the swing doors of what seemed to be an oriental Wild Western saloon bar, Lilah, high heels now carried in hand, parted the throngs of Cantonese Cowboys like Moses and the Red Sea.

"Gimmee two tinnies, Lovely?" She ordered her Fosters lager. "Make 'em real cold for a couple of *Aussie Sheilas,* will ya?"

'Shelia's' she may well have felt us both to be, but right then her demeanour was little removed from other drunken Australian blokes around the bar. Slamming onto a bench, head collapsed between her legs, pathetically she clutched her 'tinnie'. What was still a fairly alert and interesting night for me, had been one for her only to repeat old habits. Making a quick and easy buck, getting smashed and trying cure all her pain with a big old 'Band-aid' of a lover for however long she could make that last, was the same old goal. It stupefied me really, to see that someone who had once been so young and beautiful, could have had it all. Yet still, around and around in circles she'd go, aging all the while... repeating the same old mistakes yet expecting different results. Is it true perhaps that this the definition of insanity? Truly pitying Delilah, now on the verge of passing out, I hoped such insanity was transitory as I envisioned Master Po from "Kung Fu", materialising before us saying-

"Grasshopper, Western woman not pretty sight in altered state of consciousness." Leading her barefooted, into the weak morning light, she didn't mind stepping on the piles of mucky garbage, kicking out at the odd rats working their night shift. She scattered them along the way!

At least 'Lilah was loads of fun on her daily sojourns into oblivion, keeping us endlessly entertained with her own tales of adventures as a stripper both in Australia and Asia. Introducing me to many other new friends, mainly hookers and other strippers who seemed to work in much better clubs and bars than we did, it was surprising to realise how many too were 'girls' like myself... all feeding an industry of flesh. Often we'd do 'High Tea' at the Peninsula Hotel, gossiping and joking about our week's escapades in the sumptuous splendour of this colonial institution. Well-heeled, handsome strangers cruised by, offering drinks and often their company, as I often found myself forgetting that I was in Hong Kong with my boyfriend. Even though things were strained with Greg, I did not want to lose him or conceive of what I could or *would* be without him, vowing to find a way back to closeness and understanding.

Yet, there I sat drenched in my favourite perfume, "Maroc" from Ultima with a heady Middle Eastern floral note, over scones, cream, jam, and endless cups of tea. Heaving my chest in a breathless tease toward the ornate ceiling fans to be gently brushed by their

BODYCAGE

coolness, I noticed the scent would increase its toxicity with my perspiration and all the humidity. Whether that, or mixed with natural pheromones, it lured men like little honey bees. Just one more exotic stranger needed to kiss my hand, offering nights of style and charm in Hong Kong... and Greg and I would be in serious jeopardy. Somehow, a realisation had dawned that Greg was actually dependant on me.... and, unsettlingly, it changed things within me.

All that glamour and frustrating temptation were soon to be cut short as Greg had the pleasure of announcing we were about to leave for our stint in Korea.

'The Journey to the Seoul', I'd called it, wondering if it was a metaphor for a strange place I was yet to visit and discover, yet laughing it off all the same!

"Give 'Boobs in the Basement' a week's notice, OK?" he commanded, "I was talking to Jeremy about it and he's arranged our flights and new work to start in 10 days." Walking out the door with his swag bag to UA, he left me to ponder without even hearing a reply, as Jeremy reclined smirking on the couch.

"Greg's only trying to help you realise that a man should wear the pants in a relationship, Ri. Besides, it'll do you both good to have some time away from all your *distractions* in Hong Kong. You can concentrate on a second show together as you'll need two... and patch things up between yourselves." Hardly having time to get angry about such 'Agony Aunt' advice being dispensed from an amoral Jabba the Hutt, panic seized me, contemplating three months in a strange country, without my friends... alone to face Greg who had clearly conspired with Jeremy. Smirking and gloating, he savoured my bewilderment, knowing full well that both he and Greg had their reasons for not wanting me happy, exploring and growing in Hong Kong.

Rehana Incognito

Performing our show as ever at UA, we got to the part in the song 'Suffer', where I was to flick my head from side to side as Greg faked the 'take that... and that' slaps. Yet the second slap connected harshly to my right cheek... even noticeably heard by everyone near the stage. Though slightly stunned, I played through to the end, smiling and skipping hand-in-hand from the stage as ever. Unwilling to even acknowledge what he'd done to make his point that night, I let him enjoy his strike for dominance, making love with him 'til he fell asleep. Unwinding from his arm and leg across me, I slithered quietly from the bed to wash it away whilst holding on to the resentment, pulling the door quietly behind.

Turning to walk across the living room, in the half light of dawn, sat Delilah. Dazed, almost slumped on the sofa, I was stunned to see her eyes gazing into nothingness as a Chinese boy startled from between her splayed legs, finished his prodding at her exposed genitals. His black eyes caught a glint of light pouring slowly in as he darted to the door, pulling up his pants, reminding me of the rats fleeing from the garbage. Setting 'Lilah back on the sofa, with a cushion under head and covering her with a sheet, I left her obliviously snoring, not even noticing her beau had departed. After taking my shower, I uneasily crept back to bed.

Pat took the news quite badly, as she would find it hard to replace a young, attractive Western woman behind the bar and had become very used to the increase in clientele of my regulars over those couple of months.

"Just be sure, Riannon... that if anything goes wrong, you can call me from anywhere and your job will be here for you." Pat truly flattered me, knowing that I had literally materialised from nowhere with no experience

BODYCAGE

of such a job, yet managed it successfully. At the point of leaving it for then, it was surprising to myself to have actually accomplished that... if it could be called so.

"I'll even send you a ticket... from anywhere." I wondered what premonition she may have had, or did she just know something more about all this which I didn't, yet was either too gracious, honourable or *afraid* to tell. Letting slip a little more, slightly hushed... things became clearer.

"I might have known Jeremy would pull something like this. It eats him, seeing you enjoy yourself and getting so much attention. His problem is... and don't let it bother you... he told me about your past... But he wishes he could be a woman himself and do half the things you can do." Simply giving a big sigh and a disparaging nod, I stood incredulously as she revealed more of this man's poisoned heart.

"Be careful of him, Ri... watch that one. They do get very bitter and twisted over the years."

Not one to be a 'whipping boy' or even a 'sacrificial lamb' for anyone else's dysfunctional misery, if it could be helped, I promised to take care, finishing my week at Boobs in the Basement with a slightly heavy heart that it was to end so soon.

CHAPTER THREE

 A Mr Park (well... about *who else?* Nearly everyone in Korea is called Park... or Lee... Kim) in his crumpled suit, disheveled from having been caught in the rain, collected us from Kimpo Airport to chauffeur us on a perilous ride through the darkening streets of a glittering Seoul. Not until he bent close to hoist one of our bags from the back seat did I smell the overpowering reek of Soju on his breath. I wondered how he'd managed to drive us to this cute little 'Daisy Hotel' in Yongsan with all that Korean Sa-ke in his system, winding along huge expressways, dodging buses and weaving between lorries and cabs. We were surprised there were not piles of mangled wreckage on all the roads, as it transpired that this level of drinking and driving was quite normal in Korea.
 Greeting us like royalty, an elderly, grandma concierge left a banquet waiting in our comfortable suite. Picking cautiously at the unfamiliar treats, lest we inadvertently eat a dog... which we heard Koreans *did*, we felt a little guilty that the sweet old lady, called Jong-Sook busied herself unpacking all our luggage! Although she spoke no English, fortunately older Korean generations speak good Japanese... so at least I could ask her for strictly no meat. Jong-Sook found it hilarious that she spoke no English and I no Korean, yet found ourselves managing through a third-party tongue which we both managed to hilariously mangle. I did wonder why she had turned scarlet, yet bowing politely, thinking my request that she wake us up at eight in the morning was quite reasonable. Unfortunately though, I had mixed up the Japanese words 'O-ko-shi-te' and 'O-ka-shi-te', respectively meaning 'wake me up please'.... and 'please violate me'. Thankfully that was solved in time, as Korean people are very accommodating. Such

BODYCAGE

a harrowing awakening by an old Korean grandma would certainly have dampened our shopping excursion to Itaewon for new costume material for our next show.

After a cosy night, feeling more at home in our own space with something of a 'home' around us, we felt finally like we were away on a honeymoon. With our maps and travel tickets in hand we were shown how to use the Subway and buses to easily get around, having decided on a 'Jungle Jezebel' theme to accompany the show we'd already learnt. We had the music already on some cassette tapes we'd brought over and found it an easy enough number to devise a routine of Greg being a kind of Tarzan, chasing me around the stage as some kind of Jane... all the while losing our kit along the way! We found heaps of animal-printed materials, leather thongs and various shells and beads to get a whole image together, babbling on about how we'd make the routine go from start to finish.

Holding hands in the busy shopping and bar area, we noticed so many more foreigners around us, though all were men with buzzed hair-cuts, some in their uniforms and some in the standard uniforms of American servicemen when not on duty! Making our way through the throngs of hustling Koreans and meandering servicemen, Greg clasped my hand ever more tightly as each of these men stared as I went by, almost forgetting they all had the same styled Korean girlfriend in tow. Often looking back myself, more often than not, these guys kept turning to watch me disappear too, with the Korean girls just as often beating them savagely about the ears for leering at the tall, Western blonde... and making their interest so obvious.

Rehana Incognito

"You'd think these guys were out walking their bloody dogs," Greg loudly announced when the leering became too much as I shushed him to lower his voice.

"They'll get a hard enough time when they get back to the States for it anyway, I'm sure... So don't worry about it." Disdainfully, I watched these guys stroll by, not really even knowing the girls, stuck to them like glue with only the hope of a visa out of Korea on their minds. Hordes of guys just hitched up with them in the absence of anyone around from their own culture, looking longingly at what they didn't have. Notching up another deep nick in my 'Men are Pigs' belt, I let the nasty glares of the Korean 'Stepford' *girlfriends* pass me by.

"They'll deserve it... Dickheads!" he cruelly added as I realised he was just feeling insecure about all these buffed-up guys around with no other Western women in sight, I was clearly an attraction. Reaching a shaded spot under a tree, popping down my bags of goodies on a bench, I decided in a moment of spontaneous affection, to give him a big hug and kiss... as sirens began to wail.

Yes, it was actually sirens... air-raid sirens! Suddenly shutters were coming down on shops, buses stopped, passengers ran out, disappearing quickly into shelters and subway stations. Mortified, we stood there as even the traffic lights and a fountain ceased spraying and military jeeps were all that were left speeding up and down emptied streets. In a matter of seconds everyone in Seoul had become troglodytes, disappearing beneath the surface, with only Greg and I standing there wondering what we could say to each other... sure there was about to be an almighty burning, big flash and all would be over. Only feeling heavy remorse to have come all that way with my lovely boyfriend and equally lovely new body, now to be

BODYCAGE

nuked by the Communists North, we obeyed a heavily armed, mean-looking soldier in a jeep's stern bark to go into the shelter too.

Down there, huddled in the crushing heat with a horde of Koreans heady with the smell of Kimchee and Soju on their breaths, it was a while before we realised that no-one was actually on their knees saying their last goodbyes. Kindly, a pretty young girl in her smart, bright yellow office uniform and shiny gold name tag, told us in perfect English not to worry as it was the compulsory Monthly Air Raid Drill. We did wish someone had warned us about that, but it must have slipped by in the excitement of our arrival, or else it was just too routine in a country still officially only in 'ceasefire' with its enemies in North Korea, to bother mentioning. Stumbling out into the brighter light after the 'all clear' siren, it did make us realise how short life could be and how quickly everything could really be over. It had served only to goad me more towards questioning and discovering about all we could enjoy and be here for... whilst we have a life... and deep down, the sirens and the sudden facing of disaster were perhaps a warning of blowing apart in other ways too. Things were becoming 'all clear' in a misty, warped 'Seoul Kind of Feeling' way.

Putting the music and costumes together with our routine went way too smoothly in the two days we had to prepare for our first show at a United States military base on the outskirts of Seoul. Mr Park was like a kid with new toys, regaling us through security gates, with introductions to officers and setting us up in our lavish change room to prepare to 'entertain the troops'... albeit not ours! Feeling all the more confident to be performing before a Western audience, their appreciation and encouraging applause, brought out my strongest desire in to make eye contact, to flirt, smile and tease them. Like invisible strings, their adoration pulled and played with my body to perform from a depth of movement and expression I was not even aware of it. Coming from somewhere deep inside, primarily manipulated by pounding drums, like a dance which was always there... perhaps performed lifetimes ago... it revelled in its chance to live and star again.

"TITS AT LAST!" yelled a sloshy Serviceman, who'd clearly tired of diminutively-endowed Korean dancers and had way too much to drink as I slunk past his rowdy table. Two burly Military Police had him dragged out before I could barely blink, as one of his company, in a high-ranking uniform, mouthed the words "Sorry Ma'am." What a comforting touch of gentlemanly manners in a sea of semi hard-ons, I thought. He must be from the South. Having made my way close to the tables around the stage, collecting the whirlwind of fluttering green and grey US notes, I lost count of the ones accompanied with phone numbers scrawled on pieces of paper for me. Greg had spotted them too, screwing them up and making sure they'd gone in the rubbish bin. With the air heavy with booze and testosterone-charged servicemen quickly getting out of control, it was like a release from prison as those huge gates lumbered open, freeing us into the night, half asleep, for the long drive back to the 'Daisy'.

For a compensatory, grounding reality check, Greg suggested we visit Seoul Zoo the following day. Scuttling straight for the Australian wildlife enclosure, we couldn't wait to find the emus, kangaroos and crocodiles, talking to them loudly in our most heavy Australian accents in case they were 'homesick'. Then Mr Park old us that they were born in Seoul Zoo, guessing it was probably ourselves who were homesick. Finding a row of more dilapidated, old-fashioned cages with concrete floors and thick steel

BODYCAGE

bars, we noticed a bunch of Koreans making a fuss as a young lady poked and prodded at an exhausted-looking jaguar, panting pathetically by the bars, with the point of her umbrella. It was clearly accustomed to such torment, yet... blindly, I snatched the umbrella from the girl, laying into her with it as she screamed loudly and the Koreans ran for a guard. As the crowd fled and the teenager disappeared along with them, Mr Park had a jovial, rapid-fire exchange with the guard who walked off laughing.
"Isn't he going to do anything to me, Mr Park?" I thought I'd be arrested.
"I told him it was 'your monthly time' and you had gone crazy for little moment." Too steamed with anger and embarrassment still to even comment on that, it felt to me that I had made my point... well a nasty, sharp umbrella point at least... probably on the sadistic little lady's backside.

To cool me down, Mr Park led us down some stairs into a huge chamber to peer through the massive thick windows into, what surprised me to be, the Dolphin tank. A little group of Korean visitors were also surprised as Greg and I pressed our faces to the glass. One dolphin had spotted us, flipping himself around for an abrupt 'about face' with the entire pod doing the same. Torpedoing straight over, this entire little tribe swarmed in front of us, surveying us up and down... from side to side.
"They've probably only ever seen Orientals before," said Greg, laughing with Mr Park as they tapped on the glass. Walking along the full length of the window, they stalked us. Longing to just walk through the glass to swim and play with them as I had done in a world which seemed now a long way away, I wanted to believe they saw or felt more than just someone with different coloured hair and eyes than what they were

used to. Feeling magically blessed with a special reunion, in that dim cavern, I lost awareness of anyone else there. Just teleported back in my mind to be the loneliest child in town, sitting by the banks of the Collie River, I was again watching my special true friends cavorting naturally and free. *Knowing* they understood me, I felt less alone there in the silence with my smile to match their permanent, fixed-by-nature, grins. Turning back a few times as I ascended from the cavern, my heart ached to see them milling about, slowly flapping their tail flukes as they hovered, watching me disappear up the stairs and away from them.

In 1987, Korea was having about the worst floods in its history, as Greg and I were moved about all over Korea to the likes of the exotic ultra chic resort of Chegudo to industrial towns like Inchon and Busan. Time flew by surreally, with way too many weird, alien experiences to even recount. Except to say, I found it slightly bizarre that in Korea, even wives and children turned up to watch our shows, which all seemed perfectly normal and healthy to them. Having even become blasé about submitting to Korean women helping themselves to a good squeeze or look at my breasts, this also fascinated them, seeming quite a healthy and natural thing for them to be doing! With few people going out in the floods and businesses losing money everywhere, we appeared in some very dodgy clubs with the absolute pits being one in which we are sure we met the Snake Woman who had sprayed the entire contents of a dead serpent across her audience in Felicity's exciting tales.

In a mad rush, finishing her show with a little bunch of snakes, doing all sorts of wild and wonderful things as she twirled them about, our music started. As she brushed by me, clipping the snake basket shut I

noticed her willowy body and extra thin, extended eye-lids. She herself had a cold, reptilian demeanour though I tried a smile as I took to the stage, noticing the Elastoplasts covering her nipples. In fact, noting the Elastoplasts on her nipples, she also had smaller Elastoplasts coving various little points on her body where she'd clearly been nipped by her snakes. With that chilling thought in mind, I burst onto stage as the 'Jungle Jezebel', bumping and grinding along its full rendition before turning away from the audience, facing the curtain to launch into a long ass-shaking shimmy. Following my hands with a sideward gaze down to highlight the direction of my trembling hips, then a big swish of my hair to fling myself back around to face the mob, two coal black eyes and darting, forked tongue came slithering out from behind the curtain!
 Snake Woman had forgotten one of her little friends as she'd swept up her discarded pieces of costume. Screaming as the thing slid towards me with its demonic little head slightly off the ground, I leapt from my high heels completely. There was little chance of me performing that night until I'd downed nearly a litre of hot Sa-ke, even though it had brought the house down to see Jane, the Jezebel of the Jungle, could be scared off by a children's python! Thankfully, the abnormally heavy rain and the ensuing floods, had come at a good time as we were well ready to cut Korea short, for the next leg of our Oriental Odyssey. We were off to Taiwan in a flash... of never-ending lighting... and booming thunder. The flight was about the scariest thing in my life (apart from almost marrying an 80 year old billionaire the size of a sofa) as I made my peace with God, fearing the end several times before we touched ground in Taipei.
 The 'Wonders From Down Under' show toured merrily around Taiwan for weeks, again with time to take in

tourist pursuits, discovering new and exciting cultures. Yet another agent, this time much younger, trendy, Westernised man called Ricky played excellent host, keeping us in the nicest hotels whilst caring for our every need. As in Korea, children showed up at our early performances, sitting with their parents, dining and chatting like an evening at the movies. Beginning to feel more uncomfortably anguished about being paraded even before children like this, it was an incident in a department store in Taipei which helped me realise how these people saw us.

Waiting for Greg to look through a magazine stand, I stood patiently taking in the strangeness, and familiarities, of this store. Alarmingly, I felt a woman running her fingers through my long, loose, cotton sleeves as I turned my head sharply, believing her to be a pickpocket! She screamed loudly as I gasped too, jumping back to see her clutch in panic her husband, now roaring with laughter. Not being used to seeing Westerners, she had thought I was a shop dummy and had come for a feel of my clothes. Poor woman had nearly died when I moved, realising that I was not as plastic as some might think! It registered then, that no matter who or what we felt we were... to these people we were aliens and may just as well have been exhibits in a display at a Natural History Museum.

Feeling that way, I no longer bothered to make much friendly conversation with the people we met in Taiwan, although I do believe they were the kindest and most friendly people I had ever met. When Ricky proposed that in some of the clubs, where he had somehow worked out a measure of assurance that it was OK for me to finish my show completely naked, he at least sought my opinion about whether I would do it or not. Greg and I decided it was fine as we only worked on stages there, so I was not too close to be peered at like a trip to the gynaecologists and our fee was bumped up by an extra $100 Australian for finishing so. Not caring at all, as I knew I'd not see any of these people again for the rest of my life, it kind of felt triumphant to unclip the g-sting, quickly flinging it aside to stand there totally naked except for high heels, whole and complete, deserving of admiration. As dozens of beaming faces smiled their approval, I grinned to myself giving the 'vertical smile' for the briefest of moments back!

Seeing huge posters of us outside venues where we'd perform, always took me by surprise. Having no idea what was written in Chinese about us, it never really completely registered that the two dancers featured were *really* Greg and myself. Often I had actually thought they looked really good and how much I would love to go see them! Gazing at a new poster in the lobby of our hotel early in an evening as we rushed back to get ready, a bit of a fuss and excited raised voices seemed to come from the main street over the racket of the traffic. The hotel staff, picking up what was being said, rushed past us, out into the street with Greg and I following too. In the direction the gathering crowd looked up to, we saw the top of the office building where the clubs we performed in were. To our horror, acrid, black smoke billowed from all the windows on about the tenth floor.

The clubs were all just burnt out shells in a few brief minutes, as Ricky had arrived at our hotel not long after the fire engines, police and ambulances. Ricky raced to and from the phone, then back to us at the bar. Steeling our nerves to hear if *anyone* had been hurt, we knew it was bad news when he finally returned, shaking his head back and forth between his hands. Some dozen or so dancers and singers had lost their lives in the fire as they finished their day shifts and prepared for the evening's shows. Some of them were our sweet, dear friends who had shown us so much kindness and help up there on those top floors for many weeks, leaving us both feeling nothing but a tragic misery about the whole business.

Ricky understood how sickened we were and had no choice but to annul our contracts anyway as the venue was burnt out. For a small fee, we were able to change our airfares for a sooner return, leaving Taipei on that hideous note. Overwhelmingly, I felt such helplessness as well as gratitude that this fire had not happened an hour later. Yet, somehow I believed that may have been life's way of warning us, about something dire and sinister, which I was too out-of-touch or lacking the self-awareness to look further within to know.

BODYCAGE

CHAPTER FOUR

Greg's parents met us at Tullamarine Airport upon arrival back in Melbourne. Reunion with our dog, Bomber, was rapturous, as he peed himself all over with excitement... and I almost wished they'd brought Pepsi the budgie to greet us as well. Having saved enough for a healthy deposit, and perhaps lost in the positive mood of Greg and I having gotten through this trip with loads to tell and still together, his parents offered to help us with the purchase of a house... to continue our life and menagerie. For several days we prowled through piles of real estate magazines, trying to decide where we might like to settle. Opting for the beautiful, forested area of the hills around Belgrave, out in the Dandenong Ranges, we accepted it would be better to buy a cheaper house, further from the city, with that little bit of land for Bomber and my proposed semi-farm of a vegetable patch.

As promised, Felicity could not wait to have me back at the Victoriana, introducing me to her bank manager as a 'respected, highly paid assistant manager', a title I felt I hardly deserved! Greg's old band were glad to accept him back too, having spent the past couple of months of his absence rehearsing and writing a lot of new stuff. Circling several quaint little cottages advertised in our price range close to each other around the hills, one stood out particularly.

'Two Bedroom "ROSE COTTAGE" on hectare of land. Through-flowing creek with established garden in bush setting.'

Arranging with a Belgrave estate agent to show us around, the Rose Cottage was first on our list. Winding down a heavily gum tree-line lane we pulled up by the white picket fence, bedecked with tiny pink and white, creeping roses... Kookaburras and magpies serenaded

from tree tops, their songs echoing all around. Almost too much to resist, I almost clawed myself out of the car for a look around. Greg pulled me back.
"Not yet, Bunny. Let's look at them all first from the outside, then decide which ones to look in." Dejectedly, I agreed, winding through the wooded roads hardly caring about any other house I saw. Nothing more needed be said, as we both agreed the agent should call the Rose Cottage vendors to see if we could look through. We did, promptly seeing no reason not to get back to the agent's office to offer a price on the house to the dear old couple who had spent decades there and were off to settle along the coast somewhere in Tasmania. Nervously, we took lunch with the agent in a gracious wooden inn overlooking an idyllic, huge lake before strolling around the shops downtown in Belgrave. Back to his office, the call had come through. The lovely old couple had accepted our offer, wishing us as much happiness in the house as they'd had.

Setting up our furniture, as well as fish tanks and bird cages, we potted up even more agriculture than was already there, feeling like we'd landed in Heaven. Not even minding the one hour train ride to work each day as Greg always showed up with Bomber after his own band rehearsals, we'd drive peacefully home to our sanctuary together. Dana who became Kylie, once rode out some 30 km on her bicycle on a hot summer's day, startling me at the front door with both some nasty, bristly whiskers catching glints of the sun and her now sing-song *Swedish* accent.

"Why the accent, Kylie? You were an Aussie Sheila from Geelong last time I saw you!" Her sweating, red hulk fell through the door.

Slugging back a giant, plastic glass of minted lemon water, the now swaggering Swede, explained that she had found her voice caused less consternation and

BODYCAGE

suspicion if she changed her accent from Australian to what was first an Irish Colleen from Donegal before finally settling for a 'Swedish immigrant', changing her name now to Astrid Mortensen. Honestly, that girl had more multiple personalities than anyone could imagine... and I am sure several of them were stalking her. Taking 'Astrid' for lunch with us to the beautiful Emerald Lake, she woefully rued her lack of success at 'snaring her hare' or even anything like a date, putting it down to her not being a 'woman yet' like me.

As Greg disappeared far enough into the middle of the lake for a swim with Bomber, Dana/Kylie/Astrid, the woman of a thousand accents, told me she'd somehow gotten approval from The Board to have her surgery in a few weeks. Not only from myself, but from many others, she'd gleaned information, rehearsing over and over, all she felt they would need to hear. Even Doctor Abrams had agreed to perform her surgery. With a sense of guilt and dread that I may have inadvertently created a monster about to unleash on the unsuspecting world, I struggled for the right words to perhaps warn her off.

"You, know... Kylie...sorry, Astrid... Even if your surgery goes OK, there's no guarantee you will find a partner who accepts you totally in his life." Not wanting to make her feel bad at her moment of impending womanliness, I tried to explain.

"Men are funny... you know... When it comes to women they choose as partners, they really like to feel proud of, showing off their prize like a trophy or princess to their friends and family." She looked quite stunned at my possible suggestion that she may not quite be either of those things. So, taking a deep breath...

"I know there's lots to love about you... really... I am sure there will be plenty after you... But their big fear is that the friends and family might find out about our past! Then it's really hard for them to cope with... and the best we can do is be their hidden little dirty secret. You got to be prepared for that."

"You got lucky with Greg then didn't you!" she sullenly replied.

"Yes, Greg is one-in-a-million but he met me as a woman and thought nothing more. He'd spent enough time with me to notice no-one knew but people we'd told knew about it... so had no hesitation to bring me into his family and social life." Steadfastly, she believed a magic wand would wave in the operating theatre where she would wake up looking like a supermodel with handsome millionaires throwing fur coats and diamonds at her feet. Trying to explain that such men were few and far between enough for biologically- born women fell on deaf ears. Promising to visit her in hospital, we changed the subject, leaving her to ignore her delusions.

Building a spacious deck on the back of the house to enjoy the panorama of our private creek, flower beds and forest, I lost track of the ideas which flew at me from "Home Beautiful" and "Vogue Living" magazines to make our world even more perfect. The credit card dizzily spiralled out of control and we fell, without really noticing, weeks behind in our mortgage repayments. Greg had devoted all of his energies to his band, gaining more and more fame in Victoria and bordering New South Wales and South Australia, yet never enough money came in from it. The more successful they were, the more they invested in bigger and better equipment, leaving me taking on extra days at the Tea Rooms to get bills out of the way. Beginning to resent this, feeling like the hardworking bread winner, I woke one morning in Felicity's office at Victoriana, slumped over her sturdy wooden desk, having finally hit the wall.

BODYCAGE

Felicity, charged for a day of organising her business, stood over me with groceries fresh from the wholesalers, not believing her eyes.

"Ri, what are you doing in so early? You're not due in 'til this afternoon." Startled, I sat up realising it was morning.

"Oh, Christ... I've been here all night! I fired the kitchen hand last night on the spot... He was bloody hopeless... making more work for us than being a help! So I called Greg and told him not to bother collecting me and stayed back cleaning up 'til four. I don't think he cared less anyway."

"Take my car, Riannon...you'll walk under a tram going out in the street like that... Take a shower and a sleep at my place before you come back." Handing me the pile of keys, I achingly squeezed swollen feet into my shoes, wobbling around the office straightening out my clothes.

"Don't come back 'til your ready, Darling... You look a mess and will scare my customers away." My understanding, big, bubbly surrogate mama stroked my back and shoulders gently.

"Thanks, Girl. You know this doesn't happen often," I said. "Greg's just being a bit irresponsible at the moment and the bills are now all up to me. I'm turning into a wreck wondering how to cope."

With a serious, subdued tone, Felicity looked me in the eye.

"Don't make excuses for him, Riannon. You make a man a baby, he'll act like one. You do too much for him and, let me tell you, when he's your baby, you become his mum and that *aint* gonna be healthy."

"I just like to be helpful and kind. You know how I am! Am sure he appreciates all I do for him." Felicity just heaved that headlight rack of a chest in an almighty sigh, knowing full well that, regardless of what I *thought*

Rehana Incognito

I was doing to make *anyone* like and appreciate me- making myself a doormat, I'd get lots of feet wiped over me!
"Maybe give some thought to going back to Asia again on your own this time. Jeremy knows you well enough now and can get much better work for you in Japan. You're a professional dancer now and your Japanese is good enough to hostess in the best clubs... you don't even have to fuck 'em." Her eyes lit up, mischievously no doubt, at the thought of terrorising me with her cane through a whole new set of solo routines. Smiling back, I promised to give it some thought, wearily staggering into the bright morning rush hour.

Submerged in the lavish tub in Felicity's packed-with-antiques apartment, I breathed in the luxury pondering the likelihood of Jeremy's contacts in Japan having anything better to offer me than the floods, fires and air-raid panic of the last trip. Tempting as it was to give the Orient a second try to improve my life and home, I still felt guilty to consider leaving Greg alone for perhaps three months, even though his parents... even grandparents ... were not twenty minutes drive away. Wiggling my fingers to make rippling, concentric waves in the water, I followed those little waves, one after the other as they washed the length of my body, to the sides of the tub and tumbled through the overflow. Whatever I chose would be like those ripples, caused by my own doing... going onwards... and outwards in directions I may not be aware of, yet having their effects felt regardless.

Thinking back to my old Japanese 'soap' about Rin Tachibana, the first Japanese female journalist, I reached for the bar of Imperial Leather with its logo on one side, lathering it up. Like Rin, who when stuck with a choice of two decisions, would through her wooden shoe into the air, making her choice based on how the

BODYCAGE

shoe landed, I decided to let the bar of soap make the decision for me. Sitting up, I dropped it from on high, letting it sink into the water like the Titanic, gliding to a halt somewhere near my heels. Reaching down, stroking my fingers across the slippy bar, I felt the logo was up. A bar of soap had decided for me to 'test the waters' with Greg on the way home to the hills when he came for me at work later that night.

Many factors may have influenced this urge to go on alone... even thinking it to be only for a while... to learn and find out more about myself and the world. With thoughts of all I had put myself through up to this point in life, to now feel like a struggling housewife, or perhaps even seeing all the material success of
Lady B, this felt like cogs again falling into a new position. Not unlike the morning Greg quietly drove me to Masada hospital, we rode in silence, both exhausted from our day and night, I found the nerve to put it to him.
"Greg... all these hours and late nights are too much for me now... and we're still way behind on the bills." Keeping his mind on the road as lights along the Burwood Highway flashed quickly by, he simply put his hand onto my leg, comfortingly squeezing it. Ever the dutifully efficient housewife, I decided to soften the blow...
"If I promise to leave the freezer full of a month's supply of meals for you and Bomber... Do you think you'd mind if I took Jeremy's offer for some more work in Japan on my own?"
With no begging or pleading, Greg simply responded that he'd be fine, rehearsing, performing with the band and writing more new material. He would be fine on his own if only for a couple of months. Veering onto the lane to our little cottage, Bomber roused himself as usual from the back seat excitedly. For whatever

reason he knew we were home to his little world and sanctuary, his basket awaiting at the foot of our bed where Greg and I too quickly crashed to sleep.

All too gleefully, Jeremy arranged flights straight away to Osaka for a two month contract with a Japanese entertainment agency.

"Jeremy, please don't let this be anything as tacky as the UA or those Korean dives you had us in before ok?! I'm not going to be sharing a change room with rats ever again."

"Oh, Riannon... you're much too sensitive, Lovely Girl... really. Everything will be just fine. You know the Japs have got more style than that!" Again, I didn't listen to any tiny, inner voice screaming in my ear that the King Rat of Hong Kong might just be at it again. Like lamb to the slaughter, Kosher, Halal or just plain stunned and hacked to bits, climbing aboard Jeremy's cattle truck, it was off to the meat market again.

Felicity donated all her costumes from her days of stardom, lamenting that she'd never be getting into those again, as I rehearsed with her a whole new repertoire of shows, including a million and one things to do with an enormous white, ostrich feather fan and matching boa. My duties were to be sitting at the tables fawning 'a la geisha' over big business bosses and tycoons and getting up to sing along to Japanese and Western songs at the karaoke. Then, reappearing sensationally to their astonishment as the fabulous foreign stripper, I could dance through them all, collecting as ever, thousands of Yen in tips both for myself and commission to the 'Mama-san', grande hostess, of whatever establishments I was assigned to. Dancing and stripping to some of my favourite songs, like "Modern Talking"s- "You Can Win if You Want", gave me the sense of power and confidence to know my performances looked very dynamic and exciting... So the theory all sounded good at least.

Our deep freeze was full to bursting as was my conscience that Greg and Bomber would not go hungry whilst I was away. Though still with a sense of numbness and dread, my two favourite guys... one perched precariously on my knee... sped me along the Tullamarine Freeway for my flight to Osaka. Bomber's claws had scratched deeply into my legs so I rolled his big form grudgingly over to the back seat, rubbing the scratches and bruises I'd thought would not look too impressive on stage in Japan.

"You're going to miss him aren't you, Bunny?" Greg asked, perhaps catching me out that I should have been making a fuss over missing him, not fretting over the dog. However, at that moment, I was not feeling it so much at all. In fact I resented finding myself in this extreme position at all, having chosen a partner I was left to support by going to a strange country again to do something I really did not want or enjoy. The fact that he didn't even mind the type of work I was doing at all as long as I did not sleep with them, made my apathy all the worse. Even uncomfortably hugging goodbye at the departure gates, I wondered why I was driven this far to hold together a dream I did not even understand.

At Osaka Airport a quite tall, good-looking Japanese man in his mid thirties met me with his little sign in front saying 'MR SATO, FOR MISS RIANNON'. Driving me to a high rise apartment in a suburban district, he left me in the care of two American girls who seemed to think they were a vulgarly vile version of "Laverne and Shirley", acting out their madcap little antics as a couple of 'crazy American chicks in Japland,' as they put it. Disdainfully, both Sato-san and I gave them plenty of distance, noticing that although we'd slipped off our shoes in the doorway entrance, these two were disrespectfully stomping around on the tatami mats still in their dirty shoes! Declining their offer to accompany them out on the town, I bowed politely to Sato-san, surprising me to say he'd be back at 9.30 in the morning to take me for a train further west to Himeji City! Rolling out a big purple futon, propping my head on the pillow and flicking off the lamp, I burst suddenly into tears, feeling far away and alone... and why on earth was I off to Himeji and not to be working in Osaka?

Waking up way too early and hungry, I did not want to risk waking the American girls whom I'd heard stagger in shortly before dawn. Spying the keys on the kitchen table, I slipped into the waking streets, hoping to find a snack bar. A lady at a newspaper kiosk told me to take three stops on the subway to the main station where plenty would be open for the morning commuters. After she politely changed a 1000 yen note for the ticket machines, I boarded a train. Some of the passengers, startled to see me, occasionally glanced over their newspapers or indiscreetly displayed *very* explicit porno magazines. Crikey, I thought, I don't want to bump into any of these guys if the train gets crowded... still horny in the morning and reading all that stuff! Wondering how many realised I was in Japan to pander just to those whims and desires, fuelling their fantasies in night clubs and bars, I truly felt like an alien. There I had landed, quietly observing their world, yet not knowing what to make of any of it, praying for some strength to cope with whatever lay ahead.

Over the sea of raven-haired passengers, one very dark brown head bobbed above the rest, his enormous pools of dark brown eyes lit up to spot me jammed between the suited men with only one foot really on the ground, the other in suspended animation. He mouthed and pointed at the door to get off at the next stop. I was

BODYCAGE

glad to. Introducing himself as Matthew, this sturdy American in the tightest sweatshirt and faded 501s, begged to accompany me to breakfast where he told me all about his world back home in Nebraska and his current trip- on leave from the military during his tour in Korea.

Matthew was like an anchor with an irresistibly mesmerising mystique and the added exotica of being quarter American Indian. In those few moments, until realising the time, I hurriedly scrawled the Victoriana Tea Rooms address for him always to stay in touch should he need someone to pen pal with for the rest of his time in Korea. Tucking the address down into his back pocket, he gave me long-lasting hug as I disappeared back into the subway to meet Mr Sato back at the apartment. Looking back for a last wave goodbye, I could see Matthew buffering like a bull against the out-pouring subway crowd, with his head held high and proud, sunlight brilliant behind him before I was swallowed away.

Sato-san bowed only slightly to my deep bow of thanks for the ride to the station, armed with instructions for the Himeji adventure, as the doors slid shut on the Bullet Train. With a little wave from the window and a shrug of my shoulders, he offered an understanding smile as I whisked away for the short journey to the port city of Himeji. Arriving there, I was easily spotted, as the only foreigner wandering to the station exit, by again a very tall-for-a-Japanese woman. With a bow so minimal I took it as discourteous, she matter-of-factly heaved up one of my bags, muttering an apology that she spoke no English. However, she advised that whilst I work in her club, I not let her clientele know that I speak any Japanese as they liked to think of the 'new girl in town', not someone who's worn out with the bars and clubs on the

Rehana Incognito

Japanese circuit. Apart from that, I already knew they liked to think of us too as just that little bit 'dumb'.

Tomiko was the 'Mama-san' of where I was to work and drove me to a small village slightly out of town where the door of the house was flung open by a gaggle of Brazilian girls. With their tarty gear, bleached blonde hair (which had kind of worked out as a rusty orange here and there) and deep-blue contact lenses (which, in a macabre way, made their eyes look like dead fish) it was clear the girls were not working as missionaries. A pretty young one, who reminded me of my little sister Gemma (apart from the ghoulishness of the fish eyes and not-quite-matching-the-skin- tone straw hair) spoke very good English, showed me to a room I was to share with her. Looking back at the three who stood at the bottom of the stairs as we went into the room, I could not help but wonder if the Japanese thought they'd gotten some weird Kabuki troupe of South American performers with the garishness of these girl's attempts to look more Caucasian!

Little Consuela, laid out my futon, thrusting jumble aside on the shelves to make space for my things.

"You *sooooo* lucky lady, have the long blondes hairs and the blues eyes. Yeah, you real lucky... Japanese mans go *craaaazy* for you." The other three girls soon curiously wandered in, though spoke only a smattering of English, yet excellent Japanese. They had been there for years, working as strippers and hookers all over Japan, finally finding their niche in and around Hygo Prefecture. Teasing and tantalising they worked quite well together, toying with drunken men at tables, dancing for their pleasure before finishing the night escorting them home for whatever prices they were willing to pay. By the time we were driven to Tomiko's club called 'Gypsy' (pronounced "ji-pu-shi" in Japanese, which had me wondering at first, thinking it

BODYCAGE

was called 'Gee-Pushy'), I realised competition was stiff between these girls too, as Consuela told me about their wealthy clients.

 This club was classy enough, as I'd hoped, with work-weary Japanese bosses, executives and their staff, pouring all the more regularly in through the evening. As each entered, we'd all chorus the welcoming 'i-ra-sha-i-ma-sse!', fussing around them like wives welcoming home their heroic Samurai, helping them from their coats before seeking out their personally-name-tagged bottles of whisky from the locked bar. Tomiko assigned the right girls for each of the arriving men and groups, giving preference of the foreign girls to the more high-ranking guests. I felt sure the Japanese girls must be sitting in some dark corner somewhere swilling down sa-ke with local bus conductors.

 Making every effort to get these men as drunk and fed as possible, we'd tell dirty jokes, getting them up to dance and sing as Mama-san Tomiko beamed approvingly while the cash flowed from their wallets. Feeling somewhat guilty, I often felt camaraderie with the younger men who had clearly come along out of protocol with their superiors, knowing too this was all a big charade and part of everyday business for them. Embarrassedly, they would join with me, knowing the superficiality and transparency of all this farce, to drunkenly sing love songs to each other... knowing we could hardly wait to escape to anywhere else but there. Some of these men had often whispered they had stood up their own sweethearts at times to undergo this sad ritual to appease and please their bosses and colleagues. I found myself at times slipping them back their tips as I knew it was a struggle for them to keep it up, telling them to buy something nice for their girls!

Rehana Incognito

Night after night it was the same boring routine, being the hostess at tables and dancing my way through their groping hands as 5000 Yen notes got stuffed into my stockings and bra. Having become by now quite hardened to drinking more and more sa-ke without getting drunk, I pushed my luck too far one evening, downing an extra bottle way too fast to cope with the rest of the night at a table of Electronics executives. Tomiko had just signalled that I head for the change room to get ready for my show as Consuela noticed I was choking back, about to heave. Excusing ourselves we rushed to the bathroom where my head was straight over a toilet bowl.

"Jeremy... you bastard..." I gurgled and gagged, coughing and spitting into the loo. Grabbing handfuls of tissues, Consuela dabbed at my face.

"Jeremy from Hong Kong?" I nodded a yes, still down the bowl. "*Oooooh,* he very bad man. He sell he own grandmamma for one dirty dollar. Always problem with girls send from Jeremy." Squaring me up to look at her dabbing handiwork, she went on...

"But you really nice girl, Riannon. Other girls here very jealousy with you. You got real blondes hairs and the blues eyes..." Seeing my astonished look I wondered what she could be on about.

"They think you go take all their customer away."

"Consuela, tell them I won't even be letting these guys touch me. I am only here to hostess and do my dancing. I got no intention of going escort with any of them!"

Wanting only to help, Consuela let more slip.

"Tomiko-san be very mad now you don't let customer touch you. If customer no touch, he not make much tip." Tomiko had clearly left it to poor Consuela to goad me into being a bit more available and free with those octopus hands at the table, while I danced to further line her own pockets with our commissions.

Being half drunk through my next show, I took the hint, letting a hand squeeze here and there though jumping back with a disapproving, cheeky glare to those 'naughty boys' as fingers wandered too far near where they were not welcome! Dancing to "Ice House" with the song "You're So Strange", it lifted me in a way... knowing to myself I *was* so strange to them... as they were to me. I was only acting it out in the dance! Tomiko surveyed my every move, looking like an Oriental Wicked Queen from Sleeping Beauty, certainly chinking up in her cash-register eyes, every note stuck plastered about me. Taking it gleefully from my hand as I past by her to the change room, she followed me in, fanning it out quickly in order as a wad of tips for a pleasing performance. Folding it tightly over, I didn't even bother to count it, stuffing it into my purse.

Days were fun though, as unlike the other girls who were off on shopping trips with boyfriends, one by one neighbourhood ladies had gotten to know me, knocking on the door when they saw my bedding hang out of the window to know I was up. Bizarrely they would just shove their toddlers through the door, sometimes up to six at a time, who'd sit in the living room watching cartoons with me, drawing pictures and writing their names as they laughed at my mistakes in Japanese and sneakily taught me too many naughty words. Becoming a Mary Poppins of a little Japanese village made me a lot of friends as I had the kids often 'til lunchtime, spoiling them all in the local noodle bar near the station until they disappeared one by one as parents collected them. Other times I just borrowed bicycles to explore the countryside... once riding as far as the old Himeji Castle, feeling the foreignness, still an alien on the landscape while wondering what Greg and my pets might be up to back in Melbourne.

One of the Brazilian girls came rushing over in the club as we were setting the sa-ke bottles into the microwave ready for the evening after taking a phone call. Someone, she said, was calling me from Australia. Greg was on the line to see how I was, yet had some bad news to tell me.

"I don't want to spoil your trip, Bunny... You'll be home soon, so maybe better if you wait 'til then...."

"Just tell me, Greg... I won't rest until I know what's happened," I could not imagine what it was, pleading 'til he relented.

"It's Pepsi. I left his cage on the front veranda during a storm last night... and he's died." My poor little budgie would not be there when I got back to chirp and chat excitedly with me.

Feeling dreadful, I told him I was really upset and disappointed, asking him to at least make sure he took the best of care of my 'boy' for me. He assured me that Bomber was being spoilt rotten by his brother and parents, even when he was away with the band. Sullenly, I returned to my table, not in the best of spirits to face my last week in Japan.

Dancing slowly, uneasily, cheek-to-cheek with an elderly Japanese executive to Frank Sinatra's "You Make Me Feel So Young", I felt completely numbed. Weeks on end of toasting with endless cups of sa-ke whilst looking with fake tenderness into dreamy-eyed karaoke crooners, had led me to forget my own world. As this man slyly groped my breasts, I pretended not to notice, though glancing into his eyes I caught his look of pure despising. He loathed going through those motions of being with me for the satisfaction of his business partners, as much as I did to be with him. Smiling my fake soft smile, I took the languous spin around so he could look me up and down before turning to see him standing before me, formally... far away like a soldier. Taking his cold hand again, I wondered what this man had done during World War Two and what torments and indignities they had inflicted on us with such mutual hatred.

Realising I meant nothing to this old man other than a trophy toy for him to play with, showing he could afford such luxuries, we whirled across the dance floor in the 'Emperor Hirohito-Bridge on the River Kwai-Death March Tango.' I had learnt that Sato and Tomiko were tall for Japanese for a good reason. They were not Japanese at all, but second generation children of the Korean slave labourers brought during the war to work in Japan. Like misfit outcastes anywhere, these Koreans had stayed on in Japan, honing the criminal underworld to their own needs, adopting Japanese names, assimilating to the culture. They were organised into the Yakusa-type gangs, ruthlessly controlling the vices of sex industry, bars and gambling. Jeremy had sold me off to a bunch of gangsters!

Reaching high into the skies above Japan, I didn't even want to look out of the window anymore at what I was flying from. It was only when I was sure that Japan was a tiny dot in the Pacific Ocean, that I looked out... with no desire to ever return. Greg and Bomber picked me up at Tullamarine.

Rehana Incognito

BODYCAGE

PART FIVE

Rehana Incognito

BODYCAGE

CHAPTER ONE

Revelling in the joy of seeing Western faces everywhere again, we embarked on whirlwind visits to Greg's relatives and calling friends I'd missed. Greg's maternal grandmother who lived quite close by, slightly admonished me for leaving Greg on his own so long. Telling me I was a foolish girl for having done so, I thought she was just being old-fashioned to say it was 'my place' to have stayed at home, catering for his every need as her generation would have done, but had a suspicion that her words may have contained more of a warning. Letting it slip by, I just happily told her I had *really* left the freezer very full for him and, with his mother and gran so close by, he was not likely to starve.

Enjoying a reunion meal from the ever-generous Felicity at the tearooms, I appreciated her discretion as she passed a little pile of postcards and letters with United States military stamps on them. Matthew had indeed remembered to stay in touch and I enjoyed reading all his heart had to say about the world and how he was seeing it. Accepting Loren's invitation to 'woman myself over', I could hardly wait to find out how things had been for her and others on the 'alternative girl about town' scene.

Pressing her front doorbell, I stood back hesitant as ever, always unsure as to what would come at me! She must have taken one big last draw on 'Witchy Poo', as I could smell the dope from the garden gate. Hearing the hoarse cough, getting ever louder approaching the door, it betrayed what she'd been up to.

The door flung open.

"ARRGGghhh," She choked and spluttered, "I am woman, hear me roar... Reezy, you dirty old codger... how the fuck are ya?"

Rehana Incognito

"All the better to see you haven't changed or lost any of your charm, Darling." Straight through the house we marched, out of the fly-wire back door to a little luncheon scenario she'd set up by the pool. Copied directly from the "Summer Celebration" section of the "Australian Women's Weekly", she proudly showed me from the picture in the magazine to her rendition on the plastic pool furniture table. Apart from the flies, it looked more or less the same!

After expressing genuine commiserations that Jeremy had conned me into another crummy contract, Loren told me she had been scheduled for surgery too with the lovely Doctor Abrams. Knowing she'd talked, all the time I'd known her, of how much she enjoyed using 'what she already had' and shocking me with her stories, I was quite taken aback.

"Loren, I'm stunned... are you sure you're doing the right thing there, Girl? It's not like having a tooth out at the dentists you know. You got to be real sure! You don't want to end up like those girls who scream around the hospital after the op that their cock's been chopped off... There's no going back you know?"

"Christ... That's too much to think about before I've had lunch." She raced back into the kitchen from where I heard the 'hubble bubble toil and trouble' as she chowed down again on Witchy Poo, perhaps manifesting some magical revelation from the hoochy haze. With her mind obviously recharged by the mystical powers, reddened eyes ablaze to match the hair, she plonked herself into the creaking chair.

"If it looks half as good as what he's done for you, I'm going to just love it. As long as I can still cum." Yes, life-changing decisions seemed simple and straightforward with a mind altered for quarter of a century smoking dope! Passing me a Pims, laden with ice and half a hobby farm of mint, fruit and veg, I wondered whether to tell her the pitfalls... for a brief moment... then did.

"There's no guarantee you'll get *any* sensation after the surgery, you know? That was made clear to me... let alone an orgasm! Is it worth the risk if you're having orgasms now with guys who are happy with what you got?" That drink felt *really* good, as I downed the whole thing.

"It's worth the risk 'cos I'm sick of these poofters who want me to be the wife in public and husband in my bedroom. If you can do it... I bloody well can."

"I don't know, Loren... it doesn't change that much in your life really... just your sex life... and who'd know if that was better or worse for you?" Not being able to look with any depth into anyone else's mind... who was I to know?

Shooting that look which said she had me cornered and the sneer of an Elvis lip, Loren toyed...

"So, you're saying having a pussy is not all it's *cracked* up to be then?!" Throwing her head back in a wild chuckle, she lifted her little denim mini, thrusting her hand into her panties. Grabbing a fist around her penis and egg-sized testicles, she waved the three-piece ensemble furiously at me.

"*I'm a womaaaaaan... W.Oh.Oh.M.A.N*" again she roared loudly enough that I hoped the neighbours were not out.

"Gee... that was girlie. Maybe you and Astrid will get a twin suite and be company for your ops." I tried to recover...

"Who's Astrid?" Loren regained some sense.

"You know, used to be Deena then Kylie... Now she's Astrid....and she's Swedish."

"Really? I thought she was from Wollongong."

"Geelong."

"She's got more multiple personalities than the sad bitch in that movie... What was it called? *Sybil*!" Perhaps just the one brain cell of memory must have been left waiting to be hit by her next suck on Witchy Poo, I'd thought, also recalling that movie too recently on televison. Possibly too, I'd taken note of those tragic consequences of such a child who had been subject to unspeakable cruelty by her own mother that her mind had split into literally a dozen or so distinct people.
"I think one of Deena's multiple personalities might be stalking her. She said she's getting hate mail from one," perhaps I'd thoughtlessly said.
"*Deena*.... Now she's what I'd call a tall man! What's she gonna end up being after she's had the chop? Just a cactus with a bloody cun..."
"Enough, Loren! Surely no doctor is going to operate on her or give her approval. She'd never get through the assessments."
"Oh, but she *has,* Girl. Tricked the lot of 'em right up, she did. She told them *everything* they wanted to hear." And that, it seemed, was that. Chillingly, smitten with guilt, I realised she'd told them everything she'd thought they needed to hear... from me. However, there was no big red button marked 'STOP' on this conveyor belt they'd stepped on for me to press any more.

Greg was off to rehearsals most days, returning home usually very tired... with hardly a cuddle in bed between us. Not even bothering to talk about it, I decided to keep up appearances and a brave face 'for the sake of the dog'. Knowing, in having gone to Japan to work and *overwork* myself still at Victoriana to save our house, I had found a greater strength and success in myself than I'd expected from him. My mother had taught me well.

BODYCAGE

"Rely on nobody, Pet," she'd often said. "If you want something doing... Do it yourself. You can't believe a word a man says. Just watch what they *do,* not what they *SAY.* You'll be left to it all by yourself in the end." Truth enough in that, I'd decided, always trying to bear in mind to watch what people actually do... despite what they say, even catching myself!

We were drifting apart, feeling less that I *needed* him. Work at the Vic was always there for me, keeping me very busy 'til all hours, though meeting a lot of Aussie celebrities and making new friends. One was a weather girl from a local TV station and close friend of Felicity. She arrived one night with a woman and her daughter who sat upstairs, not attracting much of my attention until the end of my shift when all was locked up and they sat for a nightcap with Felicity.

Judy, the weather girl, called me over at some point, introducing me to the distant relatives who had arrived from Yorkshire to start a new life. As Judy disappeared to chat with Felicity, I sat by the mother, noticing the 'daughter' was a slightly gangly, shy and uncomfortable, fair-haired boy with a noticeably large Adam's Apple. Although nicely dressed as a girl of teenage years, the mother told me that Judy had introduced us so I could give some counsel to her son who was in the process of 'becoming a woman'. With no reason to see the 'daughter', Erin, as anyone other than someone who may well have been just like myself, I took her under my wing as Felicity had done for me.

Having fled from a violent, abusive father, it seemed Erin had realised her transgender situation, so they had come to Australia to 'get on with it', far from the problems of their coal mining pit village too. Without prying too deeply, I tried to point out that it might be a case that Erin may just reject being male because her father was so distant and a poor example of anything to be like. Not being too good with such things and totally averse to the thought of hurting a sweet kid's feelings, I played along again, dispensing advice and professional's contacts to get Erin further along her chosen path.

Stepping onto the 'Express Line' of the girlie conveyor belt, Erin's mum had quickly arranged a feminising nose job and shaving of the Adam's Apple, leaving the hormone treatment to do its job in the breast department before getting those enlarged too. It was nice to have a little 'sister' to go out with clubbing, shopping and swimming for a while. Still, I simply accepted that she was just like me, flirting with boys and dating now and then though forever holding back because of her status still.

On my one day off, a bright Sunday, quietly alone with Bomber, the doorbell rang unexpectedly. Astrid stood there, hauling her girlie bicycle full of groceries in the huge basket onto the front veranda.

"Hi Astrid... this is a surprise. I thought you'd be in hospital by now having your op... or away somewhere nice recovering." She clamoured into the living room, collapsing on the couch.

"I got the bike out to ride out to the hills along the Burwood Highway, to get some fresh foods and stuff like you said, to build up my strength before surgery. It's tomorrow... Look at the calves I built up on my pins." Hoisting up a billowing gypsy skirt, there they were, covered in nicks and scratches from razor blades and waxes- a big, clumsy pair of men's hiking boots on as well!

"They're looking great, Girl. Looks like you could kick a kangaroo in half with those... But weren't you supposed to show you can hold down a straight relationship and job first?" I stood gazing at her panting in a pool of

sweat, sprawled on my sofa. "I don't think you were even dating last time I saw you."
"Oh, I don't have time for that shit," she incredibly croaked in her all-over-the-place Swedish lilt. "I bought, Stuart, the towel boy from the sauna, a few grams of speed every month and he came with me as my boyfriend to meet the family on the Gender Board. It worked really good... Tricked 'em all, Love!!"
"Looks like you're well on the way to womanhood now then, doesn't it?!"
"Yep, I'm gonna suck dick 'til I'm sick."
"That's nice, Hon," I took a deep breath, puffing it all out again in exasperation, suddenly catching the glistening whiskers glaring in the light, dancing across her face through the trees in my garden and into the living room.
"What are you going to do about that facial hair though still?"
Reaching into her satchel, she pulled out the blackened pot of wax I'd met a year or so ago.
"Wanted to let them grow up 'til the last minute then have a total wax, so I wouldn't have to lie there in hospital plucking away at them like the Bearded Woman. Would you do the honours for me, Ri?"
Several hours later, her face, neck, shoulders and back were completely laid bare. Wishing her luck, she rode off into the sunset down my peaceful lane, glowing with soreness as I promised to visit her for her 'last stand' at Masada hospital when it was all done.
 Surprisingly, the phone rang the next afternoon as I was about to head for the train to work. It was a delightful treat to hear the voice of Cecilia from Masada Hospital, the gentle Sister who had cared for me when I was there.
"Riannon, sorry to trouble you...but can you get down here straight away? Your friend Astrid is making such a

fuss here. She said you'd know what to do and would probably come down if I called you." Cecilia sounded desperate, so I called a taxi instead, heading straight to Balaclava, wondering all the way, was it a colostomy disaster which had plagued me with worry? Or perhaps she'd lost a lot of blood too and was delirious... a weird anaesthetic reaction maybe?

Arriving there, Cecilia rushed me to Astrid's private room, whispering-

"You've got to do something... For God's sake calm her down. She's making so much noise and there's women on this ward who've just had their babies."

Lying there like an insect-bitten Barbara Cartland in pink negligee and matching dressing gown with the wax welts all over her face, she was surprisingly alert, though agitatedly thrashing from side to side.

"Ri, thank Christ, you're here." I walked agog to her bedside as she limply reached for my hand, feeling pathetic with the drips hanging out. "You've got to do something about those bitches in the other rooms." Heaving herself upright, like a woman about to make a dying confession, she grasped at my hand. "I'm paying a fucking fortune to be in this private room and I can't get to sleep for those bloody babies. Tell 'em to do something about it, Ri... or I'll kill the lot of the bastards."

"But, Darling, this is a women's ward... maternity. They are newborn babies... and are going to be crying most of the time! They need to be fed, or changed... or are feeling some pain...That's what they do!" Fumbling for more words to defend the babies... just doing what babies do... I managed,

"The mothers can't be too concerned about who's getting enough sleep in here. They've just been through enough themselves with giving birth. Try and

think about that." Sitting even further up in the bed she yelled at the top of her voice,
"I don't care if they've just given birth. Anyone can... Even a rat can fucking do that and have twelve of them! I've just had my bloody cock and balls lopped off." She collapsed back into the pillows, feeling sorry for herself.
"Astrid, I think they need to bump up your sedation a bit and you'll fall asleep regardless. I'll speak to the Sister. Things just don't seem quite as they should after all the anaesthetic and stuff going on in your mind right now. You won't be able to think straight for another few days yet...ok? Just try to sleep whenever you can for now, it's going to be erratic regardless." Giving her brow a few mops with a flannel and cold water, a stubbly hard whisker caught my fingertips. The 'one that had gotten away' during my exhausting last minute check for strays after the waxing. Hoping she'd not notice it, I idly chatted 'til she fell asleep before noticing the huge shadow of a figure had manifested in the doorway of her room.

Looking like one of those big, burly, Russian women commandant guards of a Gulag, I saw the family resemblance as she loomed forth.
"I'm Danny's mum," she coldly announced. With just a gentle smile, I vacated the visitor chair to leave her to whatever she had to say to 'Danny' when awake, walking quickly from the room to leave Danny/Deena/Kylie/Astrid to deal with the throes of her own rebirth, without me for now. Thinking the mother looked more like a man than her 'son' must ever have had, I wondered how much that had to do with where 'he' now lay. Sneaking from the hospital after a quick chat with Cecilia, apologising that I had ever encouraged Astrid, I could but wonder just what type of

womanly journey she really hoped now to embark on. Predictably enough, it didn't take long to find out.

Two days later, I was again summoned to Masada by the New Woman, Astrid herself.

"Can you bring a good set of tweezers with you when you come in too, Lovey? " she crackled down the line. "My face is already stubbly again and I wondered if you could....."

"Fine, Astrid...yeah, I know. I'd just love to spend the afternoon in a hospital plucking your face." On arrival, Cecilia simply shook her head, shrugged her shoulders, exasperated for sure in despair as she watched me heading down the corridor to Astrid's room. Wondering if she'd driven the staff all crazy yet, I reached for the door as it burst open and an ashen-faced orderly bumped me as he scrambled past.

"What's up with him, Astrid?" I peeped out to see him hurrying off. "He flew out of here like a bat out of hell."

"I dunno, he was bringing in some towels and I thought he looked cute so I asked him if he wanted to take a look at my...you know...." Yes, I did know!

"YOU *WHAT*, Astrid??? You can't do things like that. He'll have nightmares for the rest of his life after that. Don't you realise how totally inappropriate that is?" Lying respondent in the untied, see-thru negligee, heaving her bosom up and down, Astrid didn't seem to think so.

"Look, Love... I got a million dollar new box and I can't wait to show the whole world. Wanna look?"

Without waiting to hear my reply, the sheets were flung back to reveal her long, pimply, splayed apart legs. Something like the mound you'd see at the rear end of one of those baboons with the pink backsides, loomed from her crotch.

"Does it look like the real thing, Riannon... Does it look like a real pussy?" Indeed it did, I nodded, perhaps unconvincingly as I thought, on closer scrutiny it looked like a cow that had just given birth... to twins. It was truly a mess of chopped meat to me and my face must have belied my comment.

"Very nice, Astrid. Am sure he's done a great job and it'll be beautiful when the swelling's gone down."

"Great!" she fell back again, contentedly. "Cos Felicity said as soon as I am on my feet that Jeremy would be able to offer me a contract to dance in Asia just like you. I can hardly wait!"

"I'm sure Asia can hardly wait for you too, Astrid." Again I smiled like this was the most natural thing for someone in that state to take on. "I'm sure you'll cause a sensation." That, I did mean!

Loren had booked in for her surgery just a couple of weeks after Astrid, same doctor, same hospital. Similar story too I guessed. To offer support, I arrived early in the morning when she'd just had her pre-med and was not quite away with the fairies, though clearly had spent a lot of her time before checking in communing in the clouds with Witchy Poo. Just before the orderly came to wheel her down that same corridor to the surgery where I was 'created', she lifted the sheet to again shock me with the grab of her willy and waving handful of testicles, which amazingly had not shrunk after years on oestrogen! Again with a wild wiggle of the shiny balls, she said

"See these... they're bloody goin' "

"Get the doctor to keep them in a jar when he's done, Loren... Have them dipped... they'll make a lovely set of drop ear-rings." Knowing her, she would have... and another colleague was rocketed off on the Oestrogen Express to Planet Girly.

On an insanely busy Saturday night at Victoriana, running up and down the stairs, answering doors and handling the kitchen, I was pleased when a little, smartly-dressed lady popped an elegant hand through the kitchen doorway with a huge glass of champagne to me.

"Riannon, aren't you?" she said as I noticed her delicate, almost oriental features, short black bobbed hair and appealing little gap between her front teeth. Clearly in her late forties, she introduced herself as Ruby and a very good friend of Felicity. The kitchen had flooded again and I was literally wading in murky water, expecting electrocution at any time, yet not even caring. Someone walked by her, kind of confused in the noise and crowds in the hallway. In my exhaustion I'd thought it was an ugly bride.

Peeping past Ruby and down the hallway, I saw the white dress swallowed up in the crowds, asking Ruby if there was a wedding party that night.

"Wedding? No, Love... why?" she looked confused.

"Wasn't that a bride I just saw go by?" She doubled over laughing, champagne flying everywhere. "Bride?! that was my friend 'The Sheik'. He's an Arab from Bahrain!"

"Crikey... thank God for that, I though she was a bit ugly.... and hairy!" Clearly I needed the drink!

"He was asking about you a few times tonight and couldn't believe you were working in a kitchen. Neither can I now, seeing you here." Almost in tears now, I was way too exhausted, knowing she was probably right and I appreciated her concern and even noticing.

"You look like you needed that, Riannon... and a good break. It's my daughter's birthday tonight and I just wanted to thank you for helping make it so special and lovely for her... Especially with this going on." She nodded down to me standing in a rice paddy. Slinking cautiously, in her towering expensive heels, onto a step to be closer to me at the water's edge, she spoke more discretely.

BODYCAGE

"I can't help wondering though what a beautiful young woman is doing working like *this*. You can come work for me and earn a fortune. I'd give you a job any day." She caught my attention firmly in the eye.

"Oh, thanks very much. I work here as many hours as I can 'cos my boyfriend only works part time in band and we got a mortgage to pay," I explained.

She sneered, a kind of disgust.

"You don't *need* to be working like this, Riannon because a guy can't look after you properly. Take my card and give me a call if you want to come and check out my place." Leaning across the dirty lagoon, I took the card reading "Malvern Ruby's- Ladies of Exquisite Pleasure" with an address in an upmarket neighbourhood. Noticing the immaculate manicure and nail polish on her over-bejewelled hands, I dared to ask,

"This is a brothel isn't it? Or a massage parlour, I mean...sorry. Greg would kill me if I went near a place like that to work!"

"Is *he* paying your bills properly, Riannon?" she swayed back with a knowing smirk, that she had my full attention. "Give me a call." She skipped off down the hallway unbelievably at ease on heels that high, to join her daughter and the 'ugly bride' upstairs.

Being another unbelievably late night, I'd let Greg go home without me, taking Felicity's offer to go home and stay at her place when we'd finally shoo-ed off the last of the stragglers. Over breakfast in Felicity's jumbled kitchen, I asked her about Ruby and if she thought there might at least be some extra work there for me as a receptionist.

"There'll always be jobs coming and going there, Ri... but Ruby will pester the hell out of you until she gets you to 'go upstairs' like the other girls... or take to the whip in the dungeon at least." She knew and awful lot

for a 'Lady', I thought slurping the big bowl of milky coffee.
"Dungeon? Whips?" What was all this about I wondered.... a little too curiously for someone not yet done with her first coffee.
"Ruby, covers the lot in there, Darling. She's got them fucking and flogging, morning, noon and night and bloody well knows she can make a fortune out of you too." I sat back to let her ramble.
"She's been at this game for twenty years now and has asked about you a few times. Do you think you could stand it though? I'll tell you now... all the girls who work for her are trannies... She bloody loves us."
"Why's that?" I really was now mesmerised at the thought of a Moulin Rouge bordello full of New Orleans- styled tarts with five o'clock shadows. "Wouldn't men paying for it prefer biologically-born women?"
"Riannon! They're not going there for love affairs or to make babies. They come in for a good raunchy time with someone who knows what a man really wants."
Starting to see where this was heading, it dawned that my dear Felicity knew way too much, as she'd begun to fidget uncomfortably.
"*LADY B*!!! You're working in there too, aren't you...? Go on... you can tell me."
"Yeah, you're right. I've worked there for years. Half the bloody showgirls in Melbourne are in there too, Riannon... with and without their willies. Ruby's runs on tranny power, my Love. And she's rakin' it in." That would explain all the extravagances of furniture and fittings at the Victoriana Tea Rooms then, I guessed. Scooping up a mouthful of Special K, I asked further...
"Why does Ruby think we'd know how to give a man a better time in a brothel than ordinary women anyway?"

BODYCAGE

"She saw it pretty obvious that the likes of the show queens go pretty over-the-top with the makeup and costumes...trying that bit harder to be more feminine...You know what I mean? The extra makeup, tartier costumes... It's what men want really... and most women don't know or bother to do that properly these days do they? And besides... and I think she's right on this one... Anyone who was a man before probably knows what a man really wants anyway, right?" She washed up the dishes as I slid my bowl into the sink.
"Bang goes that theory, Felicity...'cos I haven't got a clue how they think... or care! Anyway... I never noticed any guy I was with screaming for help though... If he had it must have been in a very soft, tiny voice! But, just a minute... what are the showgirls doing in there if most of them have got dicks?!" Felicity leaned over, whispering in my ear as she topped up the teapot,
"They're all doing 'trick' when the guys don't know. The ones who do know are lining up for it. If they come in asking for a tranny, Ruby always says 'how do you like them... with or without?'" Stifling her laugh, she saw my confusion.
"You mean she asks them if they want a girl *with a dick* or *without a dick*?"
"No, you dumb bitch, she means do they want a girl with a pussy or *without one!*" That probably got confusing with more people than me... and was way too much over breakfast. So, heading to the station, I caught some rest on the train before a weary plod along the lane to our house.

The house looked like a bomb site, with clothes strewn about and the kitchen like a tsunami had washed through. Bomber circled madly, whining around my legs... starving! Greg had not even fed him, yet he'd found time to stick the red letter final bills on the fridge door with magnets. After a long week of late nights at

Rehana Incognito

Vic and a filthy house to come home to, I was ready to call Ruby and get straight down there if Greg mentioned one more time that I wasn't keeping the house clean enough for him. With Bomber, leaping all over his bowls in the laundry as I loaded the machine with two weeks of washing, I made up my mind.

Ruby answered the phone straight away.

"The lovely, Riannon! It's so nice to hear from you. Felicity mentioned you might be interested in some work, so why don't you come on over?" Promising a shift free for Saturday or Sunday evenings on reception, I took down her directions, promising to drop by on my way to work early evening. Mercifully, the two-storey, white terraced house with all the lovely laced latticework around the awnings had a discrete side lane entrance and no neighbouring houses either side or opposite to see me coming to the door. I wished I was invisible. It was in an area zoned 'light industrial', which could have meant anything from a doggy wash to a small noodle factory.

Indeed, my New Orleans, Moulin Rouge fantasy was not far wrong, right down to the burgundy tiffany lamps, satin and leopard print lounges and gilded mirrors everywhere. Ruby kindly showed me around what I saw as a little 'sex factory', three upstairs bedrooms with two adjoining bathrooms where clients were required to shower first... and of course, most showered afterwards! Two rooms gave the impression of a hedonistic Bohemian bedroom, but the third was smaller, quite Spartan and very black. It also served as a little 'mini dungeon and fetish' room. The 'menu' was so straightforward and to the point, it reminded me of a sandwich bar... lending again the feeling that this was all just so functional and ok, that it would not be a concern to me at all to book these 'girls' over the phone or when customers came to the door. It would be just

BODYCAGE

like working in a shop or restaurant but we were purveyors of the finest filth and perversions. Meeting a couple of the girls, neither of whom I recognised, as they sat watching "The Young and the Restless", putting on outfits and make-up, I accepted the job happy enough to be one of those 'bad-assed chicks from... Malvern Rube's'. So... it was-
"Hey sister
go sister...
gotta get that dough, sister". Not quite Lady Marmalade, probably not even Strawberry Jam, but definitely, I'd taken the first steps into a lot of sticky mess I'd thought could be handled as easily as offering a menu in the Tea Rooms and running a credit card through.

Taking on both the Saturday and Sunday nights shifts, were no bother as Greg was away now most weekends. He didn't mind me doing the reception, having called it many times to make sure it was me answering just the phone and not doing anything else. As I told him he'd not need worry about that, I remember his reply quite well...
"As if you would. I know my Bunny would never do anything like that."

The stream of men who caroused through the doors seemed unending at times as this was a legal business and I felt that most men regarded going to see someone in a place like this as simple as picking up a takeaway meal on the way home. If they'd been out, not been too successful to find a girl in a bar or one of our 'special ladies... with that something extra'... it would probably have cost them less than all the drinks or even a meal and movie when all they wanted was the quick-fix sex. Perhaps they got the 'gourmet meals' type elsewhere or just weren't really big eaters! Not giving it much thought or really even letting it register what they went upstairs *for*... they may as well have been up there playing scrabble for all I cared. Although one young Greek guy, who looked like he'd stepped from the pages of "GQ" magazine came by late a few Sunday evenings as Ruby was there, doing the books. Two or three girls who'd worked the shifts engaged him apathetically as he made it clear he didn't have much interest in them each time, referring to them as 'those girls', none could tempt him.

He'd bargain with me to go upstairs with him instead, with his big, baby bull eyes, promises of sensuous pleasures like I'd never had, and each week his wad of cash thrust under my nose got bigger and bigger with the bulge in his trousers. Ruby had watched discretely each time I had introduced him to whoever was on, before letting him out the door again, usually with a laugh or a joke and a slapping of his wandering hands as he tried for a grope on the way out.

After a few of his fruitless visits, I quipped to Ruby that we always want what we can't have and that if I wasn't in a relationship I'd have given that guy some thought. She'd roll her eyes as if I were quite deranged and say the same thing over and over...

"You'll learn one day, Riannon. A man is only yours when he is in your eyesight... Other than that they are game for anyone."

As she hid behind the enormous Chinese screen in the reception room one evening, I am sure her heart must have thumped with the sound of the Greek guy's wad of notes this time hitting the desk.

"Four hundred dollars... Right there if you come upstairs with me tonight!" Looking at it, frozen in disbelief then looking at his hurt, pleading eyes, Ruby literally fell from behind the screen to bounce up like a muppet by his side.

BODYCAGE

"Jesus, Girl... This guy's just offered you four hundred bucks to go upstairs for a great time with him... And you tell me you don't even *see* your boyfriend any more, let alone get on with him. You want your head read, Sweetheart... I'd bloody well pay *him* four hundred dollars to take *me* upstairs." Not even knowing if it was the thought that I was causing her to lose her commission night after night with this guy, or if she was *right* in her experience that it wasn't such a serious matter to just go and have sex with a stranger for money, I placed my hand on his cash. Taking one more look into those mysterious, exotic eyes burning through me with horniness, I thought of all the hard work I was doing, the mess in my house and the distance now with Greg. Sliding the cash towards me and off under the counter, I turned to the palpitating Madame.
"You are receptionist for an hour, Ruby."

CHAPTER TWO

Being as good as he promised to be in the soft lights and piped romantic music, nothing about him disappointed. Closing the big shiny black door as I saw him off.... disappearing into the night, with a huge, white towel around me and another wrapped around my hair after a quick shower, Ruby sat perched on my chair behind the desk... grinning.
"Not so bad was it now?" Handing me the usual envelope with my two night's salary in it, she then passed me the thicker one... with what I had made in a tenth of the time, actually enjoying myself, feeling only a little naughty and somehow justifying it...
"Well, why not? I did without much in the way of men for a long time, so I guess it won't do much harm to have made up for a bit of lost time... for once." With little or no intimacy at all with Greg, I'd justified too the sex with others as being necessary for my own gynaecological wellbeing, as Dr Abrams had insisted regular sex was essential for keeping the muscles and depth of the designer vagina in good working order. For the most part it would be a simple matter to see these men as something to use simply as human tools, living dilators for which I was grateful... then seeing little difference between them and the glass or rubber ones the doctors provided for girls who were not involved with a male sex partner at the time.
So there sat Ruby, saying nothing, which really meant absolutely everything, just watching me get myself together... knowing I'd fallen exactly where she wanted me. I knew too, my curiosity about how far I could go in all this would get the better of me, wondering all the more how intimacy with another man felt ... and would it be different or better than what I'd only ever experienced with Greg? I'd come to the banks of a

sewer in life, ready to dive in... just to see how the waters felt and where they flowed... but didn't even have the slightest notion it was anything near so dirty.

I am not suggesting that the sex 'industry' in itself is a sewer. There are times and aspects of it which really feel like nothing but filth, degradation and guilt, if people choose to see it that way on both sides of the transaction. There are other times when it feels like a service of care and comfort to a man who may have not found it anywhere else in his life, regardless of the reason. Or even something deeper, beyond the basic needs of their bodies for sex and the worker's for money, of a unity symbolised in the joining of two bodies, blindly or subconsciously chasing a wholeness we often don't realise we are missing. In a hidden secret place, mysterious as these darkened, womb-like caves, the search repeats itself... with that air of ritual and unspoken sacredness tainted with the duality of its perceived profanity. They too need and deserve intimacy and closeness but often have neither the skills, nor time and good fortune to have a satisfactory partner in their lives. It was more the case that my own life was to be soiled by it... All of the dreams of my little house, garden, my boyfriend, the pets and the white picket fence, would be washed away in the filth and the pain of the *consequences* when it was all to blow apart.

It was, just as Ruby had expected, a short step from the reception desk to the 'Stairway to Heaven' as I'd joked to the wealthy Greek boy, following my rolling rump up the stairs. I realised, as I turned to look back at him, that he would probably have followed it over a cliff. Spending more time watching and studying the dynamics, both sexually and spiritually, of the clients and the workers in these types of places, it dawned that perhaps something more profound was really behind my so called joke of the 'Stairway to Heaven'.

Rehana Incognito

Secretly though, at that time, I wished that all the men looked like him and I could enjoy such an ideal 'job', being *loved* by them all in one encounter after the other, all the while getting rich, caring for their little needs. It's a delusion a lot of people like myself fall prey to... All too easily as well, thinking it a clever way to make the world 'pay' for all our miseries. Men fixing those 'penis-shaped', damaged vortexes in the souls again and again like elastoplasts, with the added twist that these guys were even *paying* us, to be our temporary reprieve from those feelings of rejection and inadequacy.

Still, my only hesitation to have gone from receptionist, explaining services, to providing the services myself, was the thought of being upstairs in the room with someone I didn't find remotely attractive! Feeling sure I'd have to shove some fat, ugly old man off me as he sweated and heaved, I'd imagined having to run downstairs and give him his money back as I tried to wash it all away in a good, hot shower. A call came one evening, surprising me somewhat as it was a woman on the line, asking for Felicity. Enquiring if she had the number for the Tea Rooms to call her there, she said she did not but wondered if I knew whether Felicity could help her 'with a job' the next afternoon. Telling her that I knew Felicity would be at the restaurant all day, she surprised me... asking if I myself were free in the afternoon and wanted to earn 'an extra hundred bucks'.

With friendly reassurance that there was no sex involved as it was a bondage session, Britt said I was only to play a kind of observant role. Giving me her number and address to come nice and early the next day, I thought this *was* exciting! Must be like the games we play as children where we chase each other around and tie each other up. Usually though, it was this child

BODYCAGE

who had been tormented. Sitting on the tram watching Nicholson Street fly by, I'd thought of myself bound in ropes to the Hills Hoist clothes line as 'St Bartholomew' with all the darts hanging out of my thighs and buttocks... Karen and the jeering crowd at my suburban execution looking on.

"The House of Domination" was a typical North Melbourne, little terraced town house. It didn't need to be in a light industrial zone apparently, as that was only for the sex industry. Bondage and Discipline, Sadism and Masochism, it was deemed, were not sexual! Pressing the doorbell, I could hardly wait for the leather-clad Dominatrix in thigh high boots, whips in hand, clattering with chains and studs. Footsteps approached as the door opened to reveal standing before me a beautiful blonde... like Brigitte Nielsen, statuesquely confident, yet in blue and white checked apron and tight blue jeans looking like someone's mum from "Neighbours" or the "Brady Bunch".

"Just getting a casserole in the oven for the kid's dinner tonight, Darling. Come on in... Nice to meet you." 'Carol Brady's' hands were covered in flour as she finished the preparations for her children's dinner, explaining that we had enough time to do this job, then she could pack up the prepared meal and head home to the suburbs, far from this life her family and neighbours did not know of. Our 'job' was with a regular client who wanted to meet us at his hotel in the city centre... at the bar. We were to flirt with him as strangers, luring him to the car park and bundle him into the boot, back to our lair, to become the victim of the Valkyries!!

Our prearranged goal was to strip him, tie him up and find photos of his wife which we were to abuse and burn before his very eyes. All totally bizarre of course, but the worst of it was, it was to be some satanic-styled rite... not real, just playing at it... Which I did, though felt truly dreadful as the poor, dowdy woman in the photos looked so sweet. Mistress Britt spent about the final twenty minutes alone in the room with him and I had no idea how the scenario was to end, as I sat in the kitchen watching TV. The portly, middle-aged gentleman accepted a cup of tea and a merry old chat as I dared to ask him about *his* work. He was a *very* high-ranking minister of the Church! Well, there went all my religious hang-ups and questions... right out of the window. If someone, I realised I had seen on TV and read of in the papers, was balancing out his life on a shadowy side in this way, how could *I* feel bad, judging myself or anyone else?!

Pocketing the hundred bucks, off to deal with the rushing around, grovelling at tables and putting up with the same brash treatment I often got from patients as a nurse, I wondered if it was all worth it. Accepting Britt's invitation to come any time... I wanted to learn more, lured again to an irresistible taste of power... and easy money. As she said with a girlish giggle on my way out the door-

"You'll enjoy finding your power and taking it all out on the *weaker sex*!" Wondering what she herself must have been through in life, leading her to this as a job, I could not have known that I would have her as one of my dearest friends for the next twenty years to find out.

I was sat on the tatty white-washed wall at ten in the morning as Britt stepped out of her car in front of the house.

"Knew you'd be back," she simply winked, as I picked up one of her bags, and disappeared intrepidly into the little white 'temple of the mysteries' as Pollyanna, the Princess of Perversions, Pleasure and Pain. It was shortly before afternoon tea before realising I had already trained several 'puppies', threatening to castrate them or have them put down if they ever tried to do dirty things to my leg or slippers again. Dressing a couple of elderly men like fairies on Christmas trees to masturbate themselves in the mirror as I pretended to be their aunt or sister catching them in my clothes, felt like having a few friends over to play dress ups. How turned on they got whilst dressed like that didn't bother me in the least. An aroused penis in frilly knickers seemed somehow more harmless and kind of amusing than one in men's underwear! As long as they did not want to touch me, I didn't care what they thought, felt or did. Britt and I said we were like Jan and Marsha Brady, having a few of our girlfriends over for a sleepover... but they were paying all our bills, wearing all our clothes whilst escaping their drudgery as 'quasi-lesbians' for an hour or afternoon. I like the ones who could do my ironing for me, personally. As for their 'swollen clitoris', I got them to say it was a deformity and they must have been kicked between the legs by a horse when they were 'little girls'. Or....

"Don't be embarrassed about that little old thing, Sweetie... A lot of girls have willies really... maybe even your mother had one... you never know."

The first one I actually slapped so hard on his naughty, wagging doggy toosh... I apologised to, in case I *hurt* him! From the bottom of my heart though, I swear I could never be cruel to animals... honestly! Our unruly puppies had, after all, come for discipline, humiliation and training How quickly I learnt, as I became known as a new 'Goddess of the House'- "Mistress Ultra Violent" ('Light') ... well, *light*... for the most part. Adopting a little of the persona, from memories of Barbara Woodhouse of television dog training fame, combined with recent recollections of all the discipline and training of my own dog, Bomber, such men were easy to deal with as long as they didn't pee on the carpet. They'd get their noses rubbed in it, or if caught thinking my boots were something to mount like leather in heat, they'd be pushed down onto the floor to consummate their desires with the carpet...

"And while you're down there, shagging the carpet... watch for those pins I dropped earlier." - always enough to make their blood run cold with an added twist of cruelty from their Mistress, tugging on the leash.

Not just them, but anyone who'd gotten one of my severe spankings for whatever reason were always made to see how red I'd gotten their bums... glowing in the mirror, before setting them free with a reminder that they'd think of me for the rest of the week... every time they sat down. Either that, or if I'd severely brutalised them, I always let them know that St Vincent's Hospital was just a few minutes down the road if it was needed.

"You'd never think such a beautiful hand could cause you so much pain, would you?" I'd whisper in their ears, when blindfolded, naked and bound for us to toy with. Stroking my hand, painfully slowly under their chins so they could feel its softness, they'd be commanded to kiss it, before inflicting a savage thwack on their bare behinds. That viciously sharp, stinging echo, which ricocheted around the dungeon, quickly became a sound I enjoyed more and more. As the slaps induced little, shiny, clear beads of dribbles to ooze noticeably from their pathetically dangling penis to be made fun of, if it started to stir... I'd grab it sharply...

"What's the matter, Slave... scared *stiff*?" With a sharp whack on the hardening member, I could always see they were!

"You're my little pet for the next hour," they'd hear me hiss into their ears as they stood blindfolded, trembling. "To do *anything* I want with."

BODYCAGE

It's funny how quickly I noticed that a girl really can get anything she wants from a man whilst clad in a pair of very tight, thigh-high leather boots... Providing she is capable of walking more than six paces in them! I couldn't... and usually would just sit there in them... looking mean, sexy, in control and dominant at the inferior one on his knees.

Home life was a mess, slogging it out in the restaurant was exhausting, but I had a taste of fun though now, making more money than I'd imagined. Lying to Greg whilst going through the motions just to satisfy him, I found more and more reason at Malvern Ruby's to 'do her a favour' when an attractive enough guy, I thought I could cope with, wanted only the one he thought he could not have. Pollyanna, with all her justifications of curiosity, catching up for missed experiences, with bills to be paid... was now a prostitute. Yet for every guy I entertained in those boudoirs, there was an equal amount, on all fours, naked at my feet in dog collars waiting to pay me for exactly what they were *not* allowed to have! As Felicity engaged more help at the Tea Rooms, I took on more shifts at Ruby's, both at the reception desk and many times upstairs too as it pleased me. More days than not, I also reported for duties at the House of Domination.

1989

Spending a fair amount of my spare time with Erin put a tiny slant of balance on a life, which on another level, was flying well off into a whirlwind I wasn't even aware of. So, for those few hours a week when we could catch up, it was reassuringly normal to have a 'sister' close to my own age to go shopping, trying on clothes and makeup, go swimming and flirting with guys. Also, as she had the tiny little bits of surgery to feminise her nose, remove the Adam's Apple and slightly pout out her lips, she was slight and petite enough to pass totally as a woman too. Usually in a buzz of laughter and coquettish teasing of any man in our path, we covered malls, beaches and cafes by day and carried on our act like secret 'Barbie Twins' into the clubs at night, relishing the adoration.

After dressing like the girls from "Bananarama" and putting on our 'hardons from hell' cock-tease, pseudo-lesbian dance shows for all the boys around, we mimed out all the actions of the songs of the late eighties, mouthing the words and living them out. To Madonna singing "Like a Prayer" we'd called to the Heavens or the guys leering longingly...

"*Life is a mystery, everyone must stand alone*
I hear you call my name
And it feels like home..." We danced slowly around each other... Sensuous long, stokes along each other's bare arms and thighs, before pushing each other apart to wonder who had called our names... More drunkenly, we fell about...

"*I'm down on my knees, I wanna take you there*
In the midnight hour I can feel your power
Just like a prayer you know I'll take you there..."
Feigning a willingness to go down on our knees... feeling some kind of power... near that midnight hour, we whirled around as the club did too, catching dozens of captivated eyes, yet none to really reach out and actually see us.

"*I hear your voice, it's like an angel sighing*
I have no choice, I hear your voice
Feels like flying
I close my eyes, Oh God I think I'm falling
Out of the sky, I close my eyes

BODYCAGE

Heaven help me..." As we actually loudly sang these words, I paused starkly for a brief moment... to realise... I was actually praying. 'Heaven help me.'

Thankfully, we were saved from our Madonna moroseness, as the night wound up with a rush to the dance floor and an almighty crush with the blowing of whistles and waving of neon tubes. "Yaz and the Plastic People" assured us that we might be really going somewhere with the "The Only Way is Up". Someone passed us a bottle of poppers, we both took a big sniff as I said to Erin...

"Hope the only way *is* up for these two plastic people..." I'm not sure if she had then fallen over laughing, but thankfully it was backwards... onto a group of people sat on a big sofa!

Still eager for attention, like a troublesome Madame Du Barry and Marie Antoinette, it was back to Lady B's for nightcaps at the Victoriana Tea Rooms with the late night crowd, as we'd driven past to see if the lights were still on. In a quiet sofa booth, Felicity delivered us two, not so strong, Irish coffees, joining us like a mother hen to see how her girl's night had been. It was ways a cosy scene late in the evenings, with big open fires, opulent charm and brilliantly-created bygone world right there near the centre of Melbourne. We sat smugly in agreement at how far three young, blond, 'Pommy' kids, from working class England, had come to end up sitting right there in such elegance. Noticing Erin's gaze, ever following me like a scrutinizing searchlight, noting every move I made, I suddenly noticed *her* body language and movements too, echoing my own.

Quite often, having sat down, gotten up, or simple lifted a glass or cutlery... Erin found reason straight away to copy the entire manoeuvre, like an understudy for my body dynamics. Realising, she also asked a lot

Rehana Incognito

of questions about my experiences with the Gender Board, I would tell her to consult her 'Bible'. Her 'Bible' was the page-worn autobiography of the sex-change model Tula (Caroline) Cossey, whose story became an international sensation when she was exposed as the 'Bond Girl' who used to be a 'man'. Erin, had lived and breathed every word of this book, "I Am A Woman", believing it held the mystic wisdom of all the knowledge she would need... to become just like Tula. Meeting Caroline, years later in the loo at the Roof Gardens in Kensington, looking well and content after her first marriage, she reminded me of how ridiculous such comments as 'born a man' was... As if she was born, lying there in a crib with a big hairy chest, moustache and muscles! We are all born *babies* for goodness sake. They have to try to hurt us, I guess, being the last safe target for such abuse, now that the likes of our media can't make fun of other minorities without a law suit!

Becoming anything like 'Tula' appeared immediately questionable when Erin, with total disregard for the propriety of the chic Tearooms and it's celebrity clientele, flashed her newly-enhanced breasts at two men sitting quietly sipping port, almost spluttering it across the table. Half drunk herself, Erin had thought flashing what she had to get their attention was the nearest thing she could muster as flirting. I was totally shocked.

"Erin... how could you have done that?! Those guys are going to think we are a couple of cheap whores now. It's OK doing things like that in private but not in front of blokes." An almighty (though delicate, with nicely painted nails) fist crashed on the table as Erin snarled in my face,

"Don't you fucking tell me how to behave in public. I'll do what I bloody well like." Her face took on the appearance of someone who was not an 'Erin', as she sat back, holding her cigarette and smoking it like a man as if to make her point.

"You'll never make a lady", I thought to myself, realising *that* friendship would not ever be the same. Having given her a very good chance to have some guidance, support and friendship, we'd even joked about us both being April babies, two little Lamb soldiers, fighting side by side as Aries are prone to do. That explosion of unfeminine anger and behaviour should have been the point to speak to her mother or advise her to tell the psychiatrists at the Board to be aware of. Just being too disappointed with her to care, it was no surprise to learn of her future.

She too had gone through the old world craftsmanship of Dr Abrams' transforming, magic scalpel and fine needle work. After telling me she was shocked and disgusted that I could be employed to look after clients in a brothel... and domination to *boot* (yes, thigh high, leather ones!), she herself became a 'working girl' in the very same Malvern Ruby's after I eventually left. Her mother soon joined her, working there too, closely followed by her teenage sister. Not a bad little act for mum, sister and brother/sister, all busy in a brothel after expressing their horror that I could have done such a thing myself... after thinking I was 'such a nice girl'! The worst for Erin was yet to come.

She married a man, hit the media with her story of 'triumphing over her hideously traumatic past, trapped in a male body', broke up with him then fell in love with a *woman.* With the revelation that she now loved women, 'as a man would', a tirade of blame and attempted lawsuits were made against the Board which had approved her for surgery. She now lives as man again, though struggling to find 'his' way to acceptance, yet finally true and at ease with the essence of the *person* inside... identifying as very male. Erin, who is now Aaron again, is not alone in being one of many hurt, confused boys who go around a full circle of sexuality to discover, against all they deluded themselves to be, that in the end they really are men... and quite capable of sex and love with women. Hiding behind a woman's skirts, so to speak, was a temporary hideaway to obliterate and reject anything found in themselves to resemble the distant, hated 'father figures' who never showed them how to be a healthy 'man'.

With the greatest respect for Aaron for being as vocal as he can be, he has committed to organisations which offer so much more help to people who may just be confused, to look at all the alternatives and therapies to know and love who they are without taking this gargantuan step. On that score, I can only agree, remembering that we are like colours in a rainbow, sometimes yellow, sometimes red...but there are an awful lot of shades in between and really no point where we can ever say that red begins and yellow *ends*! Regardless... what a tragic way for him to learn, but at least in all he has mentally and physically endured, he takes his chance, as I do - to help...

'If you can't be a good example... Be a terrible warning!' As far as I am concerned... you decide which one is me - I really don't mind!

As for DKA (Deena/Kylie/Astrid), she flew immediately to Jeremy in Hong Kong and proceeded to run like a bull in a china shop through his friends, professional colleagues and proposed work venues, terrorising all in her path. He was horrified, and she was back in Australia within a week. The jeers, snide remarks, despising looks and outright rudeness of everyone she came by, became all too much for her too. Last I heard she'd been given a job by Australia Post to 'man',

BODYCAGE

oops... *man*age, an isolated post office way out on a lonely stretch of 1000 km highway on the Nullabor Plain, only to see the Aborigines coming in to cash their Social Security and buy their supplies before leaving her in peace for the next couple of weeks. I often wondered what they must have made of her. Perhaps she's 'gone native' and found a perfect Indigenous Australian new identity by now! Loren said the Aborigines used her as a totem pole and she moonlighted as a cactus in the desert by night. Nasty!

The lovely Loren - What can I say? She'd had a close brush with the law, having taken home a middle aged man from the street one hot day. Thinking he was grunting enthusiastically as he performed over-exuberant oral sex on her, she'd taken little notice, puffing away at a spliff, watching TV as the grunting fell still. Thwacking him around the head a few times and extracting her willy from his mouth, she sat up to realise he had turned blue and was quite dead! Hurriedly dressing him, she called the police to say he had knocked on her door for a drink of water, felt faint and passed out on her bed before having a seizure. The police had smelt a rat, undoing his trousers to see Loren had overlooked removing the condom, at which point the game was up. She told the truth which the police seemed to find acceptable and not an unusual occurrence. The poor man's wife was only told he'd had a heart attack whilst in the company of a prostitute in St Kilda. The wife had written a card thanking Loren for 'making his last moments so pleasurable, doing what he enjoyed most'. If only she had known what he enjoyed most, to the point of such excitement it brought on his heart attack... and was something she could never have catered for.

Loren had her surgery, also with Doctor Abrams. Making an amazingly fast recovery, she went literally

straight to work in another brothel. Mainly she said it was for the sex, more than the money, as her 'loyal', ever-loving boyfriend, Roddy, had left her within a week of surgery... for another street walker who still had that one special thing he looked for in a girl... a big penis! Nothing unique or out of the ordinary in that little state of affairs, I learnt over the years. As Shantelle once put it from way up on her high horse -
"Lose your balls, lose your brains and lose your boyfriend." Sadly... too many would lose their lives too. I felt I had been a kind of Mary Poppins or Pied Piper, leading this lot on a merry dance to my tune... and one by one, they'd followed like Lemmings over the cliff and into the sea. Things were not to be quite the dream boat journey out there on the seas I'd hoped for myself either.

On a certain level, perhaps I'd subconsciously set the stage for Greg to catch me doing more than I had told him I did, up in the rooms at Ruby's. Blindly unaware of *why* at all, I had used the images of my partner, my home, *his* family and everything else I'd tried to make right in my *outer* world, paint an acceptable, *normal* picture - Illusions, to cover all of the mess, darkness, pain and confusion inside... in the unconscious effort to make myself whole from the outside in. Greg had the car and all my keys late one night, letting himself into the 'parlour' as usual to wait in the TV lounge until I came down to be driven home. Creeping quietly up the stairs, as he was told not to do, to use the bathroom, he noticed the 'dungeon' door was open and the lights were off. Obviously I was *not* working in there. For the first time ever, I had not locked the door in the luxurious boudoir where I was happily having a vigorous 'thigh workout', as ever pardoning myself as merely having a 'dilation exercise', bouncing up and down on yet another horny, local Greek God.

BODYCAGE

Seeing Greg's face as he called out for me, flinging open that door to end the little piece of paradise dream we'd shared, his disbelieving, unforgettably broken look must have mirrored exactly the look on mine. Yes, time stood still, literally... and I just wished so hard I could have turned back the clock... Not just a few minutes to set the scene to hide what I was up to, but to turn the clock back to before we drifted so far apart that performing these acts did not bother me. I can still recall the gasping sigh of utter desolate grief from Greg, as both his hands hit his forehead, falling backwards from the doorway towards the stairs. Hearing all of Greg's shouting, in a split second, the Greek boy had realised what had happened.

"Is that your boyfriend?... He isn't going to kill me is he?"

"I honestly don't know." Totally sickened and cold to the core, it was an impossible dilemma which to deal with first... but I turned to the client, scrambling into his trousers. "He may kill *me*... just go... wait downstairs... keep away from him... I'll get your money back for you." Bound tightly in a towel, I bolted down the stairs to see Greg standing, just sobbing alone in the lounge, trying to stuff all of my strewn clothes into the big carry-all bag.

"Get together now, Riannon. *NOW* !!" he roared at me, bashing his fists into the walls, shattering the plaster. Making a quick grab for the handful of twenty dollar bills which were placed in the record book, I sped them out to the trembling Greek boy who thanked me and ran off! Christie, the other girl who had been busy too, raced downstairs at the same time to see the whole scene, knowing immediately I had been caught.

"Christ, Girl... you gonna be OK?... My guy's up there packing himself." She disappeared up the stairs just as quickly, Greg shouting all the more at us both,

"You fucking whores... both of you. I can't believe you were covering for Riannon, Christie... you FUCKING BITCH... I hope you die, you fucking whore." Grabbing me by the arms, he pulled them tightly back, pushing me stumbling up the scarlet, shag-piled carpeted stairs, slamming open the bathroom door.

"Get in there!" he flung on the tap, not caring if it were scalding hot or freezing cold. Pushing me into the shower, he picked up the antiseptic liquid soap bottle, broke off the lid and poured the lot over me.

"Clean yourself up... you filthy, fucking treacherous bitch. Clean *everything*... and you get yourself right fucking out of here tonight." It had seemed like only moments before that I had stepped from my candle-lit bath, all new and born to love him forever, to finding myself again in a bathroom scene giving him the complete opposite. Speechless, unable to even reply, I scoured myself red in the freezing water before going back downstairs where he sat on the sofa, not even looking up as I dressed.

"You're right... about everything you said and called me, Greg. Explaining why... and saying sorry is never going to help is it?" I sullenly whispered.

"Get in the car." Pulling out onto the freeway, he still had not spoken.

Passing the speed limit of 80 km/h, I watched the needle quickly get to 110. His eyes just looked intently straight ahead with such anger and hatred. Knowing a curve was soon coming up, bracing my hands tightly on the dash board, I was convinced he was about to crash the car with himself, our dog and me, into the big metal barrier on the bend. Perhaps noticing, my sudden move, he became more aware of his speed... dropping back to just on the limit. Over and over in my head, I said... "Thank God... thank God, he's let me live." Truly though, I felt I deserved to die for what I was doing... I wished I was dead... but not him... not our lovely little Bomber... and not like this. Reaching one arm back, I grabbed for Bomber's paw and held it tight.

CHAPTER FIVE

Perhaps Greg had noticed the sliding grasp for the security of our dog's paw, tightly gripping it as I squeezed shut my eyes, thinking only of the upcoming wreckage of the car and a sudden end to any dreams we'd had. In that split second as I'd wondered what on earth I had done to myself and my partner to end it all this way, there was no shattering boom of metal and glass before I felt I'd open my eyes to see the tunnel of light or smiling ancestors waiting to show me to some place I'd be going to face some judgement or assessment of every choice I'd made in life. With eyes wide open, I clearly saw Greg take a deep breath too, as I realised something had dawned on him somewhere to spare us all. He drove on, still without a word, parking the car abruptly to march straight into the house and into our bedroom, collapsing face down into the pillow on our unmade bed. Being only aware at that time how much pain, betrayal and disgust Greg must have been feeling for me, once again my instinct just compelled me to try and somehow make myself clean again.

Quietly lighting candles around the bath tub, I filled it up with all the oils and salts I could find. It was no time to lie back, luxuriating, pondering the day gone by with dreams of the next. With a little soap dish, scoop after scoop, I poured the water over my head, hoping it washed away the guilt from where it had started. Bubbles, salts or oils... or even soap, had gotten into my eyes. They burned and streamed, doing the job I had hardened myself too much through practicality of dealing with financial struggle and justifying turning my body into a commodity, to bring tears tumbling forth, releasing the cascade of misery I was truly feeling for myself and for Greg. I cried until the bath water had drained away, holding the shower nozzle over my head, rinsing off in the naive hope or even delusion I was starting myself afresh and cleansed. Towelling off my hair, slipping into a light dressing gown, I pulled the cord tightly around my waist as if to brace myself, turning the corner to go into our bedroom, one of the little scented candles lighting the way. Greg had closed the door.

With nothing to think or say for myself any further, it took a few seconds, starring at the door to realise our world had changed. Placing the candle on the bedside table in our spare room, devoid of any sensation at all, I slipped under the quilt. Before almost blowing the candle out to hope for sleep to come quickly, I hesitated, leaving it to glow blurrily through still reddened eyes. Peering into those streaks of rays, softly shining out in every direction of the room and the differing layers of circles surrounding the rays like concentric wheel after wheel, it felt like the candle and its light were my only link to anything alive anymore... because inside it felt like part of me now had died. In and out those worlds where we slide between dreams and reality, happy pictures and moments played out of all the good times and special moments I had been fortunate enough to share with Greg... every single event relived or just let dance around in my mind. Then the dance itself of our tour of the Orient shattered me back to that moment of running from the stage in our finale, naked, vulnerable and... deep down... feeling totally guilty. The 'Adam and Eve' moment, falling from grace to flee the Garden of Eden, led me to a fitful sleep where I woke again and again feeling across for a pillow next to mine which of course was not there in that single bed, nor was the person I'd felt sure still breathed deeply in contentment by my side.

Rehana Incognito

Kookaburras, parrots and magpies sang madly as ever, echoing through our trees and the little valley of our garden, as the stronger, bright morning light from that side of the house stabbed at my eyes through the trees and the tiny slats in the cane blind. It was enough to remind me the previous night had been no nightmare... it was all real and I was alone in the spare bedroom not even knowing where to search for a way to deal with what had taken place. Nauseatingly sickened from the space around my belly, where I felt at least able to identify a welling source which bubbled up to form a tsunami of grief sweeping emotions up to the space behind my solar plexus, the wave crashed into my heart.

Pulling up the blind, I propped myself against the window ledge to peer at all the life and light in the garden and surrounding bush land as far as I could see. Soaking it all in, to lock its beauty and timelessness, punctuating that better version of reality onto my body in that starker morning light... I'd taken a deep breath again to step out into the hallway. Step by step I felt like the "Little Mermaid" who had to suffer the feeling of walking on nails forever as compensation for the miracle of having her fish tail turned into legs. Again, every thought of what Greg must be feeling stayed in my mind as I tried to put myself in his position, imagining it was me who had found out he was capable of doing to himself... and us... what I had just done. There was no way I could get around that, were the positions to be reversed, and I'd feel our lives had exploded apart... beyond finding a way back to ever being the same. So, it appeared, must have Greg. The bedroom door was wide open, the car was gone and I was left just standing like a nude statue gazing down the lane as Bomber snuffled up to my side.

BODYCAGE

Run from it all, as far away as I can... was all I felt. Lose myself in anything it would take to forget this and make it not be real. With Bomber curled up on one side and the phone placed on the other, I rested a hand on him... the other on the phone, sitting on the sofa trying to make a decision who to call first.

"Chrissie already called me last night, Riannon... after you'd left in case there was any trouble."

Ruby had realised I would not be turning up for work that morning and quite sympathetically, perhaps even with a tinge of guilt and regret in her voice too, expressed her best wishes that I be OK after what had happened at her bordello.
"If it all blows over and you find a way through it all... your job's always here for you if you need it."
 Thanking her not quite sincerely, I recalled her own bitter feelings about her husband and all his own lying and cheating which left her with young children to support and a household of bills to be paid... How Ruby had found herself renting a tiny little flat with scarcely more than a mattress and a phone on the floor and a willing stream of men to make them all *pay* for the rotten mess she too had found herself in. Feeling just slightly sad for her to have found herself going from there to building her booming empire of sex as an industry, I went then straight to the angry realisation of how easily I'd fallen into this myself with no concept at all of other avenues I might have taken to improve my lot. Right then, Ruby's offer to come back and sell my body as simply as selling a sandwich in a snack bar, to help keep her and her family rich beyond my dreams, hit home with its full repugnance. Next port of call.

Rehana Incognito

"In all honesty, Riannon," purred Felicity as maternally as ever with all the worldly wisdom my well-thought-of mentor could muster,
"I don't know how you lasted so long thinking you could have your cake and eat it. He'd have found out sooner or later... you know that really, don't you?"

She was right... deep down I did realise that, stupidly thinking I could twist and turn around all kinds of corners in my mind to make that work be justifiable. Holding down the only semblance I'd ever had of a stable life... and a partner who'd sooner have died than do to me, even once, what I was doing on a daily basis, seemed all the more abhorrent.

"I don't know what he'll go through today and make of it when he comes home, Lady B. Usually, even if we just have a small argument, he takes some time away... a few hours... and we always manage to make it up... or laugh it off. But really, I don't think this one can be the same."

Hours passed with no call from Greg and I felt sure he'd either gone to see his parents or his mates from the band, losing himself in his music with no way to tell anyone about the situation I'd put him in. Tired of looking at the silent phone, I picked up the receiver as the house grew dark, in total silence. Dialling Karen's number in Western Australia, with the sudden urge for the company of a close relative, a young man answered the phone as I asked to speak to Karen. Somewhat surprised, this man asked who I was. I replied "just a friend in Melbourne." Although still often sending money to Karen when I could to help out with little extras for her two children, we rarely spoke to each other after I'd called the Pastor at her church, in a moment of despair at my sister's condemning, judging and crucifying attitude for my 'heinous sins against the Lord', and I guess he didn't appreciate me angrily asking him "what the hell type of Christians he was turning out in his church over there?!" We still managed civility when reminded time and time again that she didn't show much aversion to accepting any amounts of money I could send to help her whenever a hint was dropped it might be needed.

Karen had kind of softened too when I spoke often of the progress of my sponsor child in South America which I had taken on board as a good idea, knowing it would be doubtful any child of my own might come into my life. Karen appreciated the point that whatever she may think of how my life had turned out, my 'misfortune' was someone else's gain, because I had also managed to convince several other transgender girls to do the same. We'd always call each other and excitedly exchange new photos and little letters or pictures from these children to us as 'Sponsor Mothers', realising it would be the nearest we'd get to parenthood and, for most of us, were sincerely grateful that we were making a huge difference in these children's lives... no matter how we came about the money. For my part, no matter what financial struggle I ever faced, I always made sure that the standing order for my Sponsor Child's support was there in the bank for fifteen years!

"Who was that guy who answered the phone? Haven't got yourself a new toyboy there have you?" Karen's husband worked away most of the time, so I'd not have blamed her.

"No, that was Geoff! He's sixteen now and towers over me."

My nephew had just spoken to me on the phone and neither of us knew who each other were. Between thoughts of my blown apart world up there in the hills and longing to see and get to know my own nephew and a niece I had not even seen yet either, I told Karen that I needed a break from working two jobs, suggesting that I fly over to Perth where the Spring had already started with enough warmth for beach weather. More likely out of curiosity than a genuine desire for my company, Karen said she'd be happy to come to Perth, stay at my mum's for a few days and catch up with me.

"I don't mind you meeting up with me and Allegra. She's only three and doesn't know who you are... but if you don't mind, I'll leave Geoff at Mum's because he's at that age where it might affect his mind seeing you like you are now... You know what I mean?"

"He's your son, Karen... I can't tell you what to say or how to bring him up. Just bring lots of photos for me... OK?"

At least she'd agreed to that, with a promise to look through the Yellow Pages to book a hotel for me when I knew a date. Deciding on the date would all depend on what happened when Greg got home.

Still sitting in the dark, with just the light of the television, taking in nothing that was said on any station, I felt like the rabbit caught in the headlights as a car turned into the driveway, flooding the living room in the high beam. Bomber had bounded from the sofa, squirming and whining at the front door as he'd recognised the sound of Greg coming home. Not even caring if he came in with an axe to finish me off, I sat still, starring at the TV as he fussed about Bomber before sitting beside me. Still, I was numbed and speechless, looking over to see that he still wore the same clothes he stood in the night before when his world exploded. He hadn't washed or shaved, his breath smelt of a lot of drinking. Unable to bear the silence, I had to say something.

"I'll leave tonight if you want, Greg... I can't expect you to understand or even forgive me. I know I wouldn't... that's for sure."

BODYCAGE

"It's been the most painful shock and hurt in my life, finding out about this you know, Riannon."
He'd slid his arm up and around me as I could hardly believe his words.
"But probably, deep down, I'd already suspected you would try something like this all along because of the crowd you are around and I always knew I was your first."
By then tears were falling in unison from both of us.
"I've had lots of experience before you... in fact I reckon I was a bit of a slut myself... to be really honest. It was the same for me and everyone around me to try all we could while we could... and that only led me to realise how much I didn't want to be like that and just do the right thing by you. For all those nights of picking up strangers and waking up in their beds, not even knowing their names, it just felt like Heaven to me when I met you... and wanted to only wake up and find you there with me and for me every day. But I only came to knowing that from all I had done in the past... So, as much as it's hurting me still now, I can't really judge you for needing to learn and experience what you need to learn and experience for yourself either."
 His bravery and even willingness to try and understand what I had done left me feeling nothing but ashamed at how maturely he was able to deal with this. Too stunned and stupefied by all he'd said, anything *I* might say could only seem pathetic in comparison, so I accepted his hug as we held each other for a long time until I was able to draw back and promise him I would not be returning to Malvern Ruby's.
"Hold on then." He managed a huge smile as he and Bomber disappeared quickly out of the front door, up to the car. Just as quickly they appeared back in the living room, Bomber looking all out of sorts that he hadn't

been whisked off for a ride in the car as he'd undoubtedly hoped. From behind his back, Greg handed me a little box package, beautifully wrapped up.

"Promise me again you'll never go back there."
I promised, accepting the package I didn't deserve, to find a huge, purple bottle of perfume... called *Poison*.
"Oh," I managed to softly say, still numbed and with what felt like a baseball stuck in my throat... "Do you want me to drink this?"
"Ahhhh... *NOoooo*, I never thought of it like that... I just remember seeing you spray it on when we walked through Myers one day... and how nice it smelt on you... changing throughout the day as it got hotter and when we got to bed that night I could still smell it on your neck, yet it smelt different by bedtime..."
 Just giving myself the lightest spray on both sides of my neck, I thought to wait 'til morning to tell him I needed to connect again with my family. It was slow, hesitant, almost feeling like a dangerous encounter to be making love with Greg again. When finished, he rolled over with one arm left across my belly. I felt like I had just done one more client. I was doused in poison... both on the surface of my skin and beneath it.

BODYCAGE

PART SIX

Rehana Incognito

BODYCAGE

CHAPTER ONE

Greg was up and showered before I had hardly started adjusting my eyes to the daylight. Sitting on the side of the bed, pulling on his boots, he said he was off to band practise. I wasn't to forget the builders were coming sometime that day to get started on the huge extension to the back porch we were making into a deck to enjoy the panoramic vista of the bush land setting of our garden. Before I could even mumble that we'd need to perhaps actually *cancel* any more expensive work on our home now that I was going to be poor and struggling again, he'd kissed me goodbye and was off with Bomber leaving me alone to collapse in exasperation into the pillows, arms outstretched like I'd been shot dead.

In the solitude of the half lit room, crossing my arms over my chest, straightening my legs tightly together, I remember the client at Ruby's the week before. Trying hard as I might, to process what was going through *his* head, let alone my own. He'd asked me to pretend I was a corpse... to lie motionless, doing absolutely nothing as I feigned death whilst he undressed and violated me. I'd say I was *mortified*, but that would be obvious, being shrouded from head to toe in a sheet, playing dead. My mind had definitely filled with revulsion, not wanting to think of myself as deceased whilst he performed. So I imagined myself as a blow-up doll and somehow that felt more acceptable as that would be *me*... doing and being *naturally* what a blow-up doll was for.

Hardly breathing, not moving a muscle even the slightest, I only opened my eyes when he'd heaved almightily and was slipping off his condom. Asking if it was OK for me to 'rise from the dead' then, he laughed, saying it was and did I have a cigarette. "Just what you need after shagging a corpse", I'd thought, but told him I hadn't because it was the smoking which killed me. As ever, if a guy was friendly and amenable enough, my ever-curious mind would always try to find out where any fetish or perversion had come from. That was one of the other main reasons I was attracted to both the sex industry and bondage and discipline... the thirst to understand other people and, through that, ultimately more about myself.

"I'm an undertaker." His reply nearly earned him another customer! "Just curious, like any other bloke gets about different things sexually. I'd never *ever* consider touching a real dead person I deal with every day... but everyone knows about necrophilia's and I just wanted to feel what it was like with someone so helpless or incapacitated... maybe the feeling of total detachment from me... I dunno, you're a funny one you... Never really gave it that much thought and I'm surprised you'd ask."
I said it was just a relief to know he would not touch an actual dead person and wasn't sure if I felt more comfortable about playing dead (as he said it was hard to tell the difference between my having done so and half his ex girlfriends' performances in bed) or play other roles I was asked. It bothered me less, in fact, than the times when I had dressed as a teenage schoolgirl, or younger, for customer's who'd requested that. To be honest, I was grateful that those guys who wanted the young girl fantasies had come to me. Not because I enjoyed it very much at all, in fact I had a lot of difficulty knowing how to conduct a 'young girl' conversation as I had been a little *boy* myself, but more the relief of knowing they had acted it out with me and left some child alone. Always and without fail, on those

BODYCAGE

few uncomfortable encounters, I made it clear that they should never ever consider taking that fantasy any further with an underage girl... from the depths of my soul. Of all the expressions of fantasies, confused desires or just mixed up perversions, it was that one which stayed with me by consolation they had at least acted it out professionally with an adult... and that I was there to say what they may well have just needed a reminder of. Enough!

Mistress Britt! That's who I needed to call, as she would have been heading into the House of Domination over the weekend and definitely be making those 'double-domme' bookings for our eager victims and my new, adoring fan club of subservient 'gluttons for punishment'. With no idea how to let her down gently over the hole I'd dug myself into with Greg, it was still a relief to hear her matter-of-fact voice straighten me right out when I explained the unforgettable horror of being caught out at Ruby's.
"Just come and work full time here then, you dumb bitch. There's no sex here unless we insist on it," She laughed with her usual assurance that she was totally in it for her own pleasure as well as amusement, however she bloody well liked... I loved her for that.
"Hmmm, you're right, that's true... it's amazing how much guys will actually pay for what they can't have... It never stops making me smile really."
"You just smile all the way to that bloody bank, Riannon... 'cos it's buying you that house and paying your bills... Don't forget that. You got into this business 'cos Greg can't support you, remember? When any bloke's bringing in the money and supporting you like you're supporting him... then he's got a right to complain about anything. Until then, Love... you do what you got to do."

Right then, I'd agreed, feeling the panic of another few thousand dollars of bills needing paying when the deck was built. Hanging up on Britt with the promise to be in at least for the usual shifts, I decided to talk to Greg the next day and hope for his tolerance if we were to even keep our mortgage paid. As his band still was not exactly breaking even, though doing very well, I am sure that was the only reason he agreed to it. Apart from that, he found Britt to be a solid friend who he respected really 'for making money out of those wimpy bastards', as he put it. "At least she's a real woman, not like those other fucked up excuses you hang around with," he'd sneered more than once.

Being now the bread-winner in our home, and definitely the fact that I was too deeply relating to dominant roles at the H of D, served all the more to leave me feeling more and more distant from Greg. In all reality, after day upon day of a stream of men being beaten, humiliated, tied up like bugs in fine webs of feminine forcefulness, telling me relentlessly that I was a Goddess, all-powerful and deserving of the absolute best, it dawned on me –

I was a struggling *housewife* living in a cute enough little cottage in which I was building a safe cocoon, like a pretty little tomb to hide myself away from a dysfunctional past with a boyfriend who, in my mind, seemed as inadequate as my submissive, worshipping victims themselves. So, as well as feeling uneasy in this role as the bread-winner and decision maker, the responsibilities of everything to do with our lives and future resting only on my shoulders, Greg became, in my mind's eye like a dependent child. Respecting him as a man in my life was suddenly gone... in fact, I resented him.

BODYCAGE

It's not to say that delusions of grandeur settled in to my mind, being actually paid to be told how wonderfully deserving I was for being this 'powerful' woman. It was more the enforcing of the notion that I was not at all the person I was *made* to feel I was... by people who'd left me merely mistaken as a confused, undervalued child, and really not that long ago either! For those moments, standing clad in skin-tight, low-cut, black latex dresses, forcing up and out a tantalising cleavage above a set of padlocks and zip they could not touch (yet perhaps just inhale the essence of), I'd force their heads between it. Reminding them they were tied up to a crucifix on a wall and at my mercy... that child's past seemed 'cancelled'. The taste of power, being in control, was certainly a balm for all those helpless, dependent, inadequate times... yet simultaneously was equally an unnatural, confusing feeling to be dealing with men this way, when all I imagined of being a woman was to be cared for and respected. Respect, I could certainly get, when it came with a price tag at the H of D.

Like so many things, in a life of extremes, waking up to these paradigms was no different from the psychological dramas in the past which had drawn any other woman to the sex industry... And who is to say that my drawing to it was any different than some Mistress colleagues who had endured indignities at the hands of their husbands, brothers, very own fathers or any other man, leaving them burning with vengeance... acting out retribution through dominance again and again? That at least appeared more favourable than women I'd met who had been similarly abused and found themselves on the treadmill of acting it out, over and over, through becoming themselves the brutalised submissive in the Bondage and Discipline world... or simply trapped in a relationship with any man who would make them feel less worthy than they really were.

To attempt a discourse of the sexology behind all this would be well beyond my capabilities and I'd hope that anyone who feels this way can find any of the help and support out there to transcend it. But for me, and those I came across, I can only tell it as I saw it, presenting to you what was learnt along the way.

Mistress Britt could slowly slide down that zip if she liked, peel the latex to the sides, releasing the constrained bosom, to seductively fondle me, perhaps play with and suck my nipples, driving our slave wild to show how much we were quite capable of enjoying ourselves when he was tied helpless and pathetically enjoying our show.

Purring my words softly, in mock sympathy like speaking to a child who needed an injection at the doctor's for his own good... "Don't you wish this was you... touching these soft, firm, beautiful things, slave?"

I'd slowly (always slowly, to make their time pass as I was usually bored to death within the first five minutes) take Britt's exquisite hand and stroke it over my breasts, along my curves sliding it back and forth over the rounded outline of my thighs and buttocks in the tight, short dresses. With the sneering smirk, I'd make sure they knew I had seen how painfully aroused they were and quickly grab a string of long, white cord... deftly... like a machine... barely needing to even look after a while, could tie his cock and balls sharply restrained. Bulldogged!

"Look at that Mistress Britt..." I'd cup the bound 'three piece' pride and joy for a bounce in my hand... "Wouldn't that look lovely dripping with wax on our Christmas Tree this year?!" I was truly a bit bloodcurdling... scaring myself sometimes at where such perversity could come from, though I am sure the clients knew we didn't really mean any of it.

Seeing their dismay at what had happened to their pride and joy so quickly and professionally, I'd gently, then tightly squeeze, twist and stroke each of those balls I'd separated to the sides of the tragic member as they reddened and swelled. If they'd looked like they could take it or agreed to a bit of CBT (Cock and Ball Torture, not Cognitive Behaviour Therapy!), I'd dig my scarlet nails as deeply as possible into them, before a lovingly gentle stroke along their willies to nastily squeeze and slap the top when I reached it, reminding them of the fine line play between pleasure and pain I was happy to blur for them - brandishing the sceptre of total responsibility for the control thereof!

"I got top points for rope-tying and knots in the Girl Guides, didn't I Mistress Britt? It kind of looks like my 'Cross My Heart Bra' there... Separated and pushed up just nicely those balls, aren't they?!"

"Yes, Ultra... you do a lovely job," she'd wink, almost to breaking point with laughter as I'd already told her I was a Boy Scouts reject. "I do love it when you present my little treats so nicely gift wrapped." Britt would then reach for a nice firm cane each, which we took in turns using as pool cues to stab at the testicles like billiards, warning them that we might just go for potting the 8-ball if they were not careful.
 For added amusement, in our man-hating lesbian act, we could go all the more distance as Britt selected any size of threatening, rubber, black, strap-on dildo with which I'd terrorise them a little by gagging their mouths with it, commanding them to lick and make it all slippy before slapping it against their backsides, like the dirty

little sluts we'd made them acknowledge they were. Even if it was secretly their desire to be raped by the Mistress, we'd have our fun first and waste even more of their time as I'd bend over in front of them, again relishing their strains, to taunt them that they could only look, yet never touch me being so near and yet so far. Yet again, Mistress Britt could though herself, giving me a painfully slow dilation exercise 'better than any worthless worm of a man' as I usually worked out shopping lists or redecoration plans for my house whilst I feigned satisfaction.
"Don't you wish this was you too, slave....with your useless worm?"
"Yes... I do..."
"What was that whimpering voice I heard, Mistress Britt? It seemed to come from someone wishing he was a piece of rubber. It feels so much better when it's done by someone who knows what *she's* doing... And just think... you lowly dog... It might have been *you* if you weren't stuck there, tied to a cross on our bloody wall!"
 Never one to tolerate insubordination, disrespect, or miss a chance to exercise corrective services, Britt would happily stop what she was doing and slap him mercilessly to remind him he should have said "Yes Mistress!" When I'd had enough, rather... usually just plain bored, I'd mercifully release an outstretched shackled hand, one by one placing them by his side, then the spread-eagled legs from the shackles below before switching back to savage brutality mode. Flinging our victim over the gym-style jumping box I'd bind him, bent over, face down again to see himself witnessing his misery in the full-mirrored wall. Striding confidently to Britt, menacingly stroking her 'weapon of ass destruction', we'd smile cruelly at each other in the flicking light of the enormous church candles, so he

could see our reflections... The ever-present music from the classics radio station made it all the more a macabre, theatrical show. Nothing pleased me more than wasting some time slapping or caning in time to the likes of the Vienna Waltz, *thwack thwack, thwack thwack.*

"You know what to do, Britt... Rape him! I am off for a cup of tea... I'm bored with this wretch."

Like parting words from the Good Fairy, wishing a child goodnight and sweet dreams, I'd bend caringly to his ear and softly whisper -

"Never mind dear... there's a Rape Crisis Centre at St Vincent's Hospital just down the road. You're gonna need it."

Leaving him trembling, probably with excitement really, I'd leave the room to take more bookings and actually would enjoy a cup of tea, leaving Britt to the rape scene, as I really was never into B and D enough to be bothered with those kinds of antics! Around that time, I'd at least taken many opportunities to chat with waiting 'victims' or those just relieved, on their return to 'normalcy' after their session, about what drives them to the sessions themselves. It almost left me thinking how poorly-wired the psychology of men must be, weakly driven to enact and embellish, over and over the first feelings they'd had as little boys of a female in power and their link in their minds to 'Love'.

'Mummy's got to give you a very good spanking, because she *loves* you and needs to teach you a lesson!' 'You're going to be punished because you've been a naughty little boy and this is for your own *good*!' There was the most beautiful and powerful female archetype in a little boy's world, we all relate to as that first image of the feminine, the one with total control of all his wellbeing... the one he loves and adores... mixing those feelings of punishment, control, pain, guilt and humiliation... all with the fact that she *loves* him... and wants him to be *good*. Like he is born inherently *bad,* needing to be punished and corrected for it for the rest of his life? It's small wonder then, how such a phenomenal amount of men in all cultures are so drawn to this dark, yet femininely strong side of expressing their sexuality. For my part, I had merely a little sympathy, and at times totally bewildering amusement, in the realisation of such things, being sure to learn so many more reasons of incidences, no matter how small or momentous in the child's life, which blurred the boundaries between pleasure and pain, then in fact melding them into one and the same.

The 'spanky wanky' was about the best example of that little expression of fun and games with which Britt and I amused ourselves. How much savage spanking on a guy's bare arse, forcibly facing the mirror to witness what we did, could a guy take? Fondling him with slow, slippy hand to the point of almost exploding then stopping the pleasuring abruptly, as his buttocks reddened with my thwacks, I could make that last for a good hour if I had to... whispering in his ear about the 'agony and the ecstasy' I was putting him through. Roughly turning him to the mirror to witness 'Mistress's favourite colour' - the glowing pink and reddened flesh, it would then be just a few more sharp slaps or paddles before a big white squirt would shoot across his hapless image in the mirror, sliding down in a mighty mess, as they buckle under in exhausted relief. Mistress then offers a comforting smile and pop-up Baby's Wet Wipe from the dispenser tucked away between the assorted array of torture implements, ropes and dildos. It was easy enough, but I'd much rather beat 'em up than beat 'em off. If they'd tried to clean up their mess on the mirror, I'd always tell them to leave it...

BODYCAGE

"The *maid* will be in when she's finished making us our afternoon tea to clean this up. It's all she deserves." Usually the 'maid' would be readily waiting if he'd gotten into his outfit in time for his domestic humiliation to start. What better way than having 'her' clean up after another man? I think I was naturally just a bit twisted with this type of thing... and as far as I was concerned, it was making itself work for me.

I can't even get started on guys I'd met who'd lodged these aberrations into their psyche through the actions and deeds of their big sisters, Aunties and Grandmas as well... that would take a whole other book and, as I have said before, I am far from qualified to write any great thesis on the psychology of human sexuality. Suffice to say, I saw men as pretty simple creatures really, to be coming to the H of D in endless streams, whilst Britt and I worked out if we were his big sister, to sit on him and tickle him 'til he comes, or force him to wear our panties as one of us, acting the shocked and disgusted 'Aunty' or 'Gran' had caught him going through our underwear drawer!

Having already amazed myself at getting this far in life like some sort of chameleon, it was absolutely no problem, once I had quickly worked out the fetish (or even not) to be any of these women I need be. 'Ultra' could be the high-powered bitch in a boardroom interview tearing a failing employee to pieces during some office worker's lunch break. Then she was the image of total fitness and strength as a High School gym instructress. In leotard and trainers by dinner time, some 'insecure teenage boy', still with his gym bag and kit, would be humiliated by my cruelty before going home to his wife, kids and probably grandchildren, with the fantasy still being stuck on a continuous loop of replay there in his mind. For me, it was simple-

Rehana Incognito

Get 'em in, get the money, get 'em off, get 'em out! Bzzzzz. BANK!

All not too bad, I'd figured, for a boy from a pit village in Northumberland. To think, if I'd stayed there I might have ended up being a coal miner instead of a powerful, blonde bitch of a sex Goddess... Who'd ever have thought, as they handed over the cash without much of a struggle (that would be extra!), that their tormentor, rescuer and redeemer was probably as much of a mess inside as they were? Maybe even *more*, but as much as it may well have been therapeutic (with all the benefits thereof) for them, it also served to strengthen and balance somewhat myself.

Coming into the TV room, no... not where the telly was, but the girly dressing room for the TVs as in TransVestites, to finish a 'job' for Britt as she was preparing for a torture session with a slave, the sight of my client had me unable to stop fits of laughter. Abruptly backing out of the room lest he see the tears from my eyes, I had to leave this elderly, tall skinny man in his red, lacy leotard, kaleidoscope of eye shadow colours across his lids and brows with the lipstick about everywhere except within his lip line! He looked like a cross between a starving, emaciated Santa and Lily Savage caught in a rainstorm. I tapped Britt out of the dungeon for a brief moment.

"Girl, I can't go back in there... I can't stop cracking up. Shall I give him his money back?"

"Oh, yeah...she's quite a looker, isn't she. Should have warned ya... but thought you were OK with the vesties," Britt whispered from around the door as I caught a glimpse of her client swinging from a hoist on the ceiling in a kind of leather body bag, like some insect wrapped and hanging by Queen Spider for her later 'attention'.

BODYCAGE

"Just try not to look him in the eye... Keep your head down and don't look above his shoulders when you go back in, thinking of some of the worst, saddest or embarrassing things you can recall... Then you won't laugh again. OK? You'll see all sorts here... you know that... Christ, you could write a book." Door closed, I heard muffled groans from within the 'body bag' and that music to my ears of Britt's cane swishing through the air to resound viciously about the room.

In the few steps down the hallway to the 'TV lounge'... there were enough bad, sad and embarrassing things to think of before turning the handle to check on my lacy 'lady'. What stayed with me though, was Britt's comment about writing a book. Certainly I had read the "Happy Hooker" by Xaviera Hollander when I was at High School, leaving quite an impression on my teenage mind about the whole subject of prostitution and the sex industry as such. Never though, could I have imagined finding myself drawn to it, tearing it to bits in my head and making a perhaps not exactly *good* (though lucrative) living out of it. Making a point to write in and update a five year diary I had indeed kept, thinking myself as much a tragic victim as Anne Frank imprisoned there in her Amsterdam attic, I wondered if anyone had written books about the interplay of Mistresses and their slaves. Notice the capital 'M' for Mistress and the lower case "s" for slave? You've got to remember, even in print, the game has to go on!

Planning to sit down with my TV client and flick through some of the B and D magazines with him to get some ideas for further sessions and gauge what has been written, I entered the room to find he'd already gone 'Self Service', applying his own lovely little wooden clothes pegs we'd stuck tiny little bells on to make a bit of jingling noise, to his nipples poking through the red lace. Without a glance at his lined face

and the hideously applied 'make over' (this would be Trinny and Susannah's nightmare Halloween house call), I noticed the saggy little willy and droopy balls exposed from the crotch of the body stocking. So, making some time pass, slowly pinching on the pegs to the battered 'three piece', I got the 'tortured tranny' to entertain me whilst I flicked the pages of the magazines with a little disco dancing, lots of shaking about so I could hear those bells jingling....
"Yes, that's it...you dirty little slut... Mistress loves a bit of music while she *works*." Yawns dismissively, turning another page.
 Sipping a cup of tea, the flashes of a figure prancing around in a red body stocking like Cher's granddad gone oh-so-horribly wrong, hardly registered. I'd make a note in the five year diary when I got home, to try and make sense of all of this one day... and I did. Well, not make as much sense as I'd like to, but kept the notes all the same. Finding it at times quite sickening, harrowing and even painfully sad and pathetic to relive over in my own mind so much of the dynamics that had brought our clientele to the dungeon door in Nicholson Street, a steady stream of letters from Matthew the American marine I'd met in Japan, always seemed to arrive at the Victoriana Tearooms.
 Flung at me by Felicity, my 'Poste Restante' delivery lady, Matthew's letters made a suitable antidote... or at the very least a balance between getting myself too lost in seeing men as the victims of their own weird wiring and the opportunity of seeing one with a healthy outlook on his own life... and the world in general. Keeping them all well hidden from Greg, I'd often pick one up in a moment of recovery from a day of absolute insanity at the H of D, with a glass of wine, some soft music and candlelight, wishing I was living in Matthew's little home town, with a guy like him who was well and

BODYCAGE

truly capable to look after me and fulfil the illusion of what I thought a man *should* be. His letters were a quick trip escapism to "Walton's Mountain" or "Little House on the Prairie".

Arriving home again early, one still cold evening, to an empty house with Greg away for the weekend, I realised I still had those extra Christmas kilos sitting on my hips, thighs and backside needing shifting before my pre-Summer workout back in Perth. That's one thing to be warned about, being on oestrogen tablets for years - If you've started early on them and they are doing their job right, yes, your hair will grow long and lustrously rich with feminine gloss, your skin will soften and glow, curves will show up more or less where you wanted them... but, just like your mother and sisters, there'll be more of them in places you're not always going to want them! Packing a swimsuit, goggles and towel into my gym bag, I drove off to a swimming centre with large open-air heated pool set in wooded parkland for a good couple of hours of laps in the hope of quickly getting back in shape.

Wondering if I could still do the High School routine of four laps of a fifty metre pool (of the four strokes I was good at), I'd started with a slow and easy two hundred metres of breast stroke, then managed the free style as the small crowd slowly disappeared home, one by one, with the fast lane now almost empty. Pausing at the deep end to catch some breath, treading water, I steadied myself against the floating barriers between the lanes. Watching the silent expanse with just a few arms flailing about to break the stillness, I took a deep breath of that smell I've known nowhere else... of chlorine, heady with the eucalyptus scent of all the gum trees around in the landscape setting of the pool. The mist from the cold night drifted and danced over the surface with the warmth of steam from the pool.

Rehana Incognito

Pulling the goggles back over my eyes, I drew in a deep breath, kicking over to face the stars above before launching myself away from the poolside to attempt the four laps of back stroke. Very slowly, I'd managed one more lap, even slower on the way back up for the second, windmilling my arms and kicking ever slower to almost give up and finish the lap with some easier breast stroke again, heading for the end of the lane.

Flipping off the goggles, as my head would no longer be under water, to enjoy the final few stokes without the blurring, I noticed the figure of the lifeguard's red ski top and white shorts moving towards my lane, squatting down to catch me as I reached the diving block at the end. Wondering what reprimand I might be about to face, I looked up at the huge clock over the stands, realising that it was past closing time. As my head had been under water for the back stroke, I'd missed the public address announcement that the pool was closing! Spluttering out half a mouthful of ghastly water, I arrived... hairy legs and knee-level, about to address the lifeguard's shorts. On looking up to catch his eye before opening my mouth with excuses, his jaw dropped at the same time as mine in recognition.

Breaking into almost a laugh, he beat me to anything I could possibly mutter,

"*Was* going to say, I didn't recognise you with your clothes off." The cheeky monkey's eyes had me feeling trapped like that rabbit in headlights... completely stunned on recognising him and not knowing what to say either.

Somehow, "Well, it's a small world!", seemed right. "I always wondered why you were wearing an aftershave with a hint of chlorine to it when you dropped in to Ruby's late at night." It was my Greek Adonis who had hounded me all that time back to eventually accept him as my first client at Malvern Ruby's, setting me off on my 'road to ruin'... kind of! Too cold outside of the water to continue any chat, I bobbed up and down before him, seeing no-one else around and ventured to ask why he never came back to see me there. Bashfully, his reply kind of shocked me really then, as I had not a clue how any man could really feel about such things... nor bothered much to consider it.

"Well, I wanted you..." he looked around making twice as sure we were the last people at the pool, "because you were the one I thought I couldn't have... and it made me want you all the more. The more you said no, the more I was determined to be with you... even if I had to pay anything."

Then I 'got it' - Men like to hunt and chase what's worth a struggle, a unique and special prize to catch and hold like a trophy.

His next comment also took me unprepared and unaware...

"Then, like an idiot, I thought... I'd had you... and then you were just like any of the rest there to me... I went home, glad of the time we had but felt awkward about it all as I'd gotten to know you over the weeks... And, well, I dunno...." He was as stumped as I was! To him, I'd become a piece of dead meat (my indignation must have shown), not part of the hunt anymore and certainly no trophy to bring home.

Flipping about still in the water to stay warm, I felt it was a chance in a million to see him again. With a desire to settle the score perhaps a little... and definitely pretty annoyed he'd thought me just like any other 'working girl', I reached up an arm to see if he'd drag me out of the water to save me swimming to the steps and just laughed uncomfortably as he actually did. Teeth chattering, he knew I'd be ready to flee to the towel and off to get changed. Catching me straight

in the eye before letting me go, my head was spinning as I wasn't quite sure what he or I were saying, but I'd heard somewhere, myself say -
"Not that it probably matters to you... but I didn't stay in that line of work. It wasn't for me." I'd kind of lied... kind of not. It wasn't really what I'd considered a viable career and was fast thinking I was close to becoming the 'face that launched a thousand orgasms' anyway."
"Really? Was I that bad and put you off it?" He quickly smiled as I pulled away ready to flee...
"No, I got caught by my boyfriend! So that was over... and so were we... Anyway, that type of job was really not for me."
"Hah, I thought so, that's why I liked you... Got time for drink before you go home?"
With the prospect of a weekend on my own with a dog and a budgie, still not believing my luck that he'd even ask me, we quickly arranged to meet outside the Aquatic Centre entrance in a few minutes. Following his car along the Burwood Highway towards the hills where I lived, his indicator came on to signal I follow him into the car park of a quiet bar where we continued our chat and re-acquaintance over hot chocolate with marshmallows in a cosy booth.
"I bet your real name's not *'Steve'* then is it?" I huddled into the corner, shaking a little with the cold as my hair was still wet!
"Bet yours isn't *'Tara'* either... And how'd you guess?" He was right, we all make up names to work in the sex industry, to both cover our tracks with an alias name, theoretically reducing our chances of being found out... and inventing a whole different persona for work purposes. It is *she* who does that dirty job, while the real *us*... whoever we may be... is somewhere there, taking a back seat waiting to go home to be wife, mother, sister, daughter or girlfriend to someone. What

that tart does in the brothel, strip club or bondage studio was someone else entirely... and there it starts, digging deeper that chasm of a groove of an almost schizophrenic compartmentalising of parts of ourselves and the many aspects of being a woman.

"It wasn't a guess... I learnt pretty quickly, it's kind of best not to ask the guys their names at work. Or to shock them with guilt asking how was the wife and kids! They get a bit flustered really because they then have to accept it is *them* doing something a bit naughty..." I tried to focus on what else to say, not wanting to start to make him feel guilty either... if at all he did.

"When I asked their names... which I thought was just being friendly and polite really. (I mean, what can you say after massaging a guy's back for half an hour? - 'Hey Punter, would you like to roll over now so I can get to the fun side...?') They'd always quickly and obviously make up one of three names... It'd either be 'Mike, Steve or John'... and that kind of solved the mystery straight away why American working girls referred to their clients as 'Johns'... It is the first name which comes into a guy's head when he gets caught off his feet and brought back to reality by a girl asking his actual name."

Clearly I was now rambling like a lecturing authority on the protocols of prostitution. I did always snicker though when they came out with the 'Steve, Mike, John' thing, saying more than once... "Yeah, so's mine!" Just to let them know that I knew their game and couldn't really have cared less what their names were! Like a cat with a mouse to toy and tease in moments of complete boredom with clients, I'd torment them all the more saying- "Would you like a shower now *MIKE?*... There's a towel on the bed there *MIKE*... and I'll see you back here in just a few minutes... OK

MIKE? " It was fun to notice how many of them would crack and say "OK, OK... my name's David... alright!" An awful thing to do really whilst I still wanted them to believe I was named after a sprawling plantation in Confederate Georgia with Scarlett O'Hara swishing around in huge billowing dresses and hats, panting over Rhett Butler!

"My real name's Riannon... and you then... *Really*?" Offering my hand to shake seemed pointless after what we'd already done.

"It's Evan." He pierced me right through with words that hit straight to my heart with a feeling like some kind of relief. This young man had made who he really was truly known to me, instead of all the faked exchanges in the rooms at Malvern Ruby's, acting out again and again moments of intimacy, which in all the movies and romance stories I wanted to believe, were acts of love between people made for each other and actually *in love*. I surely did not love them, yet acted as if I did for the time they'd paid for... and they surely did not love me because they never knew *me* either, but for the moment they were paying for me, I was their most beloved of all.

"Evan? Isn't that a Welsh name? I thought you were Greek." He did definitely tell me he was Greek... Actually, he'd said 'a typical Greek boy', an only son, still living at home, as good Greek boys do, with mum and dad until he is off to please them by marrying a 'nice Greek girl'.

"Don't know if it's Welsh... but my whole name is Evangelos... but I like Evan for short."

"Well... with you the Life Saver 'n all... you can be my 'Evan from Heaven'... in case I ever need saving at the pool, OK?"

With no wish for my time with Evan from Heaven to end at all, I must have thought a chance was there to be a bit of a Julia Roberts and a real life 'Pretty Woman', daring to ask if he'd like to come back to my 'house in the hills'... which he did. If it were not just the fact that I craved some real intimacy after all the detached, farcical parodies of closeness at work and the emptiness I'd felt with being with Greg, I felt guilty too that Evan had saved up $400 as a Life Guard just for that hour with me. In knowing a little more of the real me... and me knowing the real him, *proving* that there was something more valuable than what he'd thought he was buying at Ruby's, was as much the reason for us making it straight to the spare bedroom.

To say it was even better than the time we'd spent the night he'd set me on 'the road to ruin' was not only borne testament by the futon bed collapsing in the passion of it all, but my falling deeply asleep with his sturdy, comforting arms holding me tightly around. Also, I had been completely taken by surprise to have simply reached complete sexual satisfaction with Evan... effortlessly, without even thinking about it or trying at all. Remaining peacefully still, I'd enjoyed that most satisfying sleep I could ever remember, to wake up enjoying him all over again... and still find he wanted to stay for breakfast.

Evan took my number at the House of Dom to be able to keep in touch, with my understanding that I could not contact him at home for the obvious family reasons - His parents, having arrived from a Greek country community in the same immigration boom in which I'd arrived, were still very old-fashioned, spoke hardly a word of English and expected him, true to form, to marry the Greek girl of *their* dreams. Continuing the affair with Evan, we went from meeting at home as often as we could while Greg was away... yet never in the bed I'd shared with Greg... to the more routine dates of dining out, movies and all the rest. Promising he would not hold it against me that I had worked at Malvern Ruby's and was still making a living as a professional man-handler at the H of D, I promised equally not to hold it against him for going to find his fun at places like Ruby's. After all, I'd always known the brothels were busy everywhere late at night with horny lads having their fun on the way home from a night out if they hadn't found what they wanted in bar, as easy as stopping off for a kebab before heading home!

We had fallen in love by time I got sick of asking him why he would not tell me his age. His stock reply was that he felt and lived older than he actually was and that I was a bitch anyway for not telling him *my* age. He was right on both accounts, as he was mature both in looks and ambition, whereas on the other hand, I looked and felt much younger than my age. Somewhere I'd justified I had only recently become who I was... and that special event at Masada Hospital was my new date of birth. Experience-wise, of emotional and intimate maturity... I was little more than a teenager myself. Sneaking a look into Evan's wallet whilst he showered one morning, I'd taken a sudden deep gasp to see his date of birth on his driver's licence. He was only 20 years old!

Seeing his age in print, I was both fantasizing as ever, finding signs and symbols in realising he was a Cancerian to flip desperately through pages of my Linda Goodman astrology books. Clinging to any thread that there'd be justification to make this work, a cold light of day realisation dawned – I still lived with a man who was rarely now home, was well and truly out of love with and neither of us even considered addressing the fact! Were we really just staying together for the sake of the dog and budgie?! It looked like it.

BODYCAGE

On a long flight back to Perth to finally meet up with Karen and her daughter, there was plenty time for reflection... Not in the least gazing at my own in the window of the plane as it circled around the Christmas Tree expanse of the lights of Perth by night twinkling away below. Only my eyes were recognisable peering back at me like a disembodied spirit hanging in the black night out there, with the Milky Way for a back drop contrasting again with the lights of Perth. The enormous black void in the middle of it all was the Swan River, where a little boy had learnt to swim and catch fish... trawling the net whilst brandishing the torch for prawns! There, after arriving in this world like some little pale misfit with all the newness of adventure and discovery... he still held longing for somewhere lost. Travelling to the city hotel, felt quite surreal, along streets I'd last journeyed as a slender, timid youth with long blond hair on his way to sell cosmetics in a department store. With very little sleep, I'd be up in the morning to meet a woman who had not seen me since I was her *brother* and a little niece who'd not even met me at all.

After all the hours, which seemed like years, when working on stage in Asia... having to look glamorous for work at either the Victoriana, House of Domination and, definitely, Malvern Ruby's, I had little time or inclination towards going to a lot of trouble with make-up, hair styling, accessories or clothes. Wishing to appear as much like my old self as possible so as not to shock Karen too much (having no idea of her reaction when finally face to face), I chose a pair of tight faded jeans, a plain white blouse with buttons undone enough to show that I did now have a healthy cleavage... so she'd hopefully get the message. Lastly, I stepped into a simple pair of sandals.

Rehana Incognito

Being a glorious warm day, I decided to walk through the back streets of the little Northbridge bohemian neighbourhood... with a lot of fun memories of the many gay friends I'd known, probably still living there. Passing the gay bar and its beer garden, where I could only smile quite contentedly that I was no longer the person standing around there making pointless conversations where I was uncomfortable enough being anyway, I bee-lined down another quaint street, leading up to the park. There, by its lake, Karen would be waiting at the opposite side by the bus stop where we'd arranged I get off.

In the distance Karen's long hair down to her hips hung over the back of the park bench where she sat, checking the buses as they came, letting people out and driving off. By the end of the road, as I was about to cross the street, into the park to sneak up on my big sister, a little girl was fussing about trying to climb out of a window in the back seat of a car parked facing the lake. A smartly dressed older woman had turned to settle her, quickly turning back to peer intently across the park to where Karen sat. It was my mother.

Stopping dead in my tracks, almost on the road, I had in no way expected this or knew what to think, let alone do.

"Allie... Will you just sit still for a minute, you're mam'll not be long."

Words my mother must have said a thousand times to me sounded softer now after all those years. The voice, instantly familiar, was certainly her... but different now too - compassionate... understanding and comforting to the child I'd realised was my little niece. As much as I was another person now, standing a few steps from her, in a flash of a moment I felt she might have changed a lot too. With it all happening at once in my head, I was annoyed to think she would disown me

BODYCAGE

as Karen had said. Wishing her to see I was a fine enough person with who I was now and not come to any harm, I also felt it was no co-incidence I had decided to walk that way, down that street and come so close to my own mother... without making myself known and having something, if not final, to say to her.

With a deep breath, shutting my eyes tightly, I took a step backwards, steeling myself, to turn around, marching right up to the window where my mother sat. Glancing quickly at me as I approached the window, she just as quickly looked away not wanting to take her eyes off her vigil across the park!

"Well, Mum... you had to come didn't you...?" Ready for all kinds of hell to break loose, I stepped back, my mum's face turning from me to the park, from the park to me quickly several times before she'd burst into tears, scrambling to get the door open and hold me like she was drowning, sobbing like I'd not ever heard.

"You're my *child,* Love... you're my *CHILD*... why did you go through this on your own? You could have told me... you could have." When we'd both managed to stop crying and settling the shaken little niece in the back of the car, I explained to Mum what Karen had said were my mother's thoughts about what I had done - That she had hoped I would die on the operating table. The look on my mother's face was one again I instantly recognised... absolute rage and indignation.

"She said *what*? When Karen told me about you going to have this operation I said the person you *were* will die on that operating table... and you'll want to start your life all new. I always *knew*, Ian... always... Eeeee, I'm sorry, Pet... I felt stupid calling you that... I know you're not Ian now... I feel daft!"

I could only think of what my niece must be making of this strange conversation, the crying and hugging as her own mother sat alone on a park bench far away.

Rehana Incognito

Karen stood looking for me getting off a bus, still blindly unaware that I knew now she had lied for years to keep me away from my own family! I let my mum continue.

"Karen said you didn't want anything to do with me... so when she said she was meeting you... all I could hope for was a glimpse of you across the park and know you are alright. I thought you were a lost lassie coming up to the window to ask for directions and was annoyed I might miss a second of seeing you across the park... and she was *you*! I mean the woman who was going to ask me something... who was you... You look so lovely... Look at you... You don't even need makeup or anything... you just look lovely."

She really was beaming... and I could see very proud of who I was, as we both laughed so hard when she reminded me she had three daughters and how ironic it was that her *son* had turned out to be the one looking most like *her*! Any words which any man may have said about what good or value I was as a woman held little or no merit to me right then... knowing my own mother knew and accepted me for who I was. This moment filled me with a new sense of strength, security and determination.

"Oh, I said that years ago to Karen when she told me," said Mum, "but I tell all my friends that I was so good at making daughters even my son became one."

Glad to see the twisted sense of humour still ran in the family and where mine must have come from, I still had the matter of Karen to deal with, who obviously had hoped to keep me away from contact with the rest of my family, whatever her reasons. Telling Mum not to worry... she would not lose me now, she let me go, settling back into the car to let me handle Karen whatever way I felt best. Tidying myself up with some tissues from Mum's handbag in the side mirror of the car, I walked around the lake, along the path, to where

BODYCAGE

Karen sat on the bench. Like my mother, she glanced up with an unknowing smile then turned away back to eagle-eye the bus stop. Before I could say a word, something must have suddenly sparked recognition as she darted a glance back at me with her jaw dropping.
"Crikey... you've changed a lot!" She nervously smiled with an uncomfortable hug, like two strangers really... on both parts.
"Yes, put on a bit of weight... here and there." Bumping out my chest with a slap across my own buttocks, I made my point that this was how I am now.
"I see you inherited Mum's bum then... like the rest of us." Karen scanned me up and down like lab specimen... clearly taken very much aback.
"Yeah... a bit too much of it actually," I managed to reply, yet not wanting to get into small talk as I was still seething, preferring to cut to the chase.
"Look Karen... I came from that side of the park," I pointed straight over where her car was visible to the side of the trees. Karen turned white.

"I've spoken with Mum... and met your daughter." I don't know how long her silence lasted... it must only have been seconds and she was speechless.
"Karen... you're a mother... how could you have done that?" She sat back on the bench, sobbing too as I gazed down at her while she blubbered about not wanting people hurt and confused about what *I had become* or her son being upset about what's happened to me if I was around in the family... her neighbours... and her church. For a moment I felt like the 'St Sebastian' Karen had made me... as her subservient understudy sibling, tied to the "Hills Hoist" clothes line when she'd organised my condemnation and execution by the arrows of my father's darts for all the world to see... punished for my crimes. With that indignant

memory in mind, I wanted to walk away from her right then and back to the car to repair or salvage what I could with my mother. So I did!

Back to the car, with Karen many paces behind, I knew my mother would be in a fury when she realised the truth. Not wanting to escalate this into anything anymore unpleasant, I quickly explained my sister's poor decision and reasoning for what she had done was her fear of what people would think... and trying to protect those around her. Mum stepped from the car to boldly challenge Karen.

"I'll never forgive you for this, Karen... Come on, Love," she pulled me away. "Let's get a taxi home. Your sisters and nephew are sitting there waiting to hear about you."

Mum and I walked off arm in arm, knowing it would be a race for us to get a taxi back home to meet up with my sisters and *nephew* before Karen could get there to drag him away from the 'traumatic experience of seeing his *uncle* in the state he is in'. Whatever the taxi driver thought of the conversation, neither of us cared... as my mother astounded me, speaking of years of reading every book or article about Transgenderism she could... even taking the time to speak with a psychologist to help her come to some understanding, if not acceptance, about the whole thing. When she had explained to the psychologist about her condition during her pregnancy with me, about how I looked and behaved as a child, the family background and no father around to speak of as well, she had let go of any guilt or blame she'd inflicted on herself. The psychologist had said, after all she'd told her about her 'son'-

"Madame... there was little else he *could* have turned out to be!"

BODYCAGE

My youngest sister Gemma, and Colleen, just a year younger, had both taken the day off work to be with Mum and were both overjoyed... though nervous and giggly... at seeing me again, still trying to be like a confident 'big brother' in a new 'big sister' kind of way! The nephew, who now towered over me too, gave me an embarrassed bear hug before sitting back on the sofa to watch TV and simply said it was great to see me, but what was for lunch? Hardly the traumatised teenage boy with all manner of hormonal ragings going on about what had become of *me* ! Leaving Geoff to whatever he was watching on telly, Mum, still abuzz with excitement, tried to get a pot of tea together as three of her daughters sat about trying to make sense of a few missing years.

Both my little sisters said it had not surprised either of them... and they were relieved that I could enjoy life feeling comfortable about how I was, but Colleen was perhaps way more enthusiastic about it all than I could even have been.

"Christ... you got a better figure than the lot of us, 'Ia-'... I mean, Riannon... shit this is going to take a while. No wonder Karen didn't want you around... did you see the size of her arse?!" Colleen, raucous and bawdy as ever, bubbled on about the time Karen had come to tell them some 'special news'... about four years ago.

"Oh, you'll love this," Gemma was prodding at Colleen... "yeah, go on tell her..."

"Karen walks in and says 'I got to tell you all some news... well two bits of news really.' She was really being smug. She said she was pregnant again and we both were saying how happy and excited we were for her. Then she says..... *'Aaaaaaaaand*... you're not going to believe this- Ian's gone and had a sex-change operation and he's a woman now!"

"We were both all over the place," gushed Gemma... "asking how you were, did she have a photo of you... how is it all going and stuff. Then she goes...'Aren't you going to ask me anything about my baby? I just told you I am pregnant again... Pregnant! Isn't that great?!' " When Colleen finished the story, I thought it no wonder Karen wasn't so embracing.

"I said 'Yes Karen... that's lovely that you're having a baby and everything... yeah, really nice... good on ya... But *my brother's a transsexual*... I can't believe it... how special's that?!" Colleen was almost frothing at the mouth with excitement. Gemma finished the tale as I sat speechless.

"Anyway...Karen was furious and stormed off with Colleen going on and on about being able to buy outfits and dressing up to go on the Gay Mardi Gras float with all the families and friends of gays!"

Well, it wasn't quite what I'd expected would go through the minds of those two, but all the same it was overwhelmingly assuring to know that they too knew and understood the whole thing well enough... well kind of! Already knowing... and meeting more and more people from 'Transworld Alliance' in years to come, I appreciated my good fortune to have such support then at last, even though it had gotten delayed in the pipelines! Way too many people in my position do certainly face rejection from all their family, often friends... and certainly work colleagues. It's only to be kind to mention, although sounding quite harsh, for anyone considering this giant step, that my path of acceptance and support with my family was made all the easier because of two major points –

I'd always already appeared to them deep down in their psyches as more towards a feminine nature, never exactly looking like a masculine 'He-Man, Master of the Universe' either. And, after completing my own total transition, look as acceptably female as any of my own sisters.

Without having the benefits of those two factors playing balls (so to speak) in your court, taking this step and expecting total acceptance from everyone around you might just be expecting a little too much. No matter how much anyone considering this step might *feel* they would be better off presenting themselves through life's journey as a 'woman'... if you don't look it, have never really *exuded* it from the very core of your being, undoubtedly, deep down they know they are not in fact a female at heart either! Again, I'd mention the middle-aged man, the husband and father with the totally masculine job who suddenly decides all his problems will be forgotten as harsh memories are wiped away by throwing on a wig, Laura Ashley print frock and calling himself Susan or Jenny! There, comforted in clouds of perfume, sugar 'n spice 'n all things nice with an Alice band perched on his head... he creates a lovely hiding place behind his mother's skirts forever.

There in the carnage of this decision sit the parents, wives and devastated children, who (no matter what anyone thinks of me for saying so), absolutely *deserve* to have the image of their *father* locked in their hearts and souls forever. No matter how these people, who now say they are 'women' who were 'living a lie', feel they need to express the 'woman trapped within', a man who has fathered a child was hardly being a woman when he did so! Women have no desire to be involved in the process a father biologically performs which creates the child in the first place. That is to say making love, sexually excited to the point of inseminating a partner to result in her pregnancy!

So that's worth thinking about before embarking on the giant leap of escapism to the trappings of femininity.

Rehana Incognito

Spare costing the taxpayers thousands and wasting NHS time to end up lying on a ward full of lorry drivers and bikers, their penises removed, with no place to fit in to a world with no obligation whatsoever to accept and embrace their decision. Sorry for the cruelty of how that may seem to men who have convinced themselves or been encouraged to seek this 'treatment' for a situation there are now so many avenues to find a way out of... But once your child is in the world, no matter what you *think* you will find from life as a 'reassigned woman', your obligation to your children and their happiness should entirely come first. Justification for my wanting to say so comes only from meeting, knowing, seeing and often finding my own self cleaning up the mess these men have made... too many times at their tragic funerals.

Excellent, no, totally *brilliant,* gifted counsellors both psychologically and spiritually, are all around us now and easily accessible. I would beg any man who has been a good husband and father to find a way to seek out such help and guidance, uncovering who and what it is he is trying to deny, reject or hide about himself as a male by making a grab for symbols of what femaleness might shimmeringly offer him. It may surprise him to learn, that in this world, everything is made up of that which we call male or female, Yin or Yang energies, which can often seem unbalanced, mysterious or luring us to hide in the extremes of one or the other. That's what the mistaken transgender person is doing... Remember, nature is not out there making *that many* mistakes or we'd have troops of male Silverback Gorillas out there trying to get themselves set up as the females of the local harem! The mistake is often *choices* and *feelings* we have made about illusionary places to hide ourselves in.

BODYCAGE

And like any illusion, it's only a play... and a bubble... which, one day, nastily bursts.

For my part, where I had used my own femininity as a place to hide and comfort myself from personal past issues I was not ready to address, it was no different perhaps than a lot of women. Hiding issues, trying to find safety and protection in perfecting illusions of how they think the picture should be, I was still only focused on the 'Desperate Housewife' option like those gals.

Restoring diplomatic relations with my family, after accepting Karen's wishes to move on and wipe the slate clean for the sake of the next generation around us, I flew back to Melbourne. Karen encouraged as much of my friendship and support as possible with her children, realising that the very fabric of her universe would not be rent apart by my existence, which meant a lot to me. Feeling more aware that I'd used so much of my life with Greg as a way to create a cosy little Paradise to hide myself away, comforting myself from memories of a shaky past, I knew that bubble had burst and it was all coming to an end. Yes, maybe this *love* I thought I was now in with Evan, or having worked in the sex industry to be caught, distancing me away from Greg, were catalysts to get me moving on.

Without too much pain or fuss, that I was able to express, Greg accepted my undignified opt-out from our partnership. As a financial pay-off transaction, with him needing money for his band aspirations, and my having some to spare, I paid Greg several thousand dollars to move out of the house and sign it all over to me. As I had in fact paid the mortgage myself, as well as all the modifications and improvements, I have to be thankful that he did the right thing in not forcing me to sell it and split the profit from the sale with him. I would have been left without enough money to buy anything else... and without a nice home for our dog which we agreed to share 'custody' of!

It wasn't pleasant or on really good terms when the removal van drove off down our lane with Greg and all his personal effects to stay with a girl he had started seeing... The pain of remembering all we had gone through together in those few years and the life which had now come to an end in that half-empty cottage, hit me when I walked back into our bedroom to tidy it up after the shifting. Hitting the bed he had built for us with his own hands and skills from all his handyman books, no longer on the shelves, I cried until the room filled with darkness. Asking Evan, when he called, to stay away for a few days... while all I had now brought upon us set in, I lay there in the silence... Bomber had gone with Greg for now. My rosy picture of 'Rose Cottage' life had slipped from me. I know I fell asleep still crying, thinking back to those first moments on stage with Greg, when we ran off at the end of our strip show and I was sure I'd heard the thunder and lightning of the two people running from the Garden of Eden.

Best thing to do, of course, was lose myself in work, which somehow seemed all the easier (certainly less draining) with Evan appearing almost every night afterwards. He was a definite tonic for balancing out a day spent in seduction and sadism, torment and teasing with moments snatched to watch the soaps on telly, fitting in a little shopping with Britt in between meting out hideous inflictions on our victims. Evan did come and collect me from work quite often when I had loaned Greg the car as part of our agreement on going our separate ways.

I remember taking him in to show him the dungeon and meeting Britt too, so he was comfortable enough with what I was doing there. His face was kind of unforgettable as he entered the dimly lit room with all

BODYCAGE

the black furnishings, scarlet walls and candlelight. Taking up Britt's offer to sit himself in the enormous bulk of a purpose-built electric chair, he looked obscenely out of place with his big muscly form in a tank top and torn jean shorts, only putting up a mock struggle as we strapped him in with the leather belts. Buckling him up as she menaced him with the vicious electric cattle prod, he feigned the tortured agonies of the many who'd sat their already during that day alone!
"Men are stupid bastards, the lot of 'em," Evan laughed. "I reckon they know they are bloody scum and their lives are out of control. They need you two to punish them for it!"
"And get 'em right back into line... to face the world again," Britt added.
 They were both probably right on that one too. It's a bit extreme to realise that... though I should think it's what we all do from time to time. Flying from one end of the scale to the other, we try to balance ourselves out... and who was I to judge? I was taking their money for the sake of their 'therapy' however it was! I had also remembered to take note of such men who came to see us holding very high-powered positions of responsibility in their jobs. Coming to see a Mistress for a session, totally surrendering their will to the dominance of a woman, they found it a comfort to relinquish all thoughts of responsibility to us... and not have to deal with all the decision-making demanded of them. Whether any of us like that or not, the story has been the same throughout history - across all classes of society and in every culture. Any Mistress will tell you the same - The higher the responsibility with their jobs, the lower they need to go in the level of restriction and punishment we will be administering!
 Britt was glad to know about the trip to Perth and restoring my relationship with family, as her own two

children were moving to the West Coast themselves. Britt looked into following across to continue the bondage business in a smaller, easy-going city which suited her lifestyle with less competition than in Melbourne. We planned to make as much money out of the House as possible and I kept up as many 'guest shift' appearances at the Victoriana for extra cash too. It was only fair to tell Evan when I too decided how wonderful it would be to start a new life, with the joy of my nephew and niece around, not to mention my mother and sisters to trawl the malls with! Naïvely, I'd hoped he would jump at the chance too and possibly look into work with all the better-developed sporting scenes in the more health-orientated Western Australia. Over sensitively (yes, I'd read the manual about Cancerian men), he'd taken the news that I'd like to leave Melbourne as my being willing to abandon him.

With his head bowed into his hands alone on the sofa, I'd stood up, trying to explain I'd wanted him to come too... but he sobbed,

"Princess.... don't do this too to me..." (that was the other thing I'd read in the astrology manual... to a Cancer man, his girl is his princess - Placed, maintained and protected by him, high on a pedestal I knew I didn't deserve to be on!) "You know I can't leave my mum and dad... It would kill them."

Seeing him so vulnerable and broken, I just wanted to tell him not to waste his tears on someone like me... I wanted to tell him the whole story about my past... that I'd be no great loss in his life, as he was so young and how I would only be selfish to keep him from chances of a wife, children and undoubtedly all the things he needed... and were expected by his parents. I had stood frozen with those thoughts, thinking it would do more harm to bring any of that up right then, believing that it would be better to wait and see if this love was really strong enough for me to be able to tell him the whole picture. Standing just hopelessly at a loss of what to say or do, I let him barge past... fleeing off into the night without another word. I couldn't call him at home to explain anymore and felt absolutely dreadful - As though the Pollyanna I'd always been was now just POISON.

Britt called early in the morning asking if I could get to the House by 10 A.M as a client was going to turn up on the doorstep exactly then. He had requested that I pretend to be a housewife stranger, luring him in with a scenario... getting him into the dungeon, capture him and have a vicious tie and tease, spanking session with him. "Whatever cranks his shank", I'd thought... taking the train early enough, having not slept a great deal, worrying all night about Evan. Picking up a good bagful of groceries on the way in, I travelled by tram to Nicholson St, realising it was too-fast approaching ten o'clock. Jumping quickly from the tram, as I'd noticed a nondescript, cute kind of guy with a briefcase almost to the gate of the House. Damn... Running across the road to the footpath, the plastic bag split from the bottom, with most of the groceries spilling around the gate. The guy with the briefcase was immediately by my side, bobbing down to help me scoop up the groceries.

Thinking it was a perfect ruse to start the scenario I could hardly of planned myself, I asked him to carry the things I could not into the house.

"No worries," he'd said, looking pleased with himself.
 Placing the bits and pieces I'd dropped onto the kitchen bench, he mentioned that he'd thought I had a very nice house. So took that for the cue to really get started.

"Thanks... Am glad you like it." I was going into mischief mode. "It's quite special... Would you like me to give you a little tour of the estate to thank you for your help?"

"Hey...cool with me." He followed like a toddler down the hallway as I pushed open the dungeon door, flicking on the dull lamp, inviting him in.

"Christ... what you got going on here, Love?" Oh, he was good but I thought I'd outdo him. Grabbing one of the neatly coiled ropes hanging from the wall I brandished it before his eyes, saying...

"I am going to show you exactly what I got going on," as the doorbell rang... and rang... 'til I asked him to wait right there and not move while I answered the urgent ringing.

"I have an appointment at ten with you... Sorry I am a few minutes late."

"Fuck! I mean... shit... Sorry... go down the road to the deli and get me a cheese and tomato sandwich... then come back and tell me you're the delivery boy."

Slamming the front door, I rushed back to the dungeon where 'briefcase man' still stood rooted to the same spot, looking way too happy to see me return.

"Sorry... this is my sister's house... she likes to play in here with her husband... I just wanted to see what it was like a bit... Really... am so sorry about that... I don't know what came over me there." Composing myself after feigning a moment of madness, I led him to the door to the light of day.

"Don't worry, darlin'... I dreamed of something like that happening all my life!" Thankfully he left without another word and my sandwich, with the 'delivery boy', were soon back for the actual appointment!

Britt arrived later and we did a wicked, cruel nurse scenario, both dressed in white rubber and latex nurses uniforms. Oh, how the memories of all my

BODYCAGE

hospital work came flooding back - All the screaming, the abuse, druggies and alcohol-damaged, soiled beds and broken lives... And that was just the other nurses! Stuffing a bottle of poppers, as our 'drugging sedative medication', up the guy's nose, we'd pretended to circumcise him. After tightly sticking elastoplasts around his willy, with him tied to our examination table, so he couldn't tamper with himself of course, I'd bend over to let him see my panties and top of my stockings...

"Oh, I'm sorry, Sweetheart... Has that gone and popped all your little stitches again? What a shame... Nurse Britt's going to have to stitch you all up...all over again."

It was only on hearing the theme from "Days of Our Lives" on the telly, by late in the afternoon after all that hard work, I barely heard the phone ringing in the kitchen where it was kept, discretely out of the way so as not to be overheard by any clients sitting in the living room for whatever reason. As ever, I just answered - "Hello, can I help you?"

"Oh...hello," said a hesitant young lady. "What is this place I have called?" I had a fairly stock reply from experience with the phones way back at Lexi's and Ruby's to make something plausible up in case the number was found by wives and girlfriends in our clients' wallets.

"This is a private house. Telestra just gave us this number recently, so perhaps you are looking for someone who had it before." I felt dreadful... certainly, for this girl, lying to her with the thought that someone she loved perhaps very dearly was up to things she'd never understand. About to hang up, she quickly stopped, asking how long we'd had the number.

"Oh...just a few days... sorry...ok... bye"

Quickly she kept me... "You don't know someone called Riannon then?" My heart jumped from my mouth as I almost threw down the receiver. That was the last name I wanted to hear anyone ask for on that number.
"Well, yes... I am her... can I help you with something?"
"Do you know a guy called Evan at all?" Feeling confronted now with the possibility this may have been a girlfriend, an ex or otherwise, I immediately became even more worried, praying to avoid anything too unpleasant.
"Yes, I do know Evan... he drops in at the restaurant where I work a lot... Is he OK?"
"Well... no... not really. I am his cousin and we found your name and number in his wallet last night after he had a car accident."
"Accident.... oh my God... no? Is he OK?" Britt had rushed to my side knowing something had gone very wrong.
"Not really, Riannon... he's in a coma right now and may not survive the next few hours. He is in Intensive Care at Prince Alfred Hospital. His family thought to call your number on the piece of paper in case you were someone special to him who might know why he out on that road so late last night... He hit a post clocked at 160 kilometres an hour... "

Not even comprehending the rest of what she told me, except after confessing that I had been seeing Evan and become quite close, his cousin told me her name was Katrina and that I could meet her at the hospital in half an hour. Apologising to Britt, I had to run... taking a taxi directly to the hospital to find the Intensive Care Unit, desperately asking for a girl called Katrina. Katrina knew straight away by the look on my face that Evan had been more to me than a friend, leading me to the quiet little room where so many people must have sat before to hear dreadful news about their loved ones, beeping away on life support in the adjoining rooms.

"Look, Riannon... this isn't going to be easy. Evan told me he'd met an older woman and was in love with her... not knowing how to tell his parents. He's always been like my own little brother to me... and I know it's you, isn't it?" Her eyes were red, lined with streaks of blackness from crying as the news got worse.

"Evan's mum and dad are by his side right now... and a priest is with him. You know it's his last rites, don't you?" I nodded, then shook my head, not wanting to believe my ears.

"His parents are devastated and are sure to blame you no matter what... you can understand how mad they're going to be, but they want you to be with him as they know he loved you... I had to tell them."

"Katrina, all that matters to me right now is Evan... I need to see him."

If it was only going to be holding his hand while he took his last breaths then face whatever rage his parents wanted to hit me with, I wanted to be brave enough to go in there and do anything that was left for Evan in this world to do. Katrina disappeared for a minute or two before asking me to come out, passing the father who tried to make a swipe at me, yelling into my face in Greek. The sweet little lady, out of her mind with grief who was obviously his mother, pleaded with him in Greek, pulling him back with the medical staff as I looked back at them once more before entering the room where Evan lay. There was the face which had slept peacefully next to mine... which I'd watched in the morning light, blissfully, so many times, 'til he woke up. His hair was shaved off with dozens of stitches in his head and a breathing tube coming directly from a gash in his throat. His body shone, all golden... powerfully muscled and bare in the muted light with a sheet placed across his waist and legs, the monitors all making their noises and the priest preparing to leave me alone with him, Katrina and some emergency doctors.

"It's OK, Riannon," one of the doctors kindly said, "Say what you like to him... just very softly... There's a chance he might just recognise who you are... though he can't respond."

Touching him gently on his chest I asked if it was OK to take his hand. They said it was, offering to leave the room for a while so I could be alone with him to say what I might find to say. Katrina left with them as I took Evan's big, strong hand which had only yesterday held mine so tightly... It was limp and unresponsive. Leaning close to his ear I managed to choke out through a lot of crying -

"Evan... I am so sorry for anything you think I've done. Please... *please...* if you can hear me... Try and fight this and don't let go. You don't have to go, Evan.... just sleep for now... rest... dream nice things, Evan... And if you promise me you'll recover, I'll do anything I have to and make up for all this. I promise Evan... really promise."

Silently, Katrina and Evan's parents had tip-toed back into the room to the other side of the bed to find my head on the pillow next to Evan's, still holding his hand, soaking the pillow in tears.

"I'll go now if you like... I am so sorry about all this... just so sorry," I whispered to them all, knowing I was just as devastated, yet felt it was no place for me to be with this family in their grief. Reaching down to pick up my bag, I heard Katrina gasp.

"Did you see that?! His eyes just flickered!" His parents both quickly leaned across to check, as I sat back bolt upright to look too. No sign of any flickering... If they

had, I'd missed it, sliding my hand out of his to leave. Standing up to walk away without another word, the doctor stopped me.
"Gently take his hand again for a minute, Riannon and speak to him if you like.... I want to check something."
Slipping my hand over his, with a little squeeze, I whispered to Evan that I had to go now and leave him with his family, my face close enough to look right at his closed eyes. Very, very teeny and slightly... they both made the most fragile little flutter! The doctor followed me out into the corridor, walking with me to the lifts. There he explained the chances of Evan living through the night were very slim and I could not stop crying now that his family could not see me.
"But, you know... I believe he was responding to you in there. He didn't make or show the slightest movement of his eyelids for his parents... which could mean that somehow, deep in there where-ever he is... He is still linking to you and wanting to hold on somehow. That gives any patient like this a glimmer of hope and I am going to call you tomorrow and let you know any news." Quickly scratching out my phone number, I passed it to him as I stepped into the lift. Holding the door open, he quickly added before I disappeared...

"I will speak to his parents too and tell them if he does stand any chance in making a recovery... as unlikely as that seems, they will need you to be there and encourage him back... whether they like it or not." Taking a deep breath, I tried to force a smile and cannot even remember taking the train back home to lie on my bed, staring at the ceiling all night alone until the phone rang just after seven in the morning.
"Hello... Riannon? It's Evan's doctor at Prince Albert's... He's still stable this morning and his parents

have left their permission for you to come at any time you'd like to and be with him."

Thanking him, I pulled myself from the bed, wishing it was all a bad dream and absolutely hating myself with blame for what I'd brought to Evan's life... and what it had done to his family. Not even bothering to wash, I trudged down the sodden garden path thick with wet leaves as the sun hardly peeped over the horizon. Sitting there in the carport, watching the steam from the exhaust pipe billowing around with the fog through the misted rear window, the engine warmed up. I was thinking my life was as bad as a horror film. Feeling like Sigourney Weaver in her space capsule, alone in space with that cat, my life seemed as surreal as a musical for a moment -

A deranged tale, yet still some tragically imprisoned woman-done-wrong and done-wrong-to of "Alien" meets "Chicago" in Terri Tinsel's morphine-induced inspirations. Starring the nasty, maniacal, Queen Bitch black beast herself with the extra sets of menacing teeth, playing the scheming, blonde Roxy Hart, banged up... confused and desperate with all those other women! As this "Alien", I'd beaten myself up thinking I had come into Greg and Evan's life, planting some seed which would wait inside them... only to explode one day and blow their lives agonizingly to pieces.

I made my way to the hospital to talk to Evan as if he was really awake, listening to me whilst watching out for those occasional flickers of the eyelids. For several days I did the same trip, making up some cassette tapes of music I knew he liked... telling him that we were sitting on my sofa watching MTV or lying in bed on rainy days waiting for him to wake up and do things. All too quickly, Evan's body became very lean, then thin... as nutrition was only coming to him through the tube in his nose and into his stomach. His parents still

BODYCAGE

made no effort to converse with me... just simple sentences about nothing in particular, forcing a civil smile now and then. Until one day his father held one hand as I slipped my own into the other, telling him I was leaving for his parents to have some of his time. Evan's fingers suddenly clasped themselves tightly around mine!

From then on, it was Evan's mother calling daily, asking that I come in to hold his hands... getting more and more of this hopeful response, which I was glad to do. Work was the last thing on my mind at that time... only sleeping, eating a little, showering and travelling every day to the hospital to sit with Evan. Arriving to find him alone after a couple of weeks of this routine, I sat for my usual one way chat about the mind-numbingly, boring non-activity of my day to day life, trying to find ways to make that sound exciting. His hand, by now (only one of them though) could occasionally move up and down slightly. As usual, I took hold of his hand, whispering hello with a kiss on his lips. He suddenly shifted my hand from lying across his navel to hold it against his heart, taking me by surprise as Katrina snuck in to sit watching in amazement from the other side of the bed.

"Am so happy to feel your big heart beating so strong, still Evan... Keep it going... you will be just fine and out of here one day." I beamed at Katrina who seemed equally thrilled.

His hand moved mine, slowly, halting and stalling, yet with great deliberate effort to just about his belly button... then with one final slide it landed me right between his legs! Katrina, as stunned as I was... making a confused face at her as to what the heck I should do now, mouthed the words "leave it there". Resting my hand there, I noticed more of the flicker of Evan's eyelids and a tiny curl of one side of his mouth like a baby Elvis smile. And... incredibly slowly, in a detached sort of way in the surreality of it all, I wondered why my hand seemed to be levitating from Evan's groin towards the ceiling! Katrina knew, cupping her mouth to stifle the snicker, quickly dashing quietly from the room.

The doctor had said coma patients were often semi-conscious at various times... but there was Evan now semi-*erect,* with me fussing up the bedspread a little to disguise the tent pole before his mother walked in! I was sure she'd think I was tampering inappropriately with her son in this helpless state, so plonked a spare pillow over it, then that big old straw handbag I'd had for years over the lot for good measure. Back in the corridor with Katrina she told me she'd ran the Charge Nurse to tell her of Evan's response, thinking he was alone in some intimate moment with me. The Nurse had told Katrina it was quite common for that urge to be still alive and dominant in men, especially of that age... and in all reality... it was to be expected and encouraged to kind of 'keep them interested' and not give up! Well, I thought, as long as they didn't expect me to take it any further... I'd be happy to 'lend a hand' for the sake of his recovery. When Evan's mum arrived some time later, she must have been told. Giving me a look while biting her lower lip with a smirk that her son had been a naughty boy, I just sighed and shrugged... absolutely hoping that would not happen again with anyone else in the room.

As for his further recovery, it was exactly like the journey of a new-born baby. His eyes slowly opened, he made little gurgling noises, trying to make out words. He was put on padded mats to learn how to crawl again, hardly able to raise his head with the heavy crash helmet on it so as not to bang himself. Muttering my name as just 'R-Rhhh.-Rrrrr-RIAN-NON' took dozens of efforts, but was the first name he had recalled, although I am not sure what he knew and remembered about who exactly I was. He had looked quite panicked one day when his parents joined us whilst we played with a giant ball on the floor as I realised he must have had some memory of my being a secret from them

"It's OK...your mum and dad know me now, Evan. They are glad I am here helping you get well again." For the most part, I believe they probably were.
 A day or so later, I'd walked into his room to find him not on his bed or rolling around on the floor. Believing the worst, I rushed to the Nurses station to ask where Evan was. It was OK, he was spending the day *under* his bed as he'd been feeling a little frightened of everything around him and a little fragile. Going back to coax him out in his little blue pyjamas and crash helmet, I let him just lie on the floor with his head in my lap and cry.
 By the time he had started to totteringly walk again and make simple conversation, though just in Greek to start with (which involved grabbing the friendly tea lady every time we needed the interpreter), I had accepted everything the doctors had told me about his recovery. He was unlikely to remember much about the night of the crash. His brain had severely lost its blood supply and the part of his mind, which dealt with short term memory in particular, was dead... not able to recover. Only knowing me as something to do with closeness, sensuality or intimacy (but without the rest of the details), his awareness of who his parents were seemed less sketchy. That pained me even more than knowing any dreams I'd had with Evan were also well over.

Rehana Incognito

At his bedside, Evan sat watching the kid's shows early in the morning on the ABC, trying to mouth some of the words in the silly little songs with the "Bananas in Pyjamas"... His mum tried to spoon him a scoop of baby food. Spitting it out, he splattered his hands into the dish, angrily plastering it all over his skin and face to his mother's dismay.

"Evan... come on, you're big boy... Not a *plant*... Absorbing your food directly through your skin with osmosis isn't going to work, you know." I reached for the spoon.

Clearing up the carnage a little, I scraped up what was left onto the spoon which he accepted from me, disheartening his mother. Feeling the dreadful guilt again, I cleaned up Evan's face with wet-wipes, gathering up my bag and car keys ready to leave.

"*Evaaan..*," said his mum quite sternly "You give Riannon big kiss before she go now." And he did before quickly focusing back again on the remnants of his lunch.

Arriving back home, alone with my garden and pets, I picked up the Yellow Pages, found the number of the estate agent who'd found 'Rose Cottage' for me years ago and invited him to put it on the market for me immediately. It sold to the first couple who walked in. Newly married and totally in love, early one morning they stepped onto my huge back porch overlooking the cluster of gum trees, terraced garden and little brook winding through and under the Japanese wooden bridge Greg had built for me. I would go back to Perth, away from it all to give Evan a chance of recovering whoever he was going to be... without me there even trying to re-enforce or remind him of what we had been to each other. I waited until Evan was speaking quite well and had moved to live in a therapy and recovery centre before telling him I was going for a holiday soon

and might not be in for a while. I promised to send him a postcard now and then. Laughing, wishing me a great trip and to drop by when I got back, it was an agonising realisation that everything I thought we were was just *my* dream now and a hazy memory to 'Evan who nearly went to Heaven'! Funny, I'd thought, walking back to the car... I'd become the Lifesaver to a guy I'd thought was mine. Abba were singing "Chiquita" on the radio when I turned the ignition, falling my head onto the steering wheel and just crying it all out as I soaked up the words...
"Try once more...
like you did before...
sing a new song,
Chiquita."

# Rehana Incognito

CHAPTER TWO (PART SIX)

1990

Mistress Britt called to say she was driving out to the hills, on some business affair, with the promise to drop by to the Rose Cottage and say goodbye while I finished the last of the packing for the move to Perth. Having no wish to remain too attached to the furnishings in the cottage, I'd arranged for the Salvation Army to come by and take it all as a donation. Things I couldn't bear to part with and a few other essentials, were in cardboard boxes scattered about the empty house. Bomber anxiously whined about, knowing something even more confusing than the custody arrangements with Greg, was up. When the Salvo truck disappeared around the corner with almost everything we owned, I remembered my mother's pain when she watched all her own furnishings go, when we emigrated from England in the 1960s. Wanting to have a bit of a weep over the misery of it all was kind of scuppered as my beds had just gone, so nothing to throw myself upon to milk the misery, or just cry it all out as I'd always thought right to do.
 Instead, remembering a comedy skit with one of the drag acts from Tangles, 'Joy' dressed in a Salvation Army uniform with a tambourine and enormous false buck teeth, I danced around the living room for the dog, singing "*put a nickel on the drum...save another drunken bum.*" I believe Bomber enjoyed it immensely, though mercifully, was rescued from the performance by Britt hammering on the front door.
"You look a right bloody state, Girl... feelin' a bit rough?"

BODYCAGE

 Britt did offer a comforting presence in her stoic enough way and was happy to take my Pepsi (Number Two) budgie to keep her entertained at the House of Domination, sparing him the 3000 km drive across the Nullabor Plain back to Western Australia. Apparently she kept him there for years where his chatty repertoire of unspeakable filth, which Greg had taught him, was only augmented by mimicked sounds of rattling chains, cracking of whips, the occasional agonising screams and 'mercy Mistress!'
"The furniture's just gone... and I feel awful. I'll stay at Felicity's tonight, drop by at Greg's in the morning so he can say goodbye to Bomber and head off about lunchtime, I guess." I'd resigned myself to the misery of the next day, but, up to the mark as ever, Britt had a final surprise.
"Fancy a bit of pocket money to spend on the trip over to W.A?" she raised her brows intent on mischief.

"I haven't got time to go back down to the dungeon, Britt... am in the middle of all this."
"No need to, Love... he's in the boot of the car." Britt beckoned me to the front door. "Let's do one more for old time's sake... He wants a kidnapped-by-the-bitches and flogging scenario out in the bush... Let's go." With a high five slap each, it was fine by me.
No problem there, I'd figured, it would be a fitting finale for all I'd felt about the last few months of life in Melbourne. Besides, not really sure anyway where my next dollar would come from, every little flogging would help.
 Driving out past Belgrave, from the bitumen roads, to gravelly tracks, then barely-discernable-as-roads dirt furrows, we pulled up in a clearing of green scrub and semi-scorched trees from the last big bush fire a couple of years back. Britt's pre-bound and gagged

victim looked suitably terrorised, gazing fearfully up at the towering, blonde Valkyries menacing him in the boot. Roughly hauling him out, we stripped off his clothes, lifting his shirt to below his armpits before strapping him around the blackened tree trunk. Menacing him further, we 'robbed' his wallet, going through personal documents like his driver's licence and Medicare Card, threatening that we would tell his wife what he does if there was not enough cash for us in the wallet... and we'd have to torture him for the PIN for his credit card. After a good half hour, sharing nice paddles, canes and whips, we took it in turns to lay into him. Finally, all sooty with the charred bark of the tree trunk and red welts across his back, thighs and arse, we felt we'd done a good enough number on this crumpled, pathetic heap panting in the sand and scrub. For my part, I'd just felt it was extra fitting to hurt him extra hard on this occasion and had, in fact... enjoyed doing so.

I never really felt too bad to say goodbye to Britt, as we promised to stay in touch if she indeed moved over to Perth too... and said to everyone else I would always stay in touch, visiting when I could with the offer open for anyone who cared to visit. Greg, I was relieved to accept, left no hard feelings towards me for my part in our separation anymore. It was a tearful last hug for that timebeing, both resolved to something of starting new phases in our lives. He understood my wanting to keep Bomber with me because of all his travelling with the band. He promised to call often to speak to Bomber! Which he did... and arranged to visit now and then in Perth. As he said, Bomber always was a 'mama's boy' and bizarrely over-attached... apart from when I sent him off to be neutered, in despair after the one final appearance of the 'pink lipstick' (that shade

BODYCAGE

doggies often shock their owners with) in an amorous moment with Greg's grandma's fluffy, pink slippers.
"Well," when Greg raged about me sending Bomber off to 'lose his nuts', "if it was good enough for mama...."

We drove away from Melbourne, through all the country roads along the coast. With Bomber hanging out of the window, sniffing all the new smells of other towns and endless forests, we arrived, after about seven hours, to wind through the hills on the outskirts of Adelaide. After driving around, quite lost, I spotted some signs leading to the highway out across the emptiness of the rest of South Australia, over the vast desert of the Nullabor Plain and on to the far west coast to Perth. I should really have taken a motel room for a rest and shower, but felt still wide awake and driven like a salmon swimming upstream to get to 'home' as quickly as possible. Turning onto the highway, filling up the tank one more time, I drove into the night until thousands of headlights had hypnotised me enough to realise it would be best to pull over somewhere, put back the seat and nod off. This I did, feeling safe with Bomber in the back, somewhere overlooking the sea which roared from the distance, lulling me to sleep on an empty stretch of road.
 With the sunlight slightly filling the car in the total silence (except for the far-off occasional whoosh of a car or truck back on the highway), I tried to sit up to look out at where I might be... but feeling so exhausted, fell straight back to sleep. Hours later, with Bomber pouncing around and panting from seat to seat, I woke up thinking I'd left the heating on full. Quickly winding down the window, I looked out. The freshness of the sea soothed my face, gawking at the course of the massive curve of the Great Australian Bight. It disappearing into the distance as far as I could

Rehana Incognito

see with its huge, rugged cliffs and wildly, intimidating rolling ocean. Letting Bomber out for a little scoot, we both wandered for an hour or so, just totally alone as far as we could see across scraps of desert, a blue sky forever and the expanse of wind-whipped water which looked like it covered half the world. Lashed by an ever-warming, fierce wind, I stood by the cliff, reaching down to touch my dog's head... as his tongue hung out, with dribble flying into the breeze.

"It's just you and me now," I'd said aloud before bundling him back into the car and onto the highway to face possibly the longest stretch of straight road in the world.

For the first few hours of driving, I listened to the same favourite cassette tapes over and over. Boring myself with those, I tuned in to sporadic local radio transmissions for the handful of isolated communities out there. I soon tired of hearing, between Country and Western music, about sales of rabbit traps, hurricane lamps and news bulletins consisting of whom ever, on homestead farms in fly-blown hell holes, had been bitten by snakes. Perhaps seeing nothing but one, endlessly long stretch of a black strip road as far into the distance as I could see, had lulled my mind into some altered state. Finally giving up on the radio, with nothing but the sound of wheels on the road and only sand and sky to flank from side to side and above, I felt like I had just blended in as one with this timeless scene. Not even letting one thought bubble into my mind for God-only-knows how long, it was close to yet another sunset, defying all description, over the shimmery horizon, when I reached round to let my dog know I was still conscious.

Squeezing his paw, I looked over to see he'd taken a nap with his head resting in the lap of my huge wooden, gold-gilded Buddha propped between

BODYCAGE

cushions with a seat belt on. The burning rays, like golden, orange honey, shone all the more on Buddha like he was glowing and smiling peacefully... all-knowing in the back seat of my little Toyota Corolla. The same, now weakening, rays highlighted the tan tones in Bomber's fur as we sailed towards that sunset, blurring into the translucent haze waving up from the road and desert. In that moment, for the first time in my life, I didn't feel aware of being anyone or anything in particular... just a mind, untroubled by any worries, cares or anything else I could make up about this world. I know the sunset reminded me of the first one which moved me to cry in the movie "Jonathan Living Seagull" when I was thirteen years old. Remembering the lonely seagull "lost... on a painted sky" in a similar sunset to the one nature had put on for me then, I sang the words to "Be" for my audience of a dog and Buddha, crying until I couldn't even see the road anymore.

So, unless you're "Priscilla, Queen of the Desert", with a bus full of drag queens sailing through countryside as majestically ancient and awesome as Australia, a solo trip across the Simpson Desert... and most of an entire continent... is very good for the soul. For that time, centring my life in some stillness I didn't really understand, I am glad to remember it so vividly to write about now. It was indeed during that same movie, several years later, I'd thought about my own such trip, though no such appearances of 'Gloria Gaynor' Aboriginal drag performers, dancing to "I Will Survive" for me. Seeing that movie, as inspiringly brilliant and touching as it was, my mind was made up to keep notes often. I'd hoped to speak one day of all that leads up to how, why and what happens along the way before 'Priscillas' even need to hit the road in big, pink buses!... Just in case anyone might really, actually, be wondering.

Checking into a hick town kind of motel full of weathered, dusty crews of locals and long-distance truckers, I didn't bother with a drink at the bar or even take a snack. Mercifully, there was no Philipina bride doing a ping-pong show either and this little Queen of the Desert probably slept for an hour and half, then took the longest, hot shower before driving out onto the lonely highway again for the last leg to Perth.

Before the sun was quite up again, I had already crossed the Western Australia border, almost completely slowing to a halt to avoid the millions of rabbits which teamed across the road and wouldn't get out of the way... undoubtedly stunned by the headlights. Horrified, I learnt that the hard, traumatic way. They'd scattered a little when driving fast towards them, as brainless as rabbits are, many darted into the lights and hence under the wheels becoming genuine 'Thumpers'... thumping themselves to death! The occasional frustrated car or truck would honk past, splattering bunnies into the air and across the road all around until it was *traumatisation* by rabbit rain.

Reaching the outskirts of Perth, I'd felt like a mass murderer, having picked up speed, realising the journey could not feasibly be continued without compromising my fledgling spiritual beliefs to keep good in the Karma Bank - limiting any involvement with harm to our fellow living beings... unless, of course they were willingly paying for it! Heading onto the main highway into Perth, the fan belt went on my car. The AA man came out to replace it, remarking how amazed he was that I had driven across the country on my own (well... with Buddha and a dog) with no-one having told me that it might have been wise to at least take a spare

BODYCAGE

fan belt! Sleeping like a baby in my mother's spare bedroom, it felt good to be home.

After sharing a flat for a few weeks with a friend, I settled on the purchase of a small house in an affordable neighbourhood, close enough to my mother. Kelly, with whom I had stayed, was a pleasant enough transgender person I had met when she'd worked for a while at Ruby's, until it was discovered she was only 17 years old. She had also moved back to Perth to be close to her family. Now, at 19, she was living in her own rented penthouse in an upmarket neighbourhood with an endless stream of men coming over to play with her boobs and willy... for which she'd command a small fortune, being the 'youngest girl on the scene' in Perth. Through Kelly (self-titled on a loose delusion that she looked like Kelly Le Brock), she towered above most men... and was known behind her back as 'Kelly Le Brick' as she was about as thick, then later as 'King Kong Kelly', I met the rest of the 'scene'.

Those characters, I can only say, were the absolute feral end of the transgender scale as regards appearances and mindset. Put bluntly, for the absolute most part, these were a bunch of vicious gay men who had found a cosy niche through the lax prostitution laws in Western Australia (totally police controlled) to work legally from their own homes. As long as it was only one prostitute or escort working alone from the premises they lived in, it was fine. All sex workers... women, men or any expression in between, only needed to register at the Vice Squad section of the State Police, to have all their details recorded and photos taken. With a promise to work alone, not disturb neighbours and serve no alcohol or drugs on the premises... they were in business.

Those I'd called, at the time, the 'Feral Beryls', spent half their lives either smoking dope, peddling drugs,

Rehana Incognito

robbing clients or played dirty and often dangerous tricks on each other to protect their 'business interests'... ruining their competition by any means. Most of them saw it as something of an achievement to walk through a shopping mall and not get chased out with beer bottles thrown at them if a bunch of drunks or layabouts had 'sprung' them. An enormous hulk of Maori drag queen, known as Rotorua Rita, or simply 'Rah-Rah', had 'herself' advertised in the back of the local state newspaper with the rest. In the column of sex workers marked 'Transsexual Escorts', under the working name of 'Whitney' (yes, after Miss Houston), she'd tell her clients that's how she looked, promising all manner of alluring services to get horny guys to her doorstep with bulging... wallets. Probably from the same old school of transgender charm as Lexi Roper, Rita would stand behind the door on opening it, with a black trunk of a stockinged leg thrust out to tempt the guy in. Then beholding the horror on his face when he realised he'd been duped, a shovel of a hand would then hold the door firmly shut behind him. As he'd claw the latch to escape, Rita would bring out her baseball bat with the other hand, demanding a 'cancellation fee' if he'd try to back out... of $50. This she did up to 10 times a day, providing a massive income for drugs for herself and hangers on. I doubt she'd ever once gone into her boudoir to perform with any of her unfortunate 'clientele'. Like most of those guys working under all sorts of seductively tantalising names like 'Sexy Shyra', 'Busty Bianca' and 'Active Bambi- fully functional', they knew that not one of the guys they extorted this way was likely to go to the police. Can you imagine? - "I went to see a transsexual prostitute who menaced fifty bucks out of me at the door with a baseball bat." Not likely to happen!

BODYCAGE

These *lovely* working girls knew they had it made on an easy wicket... and I have learnt since, it's much the same where-ever these types are plying the trade. Most were astounded that I myself did not routinely rob client's wallets when they were in the shower, thinking me quite mad not to do so! Sadly then, those were the types which most men, who might have had an interest, whatever their urges to do so, saw of people 'like myself'. Their minds, and those of the public believed these 'transsexuals' were nothing but low-life men, dressing up, taking female hormones or not, to make public nuisances of themselves. As for Rita, I often thought she'd meet her match some day and he would give her (despite looking like a Polynesian warrior, club in hand, with tits), an equally unpleasant surprise back. However, she was horrified by me, as were all the others really that worked the 'escort' scene in Perth... where again I was definitely the misfit. They didn't like that I would not socialise with known criminals, go to gay bars and clubs with them to be stared at and hooted on the way there and in it, or held any fascination for destroying whatever brain cells I had left with drugs.

Rita did indeed meet her match, shortly after I found out she was arranging to have my house burnt down when my youngest, pregnant, sister Gemma was staying alone in the house whilst her husband worked away. Rita was found dead on her sofa, apparently having downed a load of bad drugs which mustn't have quite agreed with her. In the squalor of her flat, surrounded by filth and absolutely nothing of worth earned from her extortionate income, her little dog had survived a few days by chewing off her hands! Relieved that the poor little dog had not choked on the false fingernails, I could only wonder about the Laws of Karma when people are so full of hatred and resentment for other people that such things befall them. In a quick inventory of all this lot in Perth who danced around me like a bunch of crazed, gay witch doctors auditioning for jobs as Las Vegas Showgirls, it made me wonder. Another of them, who had threatened harm through some dirty trick, was also stabbed through the lungs by an unhappy client. Quickly, this little pest, backed down with the threats, convinced I had some magical power to have influenced the death of Rah-Rah Rita and his own knifing!

Having learnt to live with abusive, threatening phone calls from these men (which was what they definitely were), I never once felt like reporting them to the police or even having calls traced. Just knowing they were damaging only themselves with jealousy of myself, or anyone who appeared in their sphere of existence, becoming everything they could never be... was enough to see they were already tortured souls. They had to look in the mirror everyday and see the pathetic travesties they were and I always felt that must be hard enough for them to deal with, not going into any anger with them at all...only pity. So, in recounting this 'dossier of the dead' of the twenty or so 'transsexuals' in a small city scene in Perth, I can put names and circumstances to many of them - The few who still lived and those who either died of drugs overdoses, accidental or otherwise... and the rest who succumbed to AIDS;

Miss Robbie-Lee, the star of Perth's gay clubs and drag bar shows, died of AIDS soon after I arrived in Perth. Her boyfriend, called Tony, had notoriously slept with most of the rest of the 'girls' he could in Perth, which is the tragedy of small scenes... everyone's a step away from someone who has slept with someone who has been infected with AIDS.

BODYCAGE

Tony infected, she believes, a kindly and fun English friend called Nicky-Jayne, who I have no doubt was the typical unattractive boy, teased mercilessly throughout his childhood, who'd found 'the hiding place' in female trappings and attire. Nicky had impressed me on the phone, as I had hoped she was one not needing to fall into prostitution, saying she worked in a bank. Surprisingly, on finally meeting Nicky, I learnt she worked in the bank, cleaning them after hours. She decided to put her ad in the paper after coming to the penthouse where she met me at Kerry's, amazed at the turnover of men coming by to pay for sex. She died of AIDS related illnesses a few years after I met her. No health checks were ever required for sex workers in Perth to prove their status or not. Chillingly, clients were foolish enough not only to beg for unprotected sex with technically 'male' prostitutes, but offered to pay extra money for services 'without'... (condoms).

Ironically, these irresponsible men are actually *paying* to get infected, not only possibly with AIDS, but any other infection from a worker who 'goes through' several other such men a day. Still, to this present moment, I anguish and wish I could scream on the national news how stupid these men are, thinking so little of themselves and their own unsuspecting partners to engage in this stupidity. To any lady, I'd implore her to be very sure it's not her man who is out there taking these risks... whatever their reasons. Please don't think it's only a small amount of men doing this... sorry it is not. Remember- 'when their balls are full, their brains are empty' and 'when the little head's thinkin', the big one aint!' I miss so many of the laughs I had with Nicky as a 'good soul' really, who always reminded me of the best of Lily Savage although kind of softer with a West Country accent.

Rehana Incognito

Although I knew why she had decided to live as she did, I felt I'd probably have done the same with what I knew about life at the time, to offer some comfort to myself for a hideous, humiliating past.

The truly sweet and convincingly female Lisa was my nail lady. She, of all of them had no interest in the sex industry, being happy to work in her little salon on Beaufort St, Mt Lawley, chatting about everyday things like a suburban housewife with everyone who came in. It was all she seemed to want from life and she was my link to 'normalcy' after sliding into the company... (to feel safely accepted) with 'my own kind', which was far from the case. If I had only known.
I have no idea why Lisa killed herself, but only recently heard she did... and how I pity her, of all of them, that she didn't find peace and happiness on this path.
 Miss Kerry-Lee Curtis, yes... after Jamie Lee (they all have to have an idol!), worked both in the drag shows and sex work. Trying her hand at nail technician work through the advice of Lisa, she fell quickly away from it through boredom with the 'slappers', lamenting the loss of quick, easy money and the ready supply of the sex she liked through prostitution. I met Kerry-Lee at a cabaret night at a kind of upmarket mixed bar in East Perth where she was lip-syncing the Dusty Springfield song "In Private" wearing a large powder blue, 18th Century dress covered in enormous bows and lace.
 Kind of reminding me of one of the portraits I'd seen of Marie Antoinette somewhere, after the show, she swished over to my table with all eyes upon her, as a star rightly should have, nodding and smiling at the kow-towing courtiers. Incongruous with the Court of Versailles frock and hair-do, Kerry-Lee waved, for all to see, the bulky black form of the 'brick' mobile phone by her side to announce to the world she had one. At that

time, anyone seen carrying these new 'mobile phones' was marked immediately as a prostitute or drug dealer. In the trans-world Empire, in Perth, I'd say a good half of them were both.

Kerry's boyfriend, rough and dishevelled, being just out of jail on remand, heaved an awkward box the size a small telly, plonking it onto the table. She said that's what she need a boyfriend for, setting the 'brick' phone into the holder of what seemed not to be a car battery after all, but the phone battery! Kerry-Lee too, fell victim to accidental drug overdose within my first year back in Perth. Being called to the hospital to identify her body with another friend, her face was unrecognisable on the mortuary slab. I recall remarking to Belinda, who accompanied me, that it was really only the long salami of a bulge halfway to her knees beneath the white sheet which looked familiar.

"Well, that's what she was famous for, Riannon. Not looking too pretty-pretty now, Miss Kerry-Lee," said Belinda through the tears. At her funeral she was buried in her male name and referred to as "he" throughout the service as a final indignity. The undertakers had removed the silicone implants from her chest lest they explode during the cremation. I guessed that was better than slowly turning into a skeleton with two plastic bags lying on your bones after a few years.

Next to recall is Amanda Barrington, (the 'Barrington' being a customary habit in the trans-world as a name chosen which offers some substance and quality to who they have become.) I lost count of all the girls, met along the way, who'd conjured up even double-barrelled surnames to show on deed polls how worthy they really were now in the new identity, quashing the past in attempts to forget. Not in the least my beloved 'Lady' Felicity, who'd pretty much rubber-stamped her feminine validity with a regal title. Amanda, in the short time I knew her, went from being a pre-op trans-prostitute, back to Grant... the male body builder, then back to Amanda again as a Mary Kay cosmetics representative! Finally, having her sex-change operation after convincing the local gender psychiatrist she had definitely landed on 'woman' after ricocheting back and forward on the spectrum, she worked as a hooker again before killing herself not a year after surgery. It just hadn't worked for her at all and perhaps was Grant at the end of the day, but too late to change back this time. The psychiatrist, who had signed the documents for all of the 'girls' in Perth, whom I'd known had done so to become prostitutes mainly, also died. Actually, Dr Rose Toussaint was murdered in her own home and office in a robbery, I believe.

Diane ('The Man'), had also called me, being an English friend of Nicky-Jayne's. A sort of very crude Cockney type with claims to have knocked about with the Krays (which made me wonder how she might have accomplished that... *as a foetus*, being as she'd told me she was only in her mid 30's!). She impressed me, describing 'herself' in a demonic voice, as 'looking like Blondie'. Nicky-Jayne had picked me up in her little car, driving us way out to the sandy, scrub lands on the outskirts of Perth, down a long bumpy driveway. Singing,
*'There's a track
winding back... to an old-fashioned shack,
Along the road to... Gundagai..'*

We'd laughed through that folk song 'til 'Diane' opened her front door on the abysmal, decrepit old farmhouse. There, I immediately thought I'd met the murderous, girl-killing, body-skinning psycho from Silence of the Lambs. This one was Catweazle in a cat suit and a red paper rose tucked girlishly behind one ear with the fried, frizzes of 'Blondie' hair clipped back with an Alice band! Clearly shaken, still with the thought of her dancing around like an Aztec priest wearing my sacrificed skin, I'd remarked on her uncanny resemblance to Blondie lest she hurl me down a well to douse myself in lotion before killing and flaying me. I couldn't get Nicky to drive away, with dust flying in a trail behind us, quick enough. Diane called me often, confused about why clients ran away when she answered the door, but was soon arrested for Social Security fraud, which I'd often learnt was more the rule with these workers - Keep the benefits either coming in with the male name still on documents, or have yourself declared mentally ill and unfit for work whilst raking it in through the oldest profession. Diane too, died alone in a hideous flat she'd rented in Perth overlooking the Swan River. This one, we felt sure was deliberate heroine overdose when another tragic man, unhappy with his lot, realised he would not be passing safely through the rest of his life, disguising his true self and all his travails under make-up, high heels and miniskirts.

There were two or three others I did not personally know at that time, who had suicided or overdosed, working in Perth either as prostitutes or showgirls. The last I'd speak of was a part-Aboriginal trans who called 'herself' Kristy... or to those who loathed her as much as I did... 'Krusty'. This one was a particularly uncouth and unpleasant sex worker who had a particular interest in young, teenage boys. Stalking boy's High Schools with Kelly, who also shared the same interest, they lured boys either into their cars or back to their flats, dazzling them with the material trappings of their earnings, seducing them with dope to engage them in 'trick sex' encounters when the boys were too stoned to notice these were not actually 'women'.

Kristy, I truly despised, as 'she' knowingly engaged in unsafe sexual acts, being fully aware she had AIDS, likely to infect young boys who didn't stand a chance. It was some sort of evil 'vendetta' on her part which seemed to make her bloody-minded about 'punishing' teenage boys for whatever they'd done to her as a dysfunctional teenage boy herself. As for Kelly, she had been molested, with full intercourse, by a woman as a 14 year old schoolboy herself. This, tied in with a heavy addiction to smoking dope on a continual daily basis from that age, had undoubtedly stunted her own emotional development to the early teens... as well as adding to the twisted thoughts of feminine power and allure by the irresponsible actions of an adult woman.

Kristy also spent a lot of time with an 18 year old young man who had known Kelly at High School in his previous boyhood incarnation. This young man, I felt had the whole of his exuberant, fit, sporty life to look forward to. So catching a little time on his own while Kristy and Kelly did a 'double' at the penthouse, I warned him to be careful if he was getting sexually involved with Kristy, feeling he was being gullibly taken in. Joshua, in his captivating Texan accent, was only in Australia for a short while visiting his mother, explained that there had not been any sex with Kristy as they seemed to be trying to get to know each other more closely first before going 'that far'. Then, realising she was suckering this lad by grooming him into a more committed idea of a relationship, I caught her on her own.

"You know, Kristy... or whatever you choose to fucking call yourself." Cornering 'her' in the bathroom as Joshua sat unaware, glued to the basketball on TV in the spare room where I had set up my temporary world, I let fly with all I had. "That's just a young kid in there... and he's got every right to get through the rest of his life without getting your disease from you... out of your own selfishness for a toy to play with. Either you get in there and tell him the truth... Now... Or I bloody well will."

Having rarely seen such hatred on another's face as this vile male parody of anything remotely feminine, *Kristy* stormed away. Slamming the door for a good half hour until exiting with Joshua, both of them in tears, they wandered into the living room where I stood with Kerry, whom I had told about my intent. Joshua came to my side, as Kristy ranted what a bitch I was to have 'done that to her' as I simply stood, arms folded in disgust. Placing his hand gently on my shoulder, Joshua said "thanks", opening the front door to walk out with one last look from his baleful brown eyes with the longest lashes I had ever seen on a human being!
Not quite finished with Kristy, I spoke to several other trans-sex-workers who all agreed they wanted their lives and businesses protected by getting Kristy exposed and run out of the business. Another trans, another Renee (there was always a 'Renee', reborn into womanhood somewhere to be found) had called the local TV news channel, spilling the details that there was a transsexual prostitute working in Perth, knowingly having AIDS. As ugly as that was, the reporters were at Kristy's door in no time, showing all the viewers that hardened, bitter face and a good view of the building where she lived. Kristy fled town, predictably, where she worked on the streets in Brisbane until falling to the dreaded disease about three years later.
Joshua came by before heading back to live with his father again in Dallas. Thanking me for caring about

him enough, even though we were strangers, he invited me on a lovely night out around the bars of Northbridge until arriving back at the penthouse both quite drunk and well after the trains had stopped running. Right or wrong, lonely... or just plain attracted, I felt quite close to Joshua, whose life I may have just saved. Finding him intelligent, babbling about so much in the world we'd found unusually in common, I invited him to sleep in my bed to save going home to disturb his mum. Although quite drunk really, both of us, I do recall, in making love with him that night, my main intention was to somehow take the last chance I might have to let him know how it felt to be completely with a woman... and hope not to be tempted by predators like Kristy again. He enjoyed the 'reminder', he told me in the morning...

"Don't worry, things got a bit close there with Kristy, but you've reminded me which side I like my bread buttered on." Joshua gave me a tight hug and we both said we felt sure we'd cross paths again sometime.

I felt relieved that, as ghastly a person as Kristy was, telling Joshua about my own past was something she'd forgotten to let slip. He'd thought I was just the horny, 'older woman' any guy his age was spending almost all their conscious moments dreaming of. Although enjoying the time with Joshua, I'd seen it mainly as a mercy mission, letting it slip pretty much from my memory.

Back to the 'gallery-of-ghouls-who-thought-they-were-gals' in Perth, I could write a whole separate book on the rest of those violent, dysfunctional, drug-using/drug-dealing guys who sashayed in and out of my life and all around there and then. It is only in writing about all of these I want to warn anyone that this so called 'condition' of gender dysphoria can't totally be the reality so many believe. Of those twenty

BODYCAGE

or so I knew well, or not, in a city like Perth, none of them had made successes of their lives in the 'female' world and survived it. Not even one. I am sure there must have been some who had made this transition to enjoy stable, productive lives as 'new reassigned women', but with hand on heart, I cannot say I met one. So, although it would be easy, undoubtedly enjoyable and titillating, to write about all the girly fun and frolics as unfortunate 'little ladies' with a secret past, released from our body prisons to be the 'women we always were inside', it would be misleading and deceptive. Making the point about the tragedy of these people I'd mixed with, thinking they were 'my community', my only hope is that others will recognise it... in themselves... if about to embark on the same mistake, or in someone dear to them. Then, I'd hope, they get help to find their ways through all the misconceptions, to full and satisfying lives they can achieve without bringing disastrous embarrassments on themselves... and those dear to them in trails of carnage, crime and destruction.

I wondered whatever happened to the days when a *tranny* was just that tiny plastic, red radio I carried slung on a little black cord! Passing the time waiting in the heat for the bus to work early in the morning in Perth, to find myself standing a year later in pitch darkness, knee-deep in snow waiting for the bus to work in a mental hospital, I remembered over and over all the crazy songs listened to on that thing to which I now seemed to have lived my life! After the few months in Perth, alone with the dog in my new little house and occasional socialising with my sisters and mum, I was bored! Apart from that, I felt I'd once again built my little 'white picket fence' dream world to paint a perfect picture. Yet through the course of other people's expectations and wanting to please them all, I felt life would always be incomplete if I did not try to find the 'right' partner, maybe even finding a way to start a family with him. So, off I flew to Hawaii and married Matthew!

If this seems like a rollercoaster of irrational acts, it was! And I was on the ride... not even sure why I'd bought the ticket, which would take sharp turns, terrifying plunges, drench me in a pool or come to a sliding halt. Matthew's letters had continued to flood all that time since I met him in Japan until I felt a closeness enough to gauge telling him all about my past. Not in a letter, but over the phone, braving myself up enough, I told him I was not born a girl like others and spilt the rest of the story to him. Matthew did cry a lot when I told him, yet not out of despondency on his own part, but swept away in caring about how that must have been... for me. He asked how on earth I managed to get through my life with a past like that... to be who I had become. Claiming that he always felt he knew me in my heart and soul, telling him the whole story would test that in truth... but I was not in love with Matthew. I loved him as a wonderful and special friend with a chance to possibly grow into a lot more. Finding it a relief to hear that he would like to take a few days to process what I had told him and he would write, it was a surprise to find a letter soon enough.

It was a lovely letter, pouring out his heart with understanding, containing a poem which I wish I had kept. The last line, I recall well enough.

'I give you my love, I give you my life... I ask you, Riannon... Will you be my wife?'

BODYCAGE

1991

Perhaps not totally a heartless, selfish bitch toying with other people's lives, I was honest enough to tell him I was ready to spend time with him in either country to at least work on where things might take us. Having no desire to live in the United States, as I had just made a new life for myself in Perth, Matthew felt keener to get away from the problems he saw inherent with failed 'American Dreams', wishing to try a new life in Australia. The reason we needed to marry, on the proviso he remember we are still two friends working on how far a relationship would take us, was for the main purpose of his attaining a work visa for Australia. In Honolulu, we married on the beach in a place called Diamond Head Park with the Pacific Ocean crashing. Matthew looked like the cat which had caught the canary and I looked nervously apprehensive in a tight, white, silk and lace dress with lots of tiny pink and gold flowers here and there and in my hair. Clutching my little bouquet as we waited for a taxi back to our hotel, a young lady rode past us on a bicycle saying I looked really beautiful. I suddenly realised that I had forgotten to wear the Bluebirds of Happiness earrings Colleen had lent me. Matthew looked well pleased, with that same glint in his eyes I'd noticed as he put the wedding ring on my finger. For some reason, I thought he may as well be putting it through my nose with a chain on it to lead me away.

In no way emotionally ready for the type of loving intimacy anyone might expect on a 'honeymoon', with someone I'd really only known as about two kilos of letters, Matthew was clearly disappointed. I wasn't loving him with the enthusiasm he had hoped would just fall into being by merit of wedding rings now on our fingers. The rest of a week in Hawaii was more interesting for me to play tourist than doting wife, feeling odd at the Australian Consulate to be referred to as someone's wife and to keep mentioning this man 'my husband' there and everywhere else. Only agreeing to stay a week to see how things would go then I return to Australia to await Matthew's papers, I realised he was not going to accept us taking our time to be friends first, looking deeper into what a true marriage should be. He wanted the 'Ready-mix/Just-add-water', full-ownership scenario of the woman he had married.

The rollercoaster of irrational choices continued as I got back to Perth alone. Immediately, I was swept off my feet by an Australian golden boy football coach who always said "g'day" as I ran the dog at the local park and playing field. He had practically moved into my house... just a short walk from his parent's home where he still lived. My relationship with this young, upcoming football star... already in the local news and television on a daily basis as one of the new prospects for the state team, had started naturally with physical attraction, friendship and going out.

Totally sexually in heaven with each other, I remembered feeling guilty that I was married to another man, yet still felt justified in my assertion that it was a visa tool to work on friendship first. That situation, I had also honestly explained to Shaun, so he knew the complication I was stuck with. Clearly, I was not ready or in a position to bring Matthew into my life anymore and it pained me to tell him it had all been a foolish emotional trip on my part, whereby I certainly was using him... to considerable extent... as a quick fix, missing piece of a picture in my life. Broken-hearted for sure, then most definitely very angry with me, Matthew eventually accepted that I was still an emotionally immature person, nowhere near ready for all the

stability and commitment required for a solid, lifelong partnership. Through the Family Law Courts in Perth, I was able to have our marriage annulled to Shaun's great pleasure, claiming as we cuddled in bed the night I'd told him the news...
"Good... now you're all mine."
 In itself, that statement felt both hugely securing and a warning bell at the same time. Shaun was not only a football hero... and in Australia, that's top of the league for any man to reach... but an only young son in a family which expected, along with himself, that he become a father too. The wives and girlfriends held the same position as the "Wives And Girlfriends" of sporting celebrities in the UK, which I soon both feared and enjoyed at every football award night in his company. Too many TV cameras and newspaper reporters were snapping us together as other 'WAGs' asked way too many questions about who I was, how long I had known Shaun and where I came from. Panic finally came when one WAG from an opposing sports team, somehow circuitously worked out she had been at school with my youngest sister. The net was closing in on a secret the media would have gleefully used to ruin Shaun's career and also, without a care... his life.
 Practically turning anorexic, in a living kind of grief... knowing I loved him very much... I wished to be left alone forever with my beautiful hero. It was clear I would have to simply find a way to let him be free of me and all the devastation potentially I could bring. Losing Shaun, I knew I would need to get as far from Perth... and even Australia... for a very long time, so used the excuse that I wanted to travel the world. He wasn't buying it. Begging, crying and looking at me like his world would simply end, it was really me who wanted to beg and cry with *my* world ending. Without betraying a thing, I made myself look like the heartless

bitch I certainly was *not* in just 'dismissing him', he'd said, 'throwing him to the kerb like a used piece of trash'.

"I'm sorry you feel that way, Shaun... I really am. One day you will thank me for it... and understand it's for your good too." I needed him to hate me and not try to hold on.

There was no way I could tell him the truth about my decision. Storming off into the night after we'd been to see "Silence of the Lambs", I kind of wondered if I'd chosen the right night to tell him and be left alone with the nightmares of the movie, knowing to a certain extent I had met the caste and lived it! Hearing a few of Shaun's comments during the movie, it was signed, sealed and delivered that there was no way this guy would have wanted to deal with the movie he starred in with me right then. To top it all off, there actually was an horrendous thunder storm that night, making the mood and pain even uglier. I wanted him there with me and this world to be a different place for us to go on... as we were... with some right to have lived that life with Shaun. With the thunderstorm, memories of the movie and all the pain of doing what I thought I had mustered the bravery to do to Shaun, it was a long night. Pictures in my mind of my 'social set' of work colleagues or friends played out like a line up of criminals on "Australia's Most Wanted" criminal mug shots. The ones who had died faded in and out of my dreams as skulls with painted on glossy, red lips around the bony jaw and exposed teeth, with garish blue eye-shadow around the empty, black sockets.

With nothing but bloody-minded bitterness that a life most girls dreamt of around me had just slipped by, I felt it no wonder that transgender girls become embittered, acting out a rage against the unfairness of

BODYCAGE

it all through the sex industry and Bondage. Booking my flight to London, assured that Gemma, her husband and new baby boy would look after my dog and house, I arranged with a friend from Melbourne who had moved back to the UK, to fly over and start anew.
"Don't cry for me West Australia... the truth is..."
well... I never bloody well really liked you!
I'd done an "Evita" in my overdramatic mind, using... as ever... themes from musicals and movies to relate to life as if some hidden machinations of the Universe called the tunes for everyone to dance our lives to. Not even realising I was just a bit stunted in working out emotions for myself, mostly by proxy, through any song I could remember suiting the occasion, it took years to realise I might just have been 'life imitating art'. It kind of made me often wish I was deaf and dumb, blissfully uninfluenced... or at least lived in a world without movies, radio and television!
Jamie lived with his partner in a huge house in Vauxhall, graciously allowing me the space to catch my breath there in the cosy spare room as a base between quick jaunts around the UK and several adventures in other European cities. Travelling back to Northumberland to visit the one friend with whom I'd stayed in touch, I felt like a ghost... wandering alone through the village where I was born. Shivering in an evening chill I'd not prepared myself to stay out long enough to face, I trailed past the terraced house in which I was born, feeling a million different emotions all at once. Turning on to the main street, I almost crashed straight into a woman in a head scarf with a load of shopping in plastic bags. She smiled, saying "Eee, Ahm sorry, Pet", although I'd nearly knocked her down.
Catching the woman eye to eye, my mouth wanted to move and my arms throw themselves around her... but

Rehana Incognito

I could not say a word. It was my mother's youngest sister whom I'd always been closest to... and there I stood before her... a total stranger, respecting my own mother's wishes to not make myself known to her family for fear they would not understand. Although approaching darkness, I rushed then down a lane to the woods and river down the bottom of a hilly field.

I know I was crying quite a lot, stumbling up and down slippery, muddy hills and pathways with the trees bowed over me... fading light hardly getting through the leaves and branches. Reaching the banks of the fast-flowing river, I came to the clearing near a crossing point of blocks of stepping stones which I last recalled crossing as a five year old with my dad securely holding my hand, calling "one-two-three, Jump!", as I leapt across the swirling chasms. Onto the first one I stepped, looking to the left then right at the cold, grey water and overhanging trees almost bare before winter. One by one I crossed the rest, totally alone in the silence with just the occasional sound of an owl as I got to the other side. With much thought of a father who had not been there for me at all since last crossing this scary river, over seemingly huge expanses between stepping stones, for that brief time... I felt some elation of all I'd done without him. Marching firmly... and very briskly away, I sat upstairs on the bus back to Newcastle looking over my shoulder until the highest building in the village... the church where my parents had married... could no longer be seen. I never went back there again.

Back in London, I looked up the Chinese hooker, Jessica, from "Bottoms Up" in Hong Kong... who also owned a flat in Earls Court, flying between the two countries as the work suited her. Jessica was somewhat rushed when I dropped by as she was between 'cases', as she called them, putting in rollers and doing her nails in time to meet another working girl for a double date at Simpsons on the Strand. Amazed that I never knew of any of the similar kinds of hostess bars in which we'd met in Hong Kong, she scratched out the number of a club in Mayfair, recommending I call them about some work - getting guys to buy overpriced bottles of wine and champagne, dancing with them and keeping them entertained with the option to go out and 'do extras' if I was really up to it. It sounded like the perfect arrangement for all I could be bothered with.

The efficient, attractive blonde girl, slightly older than myself, asked me in for a brief interview early the next evening. Outlining the nature of what was expected of hostesses there... dress style, etiquette and all the rest, this Scottish 'Mama-san' was pleased I spoke several languages with plenty of similar experience in the Far East. She was happy for me start that night, setting me alone at a table to watch the live band warm up. Other girls filtered in as the charming Lebanese waiters flirted with the new girl in the Club Deluxe... which looked like a shabby rendition of how I could imagine Selfridges cafeteria might have looked in the 1960s. Some of the girls introduced themselves before it got busy, surprising me through the course of the night that another three of them, I'd quickly worked out, were ladies like myself!

One was a petite Indian girl with swept back glossy, short hair called Sunita whom I delicately asked if she was a 'Sister Act'. Taken aback that I was too, Sunita confirmed my suspicions about the very tall Irish girl with the stripped-to-death, over bleached, platinum long hair working there as 'Diva'. I wasn't sure about the Iranian girl who appeared to have rather large, clumsy hands which I'd probably not have noticed if they weren't so over-adorned in gold and gems with nails probably way too long for any biological woman I personally knew. Diva confirmed that Nushin was a close friend and had also just recently had her gender reassignment surgery. So, there it happened... all in an instant. Another little trans-world underworld (well, Club Deluxe was in a basement off Piccadilly) had materialised before me with no surprises to have found these colleagues too, like myself, working in this area of the hospitality industry.

There's no need to write so much about time spent working at this club. What this work entails has been written about in thousands of stories. I could have called myself a 'high class' call girl like all of us there, but never really thought 'class' was something to associate with fawning all over drunken business tycoons of the 1990s boom times in London. Getting guys dancing in the hope of seducing them into 'buying us out' from the club to bleed more from them at their homes or in hotels rooms, didn't merit it either.

For the most part, I'd thought of myself as a courtesan... acting in the manner of a well-trained Geisha. At the very least, with all these girls like myself around, working in the same business... that could have been a book in itself. I'd have to call it "Memoirs of a Geyser" and watch for the movie, wondering about all those men down there in 'Club De Fucks' who'd spent a fortune on us bunch of trans-girls to waste on God-knows-what! As exotically exciting as this work and lifestyle may sound to anyone, it amazed me to have gotten away with it, retaining one brain cell left in my head after all the alcohol consumed to keep the expensive bottles coming to my table, padding up the customer's bills. Yes, it all sounded like fun, but if some lives could be described as that 'Downward Path to Wisdom', as far as I was concerned, I may as well

BODYCAGE

have been on a mud chute, sliding headfirst into a cess pool.

My closest girlfriend at Deluxe was called Naiima, from Tunisia. She had helped me rent a cosy room in the house where she lived in Beaufort Gardens, Knightsbridge and kindly invited me for a trip to her home for her upcoming fortieth birthday. We thought it a good break from a hard year of nights at the club... and picking up Arabs in Harrods to buy us goodies by day. We travelled quite a way to her town, far from the more cosmopolitan Tunis, by taxi with Naiima constantly whacking the driver to keep his eyes on the road, not glued to me in the rear view, sitting in the back seat. Her family were welcoming and overwhelmingly kind, parading me from house to house and shown the sites with way too many stares for me to feel comfortable going out. Even though I'd completely covered my arms, wore nothing tight and baggy jeans, the men looked at me like I was a walking shop dummy for their perusal. An older, perhaps middle-aged woman in full black cloak with her face covered said something in Arabic as Naiima and I passed in the market. Naiima chased her, hurling abuse as shoppers looked on grinning until she came breathlessly back to my side.

"What the hell was that about, Naiima? What did that woman say?" with great concern, and not in the least a lot of fear, I'd asked in a hushed voice.

"She said we were whores corrupting the men in the Souk with the way we dressed."

"Oh no! What were you shouting after her down the street?" Franticly scanning across the women's clothes stalls, I tried to spot a burqa to walk home in.

"I said she was an ugly bitch and needn't cover her face as she'd not be likely to blind anyone with her beauty. She swore at me again so I told her she was only jealous 'cos she'd have to walk naked through the Souk for anyone to look at her."

It seemed the whole market agreed... but feigning interest in local costume, decided to buy a nice all-encompassing, black abbaya which would cover me from head to toe. The one I spotted with lots of colourful, glittery metalic, neon-like edging caught my eye and I bought that one for a well-haggled price with a matching long headscarf or veil... along with some crazy pieces of glass bauble jewellery. Naiima tucked away any wisp of blonde hair which might have strayed from beneath the nice wrapping she'd done with the head cover, decking the new jewellery here and there. Catching a glimpse of myself in a shop window, scuffing through dust to the taxi stand, I looked like a nun who'd gotten herself mangled up in a Christmas Tree!

Naiima had booked a hotel room at a resort not far from the kind of marina club house where her birthday celebration was to be held, so we would not have to travel back to her parent's late at night. Friends and relatives there, she'd told me, were educated in France and mostly successful professional people... so I could resist the urge to cloak myself, at least for the party. That was a relief, as I'd found the swathing black abbaya and head scarf heated me up so much I'd thought my own body fat would spontaneously combust. Following Naiima's lead, with the added comfort that we'd travel only from hotel to venue with a male relative escorting us, I put the rollers in, felt liberal with the makeup and wore a somewhat tight, silky green dress. Not too low-cut and just on the knee, I didn't think it would raise too much attention or detract from Naiima, whose birthday it was anyway. Still, not risking too many chances, I slung the head scarf around my shoulders as it matched quite well as a loose, flowing shawl in case a breeze came in from the sea.

Like Middle-Easterners celebrating or just socialising in the cool of evening anywhere, they got things going very late. By midnight, Naiima's older relatives had drifted home as one by one, more of Naiima's ex boyfriends and even an ex husband arrived in the later hours. With more and more toasts to the birthday girl and my constant wandering out to the deck, gazing across the sea to straighten myself out before braving the party again, I hardly noticed the few women there had all but disappeared. Naiima had forgotten me entirely as I'd worked out the motive of the party was primarily to impress her main squeeze ex-boyfriend whom she'd hoped to win back. For whatever reason, certainly not through any act of encouragement on my part... even politely rebuking the aggressive flirting with the leftover men... they took the very presence of a lone Western woman as an open invitation to groping! Coming to the point of several of them ganged around, manipulating me uncomfortably towards a cleared table. Pushing me practically onto my back whilst trying to lift the dress became enough warning for me to get out of there.

Pushing them aside, angrily grabbing my bag and the scarf, again I headed for the outside deck to scarper down a side stairway and around to the front of the marina. By almost dawn, the place was desserted, though I could see the lights of our hotel about ten minutes walk way through clusters of other buildings down an empty road. Rounding a little bend, just a couple of minutes into the walk, a car's headlights bumped towards me. In a kind of open jeep, it was a bunch of policemen in uniform doing some patrol. Asking in perfect French if I was alone... and Ok, I replied that it was only a short walk now to the hotel where we were staying. The tallest one, who spoke the best French, gallantly leapt from the jeep, insisting that he walk me back to the hotel as it was 'not good' for young ladies to be out on the road. "How lucky was that", I'd thought... as the policeman grinned at my side. The other few drove on away after a quick exchange in Arabic which I needn't have bothered trying to follow, recognising only the words *bint, hotel* and *boukra*...'girl, hotel and tomorrow'.

Rounding another bigger bend, the officer indicated I walk through a large space of land, disappearing off into blackness, which I remarked seemed a bit off course to get to the hotel. Monsieur Le Policeman explained I was thinking of the most direct route by car, but it would be quicker by walking through the space we'd now found ourselves well into. Comforted with a personal police escort back to the hotel, I didn't think it worth questioning... I mean, just how safe could I have been? Suddenly, pushed... or knocked flying... onto a pile of viciously sharp rocks, dried up twigs and sand, my gallant knight's face had turned disturbingly brutal in the light of the moon. Only able to whine muffled protest through his hand, firmly over my mouth, my panties were torn off, digging and burning into my flesh as they were wrenched away. Holding one of the larger rocks over my head menacingly, feeling as malleable as a jellyfish, he roughly threw me around to any positions he wanted, until he heaved in completion... my face buried down in the sand with bits of twigs stuck into my flesh and hair. Hearing his zip do up and the buckling of his belt, I waited 'til his footsteps had faded away.

Crawling a short distance, then struggling to my knees and onto my feet, I staggered back to the hotel room. Turning the key, looking across the walkway towards

BODYCAGE

the sea, I noticed the ink-black sky had started its slow, fading-indigo change to dawn. Still totally stunned, gazing into the mirror at the stranger's face looking back through reddened eyes circled with black, streaky eyeliner, tiny trickles of blood ran from scratched temples as bits of twiggy foliage still dug into the flesh and lodged in my hair. All the rolling tears had soaked my face, so dollops of sand had stuck to it here and there. Rubbing bits of bushes and dirt from my arms and legs, soaking towels to wash off the blood, I looked into the mirror again feeling like an iconic picture of the crucified Christ, trying to ponder how on earth I could gather compassion or forgiveness for what the betraying policeman had just done to me. Falling onto the bed, pushing aside the towel sculpture of a swan (which only hours before had frightened me from the room, thinking a goose had wandered in), the loud speakers of all the nearby mosques rang into life as the chant echoed across the water and desert silence.
"*Allah hu akhbar... Allah hu akhbar...*" the voices floated into the distance. Catching sight of the ceiling arrow, pointing in the direction on Mecca for guests to correctly position themselves for prayer, I just closed my eyes as the chanting call continued, thinking... "Yes God... You are great. It wasn't You who did this to me." Then, humming my favourite hymn, "How Great Thou Art", between sobs, I felt something of a soothing, warm wave carry me to sleep... far away from that ugly scene until Naiima returned about eight o'clock.

Perhaps instinctively, she knew what had happened, not even needing to ask. Just holding me like a child in her arms on the bed, roughly unclipping her hair extensions as if to say "what the hell do we do this for to please anyone", she clearly seethed inside herself.

Rehana Incognito

"Riannon... do you want me to take you to the hospital... the police?" Naiima stroked some drenched hair out of my eyes as I looked up.

"It *was* the police, Naiima... I just want to get home." I could only whisper... not even wanting to make it any more real by speaking it loudly... If I whispered... it might fade away like a scary story. It would have to fade anyway and be dealt with only by me. Naiima explained what I'd only understood such a little of. In a Muslim country, rape would be hard to prove as it required four male witnesses... all would need to be Muslims and of sound mind. Sadly for me and any other woman in such circumstances, that criteria is seldom met. Reporting the 'crime' of rape could well land me in trouble myself if I were accused of 'seducing' this man by the very act of what I was wearing, having been drinking and walking alone late at night. Were the policeman to have been a married man, I could easily have found myself charged with adultery. I just knew it... it was pointless to complain and I now only longed to get home to London and straight to a doctor... which I did. "Welcome to our World"... I'd thought again about that card I'd woken up to on the bedside table at Masada Hospital as I flew out, over the Mediterranean. Am I really, *really* having fun in yet?

Back into the big old dark den of Dollars, Pounds and healthy Deutschmarks, I wasn't much company at our client's tables of executive chiefs and oil dealers. Considering how much they'd paid per hour for me sitting there flirting, talking suggestively and padding out their egos to keep them spending their money, I am surprised none had asked for refunds. As the only professional former dancer I knew of there, it was always easy to escape from the drivel at the tables, yet still give them their money's worth... dancing with the other girls or anyone game enough to join me. When the band played anything exotically exciting, like a samba or lambada, I'd excuse myself to put on a brief show, winding through the other girls alone... holding my own arms around myself tightly, stroking my thighs or holding up my hair to expose my neck then let it tumble down with a swish and a shake like Jessica Rabbit in a favourite tight, sparkly red dress. On the verge of throwing up again after another £300 bottle of champagne which some grovelling Japanese upcoming manager had shocked himself in purchasing to impress his company emperor, I bowed...very low, excusing myself to head to the loo.

After a generous soaking with some flannels under my arms, dabbing around my neck... up into my hair, I was almost seeing and thinking coherently as the cubicle door opened behind me in the full wall mirror. Huskily, quite chillingly really, in a totally male voice with that heavy Persian accent, Nushin swept her gaze across my rump bent over the sink, growling...

"I wish I still had my cock... I'd fuck you with it... Soooo hard." Still staring, frozen, at her image in the mirror, I let her walk away like she'd just hit me with a baseball bat.

Although money fluttered effortlessly to me, doing a job which came surprisingly easy as not even *second* nature, I was guiltily paid to play courtesan whilst dating some of the most influential businessmen in the world. As well as the occasional aristocrat, whose names I would never put to print either, going back to suites in the Dorchester or private, luxury apartments kept in Mayfair and Belgravia for such dalliances... I still decided to give it up. Enough became enough when allowing myself to be 'bought out' of the club again, going back with the men I thought bearably tolerable or even slightly sexually attractive. I stopped cold and quit. How many nights I'd stood in front of bathroom mirrors in the most palatial homes and hotels, gathering up wads of £50 notes or adjusting makeup so porters might not register what I had done (who was I kidding? I'd always slipped them £20 on the way out every time anyway, as they'd wink knowingly), there was no way of counting.

Not really caring how many of these men had admired and used my naked flesh, it somewhere marked itself on my conscience that I cherished my body so little to willingly be exposed, yet in no way knew how to be naked with my heart and soul before any of them - Possibly ever-fearful they'd reject what they found in there, or even worse... I'd loathe it in myself. In those transactions, it was rare that either party would be aware or even care that anything of human pain, joy, hopes, disappointments and aspirations were there anyway. It was all as transient and disposable as a takeaway meal... gourmet, fast-food or otherwise.

Big, tall Kelly from Perth, along with her bisexual boyfriend, Todd and bubbly, busty Belinda had all flown over, bringing an onslaught of Australiana, for a working holiday in the UK. Their company was refreshing enough as they rented a basement flat in Royal Crescent, Holland Park to quickly set up business. With Kelly and Todd doing live sex shows, which clients could join in with either of them or both. Belinda advertised too in local papers, the "Loot" and "Exchange and Mart" as a 'Big Busty Mama' for the clients who liked it large. Quite a few days and nights we'd all spent in the basement flat between going out to buy fabulous costumes for the likes of the Kinky Girlinky extravaganzas, the Torture Gardens and The Rooftop Gardens of Kensington to wind down with celebrities of fashion and media on Sunday nights.

BODYCAGE

Kelly and Todd flew off for a weekend somewhere exotic as I promised to come and stay with Belinda to answer the phones when she was busy, maybe do some of Kelly's 'Sexy Susan' clients... if I felt I could be bothered... and go off to fetish clubs, clad in rubber, chains and leather if the mood took us. Belinda had taken way too much liking to the fetish scene, enjoying the well-deserved admiration and attention of the worshipping fan club she'd soon amassed. Excitedly she told me of a young man, with a short name I'd quickly forgotten, who was a big admirer of big ladies with whom she'd started an affair. Making my way over with a weekender bag of kit, I called Belinda from the Holland Park tube station to see if she was not 'otherwise engaged' and if she needed anything from the shop on the way, as I'd always ask.

"Just a box of chocolates, thanks, Lovey... A family box... and that block of dark chocolate... not sure what it's called... about a 500 gram block," she'd put in her order for the heart attack quantity as easily as asking me to pick up milk and a stamp.

"Got to look after that girly figure, I guess... it pays to invest in your assets, Darling." Cleaning out the corner shop's chocolate stand, I made it to the basement. Belinda stripped the cover off the chocolate block before we made it back to the living room, where a tallish young man of about 18 years old lit up to see me come in. Walking across the room about as macho as Madame Butterfly in low-slung jeans and a t-shirt, he delicately offered his hand which I was almost tempted to kiss rather than shake, as he coyly introduced himself.

"Hello, I'm Tim... Am so glad to meet you... after hearing so much about you." He looked at me as if we'd both done something terribly naughty.

Rushing into the kitchen where Belinda was carving into the cardboard of the family size chocolate box with an enormous knife, I turned her quickly around to face me.
"Girl! What the hell have you done now?! You can't be serious... He's just a kid... *and* as camp as tits." I was truly flustered.
"Calm down, Ri... that's not my boyfriend... you're thinking of RICK... He'll be over later. Tim's just a nice little queer boy, Kelly and Todd met on the bus."
With a big, relieved sigh, I returned to *Tim* on the sofa, giving birth to a friendship lasting to this day. With never a row or argument, I watched this boy, who could have been my soul twin brother...indeed in our eyes... become just that. Tim and I were one another's sounding boards, tearing apart for decades now, all it meant to be gay, straight, men or women... or just simply human beings or spirits and souls over a million luncheons at the Troubadour and Balans in Earls Court. I think we became known as enigmatic celebrity mysteries to staff and patrons everywhere who could never work out what or who we were to each other.
As for Kelly, she had every opportunity, looking as good as she did in the increasingly accepting times of the 1990s, to have pursued a successful career to make it as a supermodel, transgendered or not. Ru Paul was already up there openly being a successful clothes horse and everyone had actually already thought Kelly was a model. She chose, however, to not believe in herself enough, continuing with what she did best... smoking dope from her first moment awake to the last thing she did in bed at night... all the while still working on her back, doing all she thought capable of doing... not exactly requiring a great deal of thought or intellect. Changing into a rude, condescendingly vile person when Kelly took up a 'lesbian' affair with none

BODYCAGE

other than Nushin, she adopted her same grandiose delusions of being some estranged Persian, deposed aristocrat. Together they deemed anyone else who came into their presence as merely subservient minions. When last I actually saw those two, Nushin wore a silky, see-through leopard print jumpsuit at a Kinky Girlinky event, leading Kelly, stoned out of her box in black vinyl to match, by the hand through the crowd.
"Oh hi, Riannon... How's your old *man*gina going?" Nushin hissed in her snaky voice with an accent like a hawker in a bazaar, trying to convince me some old piece of tat was a priceless, antique fukkari rug. With her hand clamped heavily where no-one's was welcome... uninvited, I held it firmly away at my side.
 Letting my fingers trace the curved outline of a set of silicone balloons implanted in her chest like immobile footballs, I thought to give back just as good.

"It's not bad thanks, Nushin... it does what it says on the tin." I smiled, knowing she was not bright or confident enough with English to get that. "I heard yours has been officially recognised by the Royal Astronomical Society."
"OOwat do you mean, dahhhlingggg?" she boomed as all the lights came on readying them both to scupper for cover in the harsh light, like beetles from under the rock.
"They've officially clocked you as a Black *Hole*... sucking in anything that comes near you, bending even Time and Space... or maybe they were talking about your heart, Nushin." They were swept away in the fleeing crowd in the bright light.
 Poetically, last I heard, they had parted company in a massive row over an underage, teenage boy they met

when back in Australia, whom for whatever reason they both took a fancy to!

After Belinda and I had both booked clients at the same time, we swapped them around discreetly through the narrow hallway where I'd almost gotten stuck, wedged between Belinda's boobs, upon realising we had each other's guy by mistake. Kelly was advertising as a "TS Barbie Doll" who Todd had quipped did indeed look like Barbie... "well, Klaus Barbie... the infamous Nazi of wartime France!" Belinda of course was the "Mountains of Love" from Planet Big Girl, until she was outed by News of the World as "Mrs Blobby", losing the flat when the agent read it!

"Crikey... you're very good looking," the nervous little guy had said in Kelly's room when I took his money. "but you don't look like you got a 52 inch bust, if you don't mind me saying." Immediately, I'd realised the error before standing jammed between Belinda and the wall.

"Mine said I looked good too," panted Belinda... "and would never have known I used to be a *man* !" A phantom client had later booked a session with all of them. Turning out to be a writer, he forever immortalised "Barbie and Ken" as well as Belinda in a book called "Nothing Personal"!

After a couple more Euro-jaunts, soaking in all I loved about culture, history, languages and lavish hotel rooms before putting myself far away on the other side of the world, I flew back to Perth with a big cheque from Barclays Bank and some breathing space. Shaun, who had written almost every week, vowing to keep our friendship valuable and alive forever, collected me at the airport. It was painful enough for both of us to pretend we were both now just close friends... and he was also living with a girlfriend who claimed to accept us remaining supportive friends. There was nothing I wanted more though, than to keep him in the motel room I'd booked until deciding my next step. Letting him go in the night, I didn't try to stoop that low or even tempt him into the position of cheating on the girl I already resented for having a guy I truly adored... just by virtue of how she was fortunate enough to have been born.

Undoubtedly desperately insecure at my return, the girlfriend fell pregnant as quickly as she could, duping Shaun that she was on the pill. No longer able to see him at ease... or with a clear conscience, we didn't meet up very often. Their baby boy was born in due course with some terrible handicaps, putting strain on both of them. More than once, Shaun lamented that he wished we'd both fought for what we thought was really a love worthwhile... and worth fighting for. I never, to this day, told him the whole story... of why I couldn't fight back then.

CHAPTER THREE (PART SIX)

1993

Absolutely on the bright side, I returned to Perth to find that Britt had done so too. What a relief to see her commercial advertisement in the Adult Services pages of the West Australian newspaper for Mistress in her all-new House of Domination in South Perth. I'd looked in the paper to see which of the trans-crowd were still working, alive or arrested and called a few of them I could care about for the gossip. Indeed, it was just as bad as I'd thought with a couple more dead of AIDS, two or three back in jail, a drugs overdose here and there... and half a dozen new gay boys on the bandwagon with their wigs and makeup for extra money and easy sex. Nicky-Jayne was not by then sick with the virus, mentioning some American guy had kept calling her to see if she knew when I'd be back. Really having no idea who it could be, I gave it not a great deal of thought, asking Nicky to tell him to call me at the HoD should he again ask. Back to some whip crackin', arse slappin' action in no time, with renewed fervour, it was business as usual for Mistress Britt and Mistress Ultra (Violent) as often as time allowed.

Only a short distance from my home, I'd taken back to the domination and fetish work perhaps over-enthusiastically. Dashing in late, I quickly got through a brutal, double domme session of flogging and degradation, clad in a clammy, rubber cat suit. Peeling it hurriedly off before a thorough shower in the downstairs half of the house where the suites of sadism lay, I shook it from my foot like a big, floppy octopus had ravaged my legs. Running naked up the stairs and into the kitchen to answer the forever-

urgently ringing phone, there on a bar stool, popping on the kettle ready to make tea, was a little old lady of about ninety! It was Britt's mother. Spinning around on the linoleum floor, one hand across my chest and the other doing the Botticelli's Venus over my womanhood, I just as quickly bolted down the stairs.
"Why didn't you tell me your mother's sitting up there...? I've just met her... stark naked."
"Oh, she couldn't care less... She's seen it *all* down here. She's over from Melbourne for a week's break... you'll get used to her."
 Indeed I did enjoy the old lady, once I was dressed, loving all the openness with which she'd accepted the work her daughter and I were doing just beneath her. As for me, I felt somewhat dreadful not to have told my own mother anything about what I did there... other than play receptionist. It turned out that was wasted sentiment. When I finally came clean about it, only because Karen threatened to out me, my Mum accepted coming over to go to lunch with Britt and myself before taking a guided tour of our dungeon and playrooms. Way too gleefully, Colleen and Mum's eyes had lit up on seeing all the paraphernalia of the trade... mum seating herself like the queen of her domain in the electric chair surveying her surrounds in the dimmed, red glowing light. Brandishing a big, black rubber dildo in her hand like a sceptre she seemed well pleased when Britt affirmed she does indeed 'rape the bastards' with it.
"I'll stick a toothbrush up their arses if I want... and get them to scrub the floor with it." Britt stood by the dungeon door peering in with me at a respectable grandmother making herself at home in there, looking way too gleeful. Shocking me... yes, my *own* mother... said -

Rehana Incognito

"Well, I'm proud of you two lassies, I really am. I wished I'd done the same bloody thing myself years ago... instead of letting the bastards mess me around!" Britt offered this natural man-hater a job on the spot, laughing as Colleen brushed by us and out.

"Bet there's times when we were growing up, Riannon, you'd wish Mum was sitting in that electric chair," she whispered, "I could have strapped her in and flicked the switch on and off a few times myself." I think my mother had become all the more demanding as she got older, loathing men all the more as she kind of surrogated her lack of a husband to take things out on... with us!

Without that hanging over my head, I felt more relaxed in my work, both at Britt's and in the spare room of the flat I'd rented, leaving Gemma and her family comfortable in my own house. Having a genuine certification from Adult Education for therapeutic and relaxation massage, I kept that up too, balancing something of my life in contrast to the bondage work. It was sometimes difficult to catch myself in moments of being very busy, tired or just rushed when I'd forget... with a stressed lad or two on the massage table, having to always remember not to automatically start humiliating, degrading or beating them up! Still, it was irresistible not to slap their bare bums many times, because I liked the sound and knew they all appreciated a taste of that too now and then... just for a bit of fun... really.

In that hot weather of February 1993, Britt passed me the phone before fleeing off downstairs in a flash of leather and clatter of thigh-high, metal-heeled boots to inflict some imaginably brutal terror on a willingly bound victim.

"Some American guy." She'd thrown the receiver at me...

BODYCAGE

Picking it up to curiously ask 'hello?', I recognised Joshua's Texan drawl in the first syllable. Wow, that was an unexpected blast from the past. Joshua sounded a lot more grown up... and, after also having done more travelling, seemed very worldly. He too was back in Perth again, visiting his mother before going back to Dallas for university medical studies later in the year. Being the twelfth of February, just one night from the eve of Valentine's Day, we laughingly arranged a proper date to get re-acquainted and catch up on all that had transpired for us both in the three years since we met. Perth, being not the easiest place to enjoy much of sophisticated dating or anything even close to it for the most part, I was actually quite excited. Getting ready during the day for the proper date, just feeling a little cheeky about going to welcome in Valentine's Day, I really was curious to see how much more this young man had grown into himself.

Opening my front door when he rang the bell, I pulled it open with hands cupping my eyes, not daring to look until he was inside and standing before me. Dropping my hand, blinking wide-eyed open, it was jaw dropping to see this man standing half a head taller than me. Breaking into a laugh with arms thrown out to hug me, it felt like Joshua had been beamed into my flat from some big, hunky man Heaven. Hallelujah! If it was raining men, I wasn't running for my brolly. Thanking the "Weather Girls", I thought- "oh no... I'm gonna let myself get... *absolutely soakin' wet.*" ... and his aftershave or cologne left me temporarily having an out-of-body experience.

At midnight, heralding in Valentine's Day, the club's DJ said he would dim the lights as the 14th struck, and we should close our eyes before opening them again to kiss the one who would be our Valentine date. Romantically fun as that was for me, Joshua was just as happy to play along as we danced for an hour or so more. Finding it odd that we seemed to know each other's choreography like a rehearsed show, to the point where other people were staring, we realised they'd mistaken us for the cabaret act as they stood aside to watch us perform. I remember one of the songs was "White Line", whereby Joshua effortlessly lifted me, wrapping my legs around his waist for a few spins and twirls, managing to throw in one or two flawless dips as well!

Through the night, back in my bed we eventually got to sleep with the windows wide open, letting in a soothing breeze, billowing the curtains gently inward offering glimpses of the sparkling city skyscraper lights, reflecting perfectly in the lake-sized body of the Swan River. I recalled dreaming of swimming with my dolphin friends. Every sense I'd remembered about those times was still the same - the cool water, the sloping, falling depths of the sand beneath the waves, blurring into a distance out into the mysterious unknown of the ocean... And the firm, smooth feel when I dared stroke my special friends' smooth skin. Only, in that dream, I was how I am now, with very long hair drifting freely around and about like something I'd remembered of Daryl Hannah being Madison the mermaid in "Splash".

As all the other dolphins swam off into the deeper, darker sea, one came closer, circling about to eventually come by, looking deep into my eyes and beyond. Recalling that I knew he was male and that his huge, enticingly alluring eyes were saying something... I sensed a recognition and a call. Putting my arms around him, he charged powerfully through the water until rocketing from the ocean's surface, carrying us both into the sky and off to the stars. There, dancing in the vacuum, entwined like serpents as galaxies of colour and indescribable lights bathed us in magical illumination, he transformed himself too into a naked man, somehow blending into my form as one being.

Telling Joshua about the dolphin in the morning over lunch at a little boat cafe on the water overlooking the Swan River, he laughed, thinking I must have seen him somewhere in his grey wetsuit, surfing along the coast. He loved to surf as that was his passion, his favourite sport and even, he'd explained though he never understood how, his meditation. Losing him often enough over the months, as I became a 'surf widow', sitting in windy, sandblasted car parks with girls whose men flopped around in the waves waiting for the perfect thrill, I thought back to the first time I saw Joshua and recalled him having the longest eyelashes I'd seen on a human being... and those huge, Ashkenazi eyes, set in dark olive skin against his thick, wavy black mane... put me in mind of some mysterious beast.

A lot happened further along those lines... of situations I'd describe as perhaps inexplicable co-incidences or symbolic mysteries of how things were acting out in our lives. They are personal to me, most times beyond even belief for myself, let alone to write about for anyone else, but we all have them. Sometimes we just brush these things aside under the heading of 'mere coincidences' or subconscious wishes and desires playing out in our dreams, with a touch of that 'deja-vu' which shakes us to think deeper and take notice at times too. Sitting late one night again in a burger bar, where I munched into some fries and a corn cobette, I mentioned my vegetarianism to Joshua and how I just felt a deep-rooted belief it was morally wrong to kill animals for us to eat and all the reasons why. Completely insensitively, Joshua leaned to my face and breathed the smell of the burger onto my nose saying how much he loved meat and could never give

it up. Wanting to just burst into tears, I held in my shock, simply telling him there'd be no kiss goodnight for him until he'd brushed his teeth and gargled.
"You know... when you say things like that to me... you actually remind me so much of my mum." He showed more interest in the burger as he spoke. "Actually, you even sound like her... smart, fun and sexy... and you got a similar way with people. Funny isn't it?"
"I suppose it is, Josh... Should I be worried men are attracted to women who are like their mothers? Maybe I should drive you home tonight to yours."
Getting his attention away from the burger at last, he asked what I meant by that. I still seethed on the way home about breathing in the smell of the murdered animal, so jokingly threatened not to let him sleep in my bed with 'half a corpse rotting in his stomach'.
"Sorry... you know that was really bad of me... I'd just never thought of meat that way... actually, I didn't think about it all." I let him come home to my place yet again, lending him my car to go surfing again in the morning.

Over the next few months, I did actually get to meet Joshua's delightful mother who was all he said she was and more. I admired her as a woman who'd dealt with betrayal and loss of her own husband, Joshua's dad, and the added humiliation of him keeping later custody of Joshua for his teenage years of male influence, along with two further new stepmothers for Josh. When reminded how much alike his mother and I were, I told Joshua it seemed coincidental too that he shared almost the same birthday as my father in mid June making him a Gemini man also... so I'd be on my guard with him! Warning me I'd *need* to be on my guard as he considered himself a typical Gemini, though not believing any of such things!, he did mention having another Aries girlfriend who behaved a lot like me too.

BODYCAGE

"Well, Josh... Aries are all pretty much the same... Loyal soldiers, marching through life with their close comrades... friendly, generous, honest and kind. I think they wrote the text book guide on Aries women after me... or even my mother." It never dawned then that a million and one other little psychodynamics were coming into place. Those would be familiar to anyone who has read relationship studies pertaining to 'sympathetic wounds' or healing our parents' relationships through acting them out ourselves... or both! Then there's the many other complex games when we're drawn to our special 'one' we think can make us whole and complete as if we never really were to start with! Blindly we act out, through the people we find ourselves attracted to, calling it all the while this all-consuming *love* we would die for or die without! Desiring to look more into what was startling us now regularly, almost day to day, Joshua and I wandered through the "Conscious Living Expo" at the Claremont Showground.

There, amongst stands of information about every religion, New Age Healing, lectures of Polynesian Polygamy and people who communed with spacemen, Josh and I stuffed our Show-bags with all the information which took our interest. It was like stepping into a new, foreign city, where we didn't know our way around, understand the language or culture, but knew all the same our old place was not for us anymore. Picking up Louise Hay's book "You Can Heal Your Life" was the first step for me. It was the first and simplest way in which sense was clearly made about the connection of our mind, what we think and how we *feel,* which draws to us experiences and conditions around us and inside us. Whatever anyone feels about such matters metaphysically, beyond our total understanding, I'd always accept as being personal to them. We will all learn and either reject or accept such things in the time which is right to serve us.

Yet, in all of the notice I took of how things fell into place around me and others, close to me or not, it would be irresponsible not to try and explain... and help anyone along. Simply put, we all know of times we have thought of someone, then the phone rang for that person to be on the line. Or we run into someone we only just thought about, yet not seen for years. Or someone says just the exact thing we were thinking of, or that very thought comes into life in a show on TV or the words are written on a billboard in front of us. I recall walking through an area in Perth in my late teens, thinking about my parents and all the misunderstanding, the abuse and heartache caused between the sexes, wondering why people would even be gay. Looking up at a hoarding for a building site I passed, someone had written graffiti in huge letters- "Men's WARS kill Women". Next to it were the two little symbols for 'female' (the circle with the cross beneath) side by side, making the point this was a feminist, a lesbian or both. Startlingly and more chilling, in another scrawly script beneath it was written-

"GOOD RIDDANCE"... with the two little symbols for male side by side next to that!

So, in just touching on such things lightly for anyone, I'd say to look up any of the works of Louise Hay, Wayne Dyer, Harville Hendrix, Nancy Friday... or any of those heroes and heroines to me who have dedicated their life's experiences to putting back together damaged, shattered and confused souls. As for me, I read each chapter in "You Can Heal Your Life", summarising it all in a note book, like a High School project until it was committed to memory in an attempt to live it. Devouring anything I could lay my hands on by Joseph Campbell, so much more became clearer on learning about the deep psychological dramas built into our minds for perhaps tens of thousands of years, tied in with myths and symbols used in every culture. Many of these play into everyday psychological problems and misunderstandings, deeply... for us all. Others express through the different religions with hidden or sometimes very obvious meanings for our lives. Whether those religions are then used for mankind's benefit and wellbeing or controlling submission marking 'others' as less than themselves through twists in the tales, is most of the problem facing the world today. I for one, am glad this struggle is coming to the surface to be skimmed off... made clearer when realisation dawns that at the core of our beings, no matter what our race, religion or even our gender... at *that* very core...we are all exactly the same *thing*.

Then just when you think everything is pointing you in the right direction... that you've found a cosy little place to hide yourself comfortably in, blissfully enjoying the fruits of your learning... comes the time it's all put to the test. I'd thought the test was to torture me... punishing me for something I must have done in another life... or shockingly... the possibility that this one might be hideously criminal itself. Joshua needed to return to the United States for University. I wanted a happy home in the leafy suburb we lived in, cooking gourmet meals and watching endless fabulous movies. Joshua felt what we shared was a real love... how deep or where it might go neither of us really knew... but I knew that I *wished* for it to continue, growing and learning together.

In his mind, it would be a relatively straightforward transition to stay close friends, to be loving and supportive that way... even if I came for a working holiday in the United States to keep that much alive.

Part of me agreed, with the fairytale belief that the love would conquer all as all the love songs I'd ever lived out played along to my delusion. Yet, in a panic, I told Joshua I would not risk following him to the United States and didn't believe he loved me enough by letting go of our lovely life in Perth, just to be who his father expected him to be. Letting him storm off back to his mum's after many tears from both us, we really thought that was the end of our journey. The next evening, I came home to find a card from him, pushed under the door... In large letters, it was headed-
"*THE TRUTH IS...*"
Inside was a list, the full page long, of the virtues of being so many wonderful things. I cannot even remember them all. Mainly I stared at the words-
"*You Are....*
Loved,
Beautiful,
Unique,
Honest,
Kind,
Loyal,
Funny..." and on and on.

Signed...
"I Love YOU!!
 Always,
 Joshua."

He came by that evening without many words between us, just holding and crying. He'd said for the first time in his life he truly felt loved for who he was and was grateful to shift such emotions at last with tears... which seemed to give his eyes a good cleanse if not to experience raw emotions! The US Consulate stamped my passport with a five year multiple-entry

BODYCAGE

visa after first refusing it. My records showed I had married a US citizen in Hawaii, which for whatever reason, led them to believe I was going there to try and live. However, after some time sitting alone in an office whilst they reviewed my appeal, handed over the passport with permission to stay yet not work, so long as I left the US every 6 months, explaining myself at the border each time I returned. Joshua came early to my home to get ready for one last good night out, a dinner at a restaurant overlooking the river and maybe even some dancing. In the bathroom, standing in a red, satin blouse, not wanting to put on the black skirt lest I get makeup on it, I brushed out my hair. Catching his reflection in the smoky mirror when it slowly appeared like a ghost from somewhere, silently, in some kind of wonder, Josh gazed. Smiling when seeing my eyes catch his, he slowly came up behind me, squeezing me tightly. Strange as it may seem, Chris De Burgh was singing the "Lady in Red" on the radio... as Joshua gave me a kiss as we swayed, it made me start to cry.
"Don't cry, Riannon... your makeup will on run and we'll both be late again. I'll always love you...you know that... And you'll always have a friend in Texas."
A friend? I'd slightly panicked, yet said nothing. With no idea what would come of me there or the relationship with Joshua, I followed him a week later, arriving in Los Angeles late at night on Thanksgiving evening of November 1993. The airport was really eerily empty as most Americans had gone to their families for this occasion. Feeling isolated and alone, I ate the traditional Thanksgiving foods at a cafeteria by myself then boarded an early morning flight to Dallas.
With spirits lifted to be with Joshua again, we drove back to the hotel he'd booked for us, where I'd thought such luxurious surroundings would keep the feelings we had exciting enough. As we chatted away, he must

have thought, with me in the car, we were still in Australia. Turning onto a freeway with cars screaming into us, horns ablaze, he'd driven off on the wrong side of the road. Although it was a fright, I had to laugh wondering who he thought was driving... if I was in the passenger seat and he behind the wheel! At our hotel suite we ordered room service and lay on the bed where he sat glued to the basketball, hardly talking to me at all. After taking a long shower, leaving him to the game, I came back, slipping under the covers to stay warm. Joshua was not following the cue. Casually, after the game, he got up pulling his boots on... reaching for his car keys!
"You're going back to your dad's? I don't believe it." Sitting upright, I could not believe he wasn't even going to kiss me goodnight as he was almost to the door. "I've just flown across the planet to a foreign country to be near you and you're leaving me alone?!"
"Look, Riannon... I want you to make the best of a good holiday experience here... and we've got to stay *friends*. I don't want to lose you, but I am under my father's roof and he pays my tuition. He's laid down the law that I stick by his rules... and part of that is I get in when he says I do and no girlfriends unless it's right for his whole family." He was biting himself, holding back like words which seemed squeezed and forced unnaturally from a block of steel inside him.

"Well get out then.... leave me on my own! I didn't come to America for a bloody holiday, Joshua... This is the last place I'd want to be. Why didn't you tell me all this before I left Australia?" Not even realising I had taken on my mother's own expressions, tone of voice and fury when she landed in a strange country too, pleading to go home, I sat staring at the door for ages until realising he had walked out, not having the courage to say a word more. He was bound to knock on the door any second, come back, comfort me and explain it all away... but he didn't... until about lunch time. Sullenly we drove to a shopping mall where I could barely eat anything of the lunch only desperately wishing to push him for explanation and what he expected me to do next. Impatiently, I asked.

"What am I supposed to do now?" Putting down the knife and fork, I pushed the plate spilling with bits of salad away from me.

"It doesn't really matter what you do, Riannon," he coldly looked into me. "This is the time of life I have to concentrate on my studies... and I know my father is wrong in saying this... and this is really going to hurt... He blames all his marriage problems on not having married Jewish women as his first two wives. And I never had the heart to tell you... he is just seeing you as a 'no good *shiksa*' his own mother had told him they were." I wanted to laugh and tell him it's a bloody good thing he didn't know I was not only non Jewish... but not really even a biological woman... and give it to him right in the teeth. Still, I tried to reason with Joshua.

"How can you respect this man who you say put you through a horrible childhood and treated your own lovely mother as he did? I don't know what right he has to hold himself up as a virtuous example of the tenets of Judaism as a liar and adulterer himself," On I frothed. "How does that make me of any less value with *his* son? Don't you see, you are just trying to please a man who's still trying to please his own mother?!"

Joshua told me he'd walk off if I didn't try to understand the position he was stuck with as I went into a tirade about people who could be so bigoted - finding it all the more abhorrent to be coming from a Jewish family somehow seemed even more incomprehensible to me. Unable to face it or give me a humane answer back, he did storm off... with the car, leaving me to find a taxi back to the hotel. He was already by the door to my room and I was very hurt and angry.

"I am going to go home, Joshua and leave you to find out what you've done all by yourself one day. It's really nasty, this... and it's wrong." I swiped the key in the lock.

"Riannon," he stammered, following me into the room, "Coming back here has just woken me up to what life represents to me with my father and where I need to go now as a man professionally...and personally... You have to understand. Being with you in Perth, was like a dream... and part of letting go of times of freedom and fun... as a youth. I am sorry you got messed up in my experience and I *do* really love you so much... but I gotta knuckle down now." His words were like an exclamation mark at the end of an assertive sentence. That... was that.

The angry side of me just wanted to throw everything around the room and scream at him. On the other hand, perhaps just feeling glimmers of hope, I resolved to strike a compromise.

"I have come this far to America now... and maybe should find something good from the experience... and I don't have a clue what that might be... But I think I will stay on. If we're ever meant to be close again... we'll find a way and a place and a time. I'll give you what you want now, Joshua... and won't stand in your way."

Hugging, we lay silently on the bed where I felt like I'd already said goodbye to him forever really in my heart. We fell asleep until the room filled with darkness, shared a meal in the hotel restaurant and discussed what I could do next. Looking at my little map of the United States, where I'd planned all the wonderful

BODYCAGE

things I might do and see over the next five years, it was clearly not even worth contemplating Joshua wanted me to risk staying in Texas. Looking at California on the other coast, thinking how sunny and warm it would be, romanticizing San Francisco from so many films and stories as being bohemian and quite 'European', I chose to go there.

Having stepped out of my hotel room in the morning wearing shorts, a light top and sandals to sit by the pool on hearing it was a "sunny thirty four degrees", I had heaved open the sliding door and right back in again. Complaining to the concierge about the weather man having said it was thirty four, he'd looked at me as quite mad saying-

"M'am... it *is* thirty four out there... Fahrenheit!" Well, nobody had told me they were still stuck on that stuff.

Joshua saw me off to San Francisco, meaning to keep his promise that we stay in touch by letters and phone...which we did... alot. Accepting, to a great extent, the lonely adjustment to being single and on my own in America, at least that side of me still sparkled at the prospect of a new adventure, in a new city. Making it downtown, I found a nice little hotel run by Buddhist nuns, grateful in the comfort that not much could go wrong staying there. Wandering around on my own, I found San Francisco fascinating, beautiful and bone-chillingly cold! Sitting alone a couple of nights, reading some guide books I noticed the same, smartly dressed man with a lovely smile and dark hair twice sitting at a table near me at a neighbouring restaurant. On the third night he asked if he could join me. Grateful that he did, he told me his name was Michael and gave me his business card. Kindly... and with no expectations, Michael sat smiling peacefully, listening to my story of how I'd come to be alone and really quite afraid in California. At the end of the week, he said he needed to go back home and hoped he had been good comfort for me.

A few days later I did actually call his number to thank him for caring so much and listening to my misery. The recorded message said the number did not exist. Sending him a postcard to the same effect, it returned to the hotel a few days later saying "no such address". I told a lot of people about 'Michael', some of whom said I imagined him in my pain and loneliness, others said he might have been a guardian angel. I'll never know... but experiencing such kind, thoughtfulness from a man without needing anything from me was a unique experience which may have just kept me staying there. On a nocturnal wandering to another part of town I took a tram to look at the street I'd read of many times... The Castro. Perhaps, I just really wanted to see if there were any places with a gay crowd where other transgender people might be I could relate to... and make some new friends and contacts.

Perched on a stool at a quiet bar, I didn't take much notice of the young man sitting by my side until he got drunk enough to dare ask about my accent, having heard me making chit chat with the barman. He kind of reminded me of Bugs Bunny when he did his female impersonation numbers with his wit, voice and mannerisms. All the same he was dark-haired, quite olive-skinned and unfortunately (I don't know if it was the glasses) looked like Sally Jessy Raphael! His name was Seneca, he'd explained to me and was an American Indian, gay alcoholic... with AIDS. Perfect for my first new friend in a strange city, I'd thought and just my bloody luck. Seneca was kind of good luck for me, pleading that I come and stay in his big apartment in a place called the Tenderloin... which I thought must be very salaciously bohemian and all I might imagine somewhere as exotic in San Francisco to be.

BODYCAGE

Moving in straight away to *enjoy* having a 'stable' address while I look for an illegal job and somewhere more long-term to live, the Tenderloin turned out to be anything but tender! The name itself, I'd learnt, came from the early days when police were paid in extra cuts of meat by the Service for having to work in a neighbourhood that dangerous and rough! It hadn't changed either, as I soon ignored constant gun shots, becoming terrified of a pre-pubescent boy on the stairs who was dealing crack every day in our building.

On a night without Seneca, I ventured to another part of town called the Marina, again sitting alone writing postcards to everyone I could think of. A charming gentleman came over offering me to join his company when I was done, knowing by the post cards I was from out of town. This handsome man in about his late forties was a successful Jewish chiropractor with joint custody of two little children. Unbelievably, at face value, Nathan Fox offered me the guest suite of his house for a live in job if I'd care for his children in the times he had them. Not believing my luck, we chatted for hours, arranging to meet the next day over the Golden Gate Bridge in a town called Mill Valley, just a short bus ride along Highway 101 North.

*I had style... I had flair... I was...*Desperate! *That's how I became... the Nanny.* Only this nanny was English, the boss Jewish and, equally as different to "Fran Fein" in the TV series - I was not all interested in him.

Winding through the hills in which Mill Valley nestled, it had started to drizzle, as it too often does there late in the afternoon, with thick fog tumbling over the surrounding hills and Mount Tamalpais. Nathan pulled up by a long wooden staircase which seemed to go up and up forever to the huge, dark wooden house, surrounded by trees at the top of his hill. His ex wife

Rehana Incognito

dropped off the children close to night fall. The little girl of four came rushing in to the arms of 'dada' first. The mother, an angry-looking blonde girl I'd thought way too waifish and innocent to *be* a mother, plonked the little boy of three onto the porch with a gentle kiss goodbye. The children, I soon learnt were complicated little characters caught in the middle of their parent's acrimonious separation, but warmed to me ever closer, knowing that I was the one person now close to them... not involved in the battle they were aware of. Between that little boy and girl, they have no idea how unwittingly their needs and presence had grounded *me,* totally committed to their wellbeing and responsibility... almost forgetting at times, pining in my heart to build the dream with Joshua.

Putting into words those dark, empty nights in my little nanny house, gazing out of the window at all the yellow, welcoming lights of the little cottages and enormous villas set between trees and across the valley before me, would be a pain to attempt. Not in the least, we all really know what emptiness, loneliness and abandonment can feel like... and it's always the same sense of desolation for us all. The fact was, that all those little images of perfection so close, yet not *for* me, shimmered as elusively as the most expensive Thomas Kincade paintings of idyllic village paradises, tormented me all the more. With a mind stuck in a rut, digging its repetitive groove of all I *didn't* have, yet desperately wanted, Joshua's letters and calls were a life-line when they came, spilling out our hearts and minds with any new little wonder we'd discovered about the world.

Joshua flew over a couple of times to visit, lifting my spirits that there was hope of anything being rekindled, or at least he'd fall in love with the magic of Mill Valley... which it definitely had, perhaps luring him to

stay. On his first night in my bed we had felt as if it was our first time together back in Perth. Putting on a favourite sleepy time cassette called "Mariner", with haunting sounds of the ocean and sounds like the lone clank of a warning bell at sea, I drifted off thinking about being a ship with some precious cargo... not belonging safe in a harbour, but ready to sail off on a sea to who would know where. I fell into a sound sleep, believing that my hopes would be realised and we'd be back together. In the morning, I told Joshua of a dream in which we were sitting on a platform in a cavernous station. A voice had come over saying-
"Last train for the Academy is about to leave... All aboard now folks, All aboard."
In that dream Joshua was asleep on the seat and I tried to wake him. The call came again, as I then struggled to wake him, resorting to trying to *carry* him to the train as it started to pull away. Gently placing him on the platform completely unconscious, I just looked helplessly at him, realising I needed to get on the train and make the journey to this Academy without him. Taken quite by surprise, he told me he too had dreamt of a train ride in which we both sat in a carriage where 'dark', foreboding people tried to throw stones at us through the window. In that moment, it was clearer than ever, even if I didn't want to accept it myself... the Universe, or something we'd call higher and deeper, beyond our conscious minds, is always trying to tell us something!
Both times he visited, he went back and I cried for days, putting on the bravest face for little Sammy and his sister, Shannon. There is no way ever to tell those two, how... in all their squabbles, learning about their little valley life and easing their own worries and concerns, this little boy and girl represented chances to look deeper into my own childhood. Finding ways to

never let them get hurt, feel embarrassment, shame or guilt, there were countless times over three years with each triumph they made to grow... I healed wounds long buried but burning in myself.

By some great fortune, there is a bookshop in Mill Valley called the Depot, where trains used to come with passengers all the way from the fishing town of Sausalito, practically under the Golden Gate Bridge. There, every new book which was all the talk of the nation at the time were highlighted and chewed over by people sitting around enjoying the Depot and its little outside restaurant area on the town square. One such book was "Return To Love", by Marianne Williamson, which I literally inhaled the day I got my hands on it, scarcely able to put it down even to sleep. When Marianne Williamson amazingly was presenting a talk in San Francisco, I truly felt that night I had seen and heard the voice of God from this woman. With every word she said beautifully measured to perfection, only bringing an understanding of peace, forgiveness and replacing any fear with love, it became my goal to make the effort to do the same.

An effort was the right word to use because everything in my circumstances there I saw, with increasing clarity, was a challenge. Joshua may as well have come to me with a neon sign on his head saying "I AM Your Test". Even though things became horrifically ugly, I am not going to let those thoughts live again in my guts where we harbour such feelings. The dream of him being 'too heavy for me to carry' came to fruition soon enough... and as much as that brought pain to my life and undoubtedly others, his choice to go one way or another was about his journey alone. How I dealt with it all was my lesson in it. All I know is that, as Joshua turned before my eyes into a liar, a user and undoubtedly sexually 'over-explorative'... I accepted

BODYCAGE

that I was no-one to judge or complain after learning what I needed to know my own way too. Most of what he did was abreaction to his father's authority, like a naughty boy trying to do as he pleased, hitting back at daddy in any way he could. I forgave him eventually for it all, as well as myself and feelings that all men were women's enemy, spewing from some satanic nursery until the Price of Darkness himself was ready to unleash them on us all.

As for Mill Valley time, I am sure there were long weeks or even months when I could have been classified as technically insane in what we call going 'out of our minds' with heart-ache and helpless confusion. And there I was, keeping up the facade of 'responsible adult', looking after Sammy and Shannon, along with several other women's kids who'd stolen me away for the 'glamour value' of an English nanny. If only they knew... I was practically a psycho! It didn't help that I may have overloaded myself with way too many popular books about the mind connection, creating our reality and dealing with efforts to understand how falling in love with the 'wrong' men is about learning to become bigger and better, healed and whole people ourselves. What really put down roots, sustaining the rest of my life, were uncovering the schools of spiritual development and unfolding.

Through study groups of The Science of Mind, Unity School or Church of Metaphysical Christian Understanding, as well as inspiring encounter groups looking into the Course In Miracles, certainly more of this world made a lot of sense. I'd be hesitant to place importance over one path of understanding over the other because I see them as being like wells. There in deserts reaching down to what flows beneath, they help us soar with a satiated thirst... The style or structure of the well is not the focus. That 'well' could be a temple, a synagogue, a church or mosque of any religion... or simply those schools of thought which are individually right for anyone at the right time... Eventually we can realise they all do the same job, bringing the same comfort to us all. For me, and most people I met along the way who made our lives more whole again, just reconnecting to anything offering a link to something eternally wise, secure and unchanging beyond our mere selves is a great place to start. Remembering the message given to me by the gentle, accepting old lady called Grace when I was a nurse, I always now recall an older man I cared for too at the same time.

This old man must surely have been a brute of a chap, still roughly abusive in his manner to other nurses, calling them, and his own wife and children names I would not put to print. In contrast to Grace, this man sat slowly drowning in his own lungs, diseased from years of smoking as well as his alcohol-damaged other organs. Seeing what remained of what had once been powerful muscles (now hanging like bags below his bony arms and legs), I wondered how he'd used such strength while he was still able... and who he may have hurt with it. When his family had finally walked away, not bothering to come back and listen to his tirades, it was left to nurses like myself to watch and listen as his time to leave this world drew nearer in his panic. Gasping for air and clutching at anyone who got too near his bed, all he would do was call out- "God forgive me... Jesus Christ! I am sorry for everything." Then finally, in the last of his choking breaths...

"GOD help me!!"

It had been lesson enough, at that early age to somehow make sense and find peaceful understanding of the same thing which frightens us all from the moment we become aware of it - We will all die. So,

that's the main reason I'd even allude to spiritual needs beyond all we think we are as just a body and mind. Find it while we can still use it to make our lives and others' better, instead of waiting 'til we're screaming on our deathbeds for it! All I can hope is that you try... and find that which leads you to a place which works for you.
 I had spent nearly two years in Mill Valley, travelling around America in free time when I could with Joshua or on family trips to Nathan's home in Hawaii and visiting friends in Los Angeles from the movie world, who all seemed to have homes in Mill Valley too. It must have been a good half a dozen times Joshua and I had said goodbye forever and 'this time it's really over' just in telephone calls! It was 1995.
 So, while sifting through all of this, in the temporary insanity of grief and slipping loss of touch with reality... at some point I must have come to my knees. All I knew was that I was broken... down there, on the ground... and could either be there, still crying and washed away by it all... or get up and learn from it. My friend, Debbie-Lee, patiently and without the slightest judgement... only compassionate love, took me by the hand, helping me choose the latter. Having met Debbie-Lee as the immaculately groomed vision of the 'Golden Angel of the Valley' herself, this gracious lady really reached me just in time, as an angel would be expected to do! After visiting during a party at Nathan's, with her husband, Josef... who was one of his hiking friends, Debbie-Lee had dropped a long letter into the mail box explaining how grateful she was that I had shown her some photos of Joshua and myself. In one picture, where we stood arm in arm on the Marin Headlands with the Golden Gate Bridge behind us, she spotted a kind of plume of rainbow light shooting from the area of my heart. She didn't feel the

same as I did, that it was some trick of the light on the lens. No, she convinced me it was my heart chakra, whatever that was, glowing with a light of love she knew and appreciated assisting my two little charges, caught in their parent's bitterness. It was with the greatest urgency Debbie-Lee had asked me to call her and visit, hoping to discuss protection of my own self along the way... and I could not resist making that call.

At her beautiful house, which I'd describe more as a temple itself, full of wonderful angels on the walls, creamy welcoming sofas, happy, healthy plants and a different view across Mill Valley, we looked down towards the waters of the bay.

"It feels like being halfway to Heaven already up here, Debbie." I raced out to her little wooden balcony as she just smiled, pouring lovely herbal teas.

With huge scented candles and an unknown choir of music coming from her bedroom, Debbie-Lee told me more of the miracle she herself was. In her early forties, she'd only recently been given a literal death sentence by doctors, having discovered aggressive tumours of cancer throughout her lymphatic system. With no pity for herself or her condition, she spoke of her time as a famed DJ, overindulging in a lifestyle of drugs, alcohol and all other naughtiness I don't want to mention! Then she'd felt it no surprise her own body could not process what she'd brought to it... and now had started to fatally attack her. When the doctor told her how little time she may yet have to live, her own determination told her to raise her fist to it, somehow saying – "Yeah, really? I'll show you." Being led her own way to a course of positive thinking through decrees of prayer on her own spiritual path, none of it was easy for Debbie-Lee and her wonderfully adoring husband.

BODYCAGE

Keeping up the conventional medical treatments along with her rituals, she became her own miracle... clearly having *not* succumbed. In fact, Miss Lee won back a life healthy enough to astound the medical experts!

She became my inspirational mentor of hope and recovery, if not just for me... for the children... and I could write a whole novel just based on the miracles which seemed to pour out all around and for us. Instead, Debbie-Lee, whom I soon trusted enough to tell all about my journey to the point of where I sat with her then, encouraged me to harness all that I had learnt in these experiences in the form of memoirs.

"Who'd believe it, Miss Lee? So many crazy things have happened that I can hardly believe myself, let alone explain them to others, helping them or not." I walked out on the balcony to watch the last of the rain drift away as the clouds broke, exposing the deepest blue sky.

"You know what they say... Truth is stranger than fiction, right?" She came out to join me in the brightening light.

As I thought it may have been fortunate after all to have kept five-year diaries and little summaries of books I'd read relating them to experiences... I wanted to say I couldn't do it. Then, as impossible too as I thought it to be, we suddenly found ourselves standing *in* a rainbow arching from the balcony... right across the valley, the bay and all the way to the Golden Gate Bridge! With both of us jumping up and down, giggling in the wonderment of passing directly through all of the colours surrounding us, it was indescribable, except to say it felt like time, distance and everything else didn't exist for a moment... I was only a thought... aware of being made of the colourful spectrum itself.

Trailing up Debbie-Lee's particular winding road to her house on the hill so many times, I felt stronger, growing more complete, sharing things gleaned through metaphysics studies and group talks about the Course in Miracles. Delivering a couple of dozen pages for Miss Lee to look over for advice on direction and any writing style I'd hoped to have, I stopped to catch my breath. Deeply inhaling the freshness of all of the trees and flowers, one bright yellow blossom on a bush beckoned that I sniff it in a unique moment... lost in ideas about being 'one with the universe', filled to the brim and overflowing with all the thoughts and ideas of manifesting a perfect life.

Poking my nose into the flower, I was stunned to become a bit more 'at one with the universe and all its creatures' as one of them shot up my nose! Screaming and thwacking at my nose to jolt this dreadful unknown insect out of me, I had to laugh when it popped out and flew off. It may have been a coarse reminder to come back down to earth and deal with what I had to... or perhaps it was that lesson I'd recalled of the Buddhist statement – "Before you become a Buddhist, a mountain is just a mountain. When becoming a Buddhist, you don't see a mountain as a mountain any more. But then when you actually become a Buddhist....well, a mountain is just a mountain again." Perhaps my time in Mill Valley was coming to an end.

During one final visit from Joshua during a time of California's most dreadfully endless rain with accompanying floods and storms, we drove in the little old BMW Miss Lee and Josef had given me to attend Josh's half brother's wedding in Colorado. How that car got us there across deserts, through mountains and snowstorms, I really don't know. But, like our floundering vehicle of a relationship, we got there to witness this sacred event, where his brother married a 'shiksa' himself, standing up to his father's lament. Of course his grandmother stayed away, undoubtedly I thought, tearing her clothes in the grief of it all, crying and vomiting blood as she writes him out of her Will. I was proud of him for standing by the woman he loved and told him so, though not in earshot of his disapproving dad and fawning, acceptable Jewish wife, Rachel. Joshua, at least acknowledged me in his speech, commending the bride for taking on the men of his family. It was not easy to be with the guys of his father's line, Joshua told the wedding reception... "as Riannon would be the best one to probably tell you." He was right!

All the way back to Marin County we argued and fought until stopping high on a hill overlooking Lake Tahoe, surrounded by forest. Peaceful enough for a while as we took in the beauty, Joshua stopped to listen intently in the direction he'd heard the cracking of twigs. A short distance away from us a beautiful doe was gently stalking along trying not to let us notice her appearing from the woods. Reaching over to grab the camera as he quietly clicked open the door, I firmly took hold of his arm saying,

"Leave her alone Joshua... you'll just startle her and she'll run off."

Ignoring me, he spilled out of the car as the doe made three or four huge leaps out onto the highway where a small truck knocked it flying back onto the verge. Tumbling down to the side of the road, totally distraught, we reached the graceful beast as she tried to lift her head. Out of nowhere, a patrol car had stopped as a uniformed ranger merely took his pistol from the halter, shot the doe in the head... then drove off. With my head in my hands I got back to the car, too angry to even speak to him. Letting him drive almost all the way back to Mill Valley in silence, I finally had enough.

"Joshua, what you did to that deer, you're going to end up doing to me. When you lie and abuse and try to degrade me I just want to run so far, I don't care if I fall from a cliff and just die." Tears had finally rolled from his own huge, brown eyes which I'd loved and had haunted me as beautifully as the deer's.

"I'm tired now of you lighting my fuse to make me hurt and suffer so you can watch me in agony so you can learn what emotions are. I want you to go back to Texas and leave me alone... to get away from you and this country finally for good." And this time, I did mean it.

The last time I saw Joshua was at San Francisco Airport when he knew I wouldn't be used anymore... to be his partner when he wanted... and his rejected ex when he liked to play elsewhere and lie about it. It was a slow-motion moment, wishing him goodbye and good luck, this time for real now. I had the strength and the guide books to make a life without him. At the departure gate we hugged for a long moment as I choked up... feeling I would cry. Fighting it back, I only felt then like shaking his hand to thank him for bringing me to all I'd learnt about life and myself... and where I fit in by following something I thought was love all the way to America. Instead, sensitive as ever with what was evident of that old Texan charm, he thanked me... for all he'd learned which would make him a better person from then on, making him the right husband for - that right Jewish girl! Shaking my head in disbelief, I wondered if he really thought I'd be that grateful to know I had helped make this 'better man' for someone else to reap the benefit of... as he left me, alone.

Turning back for one last wave before I'd disappear from his view, I saw him standing where I'd left him - peering into the very thin crowd where he could not make out my one last wave. He just couldn't *see* me...

and that said it all. Kissing the children goodbye as they slept one last time was about the hardest thing in leaving the United States. Debbie-Lee picked me up early in the morning before they woke, to drive me to SFO, understanding my wish that she'd be the last person I spoke to and kissed goodbye there. With Debbie, I knew it would not be goodbye forever... we'd always stay in touch... and I did visit again a few years later. Seldom does much time go by without her uplifting updates... and we laughed as I said I had truly now 'been through The Mill'... down there in the Valley. Like a piece of ratty old wood, I'd been sawn down, polished and recreated into something perhaps more useful.

Gazing from the plane window, I soared over that whole Bay Area with a complete view of the bridges, fare-welling the city and my home of three years in Mill Valley. Kind of ironically humming to myself "I Left My Heart In San Francisco", I thought then again, I may have left my *old* heart... but in myself I'd found a new one. With no idea what test might come next of all I'd learnt with a new kit of tools, I slept most of the way to Sydney.

CHAPTER FOUR

NOVEMBER 1996

 Enjoying a few days rest in Sydney with Todd, the living 'Ken' doll but more anatomically correct, the bright colours, warmer weather and genuinely friendly, fun people all around was a moment to just breath in. Seeming to fill me up with each breath, expanding like a shiny, radiating ball of light, I chugged across Sydney Harbour on a ferry to Watson's Bay. Such beauty felt like an hallucination... seeing all the amazing houses and apartments in each stunning bay and cove. Being lost for some three years... pretty much in darkness... Nathan's grey wooden house, stood dimly in pelting rains, like I'd been in Dracula's castle compared to this. Letting go of a dream that all of my happiness rested on putting a dysfunctional relationship together, one of those recurring silly pictures popped into my head as they often did, tapped in from somewhere -
 Sliding back a stone wall in an Egyptian tomb, covered in pictures of idyllic scenes, I came across the golden, painted sarcophagi of a long dead King and Queen. Their faces shone peacefully at the peak of their perfection as I pushed back the lids only to see the bare bones, stretched over with parchment, brown skin and the hollow eye sockets. I wanted them to magically reconstitute themselves to their glorious heyday, as they were on the lids, to dance around in the world they remembered on the walls. Nothing happened as they crumbled when I moved their limbs, except great clouds of choking dust filled the room where they lay. Nasty bugs lodged in my eyes, stinging them and making me cry as I gagged, coughing... struggling up to the surface... and light! I was out... and all I had tried

BODYCAGE

to do with Joshua seemed clearer now. Perhaps such melancholic interpretations were a sign of sinking, vaguely aware, into some type of mentally ill state of mind, and I do believe grief does that to people. I know too, that when you have been right down on the ground, crying so hard you think you will die without someone... that eventually it all blows away like the worst ever storm. And, as everything settles again around you... with a peaceful calm, a sense of dying to something which serves us no more comes over us... and we start to revive... to build again.

Learning that I'd blindly chased around the world believing we all need some other *half* to complete our existence because... that's what the fairy tales had told us... and people *tell* us that's something which *should* be, I sat at the rugged Sydney Heads looking out over the roaring Pacific Ocean. It's true that we all seek a kind of homecoming to wholeness through love... yet it was pointless to succumb, sinking into bitterness, anger and regret that it hadn't happened in the way I'd hoped, to live a happy dream life, made up in my own head. Life's way too clever to leave us thinking like that when you realise there's a choice to think something else, just changing your mind and watching this whole new perspective like the twist in a kaleidoscope showing whole new picture. None of it was at all to waste in following the dream. The goal was *love,* with its accompanying friends of peace and forgiveness. In all the magic of knowing truly miraculous angels like Debbie-Lee... and every little hurt and pain which lured me to pick up another book, I grew in the realisation that I already *am* Love. Nothing about the type of body or what sex I could call myself, what man I might have or any piece of treasure which would decay, crumble to collapse and disappear like anything else in this world eventually, would change that fact.

Rehana Incognito

The hot wind howled, whipping my hair against my face as huge waves misted up geysers of spray hitting the boulders with a shudder, to gently tingle across my cheeks, cooling me. How could I complain, being safely back in Australia, feeling no need for anything or anyone to make me feel any more complete? Life had led me to the conditions I wanted and longed for all my life, as anyone does if they really care to admit it, though not the way I'd ever dreamt or expected. Who would know how much happiness we'd really find if life gave us what *we* had decreed was the way to go and find it, frustratingly beating ourselves up at the hardship of it along the way? No, there are higher-purpose reasons for learning the hard way, if indeed it is, and not to cowardly let go, giving up the chance to find it. I'd lived to tell the tale...and it *would* make me stronger, as I sat there remembering the gay friends I'd lost just a few years earlier to AIDS.

Not far apart from each other, my lovely friend James and the sweet, gentle-as-a-calf, Dale both turned into living skeletons before my eyes... spending their last few weeks in the AIDS ward of Royal Perth Hospital. Dale, I could only softly touch and say goodbye with a kiss on his forehead, having already slipped into unconsciousness as I whispered to him that I'd have gladly given him my worthless life that he might live. He passed away with my head lying on the pillow next to his. James smiled the same smile as ever, lighting up the room as I walked in to see him on ventilators, surrounded by cards, balloons and loads of stuffed toys. Adding a little teddy bear to the pile, in one of those 'leather guy' harnesses and a black cap with tiny black leather chaps, he took it with a wry smile.

"Girl, you look so beautiful... you just missed Jacqui," he struggled to get each word out as I said I was sorry to have missed his teenage sweetheart girlfriend who

BODYCAGE

painfully stood by him... when he'd left her for the man who gave him this disease. "You know, Riannon, I wish I had stayed with Jacqui forever instead of looking for my father's love and approval through other men... I really did sicken myself with this game, didn't I?" Only able to force a tiny smile, there was nothing I could say. "There was no love to be found in another man's pants, Riannon... none at all. I have learnt and felt more about love through the care of these nurses alone and Jacqui's forgiveness than the time I had with Michael who was cheating all along."

My heart truly sank, as I lay my head on the pillow next to his, holding his hand 'til he fell into a peaceful sleep. In the early morning I half woke up in the middle of a dream. James was standing on the bright, glimmering green banks of a beautiful river, having climbed from a canoe... smiling and waving to me across the other side.
"It's beautiful here, Riannon.... Don't come yet though.... Gotta go, gorgeous girl... gotta go..." Scrambling up the bank, he had disappeared as the phone rang next to my head. It was Jimmy's friend, Phillip.
"Sorry to call you so early..." he needn't have said more....
"It's OK, Phil... It's Jimmy isn't it... I already know." Only feeling peace, I sunk into the pillow.
"Has someone called you already?" Phil was rightly surprised.
"No, darling... Jimmy just told me... himself." I think Phillip knew what I meant.
Back to Perth again on the plane there was plenty more to reflect about, not in the least I'd still thought of having just gone through the mill in the Valley of Mills. Perhaps I wasn't yet the useful object of fine

craftsmanship envisioned, but a raw plank, sawn into the raw shape as material ready to become anything the next step might take me to be. Quickly selling my house in the suburbs, I bought an apartment overlooking the Indian Ocean, nicely situated between the river and sea at Mosman Park. Painting it throughout in an uplifting solid lemon yellow, I chose curtains as deep green as those river banks I'd seen Jimmy standing on, creating a beautiful high-rise temple to recover myself, being still in and out of moments wishing I could run back to even the insane times with the LAD (Lies Abuse and Degradation) which was about all the taste I had left now for Joshua.

Reading the local free newspaper now and then was about all the stimulation I cared to fill my mind with, mentally... and I always took note of an advertisement for a belly dance class nearby with a girl called Keti. I'd kind of fallen in love at first sight with it at a Middle Eastern dance festival at the Marin Civic Centre, just before leaving the United States. An amazingly beautiful dance was performed by a Columbian man with his German wife - a tall, slender blonde with a physique like my own, which mesmerised me, having thought such dance was only for larger ladies really. Horacio and Beate's performance had moved me enough to feel like I'd finally, if nowhere else in my life, seen the perfect combination of love between a man and a women portrayed in dance. The tease, the surrender and joy of a special union, was for me, like seeing God... performing for us. At some point, I really wanted to learn some of that... and *feel* it.

Mercifully, and right on cue, I noticed a brochure left lying on a train seat one day, heading for Fremantle's quayside markets for a little shopping and a trawl along the cafe strip. The Conscious Living Expo was on again in Claremont! Jumping off at the next station, I

BODYCAGE

caught the next train back to the Show-grounds wandering into the same hall I'd picked through years before with Joshua, collecting bits of this and that to open my mind to so much more. Seeing works by all the big names of authors whose books I'd now almost all read, it certainly amazed me how small the world can be. I'd read "Creative Visualisation" by Shakti Gwain in Mill Valley. Having finished it one day and closing the book, I'd thought how lovely it would be to meet her. I did the next evening, as she actually lived in Marin too and gave a brief talk on the subject at a book signing down the road. She had laughed when I told her I'd only hoped and wished yesterday to meet her...
"Well, that's how it works, hon... That's how it works." Shaking my hand, Shakti serenely went on her way.
After that I recalled reading "Love is Letting go of Fear", by Gerald Jampolsky and found myself working part time in a mansion, as carer for an elderly man, on an enormous estate overlooking Angel Island in San Francisco Bay. On the grounds of this estate, on a lake next to the bay itself, was the former gardener's cottage, where it transpired Gerry lived... greeting me with laughs and wishes of blessings every day. Not a ten minute walk from that estate is the town of Tiburon also situated on the waterfront looking across to San Francisco. There, it surprised me all the more, had lived the incredible women to whom the 'Course in Miracles' had poured through her mind, heart and soul to teach us so well what it actually does. As well as a delightful chat with the ethereally handsome son of Deepak Chopra, Guathama, I cherished the signed copy of that young lad's first book. There were dozens more such unbelievable 'coincidences' I could hardly write about, as it just seems too much to be true. I'd put it down to being fortunate enough to have ended up in

such a special place as 'Magical Marin'... the county where a home and a job appeared, without even trying, through pieces of a jigsaw puzzle falling into place. It was sobering, yet comforting looking at faces on the covers of those books and even their messages, just like old friends at the expo, to remember wise words -

*"Blessed are those who believe, yet have not seen the miracles...
and woe to those who have seen miracles, yet still refuse to believe."*

I'd seen miracles and wanted to keep believing there's so much more, we're not on our own... and this life is not all there is. Over the babble of the crowd, I heard a familiar, haunting piece of music. I loved to get up and dance to that tune with a crowd of wonderful people who'd started a dance night called "Zorba the Buddha" in Fremantle's "Fly By Night" club on Fridays. It drew me to a stand where loads of Arabic music CDs and belly dance paraphernalia were set up with an attractive young lady looking after the stall with a welcoming, friendly smile. I thought she looked like a cross between Elle McPherson and Kylie Minogue with that similar accent and manner... though maybe the squashed down, shorter version of the two.
Asking about the piece of music coming from her stand, as it twinkled away... kind of lulling me to sway where I stood with hips kind of coming to life, this young lady explained it was called "Bombay" by Chris Spheeris. I knew of his hauntingly moving songs and music from California, having just loved his smouldering, mysterious, Greek God looks on album covers.

"I'll write down the name of it for you," she politely offered, telling me where the music shop was which stocked it in a back lane of Fremantle.
"Why do you like it so much," she curiously cocked her head to ask.
"Oh... it just makes me *want* to get up and dance because it reminds me of a beautiful piece of belly dance music I heard in California." I stuffed the piece of paper into the show-bag of enlightenment with all the new pamphlets.
"Really? I teach belly dancing... you should come along some time." Well, that surprised me as I'd been thinking about it often as a way to ground myself too if nothing else.
"Oh wow," I replied "that sounds great... I've been thinking about going to a class in Freo with a girl called Keti... Do you know her?"
Well, I'd love to say at that point there was a terrifying clap of thunder as the place darkened with bolts of lightning flashes, but it didn't. I simply stood in surprise as she announced, as amazed as I was...
"Well, yeah... I *AM* Keti!"
That's how I fell into belly dance classes, between spending the occasional day flogging and tormenting with more of a tongue-in-cheek fervour at the House of Domination. I'd literally go in a flash from whips to hips, peeling off thigh-high leather boots to tie on my burnt orange, satin hip scarf covered in jingling little coins to balance out the teasing act of B and D of Bondage and Discipline... and the B and D of Belly Dance. Like anything else of extremes, it's a ricocheting, swing from one end to the other, but quickly absorbed, as my dancing improved that each held a power of feminine statement. Apart from that, I'd realised too that each were a tease of all a woman can be, as well as a celebration of something to respect and adore, not to

be touched, broken or taken. In both of these expressions too, I learnt that domination represented a woman being a dark side of ourselves to take control of a man and bring him to his knees in all of those games. Having my dance classes to run to with all the more determination and thirst each time, I accepted too that in such dance a woman could express the lighter side of beauty and playfulness - Both held a power and each as valid as the other.

Through Keti Sharif, in her own way, I saw that she too could not stay in that illusion of the dancer forever being just that. So many women, perhaps with lives more shattered than my own came to her classes as they do everywhere, finding that strength to dance in their own temple and find true worth. Coming to meet Keti one day in an early afternoon, just to go out and chat as a friendship quickly grew, I heard the lovely music coming from her studio. Expecting to find her dancing around vivaciously in a beautiful costume, wafting her veils about in an angelic cloudy swirl, I knocked on the door. Heavy footsteps approached as the glass door slid open to behold Keti... standing there in filthy overalls, hair in a mess with a builder's belt full of tools on her hips and an electric saw in her hand!

"Come in Riannon... help yourself to a can of beer." she pointed to them scattered all over the room. "I've just got to finish this last bit of floor I'm putting down."

Well, there went all my illusions that men would be at her feet doing anything she wanted through virtue of her beauty both inside and out. Keti was as on her own, finding her way as I was, but never once that I saw, held back any of her advice and time to any of the lonely women who came to her 'temple of dance' to heal their lives... or any other reason. Finding or even rediscovering their own beauty in all of these women, I made so many new friends with wonderful experiences to share. Admittedly, I'd still *liked* to have sought out some prince for a white picket fence scenario around then, but realised this time was about something a lot more special and of merit to my world than hiding away in the safe harbour again. Through the heartaches I'd listened to with the new tribe of ladies in my life, I was actually grateful, knowing there were no guarantees or promises down that garden path, that I was still single!

Finding my dear friend Carmel through a dance class with Keti, she became one of the greatest reasons I was glad to be free. At that certain age, when a woman has brought up two teenage sons... on her own, she seemed as run ragged as that pedigree bitch who'd had too many puppies, chewing away at her. Licking her wounds, Carmel described herself, with no other way to heal those unfortunate learning experiences we all gather. She'd felt like a dead soul, clinging to branches in a swirling river of emotions. Well, I knew what that felt like, and like myself, it led her to belly dance. I never really gave a lot of thought to the word 'belly' in all of this, but saw enough to know it's where we feel those emotions which get damaged or thrive and heal. Biologically... for women, it's where a new life comes to form... and I personally believe it is true that space is in men too, feeling things in their guts in pits of emotional agony or joy. Yes... a chakra if you want to call it that.

Carmel's relationship with a Greek man about her age had just fallen apart, inadvertently with me being in the mechanics of it, as she felt her life was like a jigsaw which had just collapsed or a beautiful vase now smashed on the ground in millions of shards. All impossible she felt for her to put back together again. There were no stars in Carmel's sky anymore...and the poetess she is needed that for sure, as any other woman. No wonder I'd found her such a kindred soul

Rehana Incognito

sister in all of that... her birthday was a week before mine, so was another soldier girl, an Aries lamb looking for the fire which came as a glimmer of hope through the dark canvas as a speck of the light of dance. Fremantle's hot, dark nights were like a womb of creation for me then, thinking of Carmel's stars and the light of dance compelling us to create something new and better like the Aboriginal's Wandjinas had done in the Dreamtime.

At a party celebrating the graduation of a few dancers, Carmel had brought her Greek knight who shockingly made obvious passes at me in her presence! Having none of it, rudely giving short, sharp one syllable answers to his flirting questions, I could not believe that Carmel simply rose from the table to take a walk outside in the fresh air alone. It's funny how we see ourselves... or actually don't, as I thought Carmel was some elegant, well-educated millionaire's wife, living in a palace overlooking the river or sea. She suddenly saw herself as an older woman about to be rejected by her man, as he worked on his next younger squeeze humiliatingly before her.

From another set of eyes, this is how Carmel saw it, not only setting me straight at how, with little knowledge, we make up an image of other's lives through the lenses of our own perception, failing to even notice about how I saw myself still. A 'floating dream' was far from any way I could have felt... more likely a shipwreck or a frozen hulk stuck in an icy sea, in that moment in time. Exquisitely, she said, in every movement... I flowed, sending orgasmic dreams and fantasies to every man in that place just by looking at me. In a world of my own, admiring the talents of the incredible dancers, I didn't even recall there being any men there other than the Greek!

BODYCAGE

Carmel had left feeling 'a lady knew when to take her leave', sure that the Greek would sweep me off my feet too, steeling me off into the night. I actually found him repulsive! But Carmel had seen me a 'wings of a butterfly', enchanting, almost appealingly frail, delicate. How could she have known that I had lost so much weight in years of stress in California and tortured myself over 'lost love' and making sense of it all? She felt, as the Greek surely did, he could reach out and touch a beauty which would fly away and disintegrate in your hands. Carmel said she'd wished she could flow like that, walking as if floating with every movement promising delights in such utter femininity. Gratefully though, she found her comforts as I did that these things could be written in the stars, enjoying too that Aries girl vulnerability, childlike naivety and curious nature. With our deep hearts, we danced in years to come in the Greek islands, around the Plaka of Athens, and even in a trip to London with her youngest son, we found enough 'Zorba's' to dance with and then set free. To her young son, I became proudly known as his Second Mum and remain so 'til this day, although now just called 'The Spare'... Well, all good boys need one!

Getting through Keti's courses of all the different forms of Middle Eastern dance, I'd have to say the tribal, troop routines... with several women powerfully performing together to heavy drums and haunting instruments... locked my place in the world quite firmly. Graduating through with certificates in each style, I have no idea if I'd perfected them or not... Keti thought so... and that's what mattered. I chose my stage name, which many of us customarily do for performances. Behind the translucent, red veil, in a golden costume straight from Sheherazade, I danced alone for an excited crowd of revellers on the bar to amazingly exotic, tantalising belly dance music... on New year's

Rehana Incognito

Eve 1999. 'Rehana', the 'Veiled Threat' danced into the new century with a whole planet anticipating what it might bring, as crowds of revellers packed the bar to watch. With a bunch of girlfriends, including Keti and Carmel, we danced into morning in a club called "The Clink", set out like a prison with bars and all... in honour of the old Fremantle jail, just around the corner. How appropriate! Grinning to myself, I stroked the painted-on bars with not even the slightest desire to accept a drink from the guys who watched us dancing in our own little world of happiness.

It was more an honour than anything else to lift the scorched, charred wings of other women, whose angel selves had fallen flat to the ground in crumpled wings which could no longer lift them, soaked in tears. That was my tribe and purpose for a short time really in Perth, before flying off with a group of twelve Aussie sheilas with Keti for a cultural, belly dance tour of Egypt where Keti lived years before as a true Star! Renting out my flat indefinitely I had the urge and a new career up my sleeve to whip (well, I packed a couple of them!) around the planet to find out what I wanted out of life... the rest of what I had.

Stashing a heap of belongings in Carmel's cellar, which I tried to get her to convert to a dungeon and make herself a little extra pocket money, I spent a day sifting through the souvenirs of my life trying to decide what to keep or throw away. Horrified, sentimental Poet Laureate of 'Freo Di Janiero', Carmel... watched as I filled a wheelie bin with photo albums, little gifts and so much else related to my past, before dusting off both hands to walk away from it all.

In her own words, the Pollyanna Poetess (yes, I threw what remained of *her* into the wheelie bin, but think her spirit may have floated out to make a home in Carmel) - I had freed myself from things which held me earthbound, clipping wings which stopped us flying through open skies, soaring high to experience new things. There, we'd see the world from the Heavens of spirituality, instead of mundane gutters of existence. Carmel learnt too about letting go of all the things which stopped her soaring again. She decided to be part of a cloud which is me, floating high throughout our lives, without shackles and knots to tie us earthbound. No, not at all... Shackles and knots I kept up my sleeve, as tools of the trade if ever I needed them! Crikey, why throw that baby out with the bath water?

Walking arm in arm with dear old Thelma who had rarely even gone from Fremantle to Perth on a half hour bus ride, we tumbled from the tour bus at Giza... Keti rounding us all along with a big shepherdess stick. A little distance from the rest of the group, Thelly and I could hardly speak as the Pyramids and Sphinx stood out before us like nothing else existed in the world. Creeping through tombs, I thought of the golden, gilt coffins and mummies in my mind which I'd try to make real and dance out the love. Glad to have that time with Thelma when she finally realised she didn't want to stay at home picking fluff off her husband and son's socks as a cooking, cleaning machine anymore, they were incredible moments like remembering past lives in the home land of our dance. She died a year later back in Perth of a terrible tumour she'd carried unknowingly with us on the trip to Egypt... but, oh my God... how that woman had danced in all the beautiful costumes she'd made in her bedroom, like Aladdin's cave!

CHAPTER FIVE

Back in London, my little soul-brother, Timmy was there for me... with his lovely partner Charlie, starting that endless cycle of lunches and walks through Brompton Cemetery, unfolding and balancing his own journeys of growth and experiences as only a Libran man would. Tim introduced me to a transgender friend, living at an Earls Court hotel to see if she'd help me rent a room there too until I found a flat of my own. It was a ghastly place really, kind of like a gay Fawltey Towers with a bar and a stench from a drain beneath it which should have been a warning! It transpired that the Philly held a night for 'trans and fans' every Monday. There was also a handy Thai restaurant at the back, overlooking the well grown-in garden and a pond, lovingly tended by James, the Glaswegian consummate barman who'd made the Philbeach Hotel his home. Guests could get world-class Thai food with a traditional welcome from a ladyboy manager in his exotic, bejewelled outfits, then a blow job in the garden or in the loo from one of many of a plague of oriental hookers who moonlighted between table service and 'love- you-long-time' massage service, in clip joints around London. In a basement room, a transvestite 'beauty parlour' offered makeovers, cross- dressing and good day of escapism for men inclined to enjoy it... or 'driven to dress', as I'd put it!
It's only claim to fame was that Kenny Everett had temporarily resided in the Sodom and Gomorrah suite down in that basement, where the ceiling had come down when a shower cubicle crashed through as two guys were shagging in it. Pierre and Giles had also stayed there, the famous gay photographers who immortalise, in mythical poses and interpretations,

BODYCAGE

celebrities usually, for many thousands of pounds per spectacular painting. In a peaceful enough room, I stayed there watching that passing parade of an endless stream of high-heeled men clacking up and down the stairs into the early hours each night. During the day, I fled to the East End, working in a dungeon in Aldgate with another woman, keeping me in fits over her lack of Mistress professionalism. I mean, how many times can you join a fellow Bitch in a torture chamber to find her there, in a leather hood with the zip mouth open, slave on a crucifix shackled to the wall getting a blow job from his Mistress?

Working behind the bar on Monday nights, I soon got too comfortable with being chatted up by men leering at my every move, gazing longingly into my eyes, wearing more make-up than I actually ever owned! Starting to have nightmares about them, those manly painted faces with whiskers coming through the grease paint after a day without a shave, had even followed me to bed. Pulling pints and pouring drinks with the same flirty banter from my Bottoms Up days in Hong Kong, I'd often catch them in the mirrors, winking at themselves or coquettishly looking away. They'd longingly pout their painted lips, making their images become marionettes, pulling a disembodied extension of themselves, acting as that tartly girl they dream of, yet seemed never to find. Incredulously, as if to emphasize the profane image they wanted these 'women' to be, 'she' always had to smoke... Tarts always smoke, but when the wigs came off and makeup rinsed down the dirty, cracked sinks in those shabby rooms, when he'd comfortingly become the man again, many of these guys were not smokers themselves!

Neither did they believe they had gay tendencies, although they had often just had sex with other men, similarly dressed... as tarts, naturally. Hypnotised by each other's stockings, skirts and boots, they'd temporarily become 'lesbians'... Though what a lesbian would want to be found sucking cocks for, I have no idea! Seeing some of them, who had actually been besotted lipstick lesbians for hours earlier, bump into each other as men with their bags on the way out, it was astounding to hear them, quickly looking away from each other saying, "oops, sorry Mate" passing at the reception desk.

Before the bar got too busy and every gay, illegal immigrant with a wig and high heels clambered down the stairs to look for sex with gullible men and make a bit of money, I'd just watch the teevees watching the TV if the football was on... Like any other blokes, letting out roaring cheers if a goal was struck, they'd all turn to look leeringly if a new pair of high heels clicked by as if a strange new, sexually available bimbo had appeared in their midst! Well, it can be summed up as half of these men loved to create the woman they wanted in their lives. If they couldn't find her...they'd *be* her, with no real problem in justifying that. The rest were mainly gay men with a pathological hatred and jealousy for women... only able to steal a little claim on the female world by cladding the trappings of the feminine to get a quick fix of money or sex.

2001
If that's a bother for anyone to accept about this game... played out, always in dark places, basements and secret little clubs, I am sorry for what you see mirrored at you. If you don't like what you see, look in a different mirror! It became tiring, speaking to army sergeants and tank drivers who sat there in frocks and wigs saying they finally felt like their 'true' selves.

BODYCAGE

Revelling in comfortable acceptance of a place like the Philbeach Hotel and all the new 'friends' it brought, it was hard to bring them back to reality. When they planned to skip around the corner to Dr Reid, the consultant psychiatrist to convince him of their overwhelming drive to become women they always believed they were, I sometimes tried to save them the troubles. I rarely met anyone, of the hundreds down there who called themselves anything from cross-dressers, drag queens, transsexual, transgender or gender 'outlaws', who were anything like genuinely 'women in male bodies'... Very, very rarely. Those girls had more chance of Boy George appearing in a puff of pink sparkling fairy dust, throwing them over a car bonnet and giving them a good seeing to than becoming a successful woman's *backside*. It was a Gender Jihad!

Unfortunately nobody tells them 'til they are alone, lost their family, jobs and dignity... sitting in desolation in dingy flats when they realise they don't wake up looking like supermodels with men throwing diamonds and furs at their feet. All they could well have done with was the right guidance and advice to accept such aspects of softness, open emotion, uninhibited fun and beauty acceptable today in any man. Learn to love that man and find, in lovingly knowing and accepting him... others will too. There's nothing written in stone which says our society will accept you when the irreversible decision has been made and you're trying to literally live in an unfamiliar universe called womanhood.

Thankfully, I had my new little flat in Holland Park with plenty of work both teaching dance and performing in clubs, restaurants and often, weddings and other celebrations. Rarely going to places like the Philbeach Hotel for the Monday nights (where I missed many people whose company I had truly grown to enjoy) just being myself too - I was soon glad to leave it behind forever. Getting out of 'Cesspoolopolis' was the best thing I could have done, relieved to leave behind that sickening world of Dungeons and Drag-Queens. I wish too often I'd not even wasted time there. It may not be nice for me to have spoken about a place I once thought a valuable, safe resource for the transgender community, but I learnt the hard way that not many gay venue owners and their staff of boys, with issues of their own, truly have our concerns at heart.

Anything I have to say about the place can be further perused at tripadvisor.com, and if any wife finds a receipt for a room at that place, I am sorry, honey... but you're probably in for an unpleasant shock! Perhaps too, I'd given false encouragement by my own success to people there too who'd clearly never make it, which only left them jealous and resentful. As Keti's teachings grew in new and exciting directions, she flew over from her base in Cairo and El Gouna, organising classes at the Fulham Dance Attic. I'd fly to France or Germany for dance festivals as her European representative... promoting her DVDs of teaching and performance as well as her own musical arrangements. Twice I went back to Cairo and down to El Gouna on the Red Sea, dancing with princes and princesses... and the interesting clique of a specially- bonded crowd who had their enormous, luxury yachts moored there!

2006
Several men, both in London and elsewhere, almost found places in my heart... one in particular. Even before leaving Perth, he nearly got to the altar, but his ex girlfriend saved me... seducing him back with the promise of instant love child and married bliss if he'd dump me. He did, just as I'd nearly bought a wedding

BODYCAGE

dress... then she left him anyway, only having acted out of spite. He's now a single dad... still looking! None of them got me down for more than a few moments of misery, simply forgiving them all at their own loss really, for letting their fears and insecurities get in the way of a chance for something special.

I *needed* none of them... and that was the difference. It's funny how, when you're walking through the world, the confident dancer in your own head, expressing all the power and allure of a body, feeling comfortable to an adoring audience, men do find you irresistibly attractive. Coupled with the assertive boundaries of respect absorbed through years of bondage (well, not my own, but satisfied victims), it served me well now being contentedly single... at the moment.

Joining in with Keti's new classes in London, brilliantly teaching belly dance through twelve simple, dynamic little routines representing the essence of every sign of the Zodiac, I couldn't quite get comfortable in memorising them all. Bits of the routines, locked in quite easily, naturally even, yet others almost clumsily evaded me. Brushing it off as belly dance thought block, I still fell back on my old work (no, not the one *on* my back... like carrying a blow up mattress, inflatable with the yank of a cord to carry on that 'oldest profession'), I had placed myself on web listings of several fetish and bondage sites.

Muddling through the basics of making a website to link with my own pictures, was something miraculous in itself, as only recently I'd thought email addresses were something people wrote on envelopes, spirited away to some special place for quicker delivery! Feeling comfortable, screening those clients on the phone, Mistress Victoria, the 'Victorious One', was happy to keep up simple fetish jobs and little bondage games which interested me enough from my own home, not requiring a fully equipped dungeon anymore. At two or three sites, I noticed the demand for transgender Mistresses. Widening my clientele pool, I listed there too, being way too selective about what I could be bothered doing or who with. Never did I need that money badly enough to compromise my boundaries... ever.

It was sometime around then I received a phone call from a member of the team at the "Trisha" show on Channel Five. The girl had found my ad on the net, asking if I'd appear as a guest on Trisha's talk show about my 'unusual lifestyle'.

"If I was heavily disguised, I might... What is she going to be discussing?" I was almost tempted to take up the offer and say my piece to the world on daytime telly.

"We were hoping to talk about transsexuals and their jobs... but we'd have to show pictures of you when you were a... a... mmm..."

"A mermaid?"

"No...I meant as a man... or as a boy even."

"Dear, as laudable as Miss Goddard's intentions may be about the subject, you may like to tell her to give me a call when she realises some of us might just be capable of doing *her* job instead of being freak-value guests for such show's ratings." She hung up, knowing she'd get no further with me.

It really left me seething that Britain is still in the position where people like myself can be openly mocked and degraded in newspapers and media, now that they can't get away with the same to the gays, people of other religions, colours or even those with ginger hair! We're left with the likes of our tabloid newspapers still making such vulgar references to the transgender character of 'Hayley' in "Coronation Street" being 'left without a sausage' and thinking that would not be personally hurtful and insulting about a condition so many are born with through no fault of our own. It's sad indication enough, as lovely as the actress is who plays a transgender character on an iconic show, that a biological woman plays a dowdy, nervy frump of a down-trodden stereotype of anything we could be!

It's the last hurdle for us here in the United Kingdom, to be accepted for beauties and talents, wit and good grace like any other woman... without needing to make the focus be on *how* we came to *be* that woman! Perhaps not in my lifetime we'll see any of the brilliant, genuinely gorgeous 'new women' I know reading the news, presenting the weather or holding her ground with a guest hosting the BBC's "Hardtalk"! Maybe I'll write to the producers of "East Enders" and see if they need a vicious new vixen of a barmaid to turn Walford upside down with her special secret at the Queen Vic. See what the "Sun" and "News of the World" start to shriek about that!

2007

On a little holiday in Dubai, escaping the cold by invitation of an Arab fan of my London shows, I went to see what all the fuss was about. Checking my work site emails, amongst the usual questions and propositions from clients, was an email from a man called Jason. Explaining that he'd be interested to look at my life story as a useful and unusual book for his publishing company, I replied rather sceptically. Enough strange people, with even stranger motives often emailed, including one guy who kept making appointments for me to strangle him. It got worse and worse until I stopped seeing him after he produced a briefcase stacked with £50 notes if I'd *kill* him... as his ultimate act of bondage and sadism from his Mistress. He's probably lying in someone's freezer right now, as a woman with less scruples than I have is off spending his cash. Jason replied with the details of his publishing company, accepting my wariness politely with understanding, expressing that he really hoped such an interesting story might help people understand themselves better. We arranged to meet up on a Wednesday when I returned to London and talk about it.

Assembling years of notes, pages of letters and cards I'd kept which were worth remembering of my life so far, I thought... "well, I'm no Nancy Mitford, Leo Tolstoy or JK Rowling (though probably look like a blend of all three after some rough nights out!), I'll try to help and tell it as I saw it, as opposed to what people think they might want to hear." Watching "This Morning" on ITV, the day before meeting Jason, I missed the whole story of what the handsome, tall man on Fern and Phil's couch were talking about. I caught that he'd transcended a lifetime lost in the confusion of mental illness with all the carnage, pain and embarrassment it brought to his life. Missing too the name of his book about it all, I wished I could have read it and just wanted to give him a really big hug.

Getting lost around Moorgate on Wednesday, I found his publishing office's building after having to call Jason from Liverpool Street and direct me. Flustered still, as he appeared from the stairs to come and collect me in the lobby, he apologised too for being rushed, as he'd been so busy after appearing on television the day before! So, after a drink and a bite in a cocktail bar to hear all about his aims in publishing, those two wishes, when watching TV the day before, came true. I had a signed copy of "A Can of Madness" by Jason Pegler and he was happy to share with me that big hug I'd wanted to give him. What a guy! So, as just one more serendipitous 'coincidence' like that came into my life, I knew it would be best to follow it.

Getting started on putting all this together, found me needing to jump back from it way too many times. Both not wanting to paint a sad picture of too many places I'd found myself in, speaking of my own life... I didn't want to rain on the parade of all those people looking for a way to hide their troubles either, using femininity as a crutch to find men to act as giant bandages over gushing wounds in shattered, lonely and confused souls. When I did go back through all those steps, processing them and letting them go, I took the time to look up Greg... and even Joshua. Letters from them both in reply, offered deep comfort that they had forgiven me for anything of my part in their lives which caused them pain. I wanted them to know too, that I'd forgiven them also for whatever they'd done inadvertently or otherwise which harmed me. Assuring them, I'd accepted we all do the best we can with what we know at the time in awkward situations where they were themselves in their own learning, I threw myself into dance.

Keti came back in summer this year, ripe and ready to start the next phase of her life too, as we met up in Brighton for the "Orient Dance Festival". Joining her class for the teachers and other students who'd found it as wonderful a concept as I did, learning routines of over a hundred different moves through each character and personality of the Zodiac, I thought of it all the more. Even if not a follower of such things as Astrology, the sensible pattern of learning this art of dance, is made all the easier to remember with them. All those little moves representing each stage of the human journey from the new 'Baby Lamb', where it all starts in a Spring born of fire, through all the rest... with

their unique lessons, elements and challenges, culminate back in the watery ocean of our dreams with the Twin Fish of Pisces. Finally, in the last of weekend's classes there in Brighton, right on the sea, I danced through each of the signs, effortlessly flowing from one to the next... not missing a beat! With a grand finale showcase of amazing dancers to finish the night at Hove Town Hall, Keti and I made our way out early after such a successful trip. As we were leaving, we came across a lovely young lady with long, dark hair in a kind of Gothic leather outfit, long burgundy skirt and a bulky black hip scarf jingling with chains and bells.
"Aren't you girls going to stay and watch my show...? It's a little bit different." Holding a coiled whip in her hand, I beamed into her mischievous grin.
"Hmmm... a belly dancing bondage Mistress huh... well... I've sort of seen that show already!" With a wink at Keti who's seen so many of our special little, inexplicable happenings over the years, we were off into the night.

www.ingramcontent.com/pod-product-compliance
Lightning Source LLC
Chambersburg PA
CBHW021757220426
43662CB00006B/86